political science is for everybody

political science is for everybody

an introduction to political science

edited by
amy l. atchison

UNIVERSITY OF TORONTO PRESS
Toronto Buffalo London

© University of Toronto Press 2021
Toronto Buffalo London
utorontopress.com
Printed in the U.S.A.

ISBN 978-1-4875-0571-4 (cloth)   ISBN 978-1-4875-3253-6 (EPUB)
ISBN 978-1-4875-2390-9 (paper)   ISBN 978-1-4875-3252-9 (PDF)

Library and Archives Canada Cataloguing in Publication

Title: Political science is for everybody : an introduction to political science / edited by Amy L. Atchison.
Names: Atchison, Amy L., editor.
Description: Includes index.
Identifiers: Canadiana (print) 20200407988 | Canadiana (ebook) 2020040802X | ISBN 9781487505714 (hardcover) | ISBN 9781487523909 (softcover) | ISBN 9781487532536 (EPUB) | ISBN 9781487532529 (PDF)
Subjects: LCSH: Political science – Textbooks. | LCSH: Political science – Study and teaching (Higher) | LCSH: Intersectionality (Sociology) – Study and teaching (Higher) | LCSH: Political sociology – Study and teaching (Higher) | LCGFT: Textbooks.
Classification: LCC JA86 .P65 2021 | DDC 320.071/1 – dc23

We welcome comments and suggestions regarding any aspect of our publications – please feel free to contact us at news@utorontopress.com or visit us at utorontopress.com.

Every effort has been made to contact copyright holders; in the event of an error or omission, please notify the publisher.

University of Toronto Press acknowledges the financial assistance to its publishing program of the Canada Council for the Arts and the Ontario Arts Council, an agency of the Government of Ontario.

Cover illustrations: Top to bottom, left to right: SOPHONISBA PRESTON BRECKINRIDGE: *Hearst's Magazine. The World To-day; a Monthly Record of Human Progress*, vol. 20, January–June 1911. Photograph by Eva Watson Schütze. ALICE PAUL: United States Library of Congress, Print and Photographs Division. Photograph by Harris & Ewing, restored by Adam Cuerden. LEYMAH GBOWEE: Photograph courtesy of Valparaiso University & Peace Is Loud. RALPH BUNCHE: United States National Archives. Photograph by the United States Information Agency. GLORIA STEINEM: Photograph © Gage Skidmore, accessed under CC BY-SA 2.0. RIGOBERTA MENCHÚ: Photograph © John Mathew Smith. https://www.flickr.com/photos/kingkongphoto/5112486475. ANNA JULIA COOPER: Frontispiece from *A Voice from the South*, 1892. Printed by The Aldine Printing House, Xenia, Ohio. Scanned by the Internet Archive.

Canada Council
for the Arts

Conseil des Arts
du Canada

ONTARIO ARTS COUNCIL
CONSEIL DES ARTS DE L'ONTARIO

an Ontario government agency
un organisme du gouvernement de l'Ontario

Funded by the   Financé par le
Government   gouvernement
of Canada   du Canada

Cover Photos

First row: Sophonisba Breckinridge (1866–1948): activist, academic, and first woman to earn a PhD in political science (and economics)

Second row: Alice Paul (1885–1977): woman suffrage campaigner who was the first to propose an equal rights amendment to the US Constitution

Third row, left: Leymah Gbowee (1972–): social worker and activist who won the 2011 Nobel Peace Prize for her role in leading a successful nonviolent campaign for peace in Liberia, Women of Liberia Mass Action for Peace

Third row, right: Ralph Bunche (1904–1971): American diplomat, first Black American to earn a PhD in political science, and first person of color to win the Nobel Peace Prize; he won in 1950 after he successfully negotiated the 1949 Armistice Agreements between Israel and four Arab states

Fourth row: Gloria Steinem (1934–): feminist activist and journalist; known for leading the American feminist movement of the 1960s and 1970s and for co-founding *Ms. Magazine*

Fifth row, left: Rigoberta Menchú (1959–): Mayan k'iche' Indigenous rights activist whose 1983 book, *I, Rigoberta Menchú: An Indian Woman in Guatemala*, brought global attention to the atrocities being committed by the Guatemalan military dictatorship against the Indigenous Mayan population; in 1992, she won the Nobel Peace Prize for Indigenous rights advocacy

Fifth row, right: Anna Julia Cooper (1858–1964): intellectual, feminist, writer, and rights activist who championed education for Black Americans and women; her book, *A Voice from the South by a Black Woman of the South* (1892), is a foundational human rights text that advocates for Black and women's rights

For Kate-O with love.

Contents

Figures and Tables

Figures

Tables

Boxes

Acknowledgments

Many thanks to the contributing authors and the editorial team (past and present) at the University of Toronto Press for their work bringing this project to fruition. Special thanks to the Brain Trust for their above-and-beyond contributions, and *extra-special thanks* to Cathy Jenkins for bringing the magic.

Introduction

*Dr. Amy
L. Atchison*

You can't be what you can't see.

– Marian Wright Edelman

LEARNING OBJECTIVES

1 Understand the approach this book takes to politics and political science
2 Think about politics from another person's perspective

KEY TERMS

extrajudicial   not legally authorized; outside the law

identity   a person's defining characteristics

identity politics   any politics based on shared characteristics that organizes groups and motivates their actions. The practice of identity politics is typically understood to be an explicit and conscientious choice, but it can be situated on spectrums of explicit and implicit choice and more or less conscious decision making.

institutions   the rules, formal or informal, that structure how decisions are made

intersectionality   the analytical framework, pioneered by Black women, to illuminate how racial, gendered, and other kinds of disadvantage reinforce each other.

The concept is that our many identities can be sources of multiple and overlapping oppressions (or privileges).

knowledge production   the process by which researchers produce empirically grounded (scientific) knowledge

marginalized   the treatment of a person or persons as incidental, or peripheral. The terms *underrepresented*, *non-normative*, and *marginal* are synonyms of this idea.

political institutions   sets of written and unwritten rules that structure politics and shape the behavior of political actors

state   a territorial entity; also called a *country* (not to be confused with *the state*, which is the full political apparatus with a monopoly over the legitimate use of violence in a given territory)

BACKGROUND TO *POLITICAL SCIENCE IS FOR EVERYBODY*

You've probably heard the old adage that history is written by the victors. As any historian will tell you, that adage is not particularly true, but it contains a nugget of truth at its core: It isn't that history is written by the *victors*; it's that, as with all **knowledge production**, history has been written by people who are viewed as legitimate and authoritative sources. And *there* is where things get tricky. Who is viewed as legitimate and authoritative?

Obviously, there are many factors at play – era, location, culture – but for simplicity's sake, let's think about people who are viewed as legitimate and authoritative research scientists (they get a lot more publicity than historians or political scientists).

1   Think about scientists who are famous because they are considered foundational to the production of scientific knowledge.
2   Take a minute to make a list of three to five scientists that you can name without thinking too hard about it.

Now, let's look at your list. If I had to bet, I would say that *if* there is a woman on your list, it is Marie Curie (bonus points for Rosalind Franklin and quintuple bonus points for Katherine Johnson or Jocelyn Bell Burnell).[1] I would also bet that *if* there is a scientist of color on your list, it is Neil Degrasse Tyson (bonus points for George Washington Carver and quintuple bonus points for Dr. Ocean Mercier).[2]

What was the point of this brainstorming exercise? To demonstrate that knowledge production, and the group of people whom we consider to be legitimate producers of knowledge, has traditionally been dominated by men of European heritage.

Figure 0.1. Percentage of Women and Scholars of Color in Anglo-American Political Science

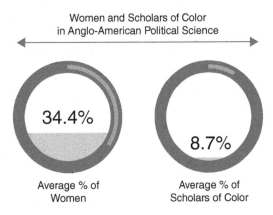

Women and Scholars of Color
in Anglo-American Political Science

34.4%

8.7%

Average % of
Women

Average % of
Scholars of Color

Source: Data from various national political science associations.

Yes, people of color and women have produced important and insightful scientific knowledge; historically, however, most have either been barred from research or had their achievements attributed to white male scholars. (See note 1 at the end of this chapter regarding Rosalind Franklin, Katherine Johnson, and Jocelyn Bell Burnell.)

As you can see in Figure 0.1, political science, like its cousins in the natural sciences, is still largely dominated by white men. The vast majority of political science textbooks are written by white men. You may be asking yourself, *Is that a problem*? In a nutshell: *yes*!

It's not that white guys don't know things – they know all sorts of cool things! It's that other people *also* know things. Members of dominant groups don't often ask how **marginalized** groups experience the political world – there's an assumption that what works for the dominant group must work the same way for everyone. But when all the knowledge that is widely shared comes from the dominant group, we get an incomplete picture of how the political world works. When textbooks are written from only the dominant perspective, you, the political science student, may be left with the impression that **political institutions** are neutral and unbiased. Except we know that's not true. Think about the fact that racial and ethnic minorities are often punished more harshly for the same crimes than the dominant ethnic/racial group in your society (more on that in Chapter 10). Think about the fact that women experience a wage gap in every country around the globe. Both of those facts are a result of social and political factors that help dominant groups and harm minority and marginalized groups.

Of course, these averages hide a lot of variation among **states**. For example, the Canadian Political Science Association reports that 40 per cent of its members are women, versus only about 31 per cent in the Political Studies Associations of both Ireland and the United Kingdom. The American Political Science Association reports that about 25 per cent of its members are scholars of color, while its Australian counterpart indicates that 0 per cent of its members are scholars of color (New Zealand reports <1 per cent and the UK <5 per cent).[3] These numbers are, of course, historical legacies of a system that was invented by white men at a time when they openly asserted that theirs was the superior form of knowledge. And it is to that time that I turn next.

WHAT IS PAST IS PROLOGUE

Just as the chapter authors and I were making the final edits to this book, the **extrajudicial** killing[4] of a Black American named George Floyd by a white police officer in Minneapolis, Minnesota, sparked #BlackLivesMatter protests not only in Minneapolis and across the United States but around the world. From small protests at the US Embassy in Lagos, Nigeria, to massive protests across Europe, people turned out in solidarity with Black Americans who have been systematically mistreated since 1619, when the first enslaved Africans were brought to the "New World." George Floyd's killing in 2020 became a symbol for *half a millennium* of racism and brutality that minority communities continue to experience regularly in their own societies.

We cannot understand the global nature of these #BlackLivesMatter protests without acknowledging that the forces against which people are protesting are products of attitudes and practices that accompanied several historical waves of European colonization (first in the Americas and then in Africa) and the trans-Atlantic slave trade. At the center of those events was Europeans' belief that they were superior to all other groups of people – and that European superiority gave them the right, even the moral obligation (!), to rule over everyone else (more in Chapters 2 and 12 on this). Nineteenth-century English author Rudyard Kipling referred to this moral obligation as the "White Man's Burden" in a poem in which he tried to persuade the United States to colonize the Philippines rather than end the Spanish–American War.

As you will see in Chapter 2, Europeans' supremacist beliefs led to atrocities that include, but are not limited to, the murder and enslavement of Indigenous peoples as well as the appropriation of their land. While colonization and the slave trade may seem like ancient history, their repercussions are with us both internationally and domestically. Here I look only at one of the domestic repercussions: race relations.[5]

Throughout their colonies, the colonial powers established, to a greater or lesser degree, what social scientists call a *pigmentocracy*, "a society ... in which skin color determines socio-economic and/or political status."[6] While our beliefs about race came about relatively recently, systems of oppression based on skin color have been around for much longer. One of the clearest examples in modern history comes from sixteenth-century Latin America, where colonial governments established racial hierarchies – a caste system – to control the population. These caste systems defined a person's rights in society based on how European they were, a status largely based on skin color, since genealogies and genetics were not available at the time.[7] The whiter the person's skin, the more rights and privileges they were afforded – including everything from which jobs they could hold to which weapons they could legally carry and which fabrics they were allowed to wear.[8]

Latin American colonies started with a few main castes (European, Indigenous, African) in the mid-1500s, but as groups intermarried those quickly morphed into 16 or more castes, all dependent on how "white" a person was. "But," you might say, "that was a very long time ago." It was. And while the role of the caste system diminished in legal importance after these colonies gained independence,[9] the caste system had institutionalized European superiority to such an extent that even revolution and freedom from colonial oppression has not eliminated the importance of race and skin color in everyday life in Brazil, Colombia, Mexico, Peru, and other Latin American countries.[10] Wealth and power are still mostly concentrated among people of primarily European descent, and poverty is still concentrated in communities that are non-European – or as one researcher puts it, "the browner the neighborhood, the poorer it is."[11]

IDENTITY MATTERS

That brief introduction to pigmentocracies is meant to get you thinking about **identity** and the role it plays in your society. In some societies, the term **identity politics** has become a kind of buzzword, with the connotation that identity politics is somehow a bad thing. And yet our societies and social relationships are structured by our identities, as you will see throughout this book. We do not all experience society and politics the same way. An Indigenous community, for example, has had far different – and likely far more negative – interactions with government than a white community has had. Why? Because *white* is the default identity in European and European-descended countries.

An entrenched power system benefits white citizens and, in many ways, simultaneously stigmatizes and erases people of color. The **institutions** of government were made by white men, who governed in eras when no one else was legally allowed to participate in governance. The histories were written by white men, who wrote the books in eras when no one else was legally entitled to seek higher education. The education systems were built by white men and are largely staffed by white women in primary and secondary schools. The histories that we teach in our schools are presented as *the* history of the country and the society, but they generally focus on *white* history and society. While it might be uncomfortable for white students to acknowledge, keep in mind that when talking about any other group, people specify the race/ethnicity: *Black* culture, *Maori* history, *First Nations* traditions.[12]

By extension, it is also the case that *politics* generally refers to *white* politics. But, because white is the default, people do not think of *white* as an identity – therefore, to many white people, only *other* politics are identity politics.

This book emphasizes an alternative: *All politics are identity politics.*

WHY THIS BOOK?

The first thing that makes this book different is that our approach is purposefully and explicitly **intersectional**. Intersectionality, a concept that was born out of Black women's lived experience, starts with the knowledge that people have multiple overlapping identities – race, ethnicity, religion, gender, socioeconomic class, and so on. From there, intersectional scholars demonstrate that our many identities can be sources of multiple and overlapping oppressions – a Black woman, for example, may be discriminated against both because she is Black *and* because she is a woman.

Kimberlé Crenshaw, the pioneer of intersectional theorizing and research, named the phenomenon after encountering the case of a Black woman named Emma De-Graffenreid. Emma asserted that a potential employer discriminated against her not because she was Black, and not because she was a woman, but because she was a *Black woman*. A judge threw out the case, saying the employer hired Black people and it hired women, so Emma had no case. What the judge ignored, though, was that the employer hired Black men to work in its factory and white women to work as administrative office support – leaving no place for Emma, a Black woman. To describe what happened in Emma's case, Crenshaw coined the term *intersectionality*, which she explains very clearly in a 2016 TED Talk:

> Maybe a simple analogy to an intersection might allow judges to better see Emma's dilemma. So if we think about this intersection, the roads to the intersection would be the way that the workforce was structured by race and by

gender. And then the traffic in those roads would be the hiring policies and the other practices that ran through those roads. Now, because Emma was both black and female, she was positioned precisely where those roads overlapped, experiencing the simultaneous impact of the company's gender and race traffic. The law – the law is like that ambulance that shows up and is ready to treat Emma only if it can be shown that she was harmed on the race road or on the gender road but not where those roads intersected. So what do you call being impacted by multiple forces and then abandoned to fend for yourself? Intersectionality seemed to do it for me.

As you will see in Chapter 2, there is more than one way to define intersectionality. For the purposes of this book, the authors have taken the approach that none of the political institutions and processes we discuss work the same way for everyone, thus we should not talk about a single way of understanding politics and government. Instead, we explain how the political world should work in theory, but also how it affects people differently in practice.

The second thing that makes this book different than most textbooks is that each chapter is written by a different person or group of people. This is because the goal of this book is to bring marginalized voices to the fore so that you get a more well-rounded view of how government and politics work. Each of these authors brings something different to the discussion, which means that you get multiple perspectives. Given that the political world is full of different – often competing – perspectives, the more perspectives you are exposed to, the better you'll be at interpreting politics.

The final thing that makes this book different is *representation* – in this case, I mean seeing people who are like you as agents of political change and as legitimate creators of political knowledge. The people who contributed to this book all believe that representation matters – which is why I borrowed a line from Black political theorist bell hooks as the title of the textbook (political science is for everybody) and why I started this section with a quote from American civil rights activist Marian Wright Edelman: *You can't be what you can't see.* That quote is true in both politics and political science.

For one thing, if you don't see your identity reflected in the pages of a political science textbook, it sends the message that people like you do not participate in politics – particularly not as agents of political change. Sadly, the evidence shows that in political science textbooks, politically underrepresented groups are largely portrayed as the people on the receiving end of policy, not the people creating policy.[13] For another thing, if you look back at Figure 0.1, it tells you that the vast majority of political science students in Anglo-American states (1) have had far more men than women as political science professors (about 3:1), and (2) have likely never seen an Indigenous, Black, Latinx, or Asian political scientist. Moreover, given the low numbers of women, the odds of you having a political science professor who is a woman of color are low. If *you can't be what you can't see*, students of color are not seeing themselves as political scientists. This is why you'll see author pictures at the beginning of each chapter: The majority of the authors are from groups that are marginalized in political science. We want students to see that political science really *is* for everybody.

THE STRUCTURE OF THE BOOK

political science is for everybody is set up in three sections. Part I of the book (Chapters 1–6) focuses on the foundations of politics, including chapters on political theory, ideologies, and political behavior. Part II (Chapters 7–11) is dedicated to comparative politics, one of the main subfields in political science – the one responsible for expanding our understanding of how domestic politics works in different countries. Here, we look at political institutions (executives, legislatures, and courts) and public policy. Finally, Part III (Chapters 12–16) focuses on international relations, also a primary subfield in political science. International relations scholars examine how states interact with each other in the global political system. This section includes chapters on security and conflict, political economy, international law, and international organizations. The book concludes with a brief summary of what the authors and I hope you will take away from this book (spoiler: *All politics are identity politics*).

FINAL NOTE

You will likely notice that some chapters are more formal than others. Some speak directly to you as a student while others leave the audience less specific. Some authors refer to themselves in the first person and others go with the more formal third person. As the editor, I think this gives you some insight into the authors as people – not to mention that the authors wrote the chapters in their preferred voice, and who am I to change that?

NOTES

1 English chemist Rosalind Franklin's work was instrumental in confirming the double-helix structure of DNA. She was not credited with the discovery, however, and three

other DNA researchers received the Nobel Prize instead. Similarly, American physicist and mathematician Katherine Johnson's pioneering work at NASA was not publicly credited to her at the time, and although Jocelyn Bell Burnell, an astrophysicist from Northern Ireland, was the first to observe pulsars, her male supervisor was awarded the Nobel Prize.

2 Black scientist and inventor George Washington Carver was an expert in agricultural science and developed techniques that helped farmers increase crop yields and preserve soil nutrients. He did not invent peanut butter, FYI. New Zealander Ocean Mercier, a Māori physicist of Ngāti Porou descent, has received numerous awards for her work on communicating Māori scientific principles and understanding to the public.

3 Data for Australia from Yasmeen Abu-Laban, Marian Sawer, and Mathieu St-Lauran, "IPSA Gender Monitoring Report 2017"; Quebec: International Political Science Association (2018); Canada: CPSA, Yasmeen Abu-Laban, Joanna Everitt, Richard Johnston, Martin Papillon, and David Rayside, "Report and Analysis of the Canadian Political Science Association Member Survey" (2012), https://www.cpsa-acsp.ca/documents/pdfs/diversity/2012_Diversity_Task_Force_Report.pdf; Ireland: Lisa Keenan, "Gender Audit of the Political Studies Association of Ireland, 2019"; New Zealand: Jennifer Curtin, "Women and Political Science in New Zealand: The State of the Discipline," *Political Science* 65, no. 1 (2013): 63–83; United Kingdom: PSA 2019; United States: APSA, "APSA Membership Data," http://www.apsanet.org/RESOURCES/Data-on-the-Profession/Dashboard/Project-on-Women-and-Minorities.

4 I cannot use the term *murder* because it has a specific legal meaning. At the time of this writing, the now-fired law enforcement officer has been charged with second-degree murder and manslaughter but has not yet been convicted of a crime.

5 The international repercussions are discussed in Chapter 12, "What Is International Relations?"

6 C.E. Cortés, *Multicultural America: A Multimedia Encyclopedia* (London: Sage Publications, 2013), 1703.

7 Ellis P. Monk, Jr., "Pigmentocracies: Ethnicity, Race, and Color in Latin America," (Chicago: University of Chicago Press, 2015), 15–16.

8 John Charles Chasteen, *Born in Blood and Fire: A Concise History of Latin America* (New York & London: W.W. Norton & Company, 2001).

9 Chasteen, *Born in Blood and Fire*.

10 Edward Telles, *Pigmentocracies: Ethnicity, Race, and Color in Latin America* (Chapel Hill: University of North Carolina Press Books, 2014).

11 Telles, *Pigmentocracies*, 3. Personal communication with Dr. Gregg B. Johnson, Valparaiso University.

12 Robin DiAngelo, *White Fragility: Why It's So Hard to Talk to White People about Racism* (Boston: Beacon Press, 2018).

13 Amy L. Atchison, "Where Are the Women? An Analysis of Gender Mainstreaming in Introductory Political Science Textbooks," *Journal of Political Science Education* 13, no. 2 (2017): 185–99; Sherri L. Wallace and Marcus D. Allen, "Survey of African American Portrayal in Introductory Textbooks in American Government/Politics: A Report of the APSA Standing Committee on the Status of Blacks in the Profession," *PS: Political Science & Politics* 41, no. 1 (2008): 153–60.

PART ONE

Foundations of Politics

CHAPTER ONE

What Are the Foundations of Politics?

*Dr. Amy
L. Atchison*

LEARNING OBJECTIVES

1 Become familiar with the basic foundations of politics:
   - Political theory
   - Political ideologies
   - Political behavior
2 Understand how affective polarization harms democracy
3 Understand the concept of democratic backsliding

KEY TERMS

affective polarization   people's increasing hostility toward their ideological
   opponents
canon   the foundational texts of a given academic discipline
civil society   all social and political organizations that exist outside the control of the
   state
cognitive dissonance   emotional discomfort/mental stress caused by the clash between our beliefs and new information

collective action   when groups of people work together to achieve a goal that an individual could not achieve alone

critical political theory   seeks to expose, explain, and remedy the social systems that contribute to oppression in all of its many forms

democratic deficit   the gap between people's idea of how democracy should function and their satisfaction with how it does function

home truths   unpleasant truths – usually pointed out to us by someone else – that make us examine who we are, our faults, and our behavior

legitimacy   people's voluntary acceptance of government

misogyny   ingrained dislike of/disdain for and prejudice against women

politics   who gets what, when, and how

racism   discrimination against persons of another race based on the presumption that one race is superior to another

social identity   a person's sense of self based on the groups (ethnic/racial, linguistic, religious, ideological, etc.) with which they identify

universal truths   things that are true regardless of time or place

WHAT IS POLITICS?

Politics: Who Gets What, When, How is not simply the title of a classic book by political scientist Harold Lasswell (1936),[1] it is also what almost all political scientists will tell you is the basic definition of **politics**. Note that this definition (who gets what, when, how) doesn't mention government at all, and that's not an accident. Politics is, at its core, about resolving conflicts regardless of where those conflicts occur. You see political currents running throughout families, church congregations, friend groups, workplaces, schools, and (yes) government because they all involve human interaction, and human interaction often involves conflict. Politics is a standard feature (or bug?) of all human relationships. Here, of course, we focus on politics as related to government – this is, after all, a political science/government textbook – but remember: The dynamics of who gets what, when, how are at play everywhere.

Focusing on government and politics means that we need to start with the three main elements that are the foundations of politics:

- Political theory, which gives us ways to think about what qualifies as the "good life"
- Political ideology, which is a set of values/beliefs that structure a person's political worldview

- Political behavior, which is how people act in the political realm

Basically, in Part I of this book, you'll be learning about how we think politics *should* work (theory), how people are often motivated to engage with politics (ideology), how theory and ideology overlap, and what people actually do in the political realm (political behavior). This chapter provides a brief introduction to all of the above.

THE BASICS OF POLITICAL THEORY

When political scientists talk about political theory, we're typically talking about works that seek universal truths while attempting to determine the meaning of the "good life," which includes answering questions like the purpose of government, the definition of justice, or the meaning of citizenship (all which you'll read about in the next chapter). Political theorists use their observations to theorize about how the political world operates. Political theory is typically aimed at a narrow audience or scholars, politicians, political commentators, and policymakers and is meant to push readers to think about (and come to their own conclusions about) politics and political processes.

Typical political science textbooks start with ancient philosophers like Plato and Aristotle and end with Marx, with stops at such luminaries as Machiavelli, Locke, Rousseau, and Bentham along the way. All of these men are part of the **canon** (the foundational texts) of classical Western philosophical tradition (read: European). In their quests for **universal truths**, these men all put forth sweeping theories of human nature and the mechanics of society. Yet feminist theorist Mary Hawkesworth notes that as these political theorists make their generalizations about humans, society, and politics, they generally "conflate the experiences of some elite, white, European men with all of human experience."[2] It isn't that they all simply ignore people of color and women. As you'll see in Box 1.1 and Chapter 2, several of the "classic" works of political theory exclude women and people of color from the benefits of citizenship and pursuit of the good life. They deemed people of color less than human and justified the exclusion of women from the political sphere because they were "mere appendages to citizen man."[3] The glaring **racism** and **misogyny** does not mean that we should "cancel" classic political theory. However, it does mean that we cannot treat the insights derived from the classics as universal truths. They may be truths for some of us, but they are certainly not truths for *all* of us.

BOX 1.1: JOHN LOCKE ON THE RIGHTS OF NATIVE AMERICANS, WOMEN, AND ENSLAVED PERSONS

Political philosopher John Locke (1632–1704) is often credited with founding the liberal school of political thought, which rejects absolute power and emphasizes the natural rights of man – European man, that is, since he considered Native Americans to be on the same level as "children, idiots, and the grossly illiterate." On the subject of "man," it is not always clear if Locke means *humanity* or *men*. Although he was more progressive on white women's rights than many of his peers, his status as a proponent of women's rights is highly contested. While he does indicate that all [white] people (arguably including women) are born equal, he does justify women's subordination to their husbands' wills on the basis that men are stronger and more able.[4]

As for his beliefs about enslaved peoples, those are made clear in the *Fundamental Constitutions of Carolina* (1669), the governing document for the then-British Carolina colony. Locke was one of the architects of the *Fundamental Constitutions,* which gave the enslaver "absolute power and authority over his Negro slaves." It also recreated hereditary nobility for the eight Lord Proprietors of Carolina, among whom the lands taken from Native Americans were divided. The *Fundamental Constitutions* also recreated a form of hereditary serfdom that tied poor whites to the Lord Proprietors' lands.

This "father of democracy" profited greatly from his support of enslavement and the theft of land from Native Americans. He owned stock in the Royal Africa Company, which controlled the British slave trade. He was also in line to become one of Carolina's Lord Proprietors, should one of them die without a (male) heir.[5] To be fair, Locke has defenders who say his writings were not a defense of slavery or stolen land in the Americas (see, for example Uzgalis, 2017).[6] There's more on Locke in Chapter 2, so stay tuned.

Critical Political Theory and Home Truths

Critical theory is the direct outgrowth of what many marginalized political theorists regard as the racist, sexist, classist, and other biases embedded in the Lockean and other more conventional streams of political thought that make up the traditional political theory canon. **Critical political theory** encompasses many strands of political thought; what these have in common is that critical theorists seek to expose, explain, and remedy the social systems that contribute to oppression in all of its many forms. Critical theorists are less interested in *universal* truths and more interested in *home* truths. On a personal level, **home truths** are unpleasant truths – usually pointed out to us by someone else – that make us examine who we are, our faults, and our behavior. Societal home truths are the unpleasant facts that force us to examine how our societies really function, how different groups are treated, and how we can be better. Just as personal home truths are pointed out to us by others, societal home truths are most often pointed out by outsiders to the system – people who have traditionally been marginalized. Two such groups, both of whom have been central to advancing critical political theory, are people of color and women. While the theories they advance, such as feminism and critical race theory, are not considered mainstream by many political scientists, they have nevertheless had considerable effects on how we think about politics.

Critical political theorists like Black feminist theorist bell hooks[7] or critical race theorist Mari Matsuda examine structural inequality, meaning the ways in which society creates and maintains patriarchal and racist institutions that oppress women and people of color, and especially women of color. These theorists also identify ways in which we can reduce oppression and increase human freedom – they then challenge each of us to do something about it. This sort of call to action is a place where theory overlaps with ideology (there's a lot of overlap), so let's look at what political ideologies are and then I'll circle back around to how theory and ideology overlap by briefly examining feminism and critical race theory.

THE BASICS OF POLITICAL IDEOLOGIES

The word *ideology* and its derivatives have gotten a bad reputation. In common use, calling a policy *ideological* is shorthand for ill-conceived and extremist. The average person doesn't want to be viewed as ideological, since it implies that we don't think for ourselves. Calling someone an *ideolog* indicates that they are closed-minded and intolerant of other worldviews. Being *ideologically motivated* is such a slur that politicians regularly deny that their words, ideas, or positions are ideological.

We need to get past the negative connotation for a moment to look at what a political ideology actually is. Unfortunately, that isn't as easy as it sounds. As ideology expert David McClellan said, "Ideology is the most elusive concept in the whole of social science."[8] As you'll see in Chapter 3, the term is so contested that political scientists don't have an agreed-upon definition for it. Here, I will simply say that we'll be focused on *political* ideology, meaning a system of beliefs about how society should be governed. In other words, a political ideology is a system of beliefs about who *should* get what, when, and how.

Unlike political theories, which tend to sound educational or "objective," political ideologies generally don't have this façade. They are typically written in simple and targeted language that is designed to convince people that *this* ideology is the right one – the proper way to govern a society. As scholar Lyman Tower Sargent puts it, "An ideology provides the believer with a picture of the world both as it is and as it should be, and, in doing so, it organizes the tremendous complexity of the world into something fairly simple and understandable."[9] This simplicity is the allure of ideologies. Adopting an ideology guides people's understanding of how society works, it tells them what they should support or oppose, it calls them to act on their beliefs, and it gives adherents a sense of community and common purpose.[10] Ultimately, adopting a political ideology embeds you in a group of people who all share a similar worldview.

Divided We Fall

The sense of inclusion we feel when we adopt an ideological viewpoint may be why, despite negative feelings about ideology as a general concept, people regularly and enthusiastically embrace specific ideologies. Being part of an ideological group defines a person as a member (us) and everyone else as non-members (them). This us–them dynamic, where a person believes their group to be superior to the other group, contributes to the increase in people who have built their ideological commitment into their **social identity** – meaning they view their ideological belief system as a fundamental component of who they are as a person.[11] Indeed, some research indicates that people's identification with a political ideology is as strong as their racial or religious identity.[12]

The increase in ideology-based identity is a factor in what we call **affective polarization** – meaning people's increasing enmity toward their ideological opponents. Affective polarization is more than simple dislike or disagreement; it is active hostility rooted in the idea that your ideological opponents are not just wrong – they're your enemy, traitors to the state, and all-around bad people. Sadly, it is becoming increasingly common for people to refuse to date, build friendships with, or even have meaningful discussions with those who don't share their political ideology and opinions.[13] This trend is problematic in democratic societies, which require willingness to compromise in order to function properly; affective polarization erodes trust in government and reduces government capacity to act. In short: High levels of affective polarization are *very* bad for democracy (see Box 1.2).

Even where people aren't feeling outright hostility to the other side, they still have a hard time accepting other perspectives. For instance, if you have ever argued

---

BOX 1.2: AFFECTIVE POLARIZATION: A DANGER TO DEMOCRACY

For democracy to work, people have to be willing to talk about their differences and compromise on solutions. Increasing levels of affective polarization in long-standing democracies are troubling because, as political scientist Seymour Martin Lipset wrote, "Inherent in all democratic systems is the constant threat that the group conflicts which are democracy's lifeblood may solidify to the point where they threaten to disintegrate society."[14] If people won't even talk to their opponents, there's no hope for compromise. Worse, as levels of affective polarization increase, trust in government decreases among people whose preferred party is not in government, but democratic satisfaction increases in people who voted for the winners.[15] In turn, legislative productivity – getting things done – declines. Since people dislike their ideological opponents and have far different beliefs about the efficacy of government, the public doesn't agree on enough to pressure parties to act.[16] Given parties' inaction, very little gets done, which the parties blame on their opponents – once more feeding into people's dislike of their opponents and increasing affective polarization.

How do we get past this if people won't even talk to each other? Perhaps, as Hobolt, Leeper, and Tilley suggest, "political scientists, and political theorists, should move beyond trying to understand how to overcome political disagreements, and focus more on how those disagreements can be sustained without yielding deleterious social consequences."[17] In other words: We have to figure out how to disagree while still respecting that the "other side" also wants what is best for the country – people have to recognize each other as fellow citizens rather than enemies.

---

politics with a particularly ideologically minded friend or relative, you've probably wondered why providing strong evidence to support your position failed to change the other person's mind. There are many reasons, but chief among them is that people experience **cognitive dissonance** when confronted with evidence that contradicts their beliefs. Cognitive dissonance is emotional discomfort/mental stress caused by the clash between our beliefs and new information. As a species, we don't do well with cognitive dissonance, and our brains are very good at figuring out how to restore mental harmony. Some research shows that we reject new evidence to reduce the discomfort of cognitive dissonance, while other research says that we actually may accept that the new evidence is true but we don't allow it to change our minds.[18]

The Overlap between Theory and Ideology

Where things may get a little confusing with political theories and political ideologies is that there is considerable overlap between the two. In the earlier sections of this chapter, I summarized some of the major differences between political theory and political ideology. However, it is important for you to understand that this is a simplification we professors often use to make the distinctions between theory and ideology more accessible. The challenge is that separating the two as I've done above – and as we've done in Chapters 2 and 3 – implies that theories and ideologies are neatly separable. While they may be separable in the abstract, that is often not the case in practice, where there is considerable overlap between the two.

It may help to use feminism and critical race theory (CRT) to show two ways that theory and ideology can overlap. In both cases, the ideology is firmly rooted in the theory. Activists use knowledge generated by theorists to tackle the many ways in which racism and sexism marginalize women and people of color.

Why use feminism and CRT as examples? Feminists and critical race theorists agree that sexism and racism intersect with other oppressive and exclusionary belief systems, such as homophobia and classism.[19] Indeed, the theory that underlies this textbook, *intersectionality*, draws from both feminism and CRT. Thus, a (very) basic overview of each will be useful to you as the book progresses (see Tables 1.1 and 1.2). That said, keep in mind that, as with all political theories and ideologies, there are *many* different interpretations of both feminism and CRT. What is discussed here is less than even the tip of the iceberg (there are suggestions for further reading at the end of the chapter).

Table 1.1. **Feminism**

As a Theory	As an Ideology
Feminist theorists have demonstrated that the canon, the foundational texts, both omits women and justifies that omission by disparaging women's capacity for political agency, free will, or reason, and even by questioning women's right to exist in the public sphere. However, women cannot simply be added to the canon since the canon is largely predicated on the exclusion of women. Thus, the feminist approach isn't to "add women and stir," but rather to question how our understanding of politics changes when women are considered as full members of society. In so doing, feminist political theory gives us new ways to think about the political world.[20] The knowledge created by feminist theorists drives calls to improve women's standing in society.	Feminists seek to end the *patriarchy*, meaning the societal hierarchy that has historically given men the majority of power in society. As a group, however, feminists strongly disagree about how to achieve the goal. They do agree, however, on three central tenets of feminist ideology: • Gender is a significant and enduring fault line in society • This cleavage is highly unequal, with women disadvantaged by the patriarchy. • Political action is required to end the patriarchal norms embedded in society.[21] Feminism has animated women's movements around the world, including the suffrage, women's liberation, and Women's March movements.

Table 1.2. **Critical Race Theory**

As a Theory	As an Ideology
CRT grew out of both the realization that the US civil rights movement had stalled and the need to understand why. CRT theory demonstrates that not only is racism the default in society, it serves the interests of the dominant group.[22] Because racism serves those interests, the dominant group has little incentive to tackle racism in meaningful ways unless doing so serves their interests. The classic example comes from Derrick Bell, who proposed that the US Supreme Court's decision in *Brown v. Board of Education*, to racially integrate the US's long-segregated education system, was less about Black equality than about serving the interests of elite Americans. Indeed, evidence from diplomatic cables and government archives shows that *Brown* was part of the US attempt to make itself more attractive to non-white countries during the Cold War.[23] CRT scholars are not content with knowledge production; the tenets of CRT demand that the knowledge be used in the fight for social justice.[24]	Importantly, CRT indicates that because racism is both conscious and subconscious, ending overt racism won't end societal inequalities. Rather than seeking an end to racism, activists work toward social justice and attempt to remedy historical and ongoing injustices. CRT theorists do so by exposing the racialization of society – the ways in which race is embedded in modern society; they then seek to rectify the harms caused by racialization. For example, CRT scholars have demonstrated tremendous racialized inequalities in the US criminal justice system, from unwarranted traffic stops of Black Americans to mass incarceration, which disproportionately affects the Black community. This knowledge animates the Black Lives Matter (BLM) movement, which started as a response to the senseless killing of Trayvon Martin and the acquittal of his killer. BLM is now a global Black liberation movement dedicated to "creating a world free of anti-Blackness, where every Black person has the social, economic, and political power to thrive."[25]

THE BASICS OF POLITICAL BEHAVIOR

As political behavior experts Russel J. Dalton and Hans-Dieter Klingemann put it, the major debates among political behavior scholars flow from the "claim that the wellspring of politics flows from the attitudes and behaviors of the ordinary citizen, and that the institutions of a democratic political process should be structured to respond to the citizenry."[26] When you consider that it's all about people and how they act in the political realm, and how political institutions respond to that, it makes sense that the study of political behavior encompasses a wide range of subjects. Political behavior scholars study everything from democratization to political communication to political culture to political participation. Since this textbook is intended for a survey course, there isn't enough space to encompass the full breadth of political behavior. In this section we focus on political participation, including civil society, political parties, and voting.

Civil Society

In the previous section of this chapter, you read a lot about people and ideological groups. Ideological groups, however, are not formal organizations with members and meetings (because, as you'll see in Chapter 3, ideologies and parties are not synonymous). Since people are social beings, we form all sorts of organizations – and you have likely belonged to several. For example, you may belong to a house of worship (church, mosque, temple), a club or student organization (or many), a philanthropic/volunteer group, or a community association. Organizations like these make up what we call **civil society**, meaning all of the social and political organizations that exist outside the control of the state.

Civil society is an important factor in *pluralistic* societies, those in which many opposing and competing viewpoints are tolerated, if not welcomed. These many viewpoints often give rise to different types of civil society organizations, a variety of which are discussed in Chapter 4. Here, I only mention two: interest groups and social movements. Both of these are forms of **collective action**, wherein groups of people work together to achieve a goal that an individual could not achieve alone.

INTEREST GROUPS

Interest groups are formally constituted organizations that seek to influence public policy related to their issue areas (the stuff they care about). Interest groups, like labor/trade unions, lobbyist groups, or issue-based groups (Greenpeace, Amnesty International, etc.), are well organized and work within the political system to achieve their goals (e.g., by lobbying legislatures or bureaucracies). But how effective are these groups at influencing policy? Do their efforts help or hurt democratic governance? These are questions that political behavior scholars regularly attempt to answer. In the interests of space, in Box 1.3 we'll look at only two ways political scientists approach the question of interest groups and democracy: pluralism and corporatism.

BOX 1.3: INTEREST GROUPS AND DEMOCRATIC POLITICS

Pluralism is the theory that politics is driven by interest group competition, and through participation in interest groups, citizens have direct involvement in the making of the laws that govern them.[27] Importantly, pluralists argue that interest groups may have differing levels of power, but none is so powerful that it dominates the rest. In turn, advocates contend that since no single group dominates, all groups are able to participate and competition keeps the power of each interest group in check – that is, pluralism is a fair and beneficial system in a representative democracy. Critics, however, counter that competition doesn't actually constrain group power and that some groups become highly powerful and influential while other interests go almost unrepresented.[28] For example, critics of pluralism point to the National Rifle Association in the United States, whose outsized political influence constrains gun control policies despite evidence that a majority of Americans support stricter gun control laws – 60 per cent in 2019, according to the Pew Research Center.[29]

Corporatism is the theory that interest groups do compete, but they also co-operate both with each other and with government agencies to achieve their goals, thus giving interest groups a formal role in policymaking. Advocates point to corporatist tripartite (three-party) bargaining in European states like Germany or Norway, in which labor and wage policy is crafted in formal negotiations between the state, labor unions, and employer federations. Proponents argue that this system is beneficial to democracy because it ensures that the interests of workers/citizens and industry are given equal positions in the policymaking process and stimulates more deliberation regarding public interest.[30] In contrast, critics argue that corporatism only gives citizens influence if the interest groups truly represent citizen interests, yet these groups are typically controlled by elites who are fairly removed from their organizations' members and may or may not negotiate with members' interests in mind.[31]

SOCIAL MOVEMENTS

Social movements are groups of people who have come together around a particular issue, such as minority rights or the environment. In general, they are less formally organized and their goals may be less specific than those of interest groups – although interest groups often participate in social movements related to their area of interest (e.g., Greenpeace is a participant in the environmental movement). Social movements typically operate outside of the formal institutions of government. Indeed, social movements challenge formal institutions through continued protest and activism on behalf of the movement's cause.

Social movement scholars attempt to answer a wide range of questions, including (but not limited to) the conditions under which movements arise, why people are motivated to join movements, how movements affect and are affected by the political environment in a given state, and when and to what extent social movements succeed in achieving their goals.

The expansion of democratic practices within societies has been a frequent topic of interest for scholars. The limited nature of early democracy makes democratization (the process of becoming a democratic state) a good example of how social movements can transform society. As social movements' expert Ruud Koopmans points out, social movements have expanded democracy in at least two ways: who can vote (suffrage) and which issues matter to politicians (the political agenda).[32] First, it's important to remember that in the initial stages of democracy, suffrage was quite limited; men without property, women, and minorities were typically excluded from the voting booth. Suffrage was only extended to those groups after sustained campaigns by labor, women's, and civil rights movements, respectively. Second, government tends to maintain the status quo rather than seek out new issues to tackle. Social movements are often responsible for putting new issues on the political agenda. Take, for example, environmental protection. The environment was not considered an appropriate subject for government action until social movements around the world agitated for better regulation of pollution, recycling programs, and a host of other environmental conservation policies.

While social movements do not always spawn political parties, the environmental movement of the 1960s and 1970s led to the development of Green parties throughout Western Europe.[33] Green parties were primarily created to advocate for environmental protection and conservation, but they also typically advocate for social justice policies that decrease oppression and discrimination. Green parties are related to both the environmental movement and to environmentally focused interest groups, but each of the three (party/movement/group) has its own role to play in terms of political participation. Interest groups work within the formal structures of government via lobbying and partnerships, social movements work outside of those structures via protest, and parties work (via campaigns and elections) to become members of government and represent the interests of their constituents.

Parties, Voting, and Backsliding

In a direct democracy, each citizen would be required to participate in decision making by voting on every law adopted by the state. As you might suppose, this could easily become a very messy enterprise. Instead, democratic states are (to a greater or lesser extent) representative democracies.[34] In a representative democracy, citizens delegate decision making to elected officials whose job it is (ostensibly) to represent the interests of their constituents. Their job is to represent the interests of their constituents, but how do they know what those interests are? How do constituents make clear what it is they want? Those are complex questions with complex answers. One part of the answer is *political parties*.

POLITICAL PARTIES

While there are many types and definitions of political parties, for our purposes they are groups that participate in elections with the goal of acquiring power to influence government outcomes (policies). If they simply sought to influence public policies, they would just be interest groups; it is the contesting of elections that separates the two.[35]

While many have disparaged parties – James Madison famously sneered at what he called "factions," warning that that they were dangerous to democracy – almost every democratic state has some sort of organized political party system. Why are parties ubiquitous in democratic societies? Because parties are what we call *linkage institutions*. Simply put, they are the primary way in which citizens connect with the state. Less simply put, parties are the primary linkages in the following ways:[36]

- Campaigns: recruiting candidates and putting them forth for office
- Elections: motivating citizen interest in the election and encouraging them to vote
- Interest aggregation: bringing together the interests of a group of citizens in a (coherent) policy program
- Representation: connecting voter policy preferences with the policymaking process
- Policy outcomes: delivering on the policy promises made while campaigning

As you can see, parties have tremendous influence throughout the political process. Without them, it would be quite difficult to hold elections or govern. First, parties simplify the choices available to voters by providing heuristics (mental shortcuts) that allow voters to make choices without having to work too hard at it – the party label itself tells people much of what they need to know about what/ for whom they are voting. Returning to the Green parties example, when voters see the Green Party label, voters know that the basic policy program centers on environmental protection and social justice, thus for many voters there is no need to do further research. Second, parties recruit and train candidates, thus helping elections run more smoothly. Finally, when parties win, they turn candidates into elected representatives and through those representatives, parties structure the work of government as they attempt to implement the policy program for which their constituents voted.

VOTER TURNOUT

At least that's how representative democracy should work – citizens' interests (as expressed by their votes) should drive the work of government. If it were that straightforward, however, voter turnout – which is in decline in long-established

Figure 1.1. **Voter Turnout in Anglo-American States, 1970–2019**

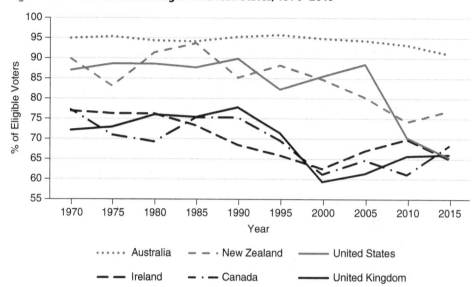

Source: Data from the Institute for Democracy and Electoral Assistance (IDEA) Voter Turnout Database, 2020.
Note: Chart shows parliamentary election turnout for the election closest to the year listed for all states except the United States. US data are for the presidential election closest to the year listed.

democracies – might look a lot different.[37] Figure 1.1 shows the voter turnout decline in Anglo-American states. Note that turnout has decreased even in Australia, where voting is compulsory.

Because voting is a central feature of democracy, scholars have been studying voting behavior for decades. Among the most important questions are who votes and why. In established democracies, age and education are both dominant factors in voter turnout. The older and better educated, the more likely a person is to vote.[38] Older people may be more inclined to vote because of a sense of civic duty, a greater stake in the system (they are more likely to own property or have children, for example), and they likely pay more attention to politics. The latter, paying more attention, likely factors into the education gap in voting as well – the better informed, the more likely a person is to vote. Education also matters because the more educated tend to be involved in more civil society organizations, which fosters political interest and learning.

Consider the following, however:

1   The median age in Western countries is increasing (there are more old and middle-aged people than young people).

2 There have been significant increases in the number of people getting university degrees.

3 Voter turnout is declining.

If there are larger numbers of older and better educated people, why is voter turnout declining? In short: We are not sure. Political scientists have explored institutional, demographic, and attitudinal hypotheses to attempt to answer this question, yet most answers have been found to be lacking.[39]

First, the institutional hypotheses fall apart given that the decline is fairly steady across most established democracies, regardless of their institutional setup (electoral systems, party systems, etc.). Second, the demographic explanation indicates that voter turnout should decline gradually as older generations die off and less-interested generations take their place; however, the decline has not been gradual – it took a statistically significant downward turn starting in 1980. However, there *is* evidence that it is among younger generations where turnout is weakest.[40] This is where the attitudinal hypothesis comes into play. Scholars hypothesize that the decrease in voting is related to a decline in citizens' belief that (1) voting is a civic duty and (2) voting matters; it may be that this decline is largest among younger citizens. The attitudinal hypothesis may have some validity. As experts Marc Hooghe and Anna Kern put it, "Citizens of liberal democracies may indeed … have stopped believing that they have a civic duty to take part in elections."[41] However, this answer is not definitive, and it leads to more questions: Why 1980? Why are younger people less likely to see voting as a civic duty? Why are people now less likely to think their vote matters? Of course, you may be wondering if the decrease in voter turnout even matters; democratic states are still functioning, after all.

DEMOCRATIC BACKSLIDING

From a normative perspective – how we think democracy should ideally work – turnout matters quite a lot. From the ideal perspective, high participation is an important part of a well-functioning democracy. Theoretically, high turnout means that more citizens have used their vote to make their preferences known and hold elected officials accountable, thus increasing people's belief in government **legitimacy**, meaning their voluntary acceptance of government.

Also theoretically, when turnout is low it may undermine people's confidence in both government legitimacy and the results of the election: They may feel that the election results themselves are illegitimate. Low turnout may also indicate a growing **democratic deficit**, or the gap between people's idea of how democracy

Figure 1.2. Executive Takeovers and Democratic Breakdowns, 1973–2018

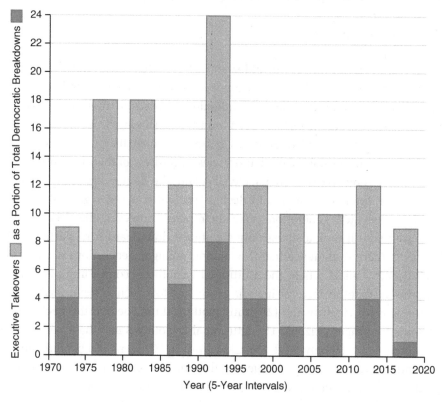

Source: Created using data from Milan W. Svolik, "Polarization versus Democracy," *Journal of Democracy* 30, no. 3 (2019): 22.

should function and their satisfaction with how it does function.[42] If the democratic deficit is high, people's dissatisfaction may drive them away from the polls. However, the research into voter turnout and satisfaction provides mixed results. While some studies demonstrate a voter turnout–dissatisfaction link, others find low voter turnout instead means that people are basically satisfied with how their state is functioning.[43] Why is it difficult to arrive at a definitive answer about how satisfied people are with democratic governance? Because questions of people's trust in government and feelings of political efficacy (feeling that your participation matters) are all tangled up with their satisfaction levels.

It is important that we keep trying to understand people's attitudes toward democracy, however, given global concerns about *democratic backsliding*. Backsliding is what happens when governments in democratic states undermine or eliminate institutions and rules that sustain democracy. It is easier to undermine democratic institutions, particularly under the guise of "reform," when people are dissatisfied with them. A good example of backsliding is *executive takeover*, in which an elected authoritarian-leaning leader erodes democratic institutions and consolidates power. In modern democracies, executive takeovers do not typically look like Hitler's executive takeover in Germany – he moved swiftly and boldly to gut Germany's fledgling democracy. Today, executive takeovers are slow; leaders gradually erode democratic institutions so carefully that their actions may lead to the total breakdown of democracy. Indeed, political scientist Milan Svolik has found that executive takeover leading to democratic breakdown has been increasing since the end of the Cold War, as shown in Figure 1.2;[44] this is what happened in Venezuela, which was once a vibrant (if imperfect) democracy (see Box 1.4).

BOX 1.4: DEMOCRATIC BACKSLIDING IN VENEZUELA

Venezuela could be called the poster child of democratic backsliding, as political scientists Stephen Levitsky and Daniel Ziblatt detail in the best-selling book *How Democracies Die*.[45] Democratic governance flourished in Venezuela from 1958 through the 1970s and 1980s, when much of the region was in the grip of military dictatorships, and into the 1990s. It wasn't all smooth sailing, though – in the late 1980s and early 1990s oil prices tanked, poverty doubled, the economy stagnated, and ordinary Venezuelans became fed up with the status quo. When Venezuelans elected Hugo Chávez as president in 1998, they expected him to shake up the system and use the state's oil wealth to reduce poverty and inequality. In the early years of his presidency, Chávez followed through on his campaign promises, implementing important economic and social welfare programs that benefited the poor (although these became highly *clientelistic*, meaning the resources were often delivered based on political grounds rather than technical reasons).[46] But by 2003–4, his authoritarian tendencies were starting to show – stalling a recall election (it would have removed him from office), then packing the Supreme Court with his supporters, and blacklisting anyone who supported the recall. In 2006, things took an even sharper authoritarian turn when Chávez had high-profile opponents arrested or exiled and eliminated term limits so that he could serve as many terms as he liked. Chávez continued chipping away at Venezuela's democratic institutions until his death in 2013, and his hand-picked successor, Nicolas Maduro, picked up where Chávez left off.[47] By 2017, all pretense of democracy was gone; Venezuela had completed its backslide into full-fledged authoritarian rule.

The specter of democratic backsliding hangs over much of the democratic world, as evidenced by the popularity of elected authoritarian-leaning leaders in supposedly democratic states. Remember: Democratic backsliding isn't a coup d'état in which outsiders take over by force. Backsliding is planned and carried out by elected incumbents. Elected leaders like Viktor Orbán in Hungary, Rafael Correa in Ecuador, and Recep Tayyip Erdoğan in Turkey have leveraged people's frustrations with their states' social problems (immigration, the economy, etc.) to win power and subsequently weaken democratic institutions.[48]

Keep in mind that constitutions cannot cover all contingencies, so democratic societies develop norms – unwritten but widely understood rules – that address regularly occurring contingencies. One of the ways politicians undermine democracy is by demolishing these norms; they know they can get away with it from a legal perspective because the rules are informal and unwritten. For example, Levitsky and Ziblatt note one of the long-standing norms in American politics was *institutional forbearance* – the unwritten rule that politicians won't use extreme tactics that are technically legal if using them violates the spirit of the law.[49] However, the demolition of the institutional forbearance norm, particularly in the US Congress, over the past few decades has helped to destroy another important American norm: *mutual toleration*. This is the idea that, although you don't *agree* with (or even like) your political rivals, you accept that they were legitimately elected and have the right to govern.[50] The elimination of these norms adds to citizens' perceptions that the "other side" is the problem; in other words, destroying these norms has helped to foster greater affective polarization.

Putting the Pieces Together: Affective Polarization, Voting, and Democratic Backsliding

Earlier in this chapter, you read about *affective polarization*, or people's outright hostility toward their political opponents. It turns out that as societies become more polarized, it becomes easier for authoritarian-leaning leaders to undermine democracy – even in states where citizens profess high levels of support for democracy, like the United States. Unfortunately, the voting behaviors of those citizens increasingly indicate that their support for democracy is limited by polarization.

In states with increasing levels of affective polarization, the shrinking pool of centrist voters means that there are fewer voters who are willing to put their principles before their partisan or policy preferences. When the choice is between (1) voting for an authoritarian-leaning politician that appeals to their interests and (2) a democratic-leaning politician whose platform is less appealing, it is democratic principles that are more likely to be sacrificed. Indeed, Svolik found that in states as diverse as the United States, Turkey, and Venezuela, "Ordinary people are willing to trade off democratic principles for partisan interests" and "voters are reluctant to punish politicians for disregarding democratic principles when doing so requires abandoning one's favored party or policies."[51] In short, when it's their authoritarian candidate, large portions of the electorate will look the other way. They know they can leverage affective polarization, so aspiring authoritarians subvert democracy by pitting citizens against each other, heightening their animosity toward each other until it is unthinkable to vote for the "other side" even in the face of growing authoritarianism. It's classic divide-and-conquer. Understanding the tactic enables you to fight against democratic backsliding.

What can you do? Here, I give you a few of historian Timothy Snyder's 20 lessons for avoiding authoritarianism.[52] The first is to "not obey in advance." By this, he means do not give your allegiance to candidates or parties that have already declared authoritarian intent. Use your vote to support candidates that support democracy. Second, defend a democratic institution – maybe it's the press, the legislature, the courts – it doesn't matter which one you pick, just pick one and defend it from undemocratic practices. Among his other lessons are to "believe in truth," "investigate," and "learn from others in other countries"; in other words, think critically, don't believe propaganda blindly, and seek outside perspectives. And finally, I leave you with one last lesson from Professor Snyder: "make eye contact and small talk." While this may seem trivial, it is people's increasing unwillingness to talk to each other and breach our divides that gives aspiring authoritarians the opening they need to weaken democracy. Each of us, no matter what our ideological bent, can help safeguard democracy. The question is whether we will all do so.

At the end of this book there is an appendix with more ideas for how you can get involved and safeguard democracy.

SUMMARY

- The basic definition of politics is *who gets what, when, how.*
- The foundations of politics are the following:
  - Political theory, which gives us ways to think about what qualifies as the "good life"
  - Political ideology, which is a set of values/beliefs that structure a person's political worldview
  - Political behavior, which is how people act in the political realm

- Many of the foundational political theory texts are riddled with racism, sexism, classism, and other biases.
  - Critical theory, largely developed by scholars from marginalized groups, pushes back against the canon, exposing different forms of structural injustice and proposing remedies to those injustices. Critical race theory and feminism are two examples of critical theory.
- Political ideology is a controversial concept and many people view it negatively. However, people frequently adopt ideological outlooks that structure their view of how the world works. It is increasingly common for people to view their political worldview as part of their identity, just as people view ethnicity or religion as part of their identity.
  - The more strongly people identify with an ideology, the more likely they are to be actively hostile to people with other ideological viewpoints, a problem known as *affective polarization*.
- Although presented separately, there is considerable overlap between political theory and ideology. The two cannot be as easily separated either in practice or in theory.
- Civil society, the organizations outside the control of government, is essential to a functioning democracy. Among the many types of organizations are interest groups, which work inside the formal institutions of government in their quest to affect public policy, and social movements, which are less-formal groups that have come together around a particular issue and work outside the formal institutions of government (e.g., through protest).
- Political parties provide the primary link between citizens and the state. Parties are involved in every stage of the political process, from candidate recruitment to policy outcomes.
- While even some authoritarian regimes have elections (e.g., North Korea), it is free and fair elections that are a hallmark of democratic governance. Voter turnout is falling in the oldest democracies; we cannot be sure if this is a sign that people are satisfied with their governments or if they are not.
- Democratic backsliding happens when governments in democratic states undermine or eliminate institutions and rules that sustain democracy. Citizens have shown that when the authoritarian-leaning leader comes from "their side" of the political divide, they are more likely to ignore or forgive actions that undermine democracy. Thus, affective polarization helps to enable democratic backsliding.
  - Knowing the tactics enables you to fight against efforts to undermine democracy.

CONCLUDING QUESTIONS

1 What types of politics do you see in your daily life?
2 Why does critical theory exist? What are these theorists criticizing and why?
3 Affective polarization. Discuss.
4 Democratic deficit is the difference between the perception of how democracy is and the idea of what it should be. Thinking about your society, is there a democratic deficit? If so, what seems to be driving it?
5 Why are political scientists and democracy advocates so concerned about democratic backsliding?

NOTES

1 Harold D. Lasswell, *Politics; Who Gets What, When, How* (New York: Whittlesey House, 1936).
2 Mary Hawkesworth, *Gender and Political Theory: Feminist Reckonings* (Hoboken, NJ: John Wiley & Sons, 2019), 61.
3 Linda Zerilli, *Feminist Theory and the Canon of Political Thought* (New York: Oxford University Press, 2009), 106.
4 Hawkesworth, *Gender and Political Theory.*
5 James Farr, "Locke, Natural Law, and New World Slavery," *Political Theory* 36, no. 4 (2008): 495–522.
6 William Uzgalis, "John Locke, Racism, Slavery, and Indian Lands," in *The Oxford Handbook of Philosophy and Race,* ed. Naomi Zack (New York: Oxford University Press, 2017), 21.
7 Gloria Jean Watkins, better known as bell hooks, chose to use a pen name and always wrote it with lowercase letters so that the reader was focused on what she wrote and thought, not her personal identity. See Debora Basler Wisneski, "bell hooks: Scholar, Cultural Critic, Feminist, and Teacher," in *A Critical Pedagogy of Resistance,* ed. James D. Kirylo (Rotterdam, Netherlands: Brill Sense, 2013), 73–6.
8 David McLellan, *Ideology* (Minneapolis: University of Minnesota Press, 1995), 1.
9 Lyman Sargent, *Contemporary Political Ideologies: A Comparative Analysis* (Toronto: Nelson Education, 2008), 2.
10 Willard A. Mullins, "On the Concept of Ideology in Political Science," *American Political Science Review* 66, no. 2 (1972): 498–510.
11 Christopher J. Devine, "Ideological Social Identity: Psychological Attachment to Ideological In-Groups as a Political Phenomenon and a Behavioral Influence," *Political Behavior* 37, no. 3 (2015): 509–35; Shanto Iyengar, Yphtach Lelkes, Matthew Levendusky, Neil Malhotra, and Sean J. Westwood, "The Origins and Consequences of Affective Polarization in the United States," *Annual Review of Political Science* 22 (2019): 129–46; Lilliana Mason, "Ideologues without Issues: The Polarizing Consequences of Ideological Identities," *Public Opinion Quarterly* 82, no. S1 (2018): 866–87.

12　Thomas A. DiPrete, Andrew Gelman, Tyler McCormick, Julien Teitler, and Tian Zheng, "Segregation in Social Networks Based on Acquaintanceship and Trust," *American Journal of Sociology* 116, no. 4 (2011): 1234–83.

13　DiPrete et al., "Segregation in Social Networks"; Casey A. Klofstad, Rose McDermott, and Peter K. Hatemi, "The Dating Preferences of Liberals and Conservatives," *Political Behavior* 35, no. 3 (2013): 519–38.

14　Seymour Martin Lipset, *Political Man: The Social Bases of Politics* (New York: Doubleday, 1959), 83.

15　Christopher J. Anderson, André Blais, Shaun Bowler, Todd Donovan, and Ola Listhaug, *Losers' Consent: Elections and Democratic Legitimacy* (New York: Oxford University Press, 2007); Pippa Norris, "Do Perceptions of Electoral Malpractice Undermine Democratic Satisfaction? The US in Comparative Perspective," *International Political Science Review* 40, no. 1 (2019): 5–22.

16　Marc J. Hetherington and Thomas J. Rudolph, *Why Washington Won't Work: Polarization, Political Trust, and the Governing Crisis* (Chicago: University of Chicago Press, 2015).

17　Sara B. Hobolt, Thomas Leeper, and James Tilley, *Divided by the Vote: Affective Polarization in the Wake of Brexit* (Boston: American Political Science Association, 2018), 27.

18　Brendan Nyhan, Ethan Porter, Jason Reifler, and Thomas J. Wood, "Taking Fact-Checks Literally but Not Seriously? The Effects of Journalistic Fact-Checking on Factual Beliefs and Candidate Favorability," *Political Behavior* 42 (2020): 939–60.

19　Devon W. Carbado and Daria Roithmayr, "Critical Race Theory Meets Social Science," *Annual Review of Law and Social Science* 10 (2014): 149–67.

20　Zerilli, *Feminist Theory*, 106–7.

21　Clare Chambers, "Feminism," in *The Oxford Handbook of Political Ideologies*, eds. Michael Freeden, Lyman Tower Sargent, and Marc Stears (Oxford: Oxford University Press, 2013), chap. 30, 562–82.

22　Note that CRT was initially an American construct, but theorists have demonstrated that it "travels" well; that is, the theory works across countries.

23　Richard Delgado, Jean Stefancic, and Ernesto Liendo, *Critical Race Theory: An Introduction*, 2nd ed. (New York: New York University Press, 2012).

24　Margaret Zamudio, Christopher Russell, Francisco Rios, and Jacquelyn L. Bridgeman, *Critical Race Theory Matters: Education and Ideology* (New York: Routledge, 2011).

25　Black Lives Matter, "What We Believe," https://blacklivesmatter.com/what-we-believe.

26　Russell J. Dalton and Hans-Dieter Klingemann, *Citizens and Political Behavior* (New York: Oxford University Press, 2009), 3.

27　Reginald J. Harrison, *Pluralism and Corporatism: The Political Evolution of Modern Democracies* (New York: Routledge, 2019).

28　Harrison, *Pluralism and Corporatism*.

29　Katherine Schaeffer, "Share of Americans Who Favor Stricter Gun Laws Has Increased since 2017," Pew Research Center, 2019, https://www.pewresearch.org/fact-tank/2019/10/16/share-of-americans-who-favor-stricter-gun-laws-has-increased-since-2017.

30　Jane Mansbridge, "A Deliberative Perspective on Neocorporatism," *Politics & Society* 20, no. 4 (1992): 493–505.

31 Harrison, *Pluralism and Corporatism*; Christian Hunold, "Corporatism, Pluralism, and Democracy: Toward a Deliberative Theory of Bureaucratic Accountability," *Governance* 14, no. 2 (2001): 151–67.

32 Ruud Koopmans, "Social Movements," in *The Oxford Handbook of Political Behavior* (New York: Oxford University Press, 2009).

33 Koopmans, "Social Movements."

34 The Swiss, for example, have a strong tradition of direct democracy, and many national issues are decided by referendum – meaning they are voted on by citizens rather than by members of the legislature. In the United Kingdom, despite the recent example of the referendum on leaving the European Union (a.k.a. the Brexit vote), direct democracy is rare. (As of 2019, there have been three national-level referendums and eight subnational referendums, according to the UK Parliament's website).

35 Russell J. Dalton, David M. Farrell, and Ian McAllister, *Political Parties and Democratic Linkage: How Parties Organize Democracy* (New York: Oxford University Press, 2011).

36 Dalton et al., *Political Parties*, 7.

37 André Blais, "Turnout in Elections," in *The Oxford Handbook of Political Behavior* (New York: Oxford University Press, 2009).

38 Blais, "Turnout in Elections."

39 Marc Hooghe and Anna Kern, "The Tipping Point between Stability and Decline: Trends in Voter Turnout, 1950–1980–2012," *European Political Science* 16, no. 4 (2017): 535–52.

40 André Blais and Daniel Rubenson, "The Source of Turnout Decline: New Values or New Contexts?," *Comparative Political Studies* 46, no. 1 (2013): 95–117.

41 Hooghe and Kern, "The Tipping Point," 547.

42 Pippa Norris, *Democratic Deficit: Critical Citizens Revisited* (New York: Cambridge University Press, 2011).

43 Filip Kostelka and André Blais, "The Chicken and Egg Question: Satisfaction with Democracy and Voter Turnout," *PS: Political Science & Politics* 51, no. 2 (2018): 370–6; Georg Lutz and Michael Marsh, "Introduction: Consequences of Low Turnout," *Electoral Studies* 26, no. 3 (2007): 539–47.

44 Milan W. Svolik, "Polarization versus Democracy," *Journal of Democracy* 30, no. 3 (2019): 20–32.

45 Steven Levitsky and Daniel Ziblatt, *How Democracies Die* (New York: Crown, 2018).

46 Michael Penfold-Becerra, "Clientelism and Social Funds: Evidence from Chávez's Misiones," *Latin American Politics and Society* 49, no. 4 (2007): 63–84.

47 Svolik, "Polarization." For a good overview of several books on the topic, see Scott Mainwaring, "From Representative Democracy to Participatory Competitive Authoritarianism: Hugo Chávez and Venezuelan Politics," *Perspectives on Politics* 10, no. 4 (2012): 955–67.

48 Levitsky and Ziblatt, *How Democracies Die*.

49 Levitsky and Ziblatt, *How Democracies Die*.

50 Levitsky and Ziblatt, *How Democracies Die*.

51 Svolik, "Polarization," 24, 26.

52 Timothy Snyder, *On Tyranny: Twenty Lessons from the Twentieth Century* (New York: Tim Duggan Books, 2017).

RESOURCES AND SUGGESTIONS FOR FURTHER READING

Delgado, Richard, Jean Stefancic, and Ernesto Liendo. *Critical Race Theory: An Introduction.* 2nd ed. New York: New York University Press, 2012.

Hawkesworth, Mary. *Gender and Political Theory: Feminist Reckonings.* Hoboken, NJ: John Wiley & Sons, 2019.

Levitsky, Steven, and Daniel Ziblatt. *How Democracies Die.* New York: Crown Publishing, 2018.

Norris, Pippa. *Democratic Deficit: Critical Citizens Revisited.* New York: Cambridge University Press, 2011.

Snyder, Timothy. *On Tyranny: Twenty Lessons from the Twentieth Century.* New York: Tim Duggan Books, 2017.

CHAPTER TWO

Political Theory and the Intersectional Quest for the Good Life

Dr. Keisha Lindsay

LEARNING OBJECTIVES

1 Define and conceptualize the good life
2 Learn how race, gender, and other intersecting markers of power shape political theorists' understandings of the good life
3 Explore the role the state plays in facilitating the good life
4 Understand how race, gender, and other intersecting markers of power shape political theorists' view of the state and its role in fostering the good life

KEY TERMS

classical liberal   an individual who promotes values such as individual liberty, freedom of speech, religious freedom, economic self-interest, and limited or "small" government

good life   a vision or understanding of what ideal human relations look like

LGBTQ+   an acronym used to describe the gender identities and/or sexual orientation of individuals who define themselves as lesbian, gay, bisexual, transgender, or queer; the + represents all the other orientations/identities encompassed within the community

Marxist   an individual who believes that capitalist economies always pay workers less than the price of the products and services they produce with the result that a wealthy few own and profit from the labor of the many

suffrage   the right to vote; universal suffrage is the right of all adult citizens to vote, regardless of gender, wealth, property ownership, education, or any other restriction

suffragist   a person who advocates for individuals', especially women's, right to vote

Western   people, practices, and ideas associated with Canada, the United States, New Zealand, Australia, and Europe

WHAT IS THE GOOD LIFE?

On the morning of December 11, 1960, Martin Luther King, Jr., approached the podium at Philadelphia's Unitarian Church of Germantown. His subsequent sermon emphasized that the United States of America would overcome racism if and when it became "a society where all men … live together as brothers and *every* man" honors "the dignity and worth of all human personality."[1] In 350 BCE, Aristotle, an ancient Greek philosopher, declared that "the good of man is a working of the soul" and that such work cannot be completed in "one day or a short time" because it requires the habitual "doing" of that which is virtuous.[2] Despite the 2,300 year gap between them, King's sermon on human dignity and Aristotle's treatise on human virtue are both examples of political theorizing or of asking and trying to answer an important question: What does it mean to live the **good life**? Or, put another way, what political values, practices, and institutions should we put in place to improve the world we live in?

As Aristotle and King make clear, there is no single or "right" answer to this query. Instead, engaging in political theory or prescribing what ideal human relations look like is a value-based activity that, by definition, yields diverse results. It is hardly surprising, then, that when contemplating what it means to live the good life Aristotle emphasized patience, truthfulness, modesty, and other applied forms of knowledge while King focused on expressing genuine concern for oneself, for others, and for god.

Other political theorists have advanced equally diverse definitions of the good life. The theorists we focus on in this chapter include:

- Seventeenth-century English philosopher John Locke,[3] who argued that wealthy people can live the good life if they voluntarily give up some of their individual freedoms in exchange for laws to protect their money and property.

- Nineteenth-century Black sociologist Anna Julia Cooper, who contended that Black women's resistance to oppression at the crossroads of race and gender qualifies them for the "inalienable title to life, liberty, and pursuit of happiness."[4]
- Twentieth-century theologian Vine Deloria, who equated the good life with fellow Native Americans' "familiarity with the personality of objects and entities of the natural world."[5]
- Contemporary Euro-American academic Martha Nussbaum, for whom "basic human flourishing" is the benchmark or the basis of a life worth living.[6]

These are very different understandings of the good life. Locke's argument is not only that such a life is available to those who acquire individual wealth, it is also that the good life belongs to those who recognize what Native American men and other non-white people purportedly fail to see – that the "earth" does "not belong in common to others."[7] Deloria contends, in contrast, that the good life is, in fact, based on "Indian knowledge." He and fellow scholar David Wilkins cite as proof Native Americans' rejection of "separate spheres" ideology or the sexist idea that women belong to the "private world of the family" while "rational" men are intended to serve in the public labor market as the family "breadwinner."[8] For Cooper, meanwhile, the good life is one in which Black women are free to occupy both of these spheres – be it as teachers and other public professionals and/or as morally uplifting mothers of the Black family.[9] Finally, Nussbaum's particular claim is that individuals' ability and desire to engage in behaviors such as marrying for love, making their own reproductive choices, and engaging in political speech are key to "human flourishing" and, in turn, to "pursuing th[e] good life."[10]

CONTEXT MATTERS

Differences in space and time help to explain political theorists' varied understandings of what it means to lead the good life. Locke's focus on private wealth and property occurred during a period, the late seventeenth century, when England's agricultural economy had reached new heights of productivity and when its trading economy was rapidly expanding. Deloria's validation of Indigenous understandings of the "natural world" took place during the late 1990s and early 2000s, when the effort to "save" supposedly dysfunctional Native American children was an especially popular topic among educators. Nussbaum's theorizing occurred within the context of two key intellectual moments in the late twentieth century – the emergence of feminism and development studies (the study of

countries once colonized or ruled by France, Britain, and other European countries) as legitimate academic fields.

Yet even if we accept that political theorists have varied opinions about what it
means to lead the good life because their views are forged in different time periods
and locations, important questions remain. Why, for example, does Locke cite Native American men as proof that the good life involves acquiring private property?
Furthermore, how are we to understand Nussbaum's tendency to associate "basic
human flourishing" with stereotypically Euro-American orientations, including
celebrating marriages based on romantic love? Lastly, why does Deloria highlight
"separate spheres" gender ideology as evidence that "Western science" is inferior
to Native Americans' ways of knowing?

Answering these and other related questions requires us to explore how the
intersection of race, gender, sexuality, and other markers of power inform political theorists' conceptions of the good life. With this goal in mind, the first section
of the chapter highlights the logic of intersectionality. Intersectional logic breaks
social groups into smaller subgroups to determine their access to power and to
decide whether this access is too expansive or too limited. We then move on to
explore a more specific but connected topic – how political theorists use intersectionality to decide which social groups qualify for the good life. The third section
goes further. It highlights how political theorists employ intersectional logic to
determine the state's role, if any, in facilitating the good life. All three sections of
the chapter pay particular attention to how woman **suffragists**, advocates of gay
marriage, and other past and present political activists concretize political theorists' intersectionally informed understandings of (1) the good life and (2) of the
state's role in facilitating this life.

THE LOGIC OF INTERSECTIONALITY: A THEORETICAL PRIMER

As a reminder, intersectionality is the analytical framework pioneered by Black
feminists to illuminate how racial, gendered, and other kinds of disadvantage
reinforce each other. To embrace an intersectional framework is to understand,
for instance, that Black women's experience of racism is informed by their experience of sexism. For example, racist whites routinely assume that Black women
are racially inferior *because* they are failed women – that is, they are lazy "welfare
queens" and hypersexual "jezebels" – rather than "real," sexually monogamous
women in patriarchal, nuclear family households. To embrace intersectionality
is to also reject a binary, either/or approach in which race, gender, and other

inequalities of power are seen as separate, independent domains. Intersectional theorizing, moreover, rejects analyses that advance a single, key oppression, like class, as the one from which all others follow. Intersectionality differs, finally, from additive models of oppression, which presume, for instance, that Native American women are subject to the double burden of racial "plus" gendered oppression.

Two streams of thought animate much of the academic discussion about intersectionality. The first and most established stream treats intersectionality as an "analytical framework within which to understand the lives of Black women" and as an important means of "challenging many of the oppressive structures confronted by Black women."[11] Put more succinctly, scholars associated with this stream assume that intersectionality and its underlying logic is *by* Black women and *for* Black women.[12] Sociologist Deborah King suggests exactly this when she describes studying multiple, intersecting domains of power as the cornerstone of "a Black feminist ideology" that Black women use to resist "the interstructure of ... racism, sexism, and classism."[13] Theorists who embrace this stream are just as concerned about what they describe as the growing "co-optation" of intersectionality. By co-optation they mean that too many scholars are using intersectionality to perpetuate a "myth of equivalent oppressions" or the flawed notion that race, gender, class, and sexuality somehow interconnect to oppress men, heterosexuals, whites, Christians, and other privileged social groups.[14]

The second, more recent, stream of theorizing challenges Black women's status as the main subjects of intersectional scholarship. It suggests, instead, that intersectionality reveals how mutually reinforcing racism, sexism, classism, and other sites of power subordinate white working-class women, Black men, and other social groups within institutions such as the welfare state and the criminal justice system.[15] This second stream also emphasizes that intersectionality can be used to perpetuate oppression. This is so because some subordinated social groups *also* have intersectional privileges that they use to cast others as inferior.[16] One example – which we will explore later in this chapter – is middle-class white women's use of their middle-class white privilege to (1) depict themselves as the most morally upstanding women and (2) to denigrate working-class Black women as social deviants who do not deserve voting rights. This more recent stream of intersectional theorizing suggests, finally, that the most privileged social groups also use intersectionality for oppressive ends. Take, for example, many white men's claim that affirmative action unfairly boosts racial minorities' and/or women's academic and job prospects at the expense of their own.[17] This claim obscures white men's institutional advantages in the job market and elsewhere, as demonstrated by their higher earnings relative to white women's and Black men's. It is, nevertheless, an intersectional claim because it presumes that white men are oppressed neither as men nor as whites but, rather, as *white men*.

WHO QUALIFIES FOR THE GOOD LIFE?

Political theorists clearly have different ideas about what it means to pursue and obtain the good life. Locke emphasizes acquiring private wealth and property. Nussbaum focuses on being able to make one's own reproductive choices along with other components of "basic human flourishing." Deloria prioritizes embracing "Indian knowledge." When we apply an intersectional lens to the question of *who* does and does not qualify for the good life, the answers that emerge are less straightforward or distinct.

The Qualified

Many theorists associated with the first, traditional stream of intersectionality described above assume that Black women deserve the good life. One such theorist is nineteenth-century Black sociologist and pioneering intersectional theorist Anna Julia Cooper. Cooper argues that Black women are especially worthy of the good life because they have a long history of challenging the flawed notion that "race, color, [and] sex," or being Black and a woman, are valid grounds for being oppressed.[18] Cooper's specific claim is that while Black women's "bark" may appear to be "resting in the silent waters of the sheltered cove," a closer analysis reveals that they have an ability "to weigh and judge" at the junction of race, gender, and class. Most significantly, this ability enables them to be "heard in clear, unfaltering tones" on various topics, including "the family, the church and the state," and "labor and capital." Cooper's argument is not just that embracing an intersectional framework empowers Black women to assert their voices in arenas where they have traditionally been silenced. It is also that their very ability to speak with an intersectional voice is evidence of their often-overlooked capacity for strategic, rational thought regarding those "interests which make for permanent good" or for a life worth living.[19]

Scholar Gloria Anzaldúa, who is also affiliated with the first and most established school of intersectional thought, makes a different claim. She asserts that women of color deserve to live a good life not because they use intersectionality in a rational fashion but, rather, because they redefine the idea of what it means to be rational. Anzaldúa contends, more specifically, that Chicanas possess a "mestiza consciousness" that enables them to shift from either/or Western "analytical reasoning" toward a more inclusive standpoint. Central to this standpoint, Anzaldúa explains, is the presumption that human beings do not exist in isolation as men, women, white, Mexican, Indigenous, and so on. Instead, we embrace attitudes and orientations at the border of masculine/feminine, white/non-white, gay/straight, and other social categories. Anzaldúa concludes that Chicanas' recognition of their own and others' location at these "borderlands" or intersections provides oppressed social groups with a more complex understanding of the relationship between race, gender, class, nationality, and other markers of power. She also concludes that Chicanas' capacity to engage in such intersectional analysis is proof that they are worthy of the good life or of a world in which "the end of rape, of violence, of war" is in full sight.[20]

The Disqualified

It is not enough, however, to simply conclude that intersectionality enables political theorists to define and expand on who is worthy of the good life. The opposite is also true. Some theorists also use the logic of intersectionality to *limit* or exclude Black women and a variety of other disadvantaged social groups from the good life. Why? The answer is twofold. First, as theorists affiliated with the second stream of intersectionality we discussed earlier explain, embracing intersectionality is not necessarily the same thing as challenging oppression. Furthermore, as these same theorists make clear, Black women are not the only subjects of intersectional analysis.

John Locke, the English theorist mentioned above, exemplifies this two-pronged reality – even though the term *intersectionality* would have been foreign to him. Locke, as you will recall, asserts that the "best advantage of life" occurs when we recognize that private wealth is ideal and that such wealth is best achieved by individuals "putting themselves under government."[21] A careful examination reveals that when Locke declares that "the earth and all that is therein given to men" is best suited for individual owners he is not referring to all individuals. Indeed, he is quite clear that Native American men do not qualify to own private property or to enjoy the good life that comes from having such property because, unlike European men, they mistakenly believe that it is acceptable to own land with others and to leave it "uncultivated" or "without any improvement, tillage or husbandry."[22]

Equally important is how Locke uses the logic of intersectionality to limit who is qualified to own private property and, in turn, to enjoy the good life. Locke's argument is not just that white men are more "industrial and rational" and thus racially superior to "wild" Native American men. It is, rather, that white men are racially superior because they alone fulfill a key tenet of traditional masculinity – that "real" men financially support their families, in part, by using their individual "labor and materials" to make land productive and profitable.[23] In other words, Locke determines who is worthy and unworthy of the good life by way of an intersectional assumption. This assumption is that European men qualify to own property and, in turn, for the good life because their status as patriarchs or masculine household heads makes them racially superior to others, including their Native American peers.[24]

The kind of intersectional logic that limits who qualifies for the good life is also evident in contemporary political theory. Political theorist Martha Nussbaum's theorizing is a case in point. On the one hand, when Nussbaum asserts that women's right to make their own reproductive choices is "the necessary basis for pursuing th[e] good life" she does so with two well-intentioned goals. The first goal is to validate women-centered "human capabilities" that have traditionally been absent from mainstream understandings of social and economic development. The other goal is to do so in ways that are "sensitive" to "cultural difference[s]" among women or the reality that race, class, and nationality intersect with and shape how women exercise their "bodily integrity or reproductive choices."[25]

On the other hand, a less praiseworthy intersectional logic also informs Nussbaum's theorizing. A prime example is her characterization of "marriage" in the "the United States and Europe" as a valuable way to "live together in intimacy, love, and partnership and to support one another, materially and emotionally, in the conduct of daily life."[26] This positive characterization of married life in the West is very different from her criticism of polygamous marriage in non-Western spaces, like "Sudan," as "a structurally unequal practice" even if "the woman's consent is required."[27] To be clear, the difficulty is not that Nussbaum values certain kinds of marriages over others. It is that she does so by privileging the kind of marriage that a disproportionately high number of middle-class people, especially in the United States, United Kingdom, and Canada, practice.[28] What results is a feminized model of development that is far from ideal precisely because it relies on a narrow, intersecting set of geographic and class-based criteria to determine who can and should live the good life.

Box 2.1 outlines the traditional history of the women's **suffrage** movement and highlights how the logic of intersectionality informed the campaign to expand and stymie Black women's voting rights.

BOX 2.1: WOMEN'S SUFFRAGE

In 1848, a group of women committed to fighting for women's suffrage in the United States gathered in Seneca Falls, New York. In the years that followed, Susan B. Anthony, Elizabeth Cady Stanton, Alice Paul, and other prominent suffragists used numerous means, including education campaigns, picketing, and political lobbying, to convince the public and government officials that women deserved the right to vote. During the early 1900s, these suffragists joined forces with the Jane Addams' settlement house movement, which also regarded the advent of women voters as a new, important means of ensuring more government funded healthcare, childcare, and education for poor urban communities. By 1920, the hard work of Anthony, Addams, and other movement leaders, in conjunction with the activities of a multiracial coalition of women, proved successful. On August 26, 1920, the US Senate ratified the Nineteenth Amendment to the Constitution, which allowed women to vote.

During the early 1900s, Emily Howard Stowe, Francis Marion Beynon, Margret Benedictsson, and other Canadian women – many of whom were lawyers, teachers, and journalists – similarly agitated for women's voting rights. Like their US peers, these women argued that women's suffrage was key to improving the social and moral well-being of the entire nation. For instance, organizations like the Woman's Christian Temperance Union and the Toronto Women's Literary Club posited a direct link between women's right to vote and reducing the prevalence of alcohol abuse and domestic violence. Suffragists were victorious in obtaining municipal or local voting rights for women as early as 1900. Women became eligible to vote in federal elections in 1918.

The paragraphs above reflect the story of the women's suffragist movement that is most often taught in US and Canadian schools. This narrative is proof that a more woman-centric version of history is now available in North American classrooms. It is also evidence of another truth – that as is the case with political theorists, political *activists* have long embraced intersectionality in ways that expand and limit who is worthy of the good life. Take, for example, the oft-repeated suffragist claim that women have the social and intellectual ability to live the good life when such a life is defined as "the right of a human being to have a voice in the government under which he or she lives."[29] At first blush, this claim seems to include all women. However, a closer reading reveals that many suffragists concluded that only white women should have the right to vote and to enjoy the good life associated with doing so. In arriving at this conclusion, these suffragists not only assumed that white women are racially superior to non-whites, they also assumed that white women's status as *women* "naturally" predisposes them to use their votes to nurture and support other whites who share their racist views. Canadian suffragist Nellie McClung captured this troubling intersectional logic when she argued that because "the woman's outlook on life is to save, to care, to help" it stands to reason that they are "naturally guardians of the race."[30] Carrie Chapman Catt, a US-based suffragist, was more explicit: "White supremacy will be strengthened, not weakened, by women's suffrage."[31]

That racist white suffragists employed the logic of intersectionality to exclude some social groups from the good life is only one part of the story regarding women's quest for voting rights. Black women suffragists' use of intersectionality to help expand multiple social groups' voting rights and, in turn, these groups' potential access to the good life is an equally important component. One such activist was Frances Harper, who argued that as "much as white women need the ballot, colored [Black] women need it more" to fight the harmful forces aligned against them. This is the case, Harper emphasized, because while all women are victims of sexism, Black women's experience of sexism intersects with their experience of racism. Put another way, while sexism is the primary reason most white women are oppressed by most white men, this is not the case for Black women. Instead, Black women are "subjected" to "ignorant" and "degraded" white men because they are *Black* women in a racist patriarchy that assumes (1) they are sexually promiscuous "bad" women, (2) their promiscuity is a sign of their racial inferiority, and (3) their sexual promiscuity and racial inferiority is evidence that they need to be disciplined and controlled by white men.[32]

DOES THE STATE HAVE A ROLE IN FACILITATING THE GOOD LIFE?

Political theorists and political activists do more than interrogate who qualifies for the good life. They are just as concerned about addressing the following question: What role, if any, does the state play in making the good life possible? The answer, not surprisingly, depends on which political theorists and activists you ask. In this section of the chapter, we look at the state's role in fostering the good life from the perspective of classical liberals and Marxists – two schools of political thought often considered to be at the extremes of modern politics. We focus, too, on gay rights activists' sometimes contrasting understandings of the relationship between the state, on the one hand, and achieving the good life, on the other. Our ultimate aim is to illuminate how a diversity of political theorists and political activists use the logic of intersectionality when contemplating the state's role in making the good life possible.

Classical Liberalism and the Role of the State in Securing the Good Life

Classical liberals have an important and influential understanding of the state's role in fostering the good life. To be a classical liberal is to promote values such as individual liberty, freedom of speech, religious freedom, and economic self-interest. Do these values sound familiar? If so, this is hardly surprising given that John Locke, whose work we examined earlier in this chapter, is a central figure in classical liberalism. These values may also sound familiar because they are part of the theoretical framework that undergirds many systems of government. A prime example is New Zealand's Bill of Rights, which declares "Everyone has the right to freedom of expression, including the right to seek, receive, and impart information and opinions of any kind in any form."[33] Another example is the US Constitution, which states "Congress shall make no law respecting an establishment of religion, or prohibiting the free exercise thereof; or abridging the freedom of speech, or of the press; or the right of the people peaceably to assemble, and to petition the government for a redress of grievances."[34]

For classical liberal theorists, the good life is one in which the state plays a small but effective role in people's daily lives. These theorists call for just enough state power to guarantee individual security but not enough to threaten individual liberty and opportunity. English theorist John Stuart Mill cautions, on this note, that a too strong state is a dangerous, coercive force that "dwarfs its men, in order that they may be more docile instruments in its hands" and, in so doing, denies them the individual "liberty" or to formulate a life plan that they deem to be in accordance with their "own character."[35] Mill, like other classical liberals, concludes that the best means of achieving the good life is to limit governmental authority by, among other means, breaking down the scope of its power into distinct executive, legislative, and judicial functions. At the same time, Mill asserts, citizens need "government" or the state to enforce contracts and other means of protecting and sustaining private wealth. These other means include laws that require children to obtain a minimum amount of schooling and that aim, more broadly, to ensure that all citizens have equal opportunity to fulfill their material wants and needs.

Most important, for our purposes, is determining how the logic of intersectionality informs classical liberals' understanding of the state's role in facilitating the good life – including those liberals who lived well before Black feminists actually coined the term *intersectionality*. Mill's theorizing is a useful departure point for achieving this goal. In 1867, he asserted that English legislators should allow property-owning women to vote because there is no "adequate justification for continuing to exclude an entire half of the community" from having political representatives "who feel specially called on to attend to their interests, and to point out how those interests are affected by the law, or by any proposed changes in it."[36] Mill's declaration is evidence that he regarded the ability to pursue one's "interests" as central to the good life. It is also evidence that he held the state responsible for ensuring that women, or "half of the community," have the opportunity for such a life.

Reading more attentively reveals something else – that Mill's declaration is also an intersectional one precisely because it seeks to provide a *specific* group of women with access to the good life. Put another way, when Mill encourages the state to grant "women" voting rights, he has in mind property-owning women who, in his view, occupy a unique and important location at the intersection of class and gender. Mill's specific claim is that although middle- and upper-class propertied women pay taxes and are thus entitled, as are all property owners, to political representation via the ballot box, their status as middle- and upper-class land-owning *women* means that they are frequently stereotyped as (1) "incapable of taking care of either themselves or others," (2) unfit to manage property, and thus (3) unqualified to handle the civic responsibility of voting. Mill's intersectionally informed analysis also leads him to a second conclusion: that women with property deserve to vote not just because they own land but also because they are land-owning women who possess certain, supposedly innate, feminine characteristics.[37] Mill's argument here is twofold. He suggests, first, that property-owning women are naturally skilled in traditionally feminine pursuits such as household management or "the judicious laying-out of money, so as to produce the greatest results with the smallest means."[38] He concludes, second, that these feminine skills are proof of middle- and upper-class women's ability to be good property owners and, by extension, to function as responsible voters with every right to enjoy the good life.

Marxism and the Role of the State in Securing the Good Life

As is the case with classical liberals, **Marxists** shed important light on political theorists' intersectionally informed views about the state's role in facilitating the good life. To be a Marxist is to assume, as did nineteenth-century German philosopher and economist Karl Marx, that capitalist economies always pay workers less than the price or value of what they make.[39] The outcome, Marxists argue, is that the owners of factories, corporations, and other means of producing goods and services are wealthy precisely because what consumers end up paying for these goods and services far *exceeds the costs of making them*. The outcome is also that capitalists' use of labor – whereby a few own and profit from the labor of the many – generates inevitable "contradictions" between the rich and the poor. Marxists predict that this state of affairs will ultimately lead to a working-class revolution that abolishes private wealth, private ownership of land, and class inequality.

If the point is to free laborers from oppression, what do Marxists regard as the good life? Marx himself imagined a world in which the state would, after a period of transition, be replaced by an egalitarian communist utopia in which people would put in according to their ability and take out according to their need.[40] However, subsequent thinkers in the Marxist tradition have not always adopted this particular portion of Marx's theorizing. Instead, many of these later thinkers emphasize that government intervention is crucial for ensuring that all are able to secure the good life. In doing so, they firmly reject the small state that Mill envisioned in favor of a communal or communist one whose primary function is to use the "proceeds" from workers' labor to establish public ownership of industry, property, and natural resources. The end goal of such a state is to meet the needs of the disabled, the elderly, and others who are unable to work; to finance transportation, schools, healthcare, and other essential public services; and to foster technological development. In short, Marxists guide us to consider state power as a generative resource to achieve a life characterized less by equality of opportunity and more by equality of social and economic outcomes.

Although contemporary Marxists and classical liberal theorists disagree about the virtues of a small state, both use the logic of intersectionality when they contemplate the state's role in fostering the good life. At first glance, this claim seems dubious given some critics' contention that Marxism fails to examine the relationship between capitalism and other sites of power and, instead, positions class inequality as the main site from with racial, gendered, and all other oppressions stem.[41] However, a more thorough analysis reveals that some Marxist theorists, particularly Black Marxist feminists, actually use an intersectional lens to conceptualize the state's obligation to nurturing the good life. One such theorist is Claudia Jones, who makes two relevant claims.[42] She contends, first, that working-class Black women's capitalist oppression is racialized and gendered. In other words, while all working-class people earn less than the value of the products they make, racist and gender-biased stereotypes of Black women as promiscuous, lazy, and unintelligent mean that they earn even less than white working-class men and women.[43] Jones concludes that the state is responsible for remedying this reality by providing Black women with access to the good life. To this end, she emphasizes a new America in which the government ensures that working-class Black women are unionized, earn a minimum wage, and lead a feminist movement that sees the "link" between eradicating sexism and ending racism.[44] Jones's ultimate goal is a world in which Black women "receive according to their needs" or live a life in which equality of outcome triumphs over intersecting racial, gendered, and other hierarchies of power.[45]

Box 2.2 discusses how an intersectional framework shapes activists', including gay-rights activists', understandings of the state's role in fostering the good life.

BOX 2.2: GAY MARRIAGE

"Like tens of thousands of other binational couples, we just want to plan our life together … The stability and security of marriage and legal immigration status opens the door to so many beautiful possibilities for our future."[46] With this June 2013 declaration, Charlie Gu – a gay, undocumented Asian Pacific Islander – defined the good life as gay peoples' ability to legally marry and positioned immigration reform as a key means by which the state could and should make such a life possible. In the days preceding Gu's statement, the US Supreme Court had ruled that the federal government cannot discriminate against gay couples when considering who qualifies for federal benefits and protections, including the right to sponsor or invite foreign-born spouses to live in the United States.

Gu's words reflect the judiciary's evolving stance on gay marriage. They also reflect the reality that, like political theorists, political *activists* have varied, intersectionally informed understandings of the state's role in nurturing the good life. On the one hand, Gu and many other gay rights activists assume that the state is obligated to foster the good life when such a life is lived at the intersection of sexuality, race, and national origin. Karin Wang, an Asian American **LGBTQ+** activist, echoes this view when she describes the Supreme Court's 2013 rejection of the Defense of Marriage Act as a significant "step towards ensuring our country lives up to its promise of equality and fairness" for Asian Americans who are oppressed not only because they are "gays and lesbians" but also because they live in a racist society that has long assumed they do not deserve the same rights as white Americans.[47]

On the other hand, many gay rights activists also use an intersectional framework to make the *opposite* argument – that the state should have little or no role in facilitating the good life if and when this life requires living at the crossroads of multiple *inequalities* of power. Scholar-activists Dean Spade and Craig Willse argue exactly this when they reject state-sanctioned marriage, including state-sanctioned gay marriage, on the grounds that marriage, so defined, is a patriarchal, heterosexist institution whose harmful effects intersect with and amplify racism.[48] In advancing this argument, Spade and Willse draw readers' attention to President George W. Bush and President Barack Obama – both of whom endorsed "Healthy Marriage Initiatives" that encouraged poor Black women to marry men. The difficulty with these initiatives, Spade and Willse emphasize, is not just that they denied "cash incentives" to Black women who choose not to follow the state's marital guidance, it is also that the initiatives were informed by an intersecting patriarchal and racist assumption. This assumption is that Black women are "bad" because they reject what Euro-Americans traditionally regard as ideal family life – namely, heterosexual marriages in which breadwinning patriarchs rule.

SUMMARY

This chapter explored how the intersection of race, gender, sexuality, and other markers of power inform political theorists' understandings of who qualifies for the good life as well as the state's part in facilitating this life. With this two-pronged goal in mind, the first section of the chapter detailed the logic that undergirds intersectional theorizing.

- We began by examining two distinct streams of intersectional thought – both of which reflect and expand upon the definition of intersectionality provided in the Introduction to this book.
- We then turned our attention to how political theorists use these streams of intersectional theorizing to determine which social groups qualify for a good life. Our focus here was on pioneering intersectional theorists like Anna Julia Cooper. It was also on John Locke and other thinkers whose work is not traditionally associated with an intersectional framework, but who clearly exhibit intersectional thinking – albeit for political and economic goals that intersectionality's Black feminist pioneers would not sanction.
- We also examined Black women's and white women's efforts to gain voting rights during the late nineteenth and early twentieth centuries. Our examination revealed that, as is the case with political theorists, political activists also embrace intersectionality in ways that seek to expand as well as constrain who qualifies for the good life.

The rest of the chapter highlighted another important reality – that the logic of intersectionality shapes political theorists' varied understandings of how much of a role the state should play in facilitating the good life.

- The final section of this chapter foregrounded two of these theorists, John Stuart Mill and Karl Marx, whose historical views on the relationship between the role of the state, on the one hand, and achieving the good life, on the other, have influenced the social, economic, and political life of many groups in United States, Canada, and beyond.

- At the end of the chapter we turned, once again, to a concrete case study. Our focus this time was on the contemporary gay rights movement and on how activists within the movement draw on an intersectional framework when considering the state's responsibility to facilitate the good life.

CONCLUDING QUESTIONS

1 How do you define the good life? How is your definition similar to and different from Marin Luther King, Jr.'s?

2 Carrie Chapman Catt's definition of the good life was influenced by her status as a white, middle-class woman. How is your definition of the good life informed by your own position at the intersection of race, class, gender, and other markers of power?

3 John Stuart Mill argued that the disadvantages of having the state play a central role in facilitating the good life outweigh the advantages. Is his argument correct? Why or why not?

4 Claudia Jones used an intersectional framework to make the case that the state is key to fostering the good life. What are the most and the least persuasive aspects of how Jones embraced the logic of intersectionality?

NOTES

1 Martin Luther King, Jr., "The Three Dimensions of a Complete Life: Sermon Delivered at the Unitarian Church of Germantown December 11," (1960).

2 Quoted in Will Durant, *Story of Philosophy* (New York: Simon and Schuster, 2012 [1961]), 98.

3 John Locke, *Two Treatises of Government* (London: Whitmore and Fenn, and C. Brown, 1821 [1690]).

4 Anna Julia Cooper, *A Voice from the South* (New York: Rowman and Littlefield Publishers, 2000 [1892]), 108.

5 Vine Deloria, Jr., "American Indian Metaphysics," in *Power and Place: Indian Education in America*, eds. Vine Deloria, Jr. and Daniel Wildcat (Golden, CO: Fulcrum Publishing, 2001), 2.

6 Martha C. Nussbaum, *Sex and Social Justice* (New York: Oxford University Press, 1999), 9, 11.

7 Locke, *Two Treatises*, 208.

8 Vine Deloria, Jr., and David E. Wilkins, *Legal Universe: Observations of the Foundations of American Law* (Golden, CO: Fulcrum Publishing, 2016), 205.

9 Cooper, *A Voice from the South*.

10 Nussbaum, *Sex and Social Justice*, 40.

11 Julia S. Jordan-Zachery, "Am I a Black Woman or a Woman Who Is Black? A Few Thoughts on the Meaning of Intersectionality," *Politics & Gender* 3, no. 2 (2007): 254–63, 255.

12 Nikol G. Alexander-Floyd, "Disappearing Acts: Reclaiming Intersectionality in the Social Sciences in a Post–Black Feminist Era," *Feminist Formations* (2012): 1–25; Sirma Bilge, "Intersectionality Undone: Saving Intersectionality from Feminist Intersectionality Studies," *Du Bois Review: Social Science Research on Race* 10, no. 2 (2013): 405–24.

13 Deborah K. King, "Multiple Jeopardy, Multiple Consciousness: The Context of a Black Feminist Ideology," *Signs: Journal of Women in Culture and Society* 14, no. 1 (1988): 42–72.

14 Michele Tracy Berger and Kathleen Guidroz, "A Conversation with Founding Scholars of Intersectionality," in *The Intersectional Approach: Transforming the Academy through Race, Class, and Gender*, eds. Michele Tracy Berger and Kathleen Guidroz (Chapel Hill: University of North Carolina Press, 2009), 61–80; Patricia Hill Collins, "Some Group Matters: Intersectionality, Situated Standpoints, and Black Feminist Thought," in *A Companion to African-American Philosophy*, eds. Tommy L. Lott and John P. Pittman, chap. 12 (Malde, MA: Blackwell Publishing, Ltd., 2006), 205–29.

15 Merike Blofield, *Care Work and Class: Domestic Workers' Struggle for Equal Rights in Latin America* (University Park, PA: Penn State University Press, 2012); Ange-Marie Hancock, "Intersectionality as a Normative and Empirical Paradigm," *Politics & Gender* 3, no. 2 (2007): 248–54; Leslie McCall, "The Complexity of Intersectionality," *Signs* 30, no. 3 (2005): 1771–800.

16 Cathy J. Cohen, *The Boundaries of Blackness: Aids and the Breakdown of Black Politics* (Chicago: University of Chicago Press, 1999); Nancy D. Wadsworth, "Intersectionality in California's Same-Sex Marriage Battles: A Complex Proposition," *Political Research Quarterly* 64, no. 1 (2011): 200–16.

17 See Frederick R. Lynch, *Invisible Victims: White Males and the Crisis of Affirmative Action* (New York: Greenwood Press, 1989); Eileen Patten, "Racial, Gender Wage Gaps Persist in U.S. Despite Some Progress," Pew Research Center, 2016, https://www.pewresearch.org/fact-tank/2016/07/01/racial-gender-wage-gaps-persist-in-u-s-despite-some-progress; Dominic J. Pulera, *Sharing the Dream: White Males in a Multicultural America* (New York: Continuum International, 2006). A related argument is that all social groups can use intersectionality for oppressive ends because while the logic of intersectionality reveals how race, gender, class, and other sites of power mutually construct, it does not specify which races, genders, classes, and so on. Social groups can thus advance very different understandings of who is intersectionally disadvantaged and how to fix their disadvantage. See Keisha Lindsay, *In a Classroom of Their Own: The Intersection of Race and Feminist Politics in All-Black Male Schools* (Champaign: University of Illinois Press, 2018).

18 Cooper, *A Voice from the South*, 108.

19 Cooper, *A Voice from the South*, 114, 117.

20 Gloria Anzaldúa, *Borderlands: La Frontera*, vol. 3 (San Francisco: Aunt Lute, 1987) 79, 80.

21 Locke, *Two Treatises*, 209.

22 Locke, *Two Treatises*, 219.

23 Locke, *Two Treatises*, 216, 219.

24 That Locke did not call for white women to be granted the same private property rights as their male peers is firm evidence that, in his estimation, whiteness alone was not enough to be worthy of the good life. In addition, Locke's failure to demand that non-white men have the same right to individual property as their white counterparts is proof that, for him, masculinity alone was not adequate to qualify for the good life.

25 Nussbaum, *Sex and Social Justice*, 47, 90.

26 Nussbaum, *Sex and Social Justice*, 202.

27 Nussbaum, *Sex and Social Justice*, 98.

28 Philip Cross and Peter Jon Mitchell, "The Marriage Gap between Rich and Poor Canadians," Institute of Marriage and Family Canada (February 2014); Kim Parker and Renee Stepler, "As US Marriage Rate Hovers at 50%, Education Gap in Marital Status Widens," Pew Research Center (September 14, 2017); *The Economist*, "Marriage in the West" (November 23, 2017).

29 Shaw, quoted in Lynne E. Ford, ed., *Encyclopedia of Women and American Politics* (New York: Facts on File, 2010), 552.

30 Quoted in Randi R. Warne, *Literature as Pulpit: The Christian Social Activism of Nellie L. McClung*, vol. 2 (Waterloo, ON: Wilfrid Laurier University Press, 1993), 158.

31 Quoted in Kathlyn Gay, *American Dissidents: An Encyclopedia of Activists, Subversives, and Prisoners of Conscience*, vol. 1 (Santa Barbara, CA: ABC-CLIO, 2011), 115.

32 Quoted in Rosalyn Terborg-Penn, *African American Women in the Struggle for the Vote, 1850–1920* (Bloomington: Indiana University Press, 1998), 47.

33 New Zealand Bill of Rights Act 1990, s. 14.

34 Amendment 1, United States Constitution (1791).

35 John Stuart Mill, *On Liberty* (London: John W. Parker and Son, 1859), 26, 207.

36 John Stuart Mill, *Speech of John Stuart Mill, M.P. On the Admission of Women to the Electoral Franchise* (London: Trübner and Company, 1867), 3.

37 Mill, *Speech of John Stuart Mill*, 12.

38 Mill *Speech of John Stuart Mill*, 8.

39 Karl Marx, *Capital: A Critical Analysis of Capitalist Production* (London: Swan Sonnenschein & Company, 1906).

40 Marx, *Capital*.

41 Barbara Smith and Beverly Smith, "Across the Kitchen Table: A Sister-to-Sister Dialogue," in *This Bridge Called My Back: Writings by Radical Women of Color*, vol. 2, eds. Cherríe Moraga and Gloria Anzaldúa, 113–27 (New York: Kitchen Table Press, 1981).

42 Claudia Jones, "An End to the Neglect of the Problems of the Negro Woman!," in *Words of Fire: An Anthology of African-American Feminist Thought*, ed. Beverly Guy-Sheftall (New York: New Press, 1995 [1949]).

43 Jones, "An End to the Neglect," 110.

44 Jones, "An End to the Neglect," 120.

45 Jones, "An End to the Neglect," 120.
46 API Equality-Northern California, "API Equality-LA and API Equality-Northern California Celebrate Supreme Court Ruling Striking Down Prop 8 and DOMA Enabling LGBT Couples to Wed and Be Recognized by the Federal Government," 2013. https://www.apienc.org/2013/06/26/api-equality-la-and-api-equality-northern-california-celebrate-supreme-court-ruling-striking-down-prop-8-and-doma-enabling-lgbt-couples-to-wed-and-be-recognized-by-the-federal-government.
47 API-Equality-Northern California, "Celebrate Supreme Court Ruling."
48 Dean Spade and Craig Willse, "Marriage Will Never Set Us Free," *Organizing Upgrade,* September 6, 2013, http://archive.organizingupgrade.com/index.php/modules-menu/beyond-capitalism/item/1002-marriage-will-never-set-us-free.

RESOURCES AND SUGGESTIONS FOR FURTHER READING

Collins, Patricia Hill. *Intersectionality as Critical Social Theory.* Durham, NC: Duke University Press, 2019.

Fraser, Nancy, and Axle Honneth. *Redistribution or Recognition? A Political-Philosophical Exchange.* London: Verso, 2003.

Nash, Jennifer. *Black Feminism Reimagined: After Intersectionality.* Durham, NC: Duke University Press, 2019.

Spade, Dean. *Normal Life: Administrative Violence, Critical Trans Politics, and the Limits of Law.* Durham, NC: Duke University Press, 2015.

Young, Iris. *Justice and the Politics of Difference.* Princeton, NJ: Princeton University Press, 2011.

CHAPTER THREE

Political Ideologies

Dr. Christina Xydias

LEARNING OBJECTIVES

1 Identify ideologies that have shaped the world we live in
2 Understand how ideologies correspond with specific institutions that reflect and reinforce those ideologies
3 Imagine alternatives to the status quo

KEY TERMS

ideology   "an explicit, consciously held belief system"[1] that consists of "a set of idea-elements that are bound together, that belong to one another in a non-random fashion."[2] More specifically, it is a set of values and beliefs that structures how people think their broader societies and political institutions should be organized.

political values   beliefs about how to rank priorities for who should get what, when, and how

social structure   the "most basic, enduring, and determinative patterns in social life";[3] the arrangement of individuals and groups according to their relative power

the state   the full political apparatus with a monopoly over the legitimate use of violence in a given territory (not to be confused with *a state*, which is a territorial entity, [i.e., a country], as noted in the Introduction to this book)

WHAT IS AN IDEOLOGY?

An **ideology** is a set of values and beliefs that structures how people think their broader societies and *political institutions* should be organized. This means that an ideology provides answers to two important clusters of questions:

1 How people believe authority should be distributed: Who should call the shots, and for whom?
2 Which mechanisms for authority people prefer: Should decision making include many people, or just a select few? To what extent, and how, should decision makers be accountable to the wider population?

Beliefs about how authority *should be* distributed strongly shape the design of societies and political institutions. We can think about ideologies in several ways. First, they function as "background criteria" for societies and institutions. A widely held ideology that includes egalitarian beliefs is likely to correspond with a political system where people view each other as equals and where political decision making includes more constituents rather than concentrating power in the hands of a small number of people. The values and beliefs that compose an ideology are therefore at the nexus of political attitudes, behavior, and institutions. Consider, for example, the Nordic countries (Denmark, Finland, Iceland, Norway, and Sweden). These societies share widely held beliefs about the importance of distributing risk and protecting people from the costs of the market (such as poverty and unemployment). These beliefs compose the ideology of *social democracy*, which infused the design of rules for political decision making prior to and in the wake of World War II. These countries' legislatures are consensual: Procedurally, they include many voices, and legislation needs lots of support to pass. And Nordic social policies are also egalitarian.

Second, ideologies provide individual people with a belief system that informs their preferences, choices, and actions. For example, a person might be ideologically socially traditionalist, believing that longtime cultural practices (such as marriage) are valuable because of their longevity and that these practices should not change. Even within societies that share widely held beliefs, individuals vary in their own ideologies.

As ubiquitous as the term *ideology* is in the news, in academic work, and in our daily conversations about politics, it has lots of different meanings. John Gerring observes in his review of the concept of ideology that these different definitions are often contradictory, even within the field of political science.[4] Giovanni Sartori has begged political scientists to stop using it, arguing that its range of meanings and applications has made it useless.[5] In spite of these challenges, Robert Putnam offers a specific definition that has become widely accepted in political science, and it is how we use the concept throughout this chapter: An ideology is "an explicit, consciously held belief system."[6]

Note that these are *beliefs*, not facts. This means that an ideology is a set of principles that are substantively interconnected by some form of meaning but not necessarily by scientific evidence or logic. People believe in these principles in the sense that they view them as true and important, and those principles justify specific policy preferences. Willard Mullins sums up the significance of ideology this way: It "[links] political thought and behavior."[7] Consider the earlier example of social democracy, an egalitarian ideology. When people view each other as equals, this belief corresponds with treating each other as equals, and this behavior corresponds with support for political institutions that aim for egalitarian outcomes. In social democratic Nordic societies, political decision making is inclusive and consensual, and there is general consensus on the idea that **the state** has an obligation for the population's well-being.

Some scholars argue that ideologies are necessary components of political life because they structure our political choices and behavior. Writing about early American democracy, Alexis de Tocqueville claims that specific values about equality are prerequisites for the emergence of democratic institutions.[8] And many contemporary political scientists view ideology simply as orderly sets of political preferences.[9]

Other scholars assert that ideologies are not merely principles that underlie our political preferences. Louis Althusser, Hannah Arendt, and Karl Marx and Friedrich Engels argue that ideologies obscure reality by indoctrinating people into a set of beliefs that keep them complacent and unable to critique the conditions they live in.[10] If you believe that you are not entitled to a living wage, for example, you will not be upset about working full time without being able to pay for basic expenses. By contrast, if you believe that everyone deserves a living wage, you will support political parties and policies that make that part of the social welfare state.

As a student of political science, you might be most familiar with the idea of an ideology in terms of the political parties that develop "around" it. Partisanship – a person's affiliation with a specific political party – is sometimes referred to synonymously with ideology. People who talk about "the left" or "the right" often mean both **political values** and the political parties that embody those values. However, not all ideologies have formal political parties associated with them. Some people have ideological commitments without a party to represent them. In the United States, for example, voters who want to support a party that prioritizes sustainability and the environment *and that is likely to win political office* are out of luck. Unlike many other countries, the two-party system of the United States does not include a Green Party that can compete effectively for office (see Chapter 6 on electoral institutions).

Some ideologies – such as patriarchy and neoliberalism – are so pervasive in society that they show up in multiple competing political parties. In other words, an ideology cannot be synonymous with a political party because some ideologies are shared by many or all parties in a given political system. In the United States, the two major political parties (Republican and Democratic) both believe in and promote free market economic policies. Free market ideologies therefore do not distinguish these two parties. This logic is known as *discriminant validity* – definitions of concepts should not overlap in a way that misrepresents how they are related to one another. Applied here, discriminant validity means that the definition of the concept *ideology* should be specific enough that it does not mistakenly overlap with definitions for political parties. This chapter makes a strong distinction between ideology and partisanship to emphasize that ideologies transcend political parties.

Many textbooks would present ideologies in terms of a left–right political spectrum. *Left* and *right* are commonly used to describe political beliefs regarding the economy. Ideologies on the left favor greater state regulation of the economy with greater redistribution of resources, and the right favors less state regulation and less redistribution. For example, *communism* is located on the far left. It prioritizes collectivism, pools resources, and produces political and economic institutions of "central planning." In turn, *conservatism* is placed on the right. It prioritizes stability, and it produces political and economic systems that maintain the status quo and its distribution of resources. Although it is a commonly used shorthand for labeling sets of beliefs and political parties, the left–right spectrum implies a simplicity that we do not find in the real world. Beliefs about resource redistribution are just one of many ideologies for differentiating between left and right. Another ideological axis that we think about in terms of left and right is sociocultural. On this axis, the ideology of social progressivism is on the left, while social traditionalism is on the right.

A political party that might be conventionally viewed as either "on the left" or "on the right" is actually much more likely to combine multiple ideological orientations that do not necessarily align together on the left–right spectrum. Consider, for example, the contemporary Party for Freedom in the Netherlands. Vossen identifies "four pillars" in the Party for Freedom's platform, some of which are ideologically "on the right" and some "on the left."[11] The Party for Freedom is *populist*, which later sections of this chapter will show is an ideology that is typically combined with other sets of values. The party is *ethno-nationalist* and anti-Islamic, accentuating Dutch national identity and expressing alarm about the presence of

Islam in the Netherlands; these are sets of beliefs that are typically considered "on the right." The Party for Freedom also emphasizes *law and order*, which is also typically considered "on the right." However, the party simultaneously supports a range of more progressive social policies, including LGBTQ+ rights, which are often associated with "the left."

In place of this conventional selection of ideologies, this chapter proceeds through a discussion of four contemporary ideologies that do not map onto political parties and which do not neatly arrange from left to right: patriarchy, neoliberalism, populism, and democracy. This selection of ideologies emphasizes two points. First, many politically relevant belief systems have significant influence over our daily lives without being part of formal politics. Second, the chapter aims to avoid misrepresenting ideologies as more coherent than they are in "the real world." Ideologies are messy, they overlap with one another, and they change over time. The selection of ideologies discussed here illustrates how ideologies create and justify our social and political systems in complicated ways, both visible and invisible.

The first two ideologies that get closer attention here are global in scope and powerfully shape all of our social interactions (patriarchy and neoliberalism); the next is a set of values that has waxed and waned over time and is gaining momentum around the world again (populism); the last is a set of values that underlies many political systems that are widely viewed as good, but which is currently experiencing decline (democracy). The discussion of each ideology covers the sets of values and beliefs that undergird it, the social and political institutions that it produces, and (where applicable) how it takes form in formal politics (e.g., in political parties). The chapter then presents a short case study of the intersection of two contemporary ideologies – patriarchy and neoliberalism – in the Me Too movement. #MeToo is a Twitter hashtag first used in October 2017 after allegations of sexual harassment were made public against entertainment tycoon Harvey Weinstein. But Me Too as a rallying cry has its origins in 2006 with a smaller-scale social movement focused on sexual abuse of young women of color. Together, these Me Too movements illustrate how patriarchy and neoliberalism create the specific issue of persistent sexual harassment and abuse of women in the workplace.

FOUR CONTEMPORARY IDEOLOGIES

Patriarchy

Patriarchy is an enduring set of values about gender and power that prioritize the experiences and rights of people received as men over the experiences and rights of people received as women. Walby defines patriarchy as "a system of social structures, and practices in which men dominate, oppress, and exploit women."[12] These **social structures** include the family, the workplace, and any organization or setting where human beings interact with one another. Similarly, Rifkin writes, "By patriarchy, I mean *any kind of group organization* in which males hold dominant power and determine what part women shall and shall not play."[13]

Describing an individual as being "received" as a man or a woman emphasizes that people interact based on what they think they know about each other and how their assumptions fit into their wider beliefs about society. People who are received as women are generally expected to conform to social expectations about women, and people received as men are generally expected to conform to social expectations about men.[14] This chapter focuses on patriarchy as it is associated with men and women and with masculinity and femininity. These are categories that correlate with persistent social expectations and with the distribution of authority across societies and across history. The chapter does not argue that the only relevant gender identities are dichotomous, either "man" or "woman." Instead, it presents patriarchy as an ideology that views men and women as meaningful categories and believes that men's experiences and rights are more important than women's. (Remember that an ideology is a set of beliefs, not a set of facts.)

If politics is "who gets what, when, how,"[15] then beliefs about gender are deeply political. Allocating resources (including power) by gender intersects with all other social structures: race, ethnicity, socioeconomic status, and so on. All other factors being equal, a wealthy woman has less authority than a man who is also wealthy; a poor woman has less authority than her also-poor counterpart who is received as a man. However, not all other factors are equal. Political scientist Laurel Weldon shows that social categories like race and ethnicity are more salient than gender or socioeconomic status in some situations.[16] An earlier section of this chapter provided the example of social democracy as a broadly shared egalitarian ideology in the Nordic states. Yet these societies are simultaneously patriarchal, showing evidence of persistent inequalities between women and men. And a sizable portion of the population holds negative attitudes toward culturally different immigrants. Sweden, for example, is globally egalitarian, but Islamophobia (negative attitudes toward Muslims) is also widespread.[17]

Although historically some matriarchal (women-led) societies exist, social expectations across the globe and across time overwhelmingly associate men and masculinity with authority. This means that even in a democratic country where women and men share equal formal rights, women's long history of exclusion has produced gendered stereotypes about what it means to be a good leader. For example, research in social psychology shows that feminine stereotypes conflict with stereotypes associated with leadership. Men benefit from the "congruency of roles" between masculinity and leadership. For women these stereotypes are incongruent.[18] These gendered, patriarchal beliefs about good leadership correspond with voters holding women and men candidates for political office to different standards.

Gendered, patriarchal beliefs about whose experiences and rights are more important also correspond with judges imposing minimal sentences on men perpetrators of sexual assault out of concern for these rapists' futures. A clear example of this is the 2015 sentencing of Stanford University student Brock Turner. California Superior Court Judge Aaron Persky sentenced Turner to six months in jail (as opposed to six years, as requested by the prosecution) for sexual assault, expressing concern about the "adverse collateral consequences on the defendant's life resulting from the felony conviction."[19]

Patriarchy is so pervasive that it is hard to find a political party that does not embody it. Parties on the left and the right perpetuate gendered hierarchies through their own internal leadership (typically more men than women are party leaders) and issue priorities. However, avowedly feminist parties have emerged in some countries since the early twentieth century, and these are parties that explicitly prioritize dismantling gendered hierarchies. In Iceland, the Women's List was a feminist party that elected women to parliament over the 26 years it existed (1983–99). Early in 2019 the Women's Party registered to be included on ballots in Australia. Their mission reflects the goal of dismantling patriarchy: "The Women's Party – is about creating equality and respect between women and men to our common benefit."[20] These parties are the exception rather than the rule, however, and they offer one illustration of the universalism of patriarchy in formal politics. At the same time as these existing feminist parties challenge patriarchy, extensive research on intersectionality and civil society shows that organizations usually advocate for their majority-status members. In the context of Iceland or Australia, feminist parties' principal focus is on issues that are of greater urgency to more affluent white women. Australia's Women's Party presents a much-needed exception to this by explicitly calling attention to the rights and interests of Indigenous women.

The principles that associate men and masculinity with authority produced and perpetuate women's exclusion from formal politics, but patriarchy is not just about public life. As the case study concluding this chapter will show, patriarchy coexists and interacts with many other social and political systems. We see patriarchy and beliefs about economic justice around us as separate forces, but the two ideologies can also interact to produce different consequences together.[21] Walby contends, "Patriarchy is not reducible to capitalism" or to any one set of economic conditions.[22] In the case study of the Me Too movements, patriarchy intersects with neoliberalism to allow sexual harassment to persist against women in their workplaces.

As an ideology, patriarchy provides these answers to the two key questions presented in at the beginning of this chapter:

1 The distribution of authority: Who should call the shots, and for whom?
   • People received as men should call the shots for their communities.
2 The mechanisms for authority: Whom should decision making include?
   • People received as men should be included in the decision-making process.
   • Women's exclusion from the decision-making process is acceptable.

Neoliberalism

Neoliberalism is a set of values and beliefs about the state's role in the economy and society. It is the twentieth- and twenty-first-century version of liberalism (see Chapter 2), with a specific preference for free market economic principles. A free market is when there are few or no rules governing economic activity. Neoliberalism asserts that "human well-being can best be advanced by liberating individual entrepreneurial freedoms and skills within an institutional framework characterized by strong private property rights, free markets, and free trade."[23] Individuals "use" their entrepreneurial freedoms and skills when they make economic transactions without rules or restrictions: They create, sell, and buy goods and services minimally restricted, or unrestricted, by laws or monitoring. Although neoliberalism is best known as a theory of political economy, Treanor argues that it "is not just economics: it is a social and moral philosophy."[24] Neoliberal values comprise "an ethic in itself, capable of acting as a guide to all human action, and substituting for all previously held ethical beliefs."[25] When profit itself is valuable, we do not need other sets of values for allocating resources. Where the money ends up is simply where it is supposed to be.

Sometimes the term *neoliberalism* is used synonymously with *capitalism* or *globalization*. This is because all three concepts derive from the same basic *classical liberal* premise that the benefits of free individual economic activities are much greater than the dangers associated with the state's intervention in economic and social life. For example, the eighteenth-century Scottish philosopher Adam Smith, one of the most influential liberal philosophers, argues that individuals' rational economic choices produce a society where everybody is better off, because profit for any one person also creates value that is available to others. Smith proposes that an underlying force, which he called "the invisible hand," motivates individuals to produce social value through their market transactions. Liberal economists and philosophers who have argued for the importance of individual freedoms, limited government in the economy, and the potential for a free market to deliver the best overall outcomes include Adam Smith (eighteenth century), David Ricardo (nineteenth century), and Friedrich Hayek (twentieth century). Liberalism is discussed at greater length in Chapter 2 of this book.

As a contemporary ideology, neoliberalism prioritizes unregulated economic activity over all other rights that an individual or group might claim to have. A neoliberal state exists to protect these rights and to preserve markets – and no more. Therefore, according to the ideology of neoliberalism, *politics* is very limited in scope, because conflict over scarce resources should not be managed by anybody. Instead, "who gets what, when, how?" should be determined through the market. Under neoliberalism, anyone who ends up with lots of money and authority deserves what they have. Because of this, Harvey argues that neoliberal policies since the 1970s have "[restored] the power of economic elites" around the globe.[26] When the state not only regulates less in the economy, but actively *de*regulates to improve the position of industry,[27] people who lack money have few alternatives for improving their lives. The effects of neoliberalism are not the same for all people, however. Neoliberalism overlaps with other pervasive ideologies, including patriarchy and racist/supremacist beliefs. When racism produces job discrimination, for example, then an entire group of people are closed off from income on the basis of their race, and a neoliberal state will not intervene to address this discrimination and the inequality it creates.

At the same time, Ong argues that countries and their governments are implementing neoliberalism in different ways.[28] As noted, neoliberalism views individuals who create profit as good and valuable because of that profit. This belief corresponds with a smaller state – one that enacts fewer laws, allowing the notional "invisible hand" to allocate resources. In some non-democratic countries, in particular, a neoliberal reduction in how much the state intervenes in society and the economy has created opportunities for non-state actors – such as humanitarian organizations – to help vulnerable groups of people. Ong's assessment is therefore that neoliberalism does not always disadvantage people who are already marginalized. This is not in line with what many critics of neoliberalism expect.

Since the late 1970s, neoliberalism has been prevalent around the globe as an economic system and as an ideology. Therefore, multiple political parties in most countries embody neoliberalism. As with the ideology of patriarchy, it is easier to identify parties that explicitly reject neoliberalism as exceptions to the norm. In the United Kingdom, for example, the largest long-standing political parties all support free market policies. However, a party established in 2005 called the Socialist Workers Network (previously called People Before Profit) explicitly rejects neoliberalism. This socialist party is active in Northern Ireland and the Republic of Ireland and has won a small number of seats at the local and regional level.

Neoliberalism provides the following answers to the two key questions presented in the introductory section of this chapter:

1 The distribution of authority: Who should call the shots, and for whom?
   - Profit is self-justifying and its own authority.
   - People should retain profit from the economic transactions they engage in.
   - Individuals who do not profit have no alternative claim to authority.
2 The mechanisms for authority: Whom should decision making include?
   - Because the state's activities should be limited, decision making is minimal.
   - This decision-making process does not need to include a representative sample of the governed population, because the state's activities are limited.

Democracy

You might be surprised to see democracy presented as an ideology when you are familiar with it as a form of government, but many political scientists argue that certain values and beliefs are prerequisites for its emergence and success. A democratic political system does not arise spontaneously. Instead, people demand some say in the rules that govern them. In order to demand opportunities to participate in governance and then to maintain these processes, they need to believe that they deserve to participate. In pre- and early-modern periods of history, the divine right of monarchs (usually kings) was viewed as legitimate. However, as societies and economies developed, more people grew to view themselves as having a right to hold rulers accountable.[29]

As a modern political system, "democracy is a system of governance in which rulers are held accountable for their actions in the public realm by citizens, acting indirectly through the competition and cooperation of their elected representatives."[30] Democratic principles are by far not the only possible basis for public decision making, and in fact most of history (and much of the contemporary world) is characterized by decidedly non-democratic governance without ways for people to hold rulers accountable for their actions.

Political scientists suggest many different terms for categorizing states that emphasize or satisfy some criteria for democracy more than or differently from others. For example, *liberal democracy* is a democratic system that specifically affirms a range of individual civil and political rights, as in the US Bill of Rights. Robert Dahl prefers the term *polyarchy* for this form of government, because it emphasizes the free participation of individuals.[31] *Social democracy* in the Nordic countries emphasizes compromise and inclusion. An *illiberal democracy* is a country that holds elections regularly – an important component of democracy! – but does not protect civil and political rights, and where the legal system is corrupt.[32]

The introductory section of this chapter mentioned Alexis de Tocqueville, an early essayist about American democracy. De Tocqueville was a French aristocrat who visited the United States in the 1830s and wrote *Democracy in America* based on his observations.[33] Unlike in France, where generations of aristocracy and financial inequality entrenched people in specific social categories, the United States seemed to be a place where individuals perceived themselves and each other to be equals. This self-perception and belief in their capacity to participate in governance corresponded with representative democracy. Of course, de Tocqueville was observing *white men* as equals; enslaved people and all women did not have suffrage at this time.

Lots of scholarship in the mid-twentieth century picked up on de Tocqueville's ideas, writing about "social requisites" for democracy. Although many of these scholars were referring to social conditions (in particular a society's technological modernization), they implicitly and explicitly also meant that people's beliefs were central to democracy. For example, Daniel Lerner's *Passing of Traditional Society* describes the transformation of how individuals understood themselves as part of their communities.[34] Lerner argues that mass communication technology makes it possible for people to develop shared feeling with large numbers of other people. The development of empathy, he argues, is a prerequisite for modern government.

Thinking about democracy as an "explicit, consciously held belief system" separately from its institutions also helps to explain how the practical definition of democracy has changed over the last 200 years.[35] Today, we generally expect a democracy to meet the following procedural criteria:[36]

1 *Effective participation*: All members of the community must have "equal and effective opportunities for making their views known."
2 *Voting equality*: All members "have an equal and effective opportunity to vote, and all votes must be counted as equal."
3 *Enlightened understanding*: All members must have "equal and effective opportunities for learning about the relevant alternative policies and their likely consequences."
4 *Control of the agenda*: All members must have control over "what matters are to be placed on the agenda."
5 *Inclusion of adults*: All "adult permanent residents should have the full rights of citizens."

Just like patriarchy and neoliberalism, democracy is an ideology that overlaps with other widespread beliefs. Even a political system that embodies many democratic beliefs about equality will still treat people differently whom it *doesn't* view as equals. Beliefs about *who counts* change over time and have profound consequences for people's rights. Many countries that are considered longtime democracies have not always satisfied the basic modern requirements enumerated above.

Universal adult suffrage illustrates both this point and the fact that ideologies intersect to produce different rights for groups in the population. Women could not vote in Canada's federal elections until 1918. However, Indigenous peoples could not vote without officially relinquishing their treaty rights until the Canada Elections Act of 1960. Earlier stages of enfranchisement required that an Indigenous person give up "being Indian" in exchange for voting, which very few people chose to do. An Indigenous woman in Canada, therefore, could not vote until 1960, unless she chose to formally exit her community and heritage.

In turn, French women were forced to wait until 1944 to vote, and Swiss women could not vote in federal elections until 1971. The United States is considered one of the longest-lived democracies in the world, but women's suffrage took 130 years to achieve, and citizens descended from slaves in the American South were disenfranchised by Jim Crow laws until the Voting Rights Acts of 1965. In her study of how we measure democracy, Pamela Paxton shows that our understanding of global political trends changes if we require that a country needs to include full adult suffrage (regardless of gender or race) in order to be considered a democracy.[37] With the addition of this requirement, the "first wave" of democratization around World War I does not exist at all, because most of those countries were political systems where at least half of the adult population did not have suffrage.

Some people will simply argue that times change. However, these changes in who needs to be included in public decision making are enormous – for example, by more than doubling the population of full citizens. These institutional changes correspond with changes in *beliefs* about who is fit to participate in politics as an equal, not facts. They are ideological changes that happen at the intersection of race, ethnicity, gender, and socioeconomic class.

Discussing democracy as an ideology also helps explain democratic backsliding, which you may remember from Chapter 1. This is when political leaders purposely undermine democratic institutions. Bermeo describes it as the "state-led debilitation or elimination of any of the political institutions that sustain an existing democracy."[38] Working from Schmitter and Karl's definition,[39] backsliding means that rulers are held accountable for their actions to a lesser degree.

Although backsliding most often happens because a non-democratic leader seizes political control, it can also correspond with voters themselves expressing different beliefs. Consider the country of Hungary. Hungary was a communist, one-party state called the Hungarian People's Republic from 1949 to 1989, but it rapidly democratized at the end of the Cold War. However, 25 years later, in democratic elections, Hungarian voters voted authoritarian-leaning Viktor Orbán into power. Orbán has proceeded to disenfranchise opposition groups and reduce leaders' accountability. Indeed, during the 2020 COVID-19 crisis, the legislature gave Orbán the authority to rule by decree – with no accountability – indefinitely.[40]

Although the legislature moved to revoke that power two months later, the legislation rescinding rule by decree creates new unlimited powers for the government, and critics contend that only the pretense of democracy remains.[41] Indeed, Hungary is the only European Union member classified as partly free in the 2020 "Freedom in the World" report, and the state is best categorized as an illiberal democracy at present.[42] When voters not just condone but *demand* less-representative institutions, then (in Lerner's language) backsliding corresponds with voters experiencing *less* empathy for one another.

Democracy provides these answers to the two key questions presented in the introductory section of this chapter:

1 The distribution of authority: Who should call the shots, and for whom?
   • Authority is held by people who are elected into representative office.
   • Political leaders' legitimacy comes from the support (usually through elections) of the people who are governed.
   • Voters should hold rulers accountable for their actions.
2 The mechanisms for authority: Whom should decision making include?
   • The decision-making process should include the people who are governed.

Populism

Populism is a cluster of beliefs that prioritize the experiences and rights of non-elites over the experiences and rights of elites. "Elites" are people who are perceived to have more material resources (money! land!). Formal education is also sometimes considered "elite," regardless of whether education corresponds with greater material resources. Canovan writes, "Populism in modern democratic societies is best seen as an appeal to 'the people' against both the established structure of power and the dominant ideas and values of the society."[43] This appeal to "the people" often accuses "the elites" of corruption.[44]

Like any ideology, populism coexists with other social structures and other sets of beliefs. But populism is especially flexible for combining with these other ideologies, because populist beliefs are oriented around subjective entities. "The people" and "the elite" are different depending on who you ask, but they are definitely central to populism.[45] Someone might be a populist and believe in the righteousness of "the 99 per cent." That person might be very well educated and read Karl Marx's *Das Kapital* and believe that anyone who is affluent has earned their money unjustly and by exploiting others. For this first populist, an elite is the person who has acquired material wealth. But another person might be populist and believe in what they would call "common sense." This person might believe that anyone who has read a lot of Karl Marx has spent too much time reading books and has lost touch with how real life works. For this second populist, an elite is the person who has acquired knowledge through formal education.

Some scholars refer to populism as a "thin ideology."[46] Stanley argues that populism on its own does not consist of any specific values or beliefs, but it does "interact with the established ideational traditions of full ideologies."[47] Put another way, "Populism is moralistic rather than programmatic."[48] It accuses the elite of being bad people who do bad things; it does not propose a specific alternative to those bad things. Populism therefore readily combines with other ideologies that do propose specific policy alternatives.

Political parties that embody populism are on the rise (see Figure 3.1) in a way that illustrates this flexibility. In Europe, for example, populism is usually found in political parties categorized on "the right," because these parties have combined populist ideology with *nationalist* ideologies that are focused on promoting their society and culture as superior. Nationalist ideologies are typically associated with the right.[49] In Germany, a political party established in 2013 illustrates the combination of populism and nationalism: the Alternative for Germany (AfD). The AfD is populist in the sense that it accuses longtime German political parties and leaders of making bad choices about the integration of Germany's economy into the European Union and about immigration policy. It is nationalist in the sense that it believes in the superiority of "German culture and society," supporting policies that limit immigration to prevent changes to that society.

In Latin America, most populist political parties are categorized on "the left," because they are focused on left-leaning economic preferences like public ownership of industries and utilities and the redistribution of wealth. Populism in Venezuela, for example, takes the form of Hugo Chávez, who served as president from 1999 until his death in 2013. Chávez was a populist in the sense that he accused longtime political leaders of corruption and bad governance, promising to replace immoral policymakers with better governance. He is quoted as saying during the 2006 presidential election campaign, "Chávez is nothing but an instrument of the people!"[50] Chávez was a socialist (a "left" ideology) in the sense that he supported nationalizing industries and implementing price controls and food distribution.

Figure 3.1. The Rise of Right-Wing Populism in Europe, 2015–2019

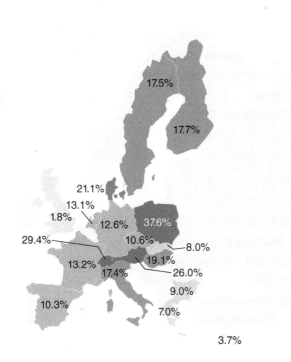

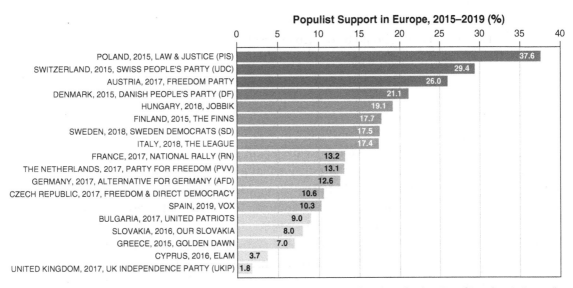

Source: Data for all countries except the Netherlands from Niall McCarthy, "The Relentless Rise of Populism in Europe," Statista, https://www.statista.com/chart/17860/results-of-far-right-parties-in-the-most-recent-legislave-elections; data for the Netherlands from IPU, "Interparliamentary Union Elections Archive," http://archive.ipu.org/wmn-e/world.htm.

In contemporary Greece, new populist parties on both the left *and* the right have emerged in the context of the Greek financial, political, and social crisis in the twenty-first century. SYRIZA (Coalition of the Radical Left) was established in 2004. This left-wing populist party defines Western Europe as "the elite." The economic elite at the heart of the European Union have, according to SYRIZA, exploited and otherwise unjustly treated peripheral, non-elite countries like Greece. On the right, Golden Dawn registered as a political party in 1993. Golden Dawn combines moralistic accusations against a corrupt government with ultra-nationalist beliefs about preserving Greek culture and society.

A quotation from Ilias Panagiotaros, a four-term Golden Dawn member of the Greek Parliament (2012–19), illustrates the party's combined populist and ultra-nationalist values. In October 2012, Panagiotaros told the *BBC*, "The Greek society is ready for a new kind of civil war. On the one side there will be nationalists like us, and Greeks who want our country to be as it was, and on the other side, illegal immigrants, anarchists and all those who have repeatedly destroyed Athens."[51] Panagiotaros is among numerous Golden Dawn politicians who have been criminally investigated on charges of physical violence against immigrants and anti-fascist activists.[52]

Populism provides these answers to the two key questions presented in the introductory section of this chapter:

1 The distribution of authority: Who should call the shots, and for whom?
   - Authority should be held by non-elites.
2 The mechanisms for authority: Whom should decision making include?
   - Decision making should be done by non-elites.

CONCLUSION

This chapter introduced the concept of *ideology* as a set of values and beliefs that shape political preferences – for individual people and for societies at large. Ideologies take form in the kinds of policies that people prefer, and sometimes in formal political parties. Most importantly, no ideology exists in a vacuum: Ideologies overlap and interact with one another. To demonstrate how this works, we close this chapter with a look at the Me Too movements in Box 3.1. This case study illustrates how patriarchy and neoliberalism combine to create an atmosphere that allows for the persistent sexual harassment and abuse of women in the workplace.

BOX 3.1: ME TOO

In 2017, #MeToo became a global rallying cry for raising awareness about sexual harassment in the workplace. The *New York Times* revealed on October 5, 2017, that over the course of three decades entertainment mogul Harvey Weinstein had made numerous legal settlements regarding sexual harassment accusations.[53] For the women Weinstein harassed, the workplace often included meetings about advancing their acting careers. The *New York Times* reported that Weinstein's accusers included such high-profile actors as Ashley Judd and Rose McGowan, as well as staff working at his production company. The article's publication prompted more women to step forward, including Angelina Jolie and Gwyneth Paltrow, two of the most powerful women in Hollywood. Weinstein negotiated a $25 million settlement with dozens of women in December 2019.[54] After a two-year trial concluding in February 2020, a jury found him guilty of two lesser charges, criminal sexual assault in the first degree and rape in the third degree, and he was sentenced to 20 years in prison.[55]

Sexual harassment and assault of women in the workplace occurs and re-occurs because a wider context allows it. Weinstein's actions were unambiguously against the law, but two intersecting sets of values had produced decades of impunity. The Me Too movements reveal that this impunity is not just about patriarchy and not just about neoliberalism. The ideologies of patriarchy and neoliberalism *together* produce outcomes that would not be explained by one or the other alone. Patriarchal values systematically prioritize men over women, and neoliberal values systematically prioritize profit over everything else.

The ideology of patriarchy meant that people around Weinstein who were aware of his behavior valued his experiences and rights more highly than the women he abused. Weinstein's apologists include men and women both, because patriarchal values infuse everyone's understanding of the world. For example, director and producer Quentin Tarantino, who worked extensively with Weinstein, admits that he knew for years: "I knew enough to do more than I did … I wish I had taken responsibility for what I heard … If I had done the work I should have done then, I would have had to not work with him."[56] These values can extend to viewing women who are assaulted as responsible for their assault. For example, Donna Rotunno, Weinstein's attorney, told the *New York Times* in 2020 that she had never been sexually assaulted "because I would never put myself in that position."[57]

In turn, the ideology of neoliberalism meant that both Weinstein and the women he abused perceived career advancement to be all-important. As the section on neoliberalism argued, the effects of neoliberalism are not the same for everyone. Women who are especially vulnerable because of their socio-economic and racial-minority status are even less likely to successfully speak out against abusers. Low-paid domestic workers such as house cleaners are more likely to be women of color, and a neoliberal society does not prioritize laws to protect their bodies and their voices in these situations.

SUMMARY

- A political ideology is a set of beliefs and values about how conflict over resources should be managed. It is not a set of facts.
- Ideologies shape individuals' preferences for what policies to support and who to vote for.
- An ideology and a political party are not synonymous. Some ideologies are shared by many political parties in the same country, while others are not part of any political party.
- Patriarchy is a set of values about gender and power that we find in most societies around the world and throughout history. The ideology of patriarchy justifies men having more authority and decision-making power than women.
- Neoliberalism is a set of values about the state's role in the economy. It is an ideology that we find in most societies and many political parties around the world today. The ideology of neoliberalism justifies an unequal distribution of money and decision-making power.
- Democracy is a set of values about individuals' equal rights to participate in creating the rules that govern them. A state can satisfy some basic procedural criteria for democracy but fall short in other ways, so there are many different qualified categories for this regime type, such as the *illiberal democracy*.
- Populism is a set of values that morally critique "elites" for making bad decisions. It is known as a thin ideology, because populism by itself does not specify alternatives to the elites' decisions. Instead, populism is usually combined with another ideology that does specify alternatives. Populism is on the rise in democracies around the world.
- The Me Too movements show that women's experiences of sexual harassment in the workplace are not just about patriarchy, and they are not just about neoliberalism. These experiences are the result of both at once. The ideologies of patriarchy and neoliberalism combine together to justify persistent sexual abuse and harassment.

- Remember, at the end of this book there is an appendix with ideas for how you can get involved and safeguard against democratic backsliding.

CONCLUDING QUESTIONS

1 What is an ideology, and how is it different from a political party?
2 To what extent are ideologies bad? Is it possible to make political decisions without ideology? What would the political world look like without ideology?
3 Briefly explain the historical origins of the following ideologies and what forms they take today:
  a. Patriarchy
  b. Neoliberalism
  c. Populism
  d. Democracy
4 The #MeToo movement is a response to persistent sexual harassment of women in the workplace. What ideologies have made sexual harassment so persistent? What ideologies might work against it?

NOTES

1 Robert D. Putnam, "Studying Elite Political Culture: The Case of 'Ideology,'" *American Political Science Review* 65, no. 3 (1971): 655.
2 John Gerring, "Ideology: A Definitional Analysis," *Political Research Quarterly* 50, no. 4 (1997): 980.
3 C. Calhoun, "Social Structure," in *Dictionary of the Social Sciences*, ed. C. Calhoun (Oxford: Oxford University Press, 2002).
4 Gerring, "Ideology."
5 Giovanni Sartori, "Politics, Ideology, and Belief Systems," *American Political Science Review* 63, no. 2 (1969): 398–411.
6 Putnam, "Studying Elite Political Culture," 655.
7 Willard A. Mullins, "On the Concept of Ideology in Political Science," *American Political Science Review* 66, no. 2 (1972): 498.
8 Alexis de Tocqueville, *Democracy in America*, trans. Gerald E. Bevan (New York: Penguin, 2003 [1840]).
9 Angus Campbell, Philip E. Converse, Warren E. Miller, and Donald E. Stokes, *The American Voter* (New York: Wiley, 1980); Philip E. Converse, "The Nature of Belief Systems in Mass Publics," *Ideology and Discontent* (1964): 206–61.
10 Louis Althusser, "Ideology and Ideological State Apparatuses (Notes Towards an Investigation)," in *Lenin and Philosophy and Other Essays*, ed. Ben Brewster, 127–86 (New York:

Monthly Review Press, 1971); Hannah Arendt, *The Origins of Totalitarianism* (Boston: Houghton Mifflin Harcourt, 1958); Karl Marx and Friedrich Engels, *Das Kapital* (1848).

11 Koen Vossen, *The Power of Populism: Geert Wilders and the Party for Freedom in the Netherlands* (Abingdon, UK: Taylor & Francis, 2016).

12 Sylvia Walby, "Theorising Patriarchy," *Sociology* 23, no. 2 (1989): 214.

13 Janet Rifkin, "Toward a Theory of Law and Patriarchy," *Harvard Women's Law Journal* 3 (1980): 83; emphasis added.

14 Kristen Schilt, "Just One of the Guys? How Transmen Make Gender Visible at Work" *Gender & Society* 20, no. 4 (2006): 465–90; Judith Squires, *Gender in Political Theory* (New York: John Wiley & Sons, 1999).

15 Harold D. Lasswell, *Politics; Who Gets What, When, How* (New York: Whittlesey House, 1936).

16 S. Laurel Weldon, "Intersectionality," in *Politics, Gender and Concepts: Theory and Methodology*, eds. Gary Goetz and Amy Mazur, 193–218 (Cambridge: Cambridge University Press, 2008).

17 Pieter Bevelander and Jonas Otterbeck, "Islamophobia in Sweden: Politics, Representations, Attitudes and Experiences," in *Islamophobia in the West: Measuring and Explaining Individual Attitudes*, ed. Marc Heibling (London: Routledge, 2011).

18 Alice H. Eagly and Steven J. Karau, "Role Congruity Theory of Prejudice toward Female Leaders," *Psychological Review* 109, no. 3 (2002): 573.

19 Sam Levin, "Stanford Sexual Assault: Read the Full Text of the Judge's Controversial Decision," *The Guardian*, September 14, 2016, https://www.theguardian.com/us-news/2016/jun/14/stanford-sexual-assault-read-sentence-judge-aaron-persky.

20 See https://thewomensparty.org.au.

21 On *intersectionality-plus*, see Weldon, "Intersectionality."

22 Walby, "Theorising Patriarchy."

23 David Harvey, *A Brief History of Neoliberalism* (Oxford: Oxford University Press, 2007).

24 Paul Treanor, "Neoliberalism: Origins, Theory, Definition," 2005, http://web.inter.nl.net/users/Paul.Treanor/neoliberalism.html.

25 Treanor, "Neoliberalism."

26 Harvey, *A Brief History of Neoliberalism*, 19.

27 Lester K. Spence, *Knocking the Hustle: Against the Neoliberal Turn in Black Politics* (Goleta, CA: punctum books, 2015).

28 Aihwa Ong, *Neoliberalism as Exception: Mutations in Citizenship and Sovereignty* (Durham, NC: Duke University Press, 2006).

29 On the development of more inclusive and participatory states in the region of Europe, see, for example, Thomas Ertman, *Birth of the Leviathan: Building States and Regimes in Medieval and Early Modern Europe* (Cambridge: Cambridge University Press, 1997).

30 Philippe C. Schmitter and Terry Lynn Karl, "What Democracy Is ... and Is Not," *Journal of Democracy* 2, no. 3 (1991): 76.

31 Robert A. Dahl, *Polyarchy: Participation and Opposition* (New Haven, CT: Yale University Press, 1971).

32 Larry Diamond, "Elections without Democracy: Thinking About Hybrid Regimes," *Journal of Democracy* 13, no. 2 (2002): 21–35; Fareed Zakaria, "The Rise of Illiberal Democracy," *Foreign Affairs* 76 (1997): 22.

33 de Tocqueville, *Democracy in America*.

34 Daniel Lerner, *The Passing of Traditional Society: Modernizing the Middle East* (New York: Free Press, 1958).

35 Putnam, "Studying Elite Political Culture."

36 Robert A. Dahl, *On Democracy* (New Haven, CT: Yale University Press, 1998), 37–8.

37 Pamela Paxton, "Women's Suffrage in the Measurement of Democracy: Problems of Operationalization," *Studies in Comparative International Development* 35, no. 3 (2000): 92–111.

38 Nancy Bermeo, "On Democratic Backsliding," *Journal of Democracy* 27, no. 1 (2016): 5.

39 Schmitter and Karl, "What Democracy Is."

40 Benjamin Novak and Patrick Kingsley, "Hungary's Leader Grabbed Powers to Fight the Virus. Some Fear Other Motives," *New York Times*, April 5, 2020.

41 Benjamin Novak, "Hungary Moves to End Rule by Decree, but Orban's Powers May Stay," *New York Times*, June 16, 2020.

42 Freedom House, "Freedom in the World: Hungary," 2020, https://freedomhouse.org/country/hungary/freedom-world/2020.

43 Margaret Canovan, "Trust the People! Populism and the Two Faces of Democracy," *Political Studies* 47, no. 1 (1999): 3.

44 Cas Mudde, "The Populist Zeitgeist," *Government and Opposition* 39, no. 4 (2004): 543.

45 Mudde, "The Populist Zeitgeist," 543.

46 Mudde, "The Populist Zeitgeist"; Ben Stanley, "The Thin Ideology of Populism," *Journal of Political Ideologies* 13, no. 1 (2008): 95–110.

47 Stanley, "The Thin Ideology of Populism," 95.

48 Mudde, "The Populist Zeitgeist," 544.

49 Cas Mudde, *Populist Radical Right Parties in Europe* (Cambridge: Cambridge University Press, 2007).

50 Quoted in Uri Friedman, "How Populism Helped Wreck Venezuela," *The Atlantic*, June 24, 2017, https://www.theatlantic.com/international/archive/2017/06/venezuela-populism-fail/525321.

51 *BBC News*, "Greece Far Right Party Golden Dawn: 'We Are in Civil War,'" October 17, 2012, https://www.bbc.com/news/av/world-europe-19983571/greece-far-right-party-golden-dawn-we-are-in-civil-war.

52 Nektaria Stamouli, "Greek Parliament Votes to Lift Immunity of Golden Dawn Deputies," *Wall Street Journal*, October 16, 2013, https://www.wsj.com/articles/greek-parliament-votes-to-lift-immunity-of-golden-dawn-deputies-1381928171.

53 Jodi Kantor and Megan Twohey, "Harvey Weinstein Paid Off Sexual Harassment Accusers for Decades," *New York Times*, October 5, 2017, https://www.nytimes.com/2017/10/05/us/harvey-weinstein-harassment-allegations.html.

54 Reuters, "Weinstein: How Events Unfolded," February 24, 2020.

55 Anna Watts, "Full Coverage: Harvey Weinstein Is Found Guilty of Rape," *New York Times*, February 24, 2020.

56 Quoted in Jodi Kantor, "Tarantino on Weinstein: 'I Knew Enough to Do More Than I Did,'" *New York Times*, October 19, 2017, https://www.nytimes.com/2017/10/19/movies/tarantino-weinstein.html.

57 Quoted in Watts, "Full Coverage."

RESOURCES AND SUGGESTIONS FOR FURTHER READING

Freeden, Michael, and Marc Stears, eds. *The Oxford Handbook of Political Ideologies*. Oxford: Oxford University Press, 2013.

Mair, Peter, and Cas Mudde. "The Party Family and Its Study." *Annual Review of Political Science* 1, no. 1 (1998): 211–29.

Mendes, Kaitlynn, Jessica Ringrose, and Jessalynn Keller. "#MeToo and the Promise and Pitfalls of Challenging Rape Culture through Digital Feminist Activism." *European Journal of Women's Studies* 25, no. 2 (2018): 236–46.

Me Too Movement. https://metoomvmt.org.

Spence, Lester K. *Knocking the Hustle: Against the Neoliberal Turn in Black Politics*. Goleta, CA: punctum books, 2015.

CHAPTER FOUR

Civil Society and Social Movements

*Dr. Erica
Townsend-Bell*

LEARNING OBJECTIVES

1 Define civil society, social movements, and contentious politics
2 Assess the relationship between institutionalized and non-institutionalized politics
3 Evaluate the function, characteristics, and consequences of civil society and social movements
4 Assess the role of power asymmetries in the organization, recognition, and output of civil society and social movements

KEY TERMS

agency the capacity to act
cisgender a person whose internal sense of gender identity corresponds with the sex assigned to them at birth
collective identity a shared sense of group belonging
frame resonance collective action frames that resonate, or appeal, to a target audience
framing the process by which social movements construct social meanings
majority group groups who have significant power, regardless of and sometimes irrelevant to their numerical size

master frame   a generic frame that connects big, widely shared ideas to specific policy prescriptions

new social movements   the supposition that contemporary social movements prioritize identities, values, and expressive goals over concrete material needs

political opportunity structure   events or broad socioeconomic processes that impact the organization of major power structures

positionality   the way in which racial, class, gender, and other salient identities interact to situate actors in the world; it is informed by both the actor's internal sense of identity as well as by identification – the way in which the actor is identified by others

power asymmetry   an imbalance in power between two sides

privilege   unearned and often unrecognized rights or advantages

public goods   a public benefit or product provided or accessible to all members of a community without exception

repertoires of contention   the array of protest tools readily available to a group at specific points in time

social movements   organized, collective, non-institutionalized challenges to specific targets seeking to achieve a common goal

strategy   the specific path or methods movements adopt to reach their goal(s)

tactics   the specific actions actors take to affect their strategies and reach their goals

unmarked   the recognition that some people, things, or ideas are designated as standard, and thus taken for granted as normal, in opposition to those people, things, or ideas that are marked by their difference

WHAT IS CIVIL SOCIETY AND WHAT DOES IT DO?

Civil society refers to the public sphere of sociopolitical life, at least partly independent from the state and the market, in which individuals are free to engage in deliberation and association and, hence, activism. The Heinrich Böll Stiftung organization, a German-based public policy think tank, is eloquent in its affirmation of civil society's democratic role:

> Civil society organizations engage in advocating the public's rights and wishes of the people, including but not limited to health, environment and economic rights. They fulfill important duties of checks and balances in democracies, they are able to influence the government and hold it accountable. Therefore, free and active civil societies are an indicator of a healthy participatory democracy.[1]

The abolition movement case study in Box 4.1 indicates that civil society has been a major presence in political life for some time. However, the popularity of civil society grew significantly as numerous countries began the transition to democracy in the period from the 1970s to 1990s. Since then, practitioners and scholars alike have lauded civil society as a major cornerstone of democracy. Why? It is the space in which people come together, debate, and make change. This means that civil society is the most common way in which the average person participates in and helps to steer sociopolitical life. It is fundamentally democratic in this way, because it allows people to exercise the basic components of democracy, such as freedom of assembly, freedom of speech, and the right to alternative information. Civil society can include charities, social service organizations, non-governmental organizations, large and small community groups, faith-based organizations, professional associations, trade unions, social movements, advocacy groups, and more. It is quite likely that you yourself have participated in at least one space of civil society.[2]

BOX 4.1: THE ABOLITIONIST MOVEMENT

The concept of civil society has metamorphosed throughout the years, with the idea shifting alongside the prevailing form of political/territorial–political organization. However, the notion of a social or political community organized in pursuit of the common, democratic good has been a constant in its meaning and attachment. One early exemplar of modern civil society is the abolitionist movement.

Like many of the civil society examples that follow, the abolitionist movement is international in scope and includes activists from varied racial, gender, and class backgrounds. As the title of Table 4.1 indicates, it also ranges in time and outcome. It has varied in its ability to make change immediately permanent with several instances of re-established slavery, or abolition in two rounds for the same location; it is also ongoing, through to the present day. The abolitionist movement is sometimes uneven in terms of the specific goals sought and achieved. For instance, abolitionists were all opposed to slavery, but their support for Black equality varied significantly, with some abolitionists supporting granting freedom followed by immediate expulsion of slaves to Africa (or other locations), others seeking the full equality of persons of African descent, and still others holding positions at other nodes of the spectrum.

Table 4.1. Chronology of the Abolitions of Slavery

1777	The abolition of slavery included in the Constitution of Vermont
1780	Abolition in Pennsylvania
1783	Abolition in Massachusetts
1784	Abolition in Rhode Island and Connecticut
1793	Abolition of slavery in Santo Domingo after the slave rebellion launched in August 1791
1802	Re-establishment of slavery in the French colonies
1803	Banning of Black slave trade by Denmark
1807	Banning of slave trade by Great Britain
1808	Banning of Black slave trade by the United States
1814	Banning of Black slave trade by the Netherlands
1815	European powers meeting at the Congress of Vienna undertook to ban the Black slave trade
1822	Abolition of slavery in Santo Domingo
1823	Abolition of slavery in Chile
1826	Abolition of slavery in Bolivia
1829	Abolition of slavery in Mexico
1831	Last French law banning Black slave trade
1833–8	Abolition of slavery in the British colonies
1846	Abolition of slavery in Tunisia
1847	Abolition of slavery in the Swedish colony of Saint Barthélemy
1848	Abolition of slavery in the French and Danish colonies
1851	Abolition of slavery in Colombia
1853	Abolition of slavery in Argentina
1854	Abolition of slavery in Venezuela
1855	Abolition of slavery in Peru
1863	Abolition of slavery in the Dutch colonies
1863–5	Abolition of slavery in the United States
1870	Moret Abolition Act passed in Spain
1873	Abolition of slavery in Puerto Rico
1876	Abolition of slavery in Brazil[2]
1880	Abolition of slavery in Madagascar
1886	Abolition of slavery in Zanzibar
1909	The British and Foreign Anti-Slavery Society founded in 1839 became Anti-Slavery International
1910	Abolition of slavery in China
1919	Creation of the International Labour Organization
1920	Abolition of slavery in Somalia

Source: UNESCO, "Table 4: Chronology of the Abolition of Slavery," http://www.unesco.org/new /fileadmin/MULTIMEDIA/HQ/CLT/images/Abolitions_02.jpg.

The Ideal of Civil Society: Characteristics and Functions of Civil Society

What work does civil society do, and what characteristics are common? Several. First, and most fundamentally, there is an expectation that individuals come to participate of their own free will. The voluntary nature of the association situates civil society as a space of reciprocity; collaboration is based on mutual dependence between the individuals or groups that participate. In this understanding, the relationship between actors is horizontal; there is an expectation of equal power between and representation of all participants. These characteristics, alongside the broad range of civil society groups mentioned above, lead us to understand civil society as inclusive and pluralist. There is a civil society group representing just about every interest under the sun. And if some priority is not already represented, then anyone who wishes to start a new group can simply start one. Anyone in a democratic setting, that is.

Given this set of characteristics, we can see that civil society is often understood as a major contributor to democracy. The following list outlines just some of the work that civil society can perform:

- It encourages or provides democratic practices by allowing space for contestation over meaning, for dissent, and for participation.
- It helps shape public policy, as a result of the democratic practices it supports.
- It promotes interest aggregation by serving as a channel for the articulation, collection, and representation of specific sets of interests.

Civil society performs this work in both democratically consolidated and democratizing countries, and it tries to do so in authoritarian countries as well. As such, there has been considerable interest in seeing the emergence or strengthening of civil society throughout the world. When civil society is robust, it can serve important additional functions that maintain or improve democracy:

- Help to constrain state power by maximizing the people's voice
- Recruit and train new leaders
- Promote tolerance and compromise
- Aid in the creation or maintenance of pluralism and cross-cutting cleavages

The Heterogeneity of Civil Society

These basic tenets of civil society help to characterize some of the work that it does. A final characteristic of civil society is its heterogeneity. As Dagnino affirms, civil society is incredibly vast and diverse, ranging from paramilitary organizations and youth gangs to unions and neoliberal non-profits, just in Latin America alone.[3]

There is a common assumption that civil society is always and only benevolent and horizontal; but, like most complex concepts, it operates on a spectrum. This means that civil society offers multiple postures that confirm and challenge its reputation for citizen engagement and democratic enhancement. For instance, compelled or involuntary group membership challenges the freedom of association assumption. Kathleen Blee describes such a situation for some of the female partic-ipants of various white supremacist groups in the United States.[4] All of the women she interviews came to the movement of their own free will, but not all feel they can leave or dissent without repercussion, including physical and emotional harm and separation from their children. A less controversial, but nonetheless still in-voluntary, mandate to perform community service is a common requirement for US and Canadian high schools. Yet there has been little discussion of whether it is ethical to make this a requirement for all students, especially those who may them-selves be resource challenged or otherwise disadvantaged in some way.

The Western conception of civil society assumes that a commitment decision is voluntary, individual, and autonomous, but these presumptions are further complicated in settings where public identity and public participation is based on group membership. Those settings are sometimes conceived as falling outside the space of civil society but may be better understood as falling outside of the Western, liberal, individual conception of civil society. Thus, formal civil society is weak in the South Caucasus region (Armenia, Azerbaijan, and Georgia), but this is partly because an alternative form of association, kinship institutions, are quite strong. Whether these alternative associations form another type of civil society then becomes an empirical question.

Civil society, like society in general, can have a tendency to prioritize the issues and perspectives of **unmarked**, often Western, actors. Unequal resource access means that these normative perspectives are often attached to funding, meaning they become the priorities of marginalized actors as well, often in lieu of their actual preferences and priorities. For instance, there is a large literature on the way that big Western donor agencies use the power-of-the-purse to push priorities that may not align with those of local, often non-Western, civil society actors on the ground.[5] Note the way in which Zambian and Malawian AIDS activists take strategic advantage of the broad, ill-defined, and inconsistently applied concept of empowerment that Western donors prioritize, and bend it to encompass the work they are already doing. Doing so allows the local actors to focus on their specific priorities and simultaneously satisfy donors' emphasis on a concept they view as tangential to the local context.

So uneven resource effects do not mean that marginalized actors have no **agency**. Underrepresented groups can and do make use of the power of redefini-tion, exit, and reorganization, among other tactics. Indeed, underprivileged actors who have felt their identities, issues, or presence to be problematic, undervalued, or overlooked in some form have frequently exercised these options, leaving, **majority**-oriented spaces and reorganizing themselves into group-specific asso-ciations that better reflect their needs and experiences. Such is the origin story of the various women-of-color social movement organizations, especially predominant in English-speaking Western countries, that organize for the purpose of more targeted activism on behalf of themselves and more inclusive and attentive (to diversity) spaces in the larger social movement community.

Democracy for Some of the People?

Such enactments of agency are important, because they serve as evidence that civil society does much of the work with which it is credited, but often in somewhat segregated spaces. Firat and Glanville find that self-help associations in the United States do a fairly good job of engaging with diverse racial groups and members.[6] Meanwhile neighborhood, sports, religious, and fraternal associations – that is, the kinds of associations that are often central to local community life and which often define our fundamental notions of community – tend to be much less integrated. And, we should remember, they may be equally likely to define community and common ground in quite narrow and exclusionary terms. Ironically, the same logic of exclusion or underrepresentation that can push minority groups to self-organize is sometimes viewed as problematic distancing. For instance, Chinese ethnic organizations in Canada report ideological pushback to their formation as Chinese-specific ethnic organizations, even though evidence shows that community-centered groups such as these are more effective at understanding and responding to the particular needs of that local community.[7] These organizations, and many like them, are accused of threatening or diluting Canadian identity, even in an officially multicultural Canada that is set up to allow and to celebrate precisely these kinds of organizations.

So, is civil society "good," democratic, and inclusive or not? The answer is somewhere in the middle. Civil societies reflect the broader social structures in which they exist, so they are not uniformly benevolent. As with other spheres of society and systems, civil society builds on practices and ideas organized around unmarked (i.e., unnoticed or unremarkable) universal subjects, **privilege**, and uneven resource access, as reflected in **power asymmetries**. Additional work on the concept emphasizes several important points. First, civil society may be necessary to democracy, but it is insufficient. Civil society is an important democratic support, but it can neither stand in for nor fix democratic political institutions. Second, civil society can have a positive valence, emphasizing transparency, autonomy, horizontality, and transformative change, but it can also fail or underperform across some or all of these dimensions. Nonetheless, the promise of civil society is its role in the consolidation of democracy and in creating meaningful spaces for social and political participation for groups and individuals. Our interest in civil society lies in our desire for empirical assessment of its contributions. More than that, it is one of the most common vehicles for the average person's participation in politics, whatever form that participation takes.

SOCIAL MOVEMENTS AND CONTENTIOUS POLITICS: DISTINGUISHING THE RANGE OF CIVIL SOCIETY

Social Movements

Civil society refers to the large, disparate variety of collective action in the world. Much of civil society operates separate from politics and political claims making. However, the politically oriented civil society associations are especially interesting to us as political scientists, because such associations exist on a continuum. At one point are **interest groups**, which are formal, explicitly self-interested associations that seek to influence public policy and do so through a framework of regularized institutional politics. Social movements, that subset of civil society organized around sustained at least partly non-institutionalized campaigns for sociopolitical change, are at another point. **Social movements** are organized, collective, non-institutionalized challenges to specific targets seeking to achieve a common goal – broadly defined. Hence, social movements, like civil society more broadly, are both public and collective:

- As with civil society, social movements are located in the sector of the public sphere, focused on questions of the common good.
- Social movements are made up of various kinds of groups and actors, including formal social movement organizations, allied individuals, transnational advocacy networks, and much more.

However, social movements are distinct from other kinds of collective action in the following ways:

- They are organized informally in loose networks of mobilization and interaction as well as formally in social movement organizations.
- They are challengers, in that movements marshal and sustain challenges against a designated target, often the state, or other authority or power holder.
- They are sustained, which is a key differentiator of social movements and other kinds of collective action. Part of what makes a movement a movement,

rather than an isolated protest, riot, individual boycott, march, or other short-term form of collective action, is its extended character.
- They hold a set of shared goals, which are often loosely defined and vary based on the how the actors themselves define them. But movements seek a particular cause of some kind or another: freedom, empowerment, lower taxes, equality, or peace, to name a few.
- They are non-institutionalized in that their primary operation is *outside* of and in contention with the sphere of governance and formal politics.

The first four of these characteristics are straightforward, but the final characteristic requires further consideration. Non-institutionalization is central to the definition of social movements, and yet this attribute can be quite variable in nature. As noted, all social movements must include some organizations or activities that operate in contention with states, specific governments, regimes, or other holders of institutionalized power such as corporations. However, just as civil society includes a huge assortment of groups, associations, and organizations, so do social movements. Within the category of social movements, some groups (such as Greenpeace and flagship women's organizations) are professionally organized and work more closely with governments than their grassroots counterparts. These high degrees of professionalization raise the question of whether they work as interest groups more clearly aligned with petitioning for, rather than contesting against, governments and other targets.

In even closer connection, the concept of state feminism originated to describe the presence of feminist actors within state institutions and the institutionalization of feminism within the state. Women's ministries, such as the UK's Minister for Women and Equalities, Canada's Minister for Women and Gender Equality, and Australia's Minister for Women, while far from the only ones, are some of the best examples of this institutionalization. The United States does not have a cabinet-level women's ministry, though state-level women's commissions are common. To have some actors who work with and in government can be a useful strategy for social movements. Nonetheless, at least some social movement actors work mostly outside of and in direct opposition to the designated target, situating them squarely within the space of non-institutionalized protest in contestation of the target. As you might guess, the kind and degree of contestation varies considerably.

Taken together, social movements are both (1) at least partly non-institutionalized and (2) distinct from other kinds of collective action, at least in theory. But the real world is a messy place, and the line between interest groups and social movements can be tricky to draw in practice. In combination, these characteristics support Tilly and Wood's argument that when we talk about movements as a broad concept, what we are really talking about is a campaign, which focuses our attention on the linkage between self-defined claimants, the target of the claims, and some form of public.[8] So, when we talk about "the feminist movement," we are referring not just to state feminism, well-known organizations, or even to specific battles, such as suffrage, women's formal legal equality, the international #MeToo movement, or International Women's Day, but to all of these as well as the less well-known aspects of the movement, such as a feminist-oriented social media post, feminist advocacy at individual workplaces, the global push for gender quotas, and too much more to list!

Social Movements and Contentious Politics

If drawing an empirical line between interest groups and social movements gives us pause, it is even less apparent that we should make either a theoretical or an empirical distinction between social movements and certain sponsors of organized political violence. In particular, terrorist movements are often treated as distinct and illegitimate forms of action, but empirically it is not clear why. We can see their connection through the concept of *contentious politics*, or "collective action used by people who lack regular access to institutions, who act in the name of new or unaccepted claims, and who behave in ways that fundamentally challenge others or authorities."[9] Such an analysis makes sense, because the actors in both cases organize in opposition to the state (or other declared target), and their goal is to access previously closed spaces of politics. Whether observers perceive this state of affairs as positive, negative, or somewhere in between is a secondary question, and it is also a subjective one.

Empirically, political action characterized as negative, such as coercive political actions of right-wing groups or domestic and international terrorism, is simply a strategic choice. The use of violence reflects these groups' perception that the goal they seek – whether that be changing or maintaining the status quo, creating a compelling and inviting **collective identity**, or both – is best achieved through violence and disruption. Such groups are often wrong in their calculations. The Quebec Liberation Front is representative of the large number of secessionist movements that engage in unsuccessful terrorism; like so many others, they began with strong backing but soon lost it because of a combination of law enforcement's effective counter-terrorism work and waning public support. The East Pakistani experience was a very different one. The Mukti Bahini, or Freedom Fighters, were also labeled terrorists and would likely have joined the list of illegitimate insurgent groups but for one thing: They won, and instead became a part of the founding story of independent Bangladesh, previously known as East Pakistan.

To be clear, collective political violence incorporates riots and other spontaneous protests, revolutions, boycotts, strikes, terrorism, insurrection, and so on. Therefore, not all kinds of political violence are social movements, and many social movements eschew violence entirely. Moreover, where political violence is used we require that the violence be a means to an end rather than the end itself; that it be explicitly geared toward a powerful institutional target; and that it seek to attain broadly **public goods** rather than exclusive goods. Still, as outlined above, groups labeled as terrorist are sometimes just social movement groups who make use of claims or tactics that people dislike.

WHAT BRINGS PEOPLE TO MOVEMENTS, AND WHAT DO MOVEMENTS DO?

How do people come to participate in contentious politics, especially social movements? Moreover, how does this participation translate to the work movements do? In other words, how do movements engage in the process of mobilization? Several theories of social movement mobilization address these questions. **Mobilization** refers to (1) the continuous process of securing new recruits and resources to a movement; (2) the varied actions that movements take, both in pursuit of these goals and for the purpose of influence; and (3) the structures that inform those processes. We focus on three major theories here: political process theory, also known as the theory of political opportunity structures; framing theory; and resource mobilization. We also consider a fourth, new social movement theory, as well.

Political Process Theory

Political process theory (PPT) addresses the interplay between social movements and the larger sociopolitical environment. It argues that large-scale structural shifts, like major economic changes, the onset of war (or peace), demographic changes, and changes in regime type, can have an important effect on the potential for mobilization. PPT has been the subject of hundreds of scholarly publications and, at times, seems to have the same amount of definitions. The general idea is that the nature of the external political system will affect social movements in a variety of ways. This includes the degree to which they can affect mobilization itself, the kinds of claims movements make, movements' strategic choices, and how much political impact movements have, among many other possibilities. One widely cited set of elements comes from Doug McAdam, who suggests that the critical dimensions of **political opportunity structures** are as follows:[10]

- The relative openness or closure of the institutionalized political system
- The stability or instability of that broad set of elite alignments that typically gird a polity
- The presence or absence of elite allies
- The state's capacity and propensity for repression

Taken together these factors indicate the "openness" or "closedness" of the broader political environment – hence the notion of open or closed windows of opportunity. Consequently, less restrictive regulations on media created an open window of opportunity. This allowed conservative Christian actors such as Oral Roberts the ability to broadcast first on radio and then on television and gain major followings. Media regulations in Canada were more restrictive, and the comparatively more closed window of opportunity is part of the explanation for a much smaller conservative Christian movement in that country.

Economic factors are often central facilitators of opportunity. Tunisia, the only one of the Arab Spring countries to successfully democratize, provides one case in which attitudes about economic shifts drove change. While economic growth was positive in the lead-up to the uprising, people's perception of the economy and its relationship to their well-being was highly negative and malaise significant when Mohamed Bouazizi set himself on fire in protest over police harassment. Thus, the Bouazizi case is often presented as the singular catalyst for the Tunisian Arab Spring, but really it was the last straw. The images of Bouazizi's protest helped to pry open a window of opportunity that citizens then burst apart.

The concept of political opportunity structures makes intuitive sense, and empirical evidence supports the idea, but a spirit of discernment is important here. One important caution is that it is inaccurate and unreasonable to treat political opportunity structures as horizontal in reach or accessibility. Consider a common scenario, in which those seeking a shift from an authoritarian to a democratic regime are much more likely to succeed in cases of severe economic downturn, because the economic collapse has the effect of changing the underlying class coalitions that structure the society. The poor citizens of the country may fight stridently against a corrupt regime without success, because they fight alone and lack power. That is, the window of opportunity is closed. This state of affairs holds until a major economic shift occurs and opens the window of opportunity by pushing economic elites who no longer benefit from the authoritarian regime's policies to take away support from the ruling regime and coalesce with the poor opposition instead. This broader, more powerful multiclass coalition manages to topple the ruling regime and install democracy, effecting a change that the poor could not make alone.

So underlying the argument of political opportunity structures is a notion that political opportunities are an objective condition or set of conditions that savvy movements can use to their advantage. Except, as we see in Box 4.2, just about every aspect of contemporary social life tempers this assumption. It appears some opportunities are more open than others.

BOX 4.2: CANADIAN SEX DISCRIMINATION – COMPOUNDING UNEQUAL TREATMENT

The story of how Canadian women achieved the inclusion of sex discrimination in the Canadian Human Rights Act of 1977 is a fairly traditional one. Numerous Canadian women's groups in the 1960s took advantage of the election of a left-of-center Prime Minister, Liberal Lester B. Pearson (1963–8) to push for government attention to unfair treatment of women in the public and private sphere; the Pearson government responded by creating the Royal Commission on the Status of Women in 1967. Three years later, the commission detailed a lengthy list of recommendations to enhance Canadian gender equality, including a clause prohibiting sex discrimination in the Canadian Human Rights Act, passed in 1977. Unequal treatment of women at the federal level was a thing of the legal past, with the critically important exception of First Nations women.

Neither the Human Rights Act nor any other legislation outlawed the sex discrimination embedded in the 1876 Indian Act. It removes Indian status from any First Nations woman who marries a non-Indigenous partner and similarly restricts the passage of status to her offspring. The act also affected widows, divorced and abandoned women, and women who married men from another band. Legislation introduced in 1985 resolved some issues but did not address women's inability to pass their status down to future generations, compromising both their and their offspring's full enjoyment of rights.

In 2017, Bill S-3 addressed this status inequality; the Canadian Senate voted in unanimous support. Left-leaning Prime Minister Justin Trudeau made First Nations rights a central part of his campaign platform. The combined support seems like a prime window of opportunity. Yet the federal government initially balked at the legislation, citing concerns about the potential cost, among other issues. Only in August 2019, after more wrangling and a public pressure campaign, did the government bring the legislation into effect. Newly entitled citizens will now have access to treaty payments, funding for post-secondary education, and healthcare, just as First Nations' males and their offspring do, who never experienced any disruption in access to these rights.

> The contrast between this battle and the contest to include sex discrimination in the Human Rights Act is stark. It is hard to pin down whether, how much, and in precisely what way it matters that the face of one movement was Indigenous while the face of the other was unmarked, but predominately white. What is clear is that the road for Indigenous women was considerably harder, even in the face of seemingly wide-open opportunities; and the losses are substantial. The untold number of offspring who have passed away, cannot be located, or lost their community ties are not addressed under the law.

Framing Theory

A focus on whether all movement actors are equally able to make use of political opportunities ignores a prior question: How do people get to movements in the first place? Framing theory offers one suggestion of how movements gain adherents and supporters. It proposes that a key task of social movements is the successful explanation of a problem for which there is a clear subject of blame (the target) and a clear suggestion of solution(s). These processes are called **framing**, a particularly useful way of understanding how social movements accomplish the dual tasks of drawing recruits to their movement and supporters to their side. David Snow and Scott Benford break down the three main components of successful frames.[11] By successful we mean frames that both persuade people to join movements and provoke targets (government, the public, other power holders) to respond to them:

1 *Diagnostic framing* identifies a problem and determines the source of the blame.
2 *Prognostic framing* identifies a solution along with who or what will fix the problem.
3 *Motivational framing* issues a call to action, often based on emotional appeals or appeals to solidarity or collective identity.

We can see how this process worked, sometimes successfully, in the US campaign for a $15 minimum wage (pictured in Figure 4.1). In this case, the frames are as follows:

1 *Diagnosis:* Economic inequality is driven by an excessively low minimum wage.
2 *Prognosis:* Corporations (and governments) should support a $15 minimum wage.
3 *Motivation:* A minimum wage would help families and help people to live lives of dignity.

Figure 4.1. $15 Minimum Wage Signing, Los Angeles, California

Source: Eric Garcetti, https://commons.wikimedia.org/wiki/File:Raise_the_Wage_LA_Signing
_(19063681245).jpg, https://creativecommons.org/licenses/by/2.0/legalcode.

This frame worked because it tied in well to a **master frame** of economic injustice. Framing choices that link clearly to master frames like economic injustice, equal rights, equal opportunities, or market choice may be more likely to achieve **frame resonance**. That is, the frame is seen as truthful and compelling and champions widely shared values and thus sways the attitudes or positions of a broad audience, including policymakers, politicians, or other targets. Again, the political opportunity structure matters to the choices movements make, including their choice of frames and whether those frames are resonant.

Canada is also home to a number of $15 minimum wage movements since at least the mid-2000s. However, unions have been less consistently supportive, and one of the main US strategies – legislative changes at the municipal level – is not possible in Canada due to the structure of government. This has led to an emphasis on achieving voluntary agreements from employers, with an unsurprisingly low success rate. The Canadian landscape also structures the need for different frames. For instance, the Metro Vancouver Living Wage for Families campaign, recognizing that employers will worry about the impact of a living wage on their bottom lines and the use of potentially antagonistic frames can backfire, diagnoses the lack of a living wage as part of larger problems with unaddressed poverty. It then suggests that part of the solution should be some employer-paid wage increases, but not necessarily to \$15. Instead, they can offset their financial burden by offering support for stronger state-level social welfare policies that could help make up the difference.[12]

Resource Mobilization

Resource mobilization theory addresses the different ways that formal movement organizations draw resources and the wide variety of resources that can help to organize and support social movement activity. Chief among these is money and elite support, but the list is quite extensive (some have argued there is too much) and includes both tangible and intangible assets. These range from office space and printer access to moral legitimacy, cultural knowledge, and the ties of solidarity that can build movements. The US civil rights movement and its combination of solidarity-based historical resources, such as Black churches and universities, is a prime example.

Again, access to resources can be quite uneven, and this distinction is found both nationally and internationally and across a variety of dimensions of privilege. Monique Deveaux has commented on the shared space of marginalization that poor social movements of the Global South and the anti-poverty and anti-globalization movements of the Global North often share.[13] Poor social movement actors in the Global South struggle with resource access in part because of a lack of language skills and access to basics like the internet and computers, which are necessary to make successful grant apps. Poor actors in the Global North experience similar struggles with resource access, such as limited virtual and physical access to transit and other effects of income inequality. Accordingly, we see shared states of uneven resource access that is experienced differentially and is unevenly exacerbated by marginalization on other dimensions, such as rights.

Figure 4.2 underscores the variation in internet access by country and by education, income, race, and geography. In the latter case, we note that the discrepancy between groups that are more and less privileged along these dimensions is double or greater. These examples challenge resource mobilization theory (and all theory) as one to understand in a more nuanced fashion across groups and issues. While there are some important elements to the concept, one trouble spot is the notion that (1) movements were not concerned about "identity" prior to this point, and (2) class movements are not identity movements. One common misconception is that only some individuals and some groups have identities – that is, only those marked as "minority" have identities, leaving some people marked as minority and others, the supposed majority, unmarked.

Figure 4.2. Variation in Internet Use and Access

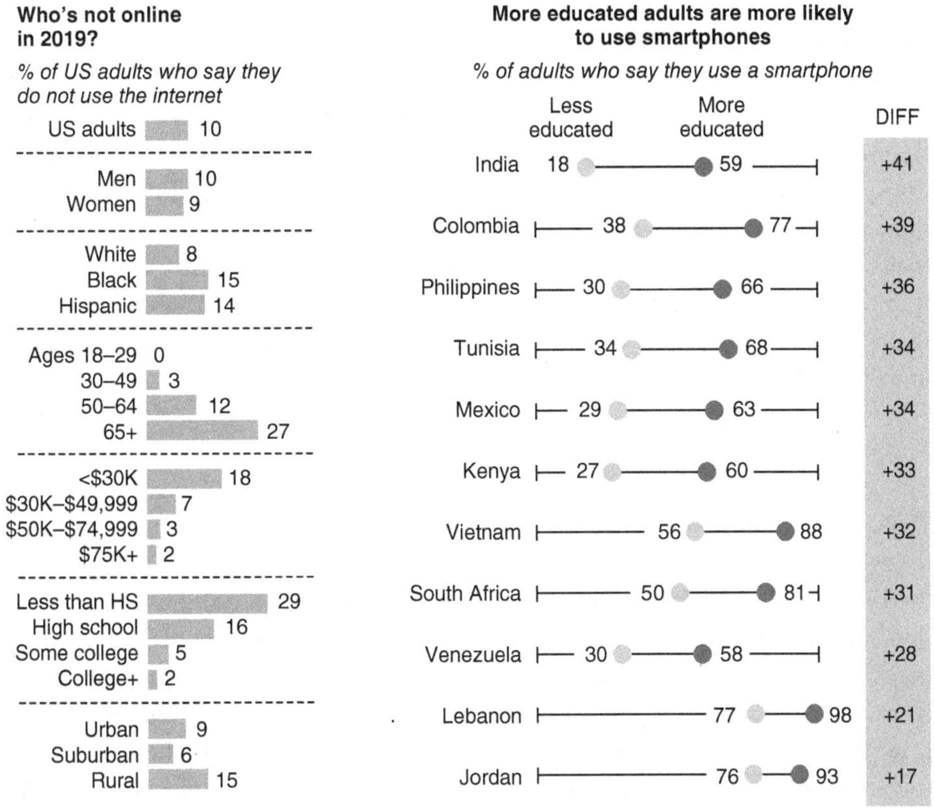

Who's not online in 2019?

% of US adults who say they do not use the internet

US adults	10
Men	10
Women	9
White	8
Black	15
Hispanic	14
Ages 18–29	0
30–49	3
50–64	12
65+	27
<$30K	18
$30K–$49,999	7
$50K–$74,999	3
$75K+	2
Less than HS	29
High school	16
Some college	5
College+	2
Urban	9
Suburban	6
Rural	15

More educated adults are more likely to use smartphones

% of adults who say they use a smartphone

	Less educated	More educated	DIFF
India	18	59	+41
Colombia	38	77	+39
Philippines	30	66	+36
Tunisia	34	68	+34
Mexico	29	63	+34
Kenya	27	60	+33
Vietnam	56	88	+32
South Africa	50	81	+31
Venezuela	30	58	+28
Lebanon	77	98	+21
Jordan	76	93	+17

Sources: *Left*: Monica Anderson, Andrew Perrin, Jingjing Jiang, and Madhumitha Kumar, "10% of Americans Don't Use the Internet. Who Are They?," Pew Research Center, April 22, 2019, https://www.pewresearch.org /fact-tank/2019/04/22/some-americans-dont-use-the-internet-who-are-they. *Right*: Laura Silver, Aaron Smith, Courtney Johnson, Jingjing Jiang, Monica Anderson, and Lee Rainie, "Mobile Connectivity in Emerging Economies," Pew Research Center, March 7, 2019, https://www.pewresearch.org/internet /2019/03/07/use-of-smartphones-and-social-media-is-common-across-most-emerging-economies/. Notes: *Left*: Whites and Blacks include only non-Hispanics. Hispanics are of any race. *Right*: Smartphone users include those who say they own or share a smartphone. For the purpose of comparison across countries, education levels have been standardized based on the United Nations' International Standard Classification of Education.

The truth is that every person has an identity – every person has a race and is classed and gendered with specific sexual orientations and religious affiliations among other "identities." Collective groups also have identities that can manifest through the specific choice to adopt an identity frame (for instance, LGBTQ+ women of color) or via the lens through which they organize. Thus, the supposedly class-oriented movements, described as being in opposition to later lifestyle and identity movements, were themselves identity movements in that the normative figure of the movement was a white, **cisgender**, Christian, able-bodied male. Indeed, sometimes this posture was quite blatant.

Throughout much of the twentieth century, a constant demand of miners in the United States, Canada, Australia, and the United Kingdom was jobs and benefits for white men. This demand took several forms, depending on the context. Sometimes the demand worked in direct opposition to other ethnic groups, as with Chinese Canadian miners and Black American miners, who white Canadian and US miners sought to exclude from work and worker protections entirely. In other cases, the issue was opposition to foreign immigrants, as evinced by Australian miners who used class-based arguments in support of a white Australia policy that kept non-whites out of the country until 1973. The demands made, and the frames used, reflected a specifically white, male, class-based **positionality** that led white miners in the United Kingdom to embrace Black miners while underground at work and ignore them when back on the earth's surface.

The Role of Identities

The same insights hold for **new social movements** theories, frequently interpreted to suggest that "new" social movements – those movements that have arisen from the 1960s on – are often identity or values based rather than economic in orientation. Historically, the understanding of mobilization into movements was primarily (1) through a class base and (2) more interest-group oriented and pluralist or corporatist in orientation. These groups were perceived as homogenous in interest, prioritizing a shared set of class-based concerns that transcended other differences such as race, gender, or location. More recently, especially since the period of the 1960s, scholars have cataloged an uptick in social movements that prioritize values, lifestyles, or identities. These are understood as supposedly expressive rather than instrumental (based on values like money, shelter, etc.) concerns.

In other cases, the normative positionality can be less clearly marked. For instance, pension and social security systems throughout the Western world defined work exclusively as full-time employment in the formal labor market. What seems a straightforward definition in fact overlooked at least two major population groups. One is white women who, by virtue of varied social expectations, were less likely to earn a full pension due to not entering the workforce, exiting it at least temporarily because of pregnancy and care responsibilities, or being blocked in some other way by societal pushback against white women working. The other is the men and women of color who experienced differential forms of societal pushback in the modes of fewer hours, lower pay, and other exclusions. In this way, a seemingly straightforward definition presumed work to be exclusively equivalent to normative white male workers in practice; this group earned pensions throughout their working careers (assuming no temporary or permanent disabilities moved them out of the normative category). All other groups experienced an inequality of full (if any) pension access. As such, the idea that new social movements are synonymous with "identity politics" or political correctness overlooks the extent to which politics is always already organized around identities that, while unmarked, are quite central to the organization of rights, responsibilities, benefits, and resources.

WHAT (ADDITIONAL) WORK DO MOVEMENTS DO? OTHER MODES OF POLITICAL ENGAGEMENT

The study of social movement mobilization helps us understand how movements form, construct frames, engage identity, and make use of resources, as well as the circumstances under which they may be more likely to effect change. It also helps us understand social movement **strategy**, which refers to the specific path or methods movements adopt to reach their goal(s). Missing still is a discussion of **tactics** – that is, what specific actions they take to affect their strategies and reach their goals. Tactics can range from more or less conventional. More conventional (institutionalized) tactics in common use include various forms of lobbying; information control or use of expertise; economic contributions to political parties, causes, or candidates; public information campaigns; lawsuits and other judicial strategies; and coalition formation, just for a start. More unconventional tactics, like those highlighted below, are less likely to be used by traditional political actors.

But there is no governing rule that determines what counts as a conventional or an unconventional tactic. The designation is more a matter of perception and context. For example, protests and rallies, while once considered outside the realm of proper politics, and still a potent tactic, are no longer so radical in many Western countries. However, they certainly remain so in many authoritarian countries. The likelihood that we would see either occur in Saudi Arabia anytime soon seems quite low.

Thomas Rochon's book *Culture Moves* addresses some of the long list of tactics that the US new left movement used;[14] Taylor and Van Dyke compile these into the following list:[15]

> petitioning, rock throwing, canvassing, letter writing, vigils, sit-ins, freedom rides, lobbying, arson, draft resistance, assault, hair growing, nonviolent civil disobedience, operating a free store, rioting, confrontations with cops, consciousness raising, screaming obscenities, singing, hurling shit, marching, raising a clenched fist, bodily assault, tax refusal, guerilla theater, campaigning,

looting, sniping, living theater, rallies, smoking pot, destroying draft records, blowing up ROTC buildings, court trials, murder, immolation, strikes, and writing various manifestoes or platforms.

Indigenous movements in the United States and Canada have similarly engaged in demonstrations and marches and made use of tactics that are more relevant to their specific sets of demands, often linked to autonomy claims or adherence to pre-existing treaties. Some of these more specific tactics include the occupations, roadblocks, and "fish-ins" that highlight the particularities of Indigenous territorial claims.

As should be clear, the variety of tactics is infinite, and different groups may use the same tactics for different reasons. An intersectional lens on modes of political engagement does not necessarily highlight differences in how some movement actors attempt to make change, but rather what meaning they bring to it, the kinds of change sought, and what strategic approach they use. In that case, we tend to see much more overlap between strategy and tactics as the same set of actions can serve both purposes.

By way of example, non-violence is a common tactic of social movements. It has often stemmed, at least partially, from an ethical or religious commitment. In addition to that emphasis, the tactic of non-violence also served a strategic purpose in the US civil rights movement. Black actors knew that any violence they perpetrated, even in self-defense, would turn public opinion against them, so their adoption of non-violence was a carefully cultivated strategy meant to garner maximum sympathy and the adherence of white supporters. Women have similarly made use of their bodies or their associations as mothers as strategic and tactical approaches meant to garner them attention. The Grandmothers of the Plaza de Mayo are one well-known example, using their status as primary caregivers to engage in simultaneous appeals for the return of children that the Argentine government "disappeared" during the 1976–83 dictatorship and to protest against the dictatorial regime itself. Naked protests have been a common and especially potent form of gendered activism in Nigeria, Kenya, Uganda, and elsewhere in sub-Saharan Africa, given their signification of women taking back the life they gave to the land and to their offspring.

WHAT IMPACT DO SOCIAL MOVEMENTS HAVE?

Social movement impact is notoriously difficult to trace. There is an obvious temptation to think in terms of success or failure. The difficulty with this approach is that trying to determine success or failure raises more questions than it answers. What does success mean, exactly? Policy change? The US feminist movement achieved this with the passage of suffrage in 1920, and Title VII and IX in 1964 and 1972, respectively, among other policy changes. Still, by the 1990s pop culture was rife with the idea that feminism was dead. So does success mean that movements accomplish the goals they set out? Perhaps, but we already made a strong case that movements are large conglomerations of professional organizations, non-governmental organizations, more grassroots associations, networks, and individual actors that loosely organized around goals that are quite broad and may be defined in different ways by different groups.

Native rights are a shared goal of Indigenous groups throughout the Americas, as well as in New Zealand, Australia, and anywhere else there is an Indigenous population, but the broadly shared goal of Indigenous autonomy can take several different and sometimes incompatible forms, such as demands for territorial autonomy and political separation in contrast to demands for affirmative action and other redistributive policies. Assigning clear and agreed upon goals is a challenging task, as is assigning intentionality.

It is equally difficult to determine who should take or be given credit for a successful movement outcome. This point is highlighted in the *Windsor* case discussed Box 4.3, and it is clear that this is a problem inherent to movements themselves. It will always be difficult to assign credit in the case of loosely linked and multigroup (and individual) populated spheres of collective action, such as we see in the *Windsor* case. The complexities are shown in Figure 4.3, an adaptation of Charles Tilly's depiction of the challenges of tracking social movement outcomes.[16]

What to do? First, a shift in language is helpful. Rather than success or failure, we can think in terms of consequences or outcomes. An important part of this is removing the requirement for assessing intentionality. Intentional or not, and whether fully credited to the movement's actions, policy change still occurred.

Yet the language shift does not fix all problems. At least one vexing issue, raised by the specter of best-selling books, is one of time. What was a clear success at one point becomes more a question later. The Australian Capital Territory imposed an early, if partial, prohibition ban in 1911, followed by the United States' prohibition amendment in 1920. Prohibition was reversed in both cases, in 1928 and 1933, respectively. However, both countries retain laws and statutes that prohibit or intervene in free access to liquor. The Australian provinces of Queensland and Victoria both enforce a blood alcohol content of 0.05 per cent for motorists; that rate is lower than the alcohol content in many kinds of kombucha. Late night restrictions and special licensing requirements remain in place through parts of Australia and the United States, and some US states

Figure 4.3. Social Movement Outcomes: The *Windsor* Case

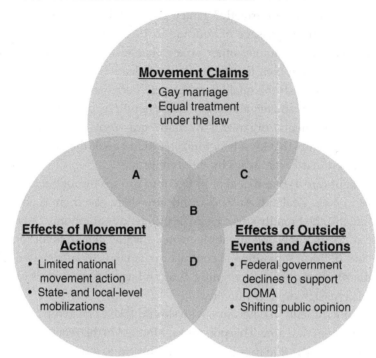

Tilly's explanation of the overlapping sections in the Venn diagram:

A. Effects of movement actions (but not of outside influences) that bear directly on movement claims
B. Joint effects of movement actions and outside influences that bear directly on movement claims
C. Effects of outside influences (but not of movement actions) that bear directly on movement claims
D. Joint effects of movement actions and outside influences that don't bear directly on movement claims

Source: Adapted from Charles Tilly, "From Interactions to Outcomes in Social Movements," in *How Social Movements Matter*, vol. 10, eds. Marco Giugni, Doug McAdam, and Charles Tilly, 253–70 (Minneapolis: University of Minnesota Press, 1999), 269.

Table 4.2. Typology of Movement Outcomes

Type	Internal	External
Political	• Power relations within	• Policy, procedural, or structural change • Agenda-setting power
Cultural	• Value or identity change • Movement spillover	• Change in public opinion, values, or attitudes • New **repertoires of contention**

Source: Adapted from Marco Giugni, "Theoretical and Methodological Issues in the Study of the Outcomes of Social Movements." https://slideplayer.com/slide/5013786.

> **BOX 4.3: *THE UNITED STATES V. WINDSOR***
>
> *The United States v. Windsor* (2013) accomplished the legalization of gay marriage at the federal level. This decision occurred prior to the *Obergefell v. Hodges* (2015) case, which made gay marriage legal across all 50 states. The *Windsor* case was brought by Edith Windsor, who sought to reduce her estate tax burden after the death of her wife. Where no such burden would have accrued for the widow of a heterosexual partner, the Defense of Marriage Act, passed in 1996, expressly outlawed this possibility for same-sex couples. Windsor, frustrated with this inequity, chose to sue, and did so successfully, but only after being turned down by multiple gay rights advocacy groups. These groups worried, among other things, that such a high-profile and big money case would scuttle their progress on another set of priority concerns, such as the progress on including LGBTQ+ individuals as protected classes in state-level anti-discrimination laws. Thus, the win was a major success for both Windsor and the LGBTQ+ movement, even though it was a lesser priority of some movement actors.

further enforce restrictions that determine where certain types of spirits may be purchased as well as what, if any, alcohol can be shipped by mail, among many other restrictions.

Thus, outcomes are difficult to measure, but it is still important to capture them. In fact, movements can bring about a variety of consequences, ranging from revolution to value change. Political and cultural impacts of the sort typologized in Table 4.2 are only some of the effects that social movements can help to bring about.

SUMMARY

- We have considered the importance of civil society and its subset, social movements, as two of the major ways in which average people engage in politics around the world.
- The two concepts may or may not connect directly with formal politics. Nonetheless, they can have important effects on public opinion and policy where they do. Consequently, they can help create and maintain democracy, among other effects.

- o In short, civil society and social movements do significant work in public life (and may translate to private life as well, though that is outside of our scope).
- Yet, or precisely because they loom so large in public life, they can be equally as messy.
  - o Civil society and social movements are sometimes exclusionary, unaccountable, untransparent, and undemocratic, just like politics more broadly. So they are no cure-all, and the work is hard. Nevertheless, they are key spaces of political participation and are likely to remain so well into the future.

CONCLUDING QUESTIONS

1 Why and how do contentious politics happen? Who is included in those processes?
2 What is the relationship between civil society, social movements, and intersectionality? How does an intersectional lens inform your answer?
3 What constitutes a public sphere or spheres? How does an intersectional lens aid in your examination and assessment of this question?
4 How democratic are these public spheres? How inclusive are they?
5 What are some of the key theoretical and political challenges to intersectional assessments of and practices within civil society and social movements?

NOTES

1 Heinrich Böll Stiftung, "The Importance of Civil Societies," November 4, 2016, https://ps.boell.org/en/2016/11/05/importance-civil-societies.
2 Slavery in Brazil was actually abolished in 1888.
3 Evelina Dagnino, "Civil Society in Latin America," in *The Oxford Handbook of Civil Society*, ed. Michael Edwards, 122–133 (Oxford: Oxford University Press, 2013).
4 Kathleen M. Blee, *Inside Organized Racism: Women in the Hate Movement* (Berkeley: University of California Press, 2002).
5 Emma-Louise Anderson and Amy S. Patterson, "Instrumentalizing Aids Empowerment Discourses in Malawi and Zambia: An Actor-Oriented View of Donor Politics," *International Affairs* 93, no. 5 (2017): 1185–1204.
6 Rengin B. Firat and Jennifer L. Glanville, "Measuring Diversity in Voluntary Association Membership: A Comparison of Proxy and Direct Approaches," *Nonprofit and Voluntary Sector Quarterly* 46, no. 1 (2017): 218–30.
7 Shibao Guo and Yan Guo, "Rethinking Multiculturalism in Canada: Tensions between Immigration, Ethnicity and Minority Rights," in *Revisiting Multiculturalism in Canada:*

Theories, Policies and Debates, eds. Shibao Guo and Lloyd Wong, 123–40 (Rotterdam: Sense Publishers, 2015).

8   Charles Tilly and Lesley J. Wood, *Social Movements: 1768–2012* (New York: Routledge, 2013), 4.

9   Sidney G. Tarrow, *Power in Movement: Social Movements and Contentious Politics* (Cambridge: Cambridge University Press, 1998), 3.

10   Doug McAdam, "Conceptual Origins, Current Problems, Future Directions," in *Comparative Perspectives on Social Movements: Political Opportunities, Mobilizing Structures, and Cultural Framings*, eds. Doug McAdam, John McCarthy, and Mayer Zald, 23–40 (Cambridge: Cambridge University Press, 1996), 26.

11   David A. Snow and Robert D. Benford, "Ideology, Frame Resonance, and Participant Mobilization," in *From Structure to Action: Comparing Social Movement Research across Cultures*, eds. Bert Klandermans, Hanspeter Kriesi, and Sidney Tarrow, 197–217 (Greenwich, CT: JAI Press, 1988).

12   Bryan Evans, "Alternatives to the Low Waged Economy: Living Wage Movements in Canada and the United States," *Alternate Routes* 28 (2017).

13   Monique Deveaux, "Poor-Led Social Movements and Global Justice," *Political Theory* 46, no. 5 (2018): 698–725.

14   Thomas R. Rochon, *Culture Moves: Ideas, Activism, and Changing Values* (Princeton, NJ: Princeton University Press, 1998).

15   Verta Taylor and Nella Van Dyke, "'Get up, Stand Up': Tactical Repertoires of Social Movements," in *The Blackwell Companion to Social Movements*, eds. David A. Snow, Sarah A. Soule, and Hanspeter Kriesi, chap. 12, 262–93 (Hoboken, NJ: John Wiley & Sons, 2004), 262.

16   Charles Tilly, "From Interactions to Outcomes in Social Movements," in *How Social Movements Matter*, vol. 10, eds. Marco Giugni, Doug McAdam, and Charles Tilly, 253–70 (Minneapolis: University of Minnesota Press, 1999), 269.

RESOURCES AND SUGGESTIONS FOR FURTHER READING

"After Paris: Inequality, Fair Shares, and the Climate Emergency." http://civilsocietyreview.org/files/COP24_CSO_Equity_Review_Report.pdf.

Climate Equity Reference Calculator. https://calculator.climateequityreference.org.

Flores, Antonio. "How the U.S. Hispanic Population Is Changing." Pew Research Center, September 18, 2017. https://www.pewresearch.org/fact-tank/2017/09/18/how-the-u-s-hispanic-population-is-changing.

Michigan Environmental Justice Coalition. https://michiganenvironmentaljusticecoalition.wordpress.com.

NRDC. "Fighting for Justice in Flint." November 13, 2017. https://www.nrdc.org/stories/fighting-justice-flint.

Ritchie, Hannah, and Max Roser. "Natural Disasters." Our World in Data, 2014. https://ourworldindata.org/natural-disasters

Strolovitch, Dara Z. *Affirmative Advocacy: Race, Class, and Gender in Interest Group Politics.* Chicago: University of Chicago Press, 2007.

Transparency International. www.transparency.org.

CHAPTER FIVE

Political Parties

*Dr. Meryl
Kenny*

LEARNING OBJECTIVES

1 Understand the definitions, origins, and functions of political parties – including
  who they represent and what role they play in the operation of contemporary
  democracies
2 Investigate the ways in which parties are organized and regulated and consider the
  costs and benefits of joining political parties
3 Explore the origins, format, and dynamics of party systems
4 Assess the challenges faced by political parties and critically evaluate whether or
  not they are still relevant in modern politics

KEY TERMS

dominant-party systems   party systems characterized by one very large party with
  an absolute majority (50 per cent) of votes and seats that dominates over other parties for an extended period of time
Duverger's law   describes how single-member plurality electoral systems favor two-
  party systems while proportional representation favors multiparty politics
electoral system   the system created by the electoral rules in their entirety

members–voters gap   the gap between the social and political profiles of political party members and voters

multiparty systems   party systems where multiple political parties have the potential to gain control of government offices, either separately or in coalition

party systems   sets of parties that compete and cooperate with each other for office and control of government

political party   there is no singular definition of a political party, but most definitions broadly center on an understanding of a political party as a group of people organized for the purpose of winning governmental power by electoral means

political recruitment   the study of how and why people become politicians, focusing on the critical stages through which individuals move into political careers

two-party systems   party systems where two fairly equally balanced large parties dominate the party system

WHAT ARE POLITICAL PARTIES?

Political parties are fundamental to the operation of modern democracy. But what are they? This chapter considers the definition, functions, and organization of political parties. We also consider the benefits and costs of joining political parties. We then move on to evaluate the competition between parties and how these leads to different **party systems** – looking at party system origins, format, and dynamics. Finally, we ask whether parties still matter in contemporary politics, evaluating whether parties have successfully adapted to their changing social and political circumstances or whether they are in decline.

Given that political parties are core to the study of politics, we might think that defining them would be a straightforward task. Yet parties around the world differ widely in terms of the ways in which they organize and behave. While there are many possible definitions of a **political party** (see Box 5.1), most share a number of common features. The first concerns the objectives of parties. Parties want *power* – specifically, governmental power "through the capture of public offices and the organization of government."[1] Second, parties seek to obtain these objectives by making nominations and contesting elections. In other words, parties operate in both electoral and governmental arenas.

Many definitions of political parties share another commonality. Edmund Burke's classic conceptualization, for example, saw a party as a "body of men united."[2] Anthony Downs defined a party as "a coalition of men seeking to control the governing apparatus by legal means."[3] This language is not accidental – for most of their "lives," parties have been dominated by men from majority groups. As we can see in Box 5.1, the foundational scholarship on political parties has also

---

BOX 5.1: DEFINITIONS OF POLITICAL PARTIES

"[P]arties live in a house of 'power.' Their action is oriented toward the acquisition of social 'power,' that is to say toward influencing communal action no matter what its content may be." – Max Weber (1922)[4]

"A party is any political group identified by an official label that presents at elections, and is capable of placing through elections, candidates for public office." – Giovanni Sartori (1976)[5]

"A political party is an institution that (a) seeks influence in a state, often by attempting to occupy positions in government, and (b) usually consists of more than a single interest in the society and so to some degree attempts to 'aggregate interests.'" – Alan Ware (1995)[6]

---

been written largely by white men. The "story" of political parties' origins, then, is not only the story of extension of political rights to new groups of people, it is also the story of the continued exclusion of others.

Early parties formed internally within parliaments. These *cadre* (or elite or caucus) parties were formed within legislative bodies, centered on individual politicians and their personal campaign and support organizations. Subsequent parties originated outside parliamentary bodies and were focused on the aim of "getting in" and gaining a voice in political institutions.[7] These *mass* parties were epitomized in the working-class socialist parties that developed and spread across Europe during the second half of the nineteenth century. In contrast with cadre parties, mass parties claimed to represent particular groups (predominantly on the basis of class) and built on pre-existing organizations (e.g., trade unions). Mass parties were organized on the ground in branches with a formally defined membership, which allowed members to participate in decision making about party governance (e.g., by electing delegates to the party's national conference).

As such, parties have been linked historically with the transfer of political power to legislatures, the enlargement of the electorate, the expansion of suffrage, and processes of democratization. Indeed, as E.E. Schattschneider famously stated: "modern democracy is unthinkable save in terms of the parties."[8] In most liberal democracies, however, the franchise was extended to a majority of adult men long before (some) women – often middle-class, property-owning women of a certain age – obtained the vote. In many countries, the suffrage of minority groups also continued to be limited through formal and informal discrimination, such as racist voting laws in the United States aimed at suppressing Black voter turnout.

Political parties, therefore, were historically interested primarily in recruiting men from majority groups as members and activists.[9]

Meanwhile, with the rise of mass parties, some groups continued to be excluded from the construction of the "working class" and its political demands. In the United Kingdom, for example, the working-class Chartist movement – a forerunner to the UK Labour Party – initially included calls for women's suffrage in their People's Charter, but then removed them for fear that this would impede the suffrage of working-class men.[10] Even after the extension of voting rights to women, male party dominance has persisted; women still tend to be underrepresented as party members and activists, and parties are generally unrepresentative of the electorate as a whole, a point we will return to in subsequent sections.

Most modern European parties take the form of what Otto Kirchheimer labeled *catch-all* parties.[11] Rather than focusing solely on rallying their traditional voter base, catch-all parties look for electoral support where they can find it, prioritizing vote-maximizing behavior. An example of this is the family of Christian Democratic parties, which sought to broaden their electoral appeal by shifting away from their religious roots to become catch-all parties of the center-right.

As parties of the traditional right and left began to converge on the catch-all model, they jettisoned some of their ideological baggage in favor of more tactical electoral considerations, becoming increasingly reliant on political professionals rather than the party membership.[12] In the United Kingdom, for example, the mass-based socialist Labour Party attempted to become a catch-all party from the late 1980s onwards, in part by targeting women voters. While historically women voters in Britain tended to vote Conservative, Labour set out to maximize its electoral support by targeting women through policy initiatives focused on "women's issues" and by selecting more women candidates to change its male-dominated public image.[13] By 1997, Labour had a 10-point lead among younger women voters – particularly among middle- and higher-income mothers.[14] Subsequent competition for women's votes has brought all of the main British parties closer together on traditional "women's issues," though they have tended to converge on a liberal feminist position – for example, focusing on women's access to paid employment – rather than more far-reaching structural change.

American parties follow a different model. Many of the American "founding fathers" viewed parties and factions with suspicion and distrust, despite playing crucial roles in creating them. Pioneering party scholar Maurice Duverger famously categorized American parties as being similar to early cadre parties in Europe – in other words, seeing them as a grouping of elites who come together to contest elections.[15] But there are also important distinctive features of American parties that make classification more difficult.[16] They are subject to extensive legal regulation; indeed, Leon Epstein notably characterized American parties as akin to "public utilities" rather than private organizations.[17] American parties also lack a formal fee-paying membership and are highly decentralized organizations, reflecting the federal nature of the country.

The models outlined above, then, represent "ideal types" and are not exhaustive. And while they are a useful starting point, they also have limitations. The comparative study of parties has been primarily a Western European endeavor, with the United States often set aside as an "exceptional case" in the literature. But studies of parties beyond these advanced industrialized cases offer important insights. Research on Latin American parties, for example, point to a huge array of party types beyond catch-all parties. Clientelist parties, for instance, in countries like Argentina and Mexico, distribute selective benefits (usually state resources) in exchange for electoral support. These kinds of parties behave differently than European parties – they are more informal, weaker, and are closely intertwined with the state – which in turn has an important impact on the functioning of electoral systems, legislatures, and democracy itself.[18] It is important, then, to both situate these stylized party models within their historical, social, and political contexts and to look beyond the "usual" cases of established Western parliamentary democracies when studying parties. Only then can we fully capture the complex universe of political parties in contemporary politics.

WHAT DO POLITICAL PARTIES DO?

Parties perform a range of different functions that are crucial to the operation of modern democracies, though these are not the only functions they perform, nor do they necessarily perform all of these functions. Stefano Bartolini and Peter Mair distinguish between a party's *representative* functions and its *procedural* functions.[19]

The representative functions of parties include integrating citizens into the "political community." In other words, parties are "agents" of political socialization that teach citizens to behave politically. Parties also do not just articulate (or express) interests, they aggregate them.[20] In other words, they take the different (and sometimes competing) demands of the individuals and groups that support them and try to combine these into a set of policy proposals and goals. For example, a party's economic policy program might have to balance the divergent interests of urban and rural constituencies, including businesses, farmers, and environmental groups.

The procedural functions of parties encapsulate the role of party as "nominator," including the recruitment of candidates and leaders, which we return to below.[21] It also refers to the exercise of political authority and the role performed by political parties in institutions. This includes the organization of legislatures and government, as well as coordination activities between these different branches of government. Parties coordinate their legislators to advance their policy agenda – for example, by subjecting legislators to party discipline and by "gatekeeping" access to legislative, committee, and cabinet power.

As parties have changed over time, so too have their functions. Indeed, while parties are seen to be crucial components of representative democracy, they are also perceived to be increasingly incapable of performing their representative functions.[22] There is a general perception that parties are not what they once were (an argument we return to at the end of this chapter). For example, the shift from mass-based to catch-all parties has made it easier for parties to enter public office and manage government, but it has also weakened the link between party leaders and their supporters. Meanwhile, the challenges of party government – including an increasingly fragmented electorate and the complexities of the legislative and policymaking process – have meant that parties have become more preoccupied with governing rather than their representative role. Yet, while the representative functions of parties have declined, their procedural functions have arguably expanded and gained greater relevance.[23]

Political Recruitment

The nomination and selection of candidates and leaders has become increasingly important over time. In most countries, political parties have exclusive control of the candidate selection process; thus, while it is voters that ultimately elect candidates, political parties have effectively already limited the options. As such, parties perform crucial functions linking citizens with government, determining the overall composition of the legislature, and structuring electoral choice.[24] The United States has often been treated as an exception to this statement, as it has a more open "candidate-centered" system in which candidates are nominated in primaries by voters. However, even though the gatekeeping powers of US parties are weak, they still play an important role in shaping patterns of representation.[25]

Why is candidate selection important? Because it is about *power*. The question of who has but also who *should have* control over selection are about "nothing less than control of the core of what the party stands for and does."[26] There has been much controversy and debate over the extent to which the **political recruitment** process is internally democratic within parties, in terms of the division of power between party leaders and grassroots members. In recent years, many parties have reformed their candidate selection procedures with the aim of enhancing intra-party democracy – for example, through the introduction of broad-based

Figure 5.1. The Vertical Ladder of Recruitment

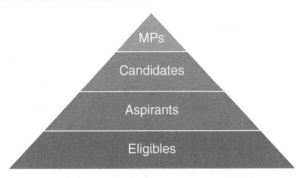

Source: Adapted from Joni Lovenduski, "The Supply and Demand Model of Candidate Selection: Some Reflections," *Government and Opposition* 51, no. 3 (2016): 513–28; Pippa Norris and Joni Lovenduski, *Political Recruitment: Gender, Race and Class in the British Parliament* (Cambridge: Cambridge University Press, 1995).

membership ballots or primaries, which allow party members or voters to choose candidates. Yet debates over intra-party democracy often fail to acknowledge disparities between different groups in terms of their access and opportunities to participate in party decision making.[27] In other words, in order to judge whether a party is internally democratic, we must consider not only whether it follows democratic processes in making candidate selection decisions, but also whether it attempts to achieve democratic outcomes in terms of the meaningful representation and inclusion of marginalized groups.

As Schattschneider notes, "he who can make nominations is the owner of the party."[28] The use of the pronoun "he" here is worth noting. The recruitment process also determines who gets into power and, as such, whether legislative bodies reflect the wider populations that they claim to represent. Some individuals succeed in moving through the "eye of the needle" into political office – moving from the larger pool of those who are eligible to run, to those who aspire to do so, and finally to the smaller group of those nominated and then elected into office – while others do not (see Figure 5.1). This process is not neutral or free from bias. Instead, it is shaped by both formal and informal "rules of the game," which generally result in legislative bodies that are unrepresentative of the wider electorate (see also Chapters 6 and 9 in this textbook).

The political recruitment process is generally a private affair designed by the parties themselves and has been referred to as a "black box" or a "secret garden of politics."[29] Party gatekeepers evaluate applicants in accordance with a range of factors, including both formal and informal selection criteria. In doing so, they take "information shortcuts" to make snap judgments about candidates they do not know well, which may take the form of direct or indirect discrimination.[30] In cases of *direct discrimination*, parties make positive or negative judgments of potential candidates on the basis of characteristics seen as common to their social group, rather than as individuals – for example, asking gender discriminatory questions in the selection process ("Who will look after your children if you're elected?"). In cases of *indirect discrimination*, party selectors make judgments on the basis of the anticipated reaction of the electorate to a particular social group – for example, assuming particular candidates will lose votes ("They won't elect a Black candidate around here").

Recent studies have challenged the assumption that party selection criteria are neutral, simply distinguishing between "good" and "bad" candidates on the basis of "merit."[31] Rather, they have argued that the model of the "ideal candidate" is shaped by informal norms and expectations that interact with gender, race, and class (among other structures of power), thereby favoring men from majority groups (see Box 5.2).[32] Candidates from underrepresented groups, therefore, face what Jenny Chapman refers to as the "scissors" problem: They are less likely to possess the appropriate "qualifications" for office, and, in turn, concerns over the appropriateness of their qualifications may prevent them from running for office in the first place.[33]

BOX 5.2: GENDER, INFORMAL INSTITUTIONS, AND POLITICAL RECRUITMENT
Scholarship on gender and political recruitment has moved from studying "women *in*" to "gender *and*" party politics, seeking to identify the ways in which parties facilitate or block access to political office.[34] An excellent example of this kind of work is Elin Bjarnegård's study of gender and political recruitment in Thailand, which takes a closer look at the political practices that facilitate and reinforce male dominance in politics.[35]

The Thai political landscape is marked by patronage and clientelism, particularly in rural areas. Clientelism – understood as the exchange of personal favors for political support – requires the building and maintenance of close-knit personal networks. These networks are crucial for social acceptance and for being considered a suitable candidate for political office. But they are also highly gendered. Indeed, Bjarnegård finds that Thai male politicians largely cooperate with other men, as male political actors are more likely to have access to the political resources and networks needed to ensure electoral success. Women, in contrast, do not have access to the crucial (and gendered) "homosocial capital" needed to build political networks and gain electoral power.

This is not to say, however, that formal party rules do not matter. Indeed, one of the most striking global trends in recent decades has been the "feminization" of party politics – evidenced in the adoption of formal rules in the form of gender quotas aimed at ensuring more inclusive legislatures. Chapter 6 discusses quotas in detail, so here we will just touch on them briefly. While legal quotas are increasingly common, the main type of quota in use across the world are voluntary party gender quotas, which are commitments by individual parties to include a specific proportion of women among their candidates. Outlined in party rulebooks, these have been used across Scandinavia, Western Europe, and Latin America and have predominantly been adopted by parties of the left. While gender quotas are the most prevalent form of quotas around the world, quota measures have also been adopted to advance representation on the basis of race, ethnicity, nationality, religion, caste, language, age, and disability, among other characteristics.[36] However, quotas for members of minority groups generally take the form of reserved seats rather than party quotas (see Chapter 9). Some countries have adopted a combination of both gender and minority quotas (often referred to as "tandem quotas"), but these measures usually evolve separately and work in different ways (see Box 5.3).[37]

BOX 5.3: INTERSECTIONAL REPRESENTATION: PARTY QUOTAS IN THE UK LABOUR PARTY

Recent elections to the House of Commons in the United Kingdom have seen increases in the number of members of Parliament (MPs) from underrepresented groups. There are, however, important differences across parties, with the left-of-center Labour Party leading on numbers of white women and Black, Asian, and minority ethnic (BAME) MPs in comparison to its Conservative and Liberal Democrat counterparts. Campaigns to increase the political presence of these groups have taken different paths, however, with Labour adopting strong party quotas for women versus a softer shortlisting rule for BAME applicants.

While the party's gender quota policy of "all-women shortlists" guarantees that female candidates will be selected in some constituencies, there is no formal requirement for party selectors to choose a BAME candidate (though they must be included in the list of candidates that parties select from). This has led to weaker results in terms of selecting and electing BAME candidates. However, when these party measures have been applied in tandem – that is, when shortlisting rules for BAME aspirants have been used in combination with gender quotas – studies find a positive effect on the representation of BAME women in particular.[38]

Many parties have also adopted internal party quotas to ensure that particular groups are represented in internal party decision-making bodies (e.g., in party executive committees). These measures can also have a positive effect on the representation of marginalized groups. For example, research by Miki Caul Kittilson finds that a higher presence of women on party national executive committees is related to higher numbers of women in legislatures and to the adoption of gender quotas.[39] In the United Kingdom, for example, studies have highlighted how the earlier adoption of internal gender quotas in the Labour Party provided the necessary bodies at party conference to pass rule changes introducing parliamentary gender quotas.[40]

PARTY MEMBERSHIP

While party membership has generally been declining (a point which we return to later), it remains important in terms of how parties understand themselves.[41] The role of a party member is a formal one – often involving membership fees (or cards) and generally requiring a pledge not to be members of other parties at the same time. As already discussed, however, parties do not need to have a formal membership to be defined as political parties. In the United States, for example, Americans can identify themselves as party supporters when they register to vote, but do not have to pay dues to the given party. There are also different categories of membership. The prototypical form is *individual* membership, where you sign up directly with the party. *Collective* membership (sometimes called *affiliated* membership), meanwhile, might come through being part of a union (or other group), though this type of membership has declined over time.

In response to declining membership, parties have started to offer a variety of new ways of joining, including "light membership" categories for "party friends" or "party sympathizers," which often offer lower dues but also carry fewer benefits.[42] An example of this is the UK Labour Party, where party rules were changed in the run-up to its 2015 leadership contest to allow members of the public who supported Labour's aims and values to join the party as "registered supporters." Supporters had to pay a (reduced) fee of £3 but were entitled to vote in party leadership elections. Many political parties today therefore resemble what Susan Scarrow calls *multispeed membership parties*, offering supporters multiple ways to engage with their given party and promoting different types of activities that they can undertake on behalf of their party.[43]

Why do parties want to recruit members and why do people join political parties? Studies of party membership point to a variety of collective and selective incentives that encourage citizens to become party members – ranging from the desire to "make a difference" and influence party decision making to social reasons to material incentives.[44] For parties, meanwhile, members may provide needed campaign support, electoral legitimacy, individuals to nominate for election and finance the organization, and a means to integrate the grassroots in decision-making and policymaking processes.

Who joins political parties? While there is much debate over how best to measure membership, in general research confirms that party members usually constitute a small proportion of the voting age population. Research also repeatedly suggests that party members are generally unrepresentative of party supporters and voters more broadly, though the extent of the **members–voters gap** – that is, the gap between the social and political profiles of party members and voters – varies across different types of parties. Party members are more likely to be male, older, better off, better educated, and (depending on the party) members of a trade union.[45] Given the costs of party membership, members tend to be well-resourced individuals who have leisure time. Indeed, some scholars argue that we should understand party members not as part of civil society but as part of an "extended political class."[46] As highlighted above, some parties have experimented with more innovative models of party membership, providing greater incentives for joining particular parties in an effort (in part) to close the members–voters gap, but this has not always been successful (see Box 5.4).

BOX 5.4: REDEFINING PARTY MEMBERSHIP
The radical-left Spanish party *Podemos* (translated in English as "We can") was founded in 2014 and quickly became the third-largest party in the Spanish parliament after the 2015 and 2016 general elections. In their study of *Podemos*, Luis Ramiro and Raul Gomez evaluate the party's innovative approach to membership.[47] The party has no requirements for membership fees, probation periods, or endorsement; nor does it require members to be citizens or to be exclusive members of the party. The party also has increased the scope for member participation in decision-making processes, many of which are carried out online.

In some respects, these innovations have been a success, with *Podemos* becoming the second-largest Spanish party in terms of members after the conservative *Partido Popular*. Ultimately, however, Gomez and Ramiro find that *Podemos*'s radical redefinition of party membership has not lived up to expectations. In particular, they have not managed to close the members–voters gap: *Podemos* members are still more likely to be men; they are more ideologically extreme than voters; and they are better resourced in terms of education and employment status than the electorate at large.

Patterns of party participation are also shaped by gender, race, class, age, and citizenship status, among other factors. This serves to empower some actors while disempowering others. For example, expectations with regard to party service – including campaigning and canvassing, attending party events and meetings, often late at night – may exclude those with family and caring responsibilities, who are disproportionately women.[48] Yet traditional indicators of political participation – like income, education, and age – do not necessarily operate the same way across or within different groups. For example, in recent elections in the United States, Black women have turned out at a higher rate than any other racial, ethnic, or gender group, despite possessing (as a group) fewer of the traditional factors associated with high levels of political participation. Seeking to explain this puzzle, work by Emily Farris and Mirya Holman demonstrates that involvement in community groups and community-based activism plays a much bigger role in stimulating Black women's political participation than it does for Black men, white women, or white men in the United States – pointing to the need to consider the ways in which marginalized groups might draw on alternative resources to engage with political parties and institutions.[49]

Why does this matter? Gaps between the composition of party membership and the wider electorate may reinforce perceptions that parties are elitist or "out of touch." These kinds of arguments have been increasingly associated with the rise of and support for populist parties, which, as you learned in Chapter 3, have sought to capitalize on anti-political sentiment by claiming that they represent "the people" against "elite" politicians and parties. It also weakens the legitimacy of party decision making and policymaking and may further discourage underrepresented groups from joining political parties, thereby making them even more unrepresentative.[50]

What do party members do? Answering this question requires an assessment of what distinguishes party members from party supporters and voters more broadly. Duverger's classic work notably made the distinction between electors, supporters, members, and militants, with partisan engagement increasing across these respective categories.[51] In Duverger's view, ordinary members, for example, are more involved in party activities than party supporters, but are not as active as party militants. The differences between these groups, however, are not always straightforward in contemporary party politics where, as already highlighted, efforts to democratize parties and the introduction of new models of membership and affiliation have blurred the lines between members and supporters.

Nevertheless, most scholars still argue that we might expect the behavior and participatory activities of party members and supporters to differ. Party supporters, for example, might be more likely to confine themselves to "low-intensity" work (such as delivering leaflets, displaying posters or yard signs, or tweeting support on social media). Party members, on the other hand, would also engage in "high-intensity" activities (like door-to-door campaigning). For example, Anika Gauja and Stewart Jackson's study of the Australian Greens found that active members of the party were more likely than active supporters to undertake high-intensity activities like fundraising, campaigning, and participating in direct action.[52] They highlight, however, that supporters have the potential to operate as a "reserve army" for the Greens, who can be mobilized when needed. Similarly, in a study of the 2010 British general election, Fisher, Fieldhouse, and Cutts argue that party members "are not the only fruit."[53] While party members still matter, supporters can play an important role in party election activities, complementing (and sometimes supplementing) member activities.

PARTY SYSTEMS

To understand the political significance of parties, we need to move beyond an examination of them as individual organizations to evaluate their connections within a system. Party systems are "sets of parties that compete and cooperate with the aim of increasing their power in controlling government."[54] As this definition highlights, interactions between parties are not only about electoral competition: They are also about cooperation (e.g., when parties build a coalition; see Chapter 8). There are three key questions that are important in classifying and comparing party systems:

1 Which parties exist?
2 How many parties exist and how big are they?
3 How do parties behave?

Which Parties Exist?

Why do some parties exist in almost all party systems (e.g., socialists/social democratic parties), while others exist only in some (e.g., religious parties)? Seymour Lipset famously observed that contemporary parties and party families represent a "democratic translation" of particular social conflicts and divisions.[55] Lipset was primarily talking about class, but this, of course, is not the only social struggle or division that has been "translated." In subsequent groundbreaking work on Western Europe, Lipset and Stein Rokkan identified four main lines of *cleavage* in the development of modern industrial societies, which they argued were

Table 5.1. Cleavages and Their Party Expressions in Western Europe

Cleavage	Party Families	Examples
Center-Periphery	Regionalists, ethnic parties, linguistic parties, minorities	Scottish National Party (UK), Bloc Québécois (Canada), Partido Nacionalista Vasco (Spain)
State-Church	Conservative and religious parties, Christian democracy	Austrian People's Party, Christian-Democratic Union (Germany), Swiss Catholic Party, Partido Popular (Spain)
Rural-Urban	Agrarian and peasant parties	Finnish Centre Party, Australian Country Party, Polish Peasant People's Party
Workers-Employers	Workers' parties, socialists and social democrats, labor parties	British Labour Party, Swedish Social-Democratic Workers' Party, Spanish PSOE
Materialist-post-materialist values	Green parties, libertarians, women's parties	Bündis 90/Die Grünen (Germany), Die Grünen/Grünen Alternative (Austria), Democrats '66 (Netherlands), Women's List (Iceland)
Open-closed societies	Protest parties, nationalist parties, extreme right-wing parties, neo-populist parties	FPÖ (Austria), Front National (France), Danish Progress Party, United Kingdom Independence Party (UKIP)

Source: Daniele Caramani, "Party Systems," in *Comparative Politics*, ed. Daniele Caramani (Oxford: Oxford University Press, 2014). Based on S.M. Lipset and S. Rokkan, eds., *Party Systems and Voter Alignments: Cross-National Perspectives* (New York: Free Press, 1967).

reflected in today's party systems: center-periphery, state-church, rural-urban, and workers-employers (see Table 5.1).[56]

Lipset and Rokkan argue that these historical cleavages have proven to be remarkably persistent, and that contemporary party systems in Western Europe have been largely "frozen" into place within this framework. However, there has been a considerable "thawing out" since the 1960s, with new social divisions and (sometimes) new parties emerging (see Table 5.1). This includes, as already highlighted, the rise of populist radical-right parties (see Chapter 3), arguably the most successful new party family in Europe.[57]

Not all cleavages exist in all countries. The Lipset–Rokkan model reflects a particular "version" of history that is rooted in Western Europe. The United States, for example, has weaker social cleavages but high levels of party polarization – in other words, party conflict divides citizens more than the social cleavages that these parties were created to represent.[58] In many newer democracies, meanwhile, parties emerged out of anti-colonial struggles and movements of national liberation – and have therefore been more shaped by "critical junctures" of decolonization and independence than by traditional historical cleavages.[59]

One of the key questions for party politics scholars, then, is why different social and political divisions have been "translated" into parties in some contexts but not in others. Class divisions are usually (but not always) translated into party politics.

Meanwhile, while ethnic divisions have often been channeled through mainstream party participation (particularly in Western Europe), elsewhere we have also seen the emergence of ethnic parties that have played significant political roles, particularly in divided societies. In India, for example, where the politics of ethnicity – caste, religion, and language – are centrally important, many parties make overt appeals to ethnic identity – including, for example, the Bahujan Samaj Party, which was formed to represent the interests of the "scheduled castes," a collection of more than 400 castes treated as "untouchables" by caste Hindu society.[60] In contrast, gender divisions, until recently, have hardly been translated at all (but see Box 5.5).

BOX 5.5: WOMEN'S PARTIES

Women's parties are designed specifically to increase women's representation in politics. Since 1987, more than 30 women's parties in Europe have contested elections at the national level. They have also had some electoral success – for example, the Northern Ireland Women's Coalition won one seat in the inaugural Northern Ireland Assembly (as well as a subsequent council seat), while more recently the Swedish Feminist Initiative (F!) won one seat in the 2014 European Parliament elections, as well as multiple seats in the 2014 Swedish municipal elections. These kinds of parties typically emerge because of the failure of mainstream political parties to include women and women's issues. Although typically small in terms of membership, women's parties can challenge mainstream parties to address women's issues while also using consciousness-raising tactics to educate women about feminism and gender equality. However, while historically some women's parties have made electoral inroads, these kinds of parties tend to be short-lived organizations lasting a few election cycles and picking up few (if any) seats.[61]

How Many Parties Exist and How Big Are They?

In answering these questions, we first need to consider how parties should be counted. In most democratic elections, there are lots of parties and candidates that do not get any votes (or get very few). Quantitative categorizations tend to focus on the *number* and *size* of parties. (Are there many small parties, or a few large parties?) Others use more qualitative approaches, focusing on the roles of parties within the system. Foundational party politics scholar Giovanni Sartori argued that parties should only be counted as relevant if they have *coalition* or *blackmail* potential. When considering coalition potential, a party should be counted if, at least sometimes, it is needed on its own or with others to form a government. When considering blackmail potential, parties should be counted if they have the potential to affect government decisions through threats or veto power.

Based on these criteria, we can identify three main types of democratic party systems. As our focus here is on both democracies and party *systems*, we do not include, for example, single-party systems with only one legal party (e.g., China).

1 **Dominant-party systems** are characterized by one large party that dominates over all other parties. It must have more than an absolute majority (50 per cent) of votes and seats for an extended period of time. In these systems, parties are legal and free to compete in elections, but no other party has a realistic chance of winning a majority. There is therefore no alternation in power, and the dominant party is able to form a one-party government without entering into coalition. Examples of this would include the Congress Party's historical dominance in India, or the African National Congress in South Africa, which was able to secure an absolute majority of votes after the end of apartheid in the early 1990s.

2 **Two-party systems** are ones in which two fairly equally balanced large parties dominate the party system. They are of similar size and have equal chances of winning elections, which often means that alternation in power is more frequent. Because of the size of these parties, the winning party is more likely to receive an absolute majority of seats (though not necessarily votes) and form a government without needing coalition partners. This doesn't mean there aren't other parties, but these smaller parties are not usually *relevant* parties, in that they aren't necessary to form a government.

   Two-party systems are not very common globally. They are more typical of Anglo-Saxon countries like the United States, United Kingdom, Australia, and Canada, particularly those that still use plurality electoral systems in single-member districts (we return to this point below; see also Chapter 6). But they have also been found in countries with more proportional electoral systems as well – for example, Austria, Spain, and Germany (often referred to as a "two-and-a-half party system"). The United States represents the only "perfect" two-party system, with Democrats and Republicans dominating since 1860.

3 **Multiparty systems** are the most common type of party system around the world, but also the most complicated, with a huge range in the number, size, and strength of parties across different multiparty systems. The number of parties can range from three all the way to the double digits, but no single

party has an overall majority in a multiparty system. This means that parties must form coalitions to support a government (see Chapter 8).

Multiparty systems, therefore, represent a different model of democracy from majoritarian contexts (e.g., the United States or the United Kingdom). This has both positive and negative aspects. For example, while multiparty systems are argued to be more representative (particularly in countries with religious, territorial, or ethno-linguistic cleavages), they can also facilitate the representation of extreme parties (e.g., right-wing or anti-immigration parties).

What causes variations in the number and size of parties across different systems? While we have already discussed the importance of cleavages, the main factor to consider are **electoral systems**, which are discussed in further depth in Chapter 6. The best-known articulation of the relationship between electoral and party systems comes from Maurice Duverger's classic work on political parties. **Duverger's laws** are simple (see Box 5.6): Single-member plurality systems favor two-party systems, while proportional representation favors multiparty systems.[62] Duverger argues that this is because of both the *mechanical* and *psychological* effects of electoral rules. For example, in single-member plurality systems, smaller parties aren't proportionally rewarded for the share of their votes (*mechanical effects*). Voters are aware of this effect, and therefore are less likely to "waste" their votes on small parties (*psychological effects*).

BOX 5.6: DUVERGER'S "LAWS" (1954)

First Law: "The majority [plurality] single-ballot system tends to party dualism."

Second Law: "The second ballot [majority] system or proportional representation tend to multipartyism."

How Do Parties Behave?

Why, in some party systems, do parties tend to converge toward the center while in others they tend toward ideological extremes? Explanations of the dynamics of party systems often start from the point that parties are *rational* actors whose main goal is the *maximization of votes*, articulated most famously in Anthony Downs's pioneering work *An Economic Theory of Democracy*.[63] To achieve this goal, parties offer platforms that appeal to voters; voters then choose to vote for parties whose platforms are closest to their own policy preferences. In two-party systems, this generally produces ideological convergence at the center. Because in these kinds of systems parties are aiming to win a majority of seats (and are not facing threats from new parties at the extremes of the ideological spectrum), they tend to propose similar policies and programs at the center to reach as wide an electoral audience as possible. A notable example here is the rise of "Third Way Politics" in the 1990s, where the US Democrats under Bill Clinton and the British New Labour under Tony Blair moved toward the center to attract moderate voters.

In multiparty systems, however, the dynamics are more complex. Sartori distinguishes between two main types of multiparty systems: *moderate multiparty systems* and *polarized multiparty systems*. In moderate multiparty systems, where the number of parties is limited, the main parties tend to converge toward the center to attract the support of moderate voters. At the center, there are usually one or two small parties with whom larger parties of the left or right can form a coalition. In contrast, in polarized and fragmented multiparty systems, there is instead an ideological fleeing from the center, with parties driven to ideological extremes.

IS THE PARTY OVER?

We began this chapter with Schattschneider's famous proposition that without parties, democracy was unthinkable. Many decades later, political parties are still central to modern democratic politics. Party actors dominate our political news cycles. We vote for representatives to look after our interests, the overwhelming majority of whom are party representatives. Meanwhile, the study of party politics is a thriving and large branch of the political science discipline, reflected in specialist conferences, research sections of professional associations, and dedicated academic journals (and, indeed, this chapter).

Despite their continuing importance, however, we also see frequent claims that parties in established democracies are "in decline" – or, at the very least, that they are experiencing dramatic change. In terms of parties' links with citizens, we see comparative trends of declining electoral turnout; the rise of voter volatility, with voters more willing to switch between parties; falling levels of partisan identification; and drops in party membership numbers.[64] We also see new actors and trends emerging that have challenged the traditional representative role of political parties – including interest groups and new social movements, as well as independent and "anti-party" candidates and campaigns.[65] Finally, while parties still play a dominant role in structuring government, patterns of increasing party fragmentation and divided government around the world raise questions as to whether parties are as effective in this role as they once were. These trends raise questions as to whether parties are still performing their key functions, while also raising broader concerns about political representation and legitimacy.

These challenges are even more acute in newer democracies, where party competition and behavior is less stable, regular, or predictable – in other words, where party systems are poorly *institutionalized*.[66] In contexts where parties appear and disappear and personalities overshadow policy programs, voters are unable to attribute responsibility for policy decisions and hold politicians accountable by voting them in or out of office. There are also negative consequences for representativeness, as weakly institutionalized parties are unable to implement and enforce policies aimed at increasing the representation of marginalized groups.[67] These systems are, therefore, more vulnerable to the rise of "anti-party" politics, with consequences for representative democracy.

Others, however, argue that these trends and challenges offer a more positive sign that parties are, in fact, adapting to the changing social and political conditions in which they find themselves.[68] As Paul Webb reminds us:[69]

> Parties continue to perform vital tasks with a relatively high degree of effectiveness and are central mechanisms of popular choice and control. If they did not exist … somebody would undoubtedly have to invent them.

SUMMARY

- Political parties are central actors in modern democracies. The definition of "party" is contentious, but most definitions focus on the objectives and functions of political parties.
- Party organizational types have developed over time, as suffrage expanded and the electorate grew. But many groups have historically been and continue to be excluded from participating in party politics, and parties continue to be dominated by men from majority groups.
- Political parties perform a range of important representative and procedural functions, including aggregating interests, recruiting candidates and leaders, and organizing legislatures and governments.
- Party membership appears to be in decline around the world. A members–voters gap persists, where party members continue to be generally unrepresentative of party supporters and voters more broadly. Some parties have experimented with more innovative and diverse models of party membership, but these have not always been successful.

- Party systems are determined by (1) which parties exist, (2) how many parties exist and how big they are, and (3) how parties behave. The format of party systems is shaped by electoral systems.
- Critics of political parties argue that they are in decline, citing trends like declining voter turnout and falling levels of partisan identification and party membership. Others argue that parties are, in fact, adapting to the changing world around them. Regardless, parties still matter in contemporary democratic politics.

CONCLUDING QUESTIONS

1 In what ways are parties central to the operation of modern politics?
2 What is the members–voters gap, and (why) does it matter?
3 What criteria should we use to classify party systems?
4 Are political parties in decline? If so, is that decline irreversible?

NOTES

1 Robert J. Huckshorn, *Political Parties in America*, 2nd ed. (Monterey, CA: Cole Publishing Company/Brooks, 1984), 10.
2 Edmund Burke, "Thoughts on the Present Discontents," in *The Works of the Right Honourable Edmund Burke*, 433–551 (Boston: Little Brown, 1889 [1770]).
3 Anthony Downs, *An Economic Theory of Democracy* (New York: Harper, 1957), 24–5.
4 Max Weber, "Class, Status and Party" (1922), in *From Max Weber: Essays in Sociology*, eds. H.H. Gerth and C. Wright Mills (London: Routledge, 2009).
5 Giovanni Sartori, *Parties and Party Systems: A Framework for Analysis* (Cambridge: Cambridge University Press, 1976), 64.
6 Alan Ware, *Political Parties and Party Systems* (Oxford: Oxford University Press, 1995), 5.
7 Maurice Duverger, *Political Parties: Their Organisation and Activity in the Modern State* (London: Methuen, 1954).
8 E.E. Schattschneider, *Party Government* (New York: Holt, Rinehart and Winston, 1942), 1.
9 Ware, *Political Parties*.
10 Teri L. Caraway, "Inclusion and Democratization: Class, Gender, Race, and the Extension of Suffrage," *Comparative Politics* 36, no. 4 (2004): 443–60.
11 Otto Kirchheimer, "The Transformation of the Western European Party Systems," in *Political Parties and Political Development*, eds. J. La Palombara and M. Weiner, 177 (Princeton, NJ: Princeton University Press, 1966).
12 Richard S. Katz and Peter Mair, *How Parties Organize: Change and Adaptation in Party Organizations in Western Democracies*, vol. 528 (London: Sage, 1994); A. Panebianco,

Political Parties: Organization and Power (Cambridge: Cambridge University Press, 1988).

13 Joni Lovenduski, *Feminizing Politics* (Cambridge: Polity Press, 2005).

14 Rosie Campbell, *Gender and the Vote in Britain: Beyond the Gender Gap?* (Colchester, UK: ECPR Press, 2006); Pippa Norris, "A Gender-Generation Gap?," in *Critical Elections: British Parties and Voters in Long-Term Perspective*, eds. Geoffrey Evans and Pippa Norris (London: Sage, 1999).

15 Duverger, *Political Parties*.

16 For an extended discussion, see Alan Ware, "American Exceptionalism," in *Handbook of Party Politics*, eds. Richard S. Katz and William J. Crotty (London: Sage, 2006).

17 Leon D. Epstein, *Political Parties in the American Mold* (Madison: University of Wisconsin Press, 1986).

18 Steven Levitsky, "Inside the Black Box: Recent Studies of Latin American Party Organizations," *Studies in Comparative International Development* 36, no. 2 (2001): 92–110.

19 Stefano Bartolini and Peter Mair, "Challenges to Contemporary Political Parties," in *Political Parties and Democracy*, eds. Larry Diamond and Richard Gunther, 327–43 (Baltimore: Johns Hopkins University Press, 2001).

20 Gabriel Abraham Almond and James Smoot Coleman, *The Politics of the Developing Areas* (Princeton, NJ: Princeton University Press, 1960).

21 Sartori, *Parties and Party Systems*.

22 Bartolini and Mair, "Challenges to Contemporary Political Parties"; Peter Mair, "The Challenge to Party Government," *West European Politics* 31, no. 1–2 (2008): 211–34.

23 Bartolini and Mair, "Challenges to Contemporary Political Parties."

24 Pippa Norris and Joni Lovenduski, *Political Recruitment: Gender, Race and Class in the British Parliament* (Cambridge: Cambridge University Press, 1995).

25 See, for example, Melody Crowder-Meyer, "Gendered Recruitment without Trying: How Local Party Recruiters Affect Women's Representation," *Politics & Gender* 9, no. 4 (2013): 390–413; Kelly Dittmar, "Encouragement Is Not Enough: Addressing Social and Structural Barriers to Female Recruitment," *Politics & Gender* 11, no. 4 (2015): 759–65; Kira Sanbonmatsu, *Where Women Run: Gender and Party in the American States* (Ann Arbor: University of Michigan Press, 2010).

26 Austin Ranney, *Pathways to Parliament: Candidate Selection in Britain* (Madison: University of Wisconsin Press, 1965), 103.

27 For an extended discussion of this point, see Sarah Childs, "Intra-Party Democracy: A Gendered Critique and a Feminist Agenda," in *The Challenges of Intra-Party Democracy*, eds. William P. Cross and Richard S. Katz, 81–99 (Oxford: Oxford University Press, 2013).

28 Schattschneider, *Party Government*, 64.

29 Michael Gallagher and Michael Marsh, *Candidate Selection in Comparative Perspective: The Secret Garden of Politics*, vol. 18 (London: Sage, 1988); Meryl Kenny and Tania Verge, "Opening up the Black Box: Gender and Candidate Selection in a New Era," *Government and Opposition* 51, no. 3 (2016): 351–69.

30 Norris and Lovenduski, *Political Recruitment*.

31 Rainbow Murray, "Quotas for Men: Reframing Gender Quotas as a Means of Improving Representation for All," *American Political Science Review* 108, no. 3 (2014): 520–32.

32 Kenny and Verge, "Opening up the Black Box"; Lovenduski, *Feminizing Politics*.

33 Jennifer Chapman, *Politics, Feminism and the Reformation of Gender* (New York: Routledge, 2004).

34 Kenny and Verge, "Opening up the Black Box"; Miki Caul Kittilson, "Party Politics," in *The Oxford Handbook of Gender and Politics*, eds. Georgina Waylen, Karen Celis, Johanna Kantola, and Laurel Weldon (Oxford: Oxford University Press, 2013).

35 Elin Bjarnegård, *Gender, Informal Institutions and Political Recruitment: Explaining Male Dominance in Parliamentary Representation* (Basingstoke, UK: Springer, 2013).

36 Mona Lena Krook, *Quotas for Women in Politics: Gender and Candidate Selection Reform Worldwide* (Oxford: Oxford University Press, 2010).

37 Mala Htun, "Is Gender Like Ethnicity? The Political Representation of Identity Groups," *Perspectives on Politics* 2, no. 3 (2004): 439–58; Melanie M. Hughes, "Intersectionality, Quotas, and Minority Women's Political Representation Worldwide," *American Political Science Review* 105, no. 3 (2011): 604–20.

38 Hughes, "Intersectionality, Quotas, and Minority Women"; Mona Lena Krook and Mary K. Nugent, "Intersectional Institutions: Representing Women and Ethnic Minorities in the British Labour Party," *Party Politics* 22, no. 5 (2016): 620–30.

39 Miki Caul Kittilson, *Challenging Parties, Changing Parliaments: Women and Elected Office in Contemporary Western Europe* (Columbus: Ohio State University Press, 2006).

40 Meg Russell, *Building New Labour: The Politics of Party Organisation* (Basingstoke, UK: Springer, 2005).

41 Richard S. Katz, "Political Parties" in *Comparative Politics*, ed. Daniele Caramani (Oxford: Oxford University Press, 2014).

42 Susan E. Scarrow, *Beyond Party Members: Changing Approaches to Partisan Mobilization* (Oxford: Oxford University Press, 2015).

43 Scarrow, *Beyond Party Members.*

44 See, for example, Patrick Seyd and Paul Whiteley, *New Labour's Grassroots: The Transformation of the Labour Party Membership* (Basingstoke, UK: Palgrave McMillan, 2002); Emilie Van Haute and Anika Gauja, *Party Members and Activists* (Routledge, 2015).

45 Susan Achury, Susan E. Scarrow, Karina Kosiara-Pedersen, and Emilie Van Haute, "The Consequences of Membership Incentives: Do Greater Political Benefits Attract Different Kinds of Members?," *Party Politics* (2018): 1354068818754603.

46 Ingrid Van Biezen, Peter Mair, and Thomas Poguntke, "Going, Going ... Gone? The Decline of Party Membership in Contemporary Europe," *European Journal of Political Research* 51, no. 1 (2012): 24–56.

47 Raul Gomez and Luis Ramiro, "The Limits of Organizational Innovation and Multi-Speed Membership: Podemos and Its New Forms of Party Membership," *Party Politics* 25, no. 4 (2019): 534–46.

48 Tania Verge, "The Gender Regime of Political Parties: Feedback Effects between 'Supply' and 'Demand,'" *Politics & Gender* 11, no. 4 (2015): 754–9.

49 Emily M. Farris and Mirya R. Holman, "Social Capital and Solving the Puzzle of Black Women's Political Participation," *Politics, Groups, and Identities* 2, no. 3 (2014): 331–49.

50 William Cross and Lisa Young, "The Contours of Political Party Membership in Canada," *Party Politics* 10, no. 4 (2004): 427–44.

51 Duverger, *Political Parties.*

52 Anika Gauja and Stewart Jackson, "Australian Greens Party Members and Supporters: Their Profiles and Activities," *Environmental Politics* 25, no. 2 (2016): 359–79.

53 Justin Fisher, Edward Fieldhouse, and David Cutts, "Members Are Not the Only Fruit: Volunteer Activity in British Political Parties at the 2010 General Election," *British Journal of Politics and International Relations* 16, no. 1 (2014): 75–95.

54 Daniele Caramani, "Party Systems," in *Comparative Politics*, ed. Daniele Caramani (Oxford: Oxford University Press, 2017), 217.

55 S.M. Lipset, *Political Man: The Social Bases of Politics* (New York: Doubleday, 1960).

56 S.M. Lipset and S. Rokkan, eds., *Party Systems and Voter Alignments: Cross-National Perspectives* (New York: Free Press, 1967).

57 Cas Mudde, *Populist Radical Right Parties in Europe* (Cambridge: Cambridge University Press, 2007).

58 Sean J. Westwood, Shanto Iyengar, Stefaan Walgrave, Rafael Leonisio, Luis Miller, and Oliver Strijbis, "The Tie That Divides: Cross-National Evidence of the Primacy of Partyism," *European Journal of Political Research* 57, no. 2 (2018): 333–54.

59 Jaimie Bleck and Nicolas van de Walle, *Electoral Politics in Africa since 1990: Continuity in Change* (Cambridge: Cambridge University Press, 2018).

60 For an extended discussion of the BSP, see Kanchan Chandra, *Why Ethnic Parties Succeed: Patronage and Ethnic Head Counts in India* (Cambridge: Cambridge University Press, 2007).

61 Kimberly Cowell-Meyers, Elizabeth Evans, and Ki-young Shin, "Women's Parties: A New Party Family," *Politics & Gender* 16, no 1 (2020): 4–25; Elizabeth Evans and Meryl Kenny, "*The Women's Equality Party*: Emergence, Organisation and Challenges," *Political Studies* 67, no. 4 (2019): 855–71.

62 Duverger, *Political Parties*.

63 Downs, *An Economic Theory of Democracy*.

64 See, for example, Russell J. Dalton and Martin P. Wattenberg, *Parties without Partisans: Political Change in Advanced Industrial Democracies* (Oxford: Oxford University Press, 2002); Peter Mair, "Democracy beyond Parties," Working Paper 05–06, 2005, http://cadmus.eui.eu/bitstream/handle/1814/3291/viewcontent.pdf?sequence=1; Van Biezen, Mair, and Poguntke, "Going, Going ... Gone?"; Paul D. Webb, "Conclusion," in *Political Parties in Advanced Industrial Democracies*, eds. Paul D. Webb, David M. Farrell, and Ian Holliday (Oxford: Oxford University Press, 2002).

65 Kay Lawson and Peter H. Merkl, *When Parties Fail: Emerging Alternative Organizations* (Princeton, NJ: Princeton University Press, 1988); David M. Farrell and Rüdiger Schmitt-Beck, *Non-Party Actors in Electoral Politics: The Role of Interest Groups and Independent Citizens in Contemporary Election Campaigns* (Baden-Baden, Germany: Nomos, 2008).

66 Scott Mainwaring and Mariano Torcal, "Party System Institutionalization and Party System Theory after the Third Wave of Democratization," in *Handbook of Party Politics*, eds. Richard S. Katz and William J. Crotty, 204–27 (London: Sage, 2006).

67 Kristin N. Wylie, *Party Institutionalization and Women's Representation in Democratic Brazil* (Cambridge: Cambridge University Press, 2018).

68 Russell J. Dalton, David M. Farrell, and Ian McAllister, *Political Parties and Democratic Linkage: How Parties Organise Democracy* (Oxford: Oxford University Press, 2011); Paul D. Webb, "Are British Political Parties in Decline?," *Party Politics* 1, no. 3 (1995): 299–322.

69 Webb, *Conclusion* (2002), 458.

RESOURCES AND SUGGESTIONS FOR FURTHER READING

International Institute for Democracy and Electoral Assistance (IDEA). https://www.idea.int
    /data-tools.

Katz, Richard S., and William Crotty, eds. Handbook of Party Politics. London: Sage, 2006.

Kittilson, Miki Caul. *Challenging Parties, Changing Parliaments: Women and Elected Office in
    Contemporary Western Europe.* Columbus: Ohio State University Press, 2006.

Manifesto Project database. https://manifesto-project.wzb.eu.

Norris, Pippa, and Joni Lovenduski. *Political Recruitment: Gender, Race and Class in the
    British Parliament.* Cambridge: Cambridge University Press, 1995.

Panebianco, Angelo. *Political Parties: Organization and Power.* Cambridge: Cambridge
    University Press, 1988.

The Political Party Database Project (PPDP). www.politicalpartydb.org.

Sartori, Giovanni. *Parties and Party Systems: A Framework for Analysis.* Cambridge:
    Cambridge University Press, 1976.

CHAPTER SIX

Electoral Systems and Representation

*Dr. Jennifer
M. Piscopo*

LEARNING OBJECTIVES

1 Understand what political scientists mean by descriptive representation and how different election rules shape different patterns of descriptive representation
2 Explain why men from countries' majority groups hold the majority of the seats in most of the world's legislatures
3 Identify how election rules and public policies influence who becomes represented, and explain how changes to the election rules matter for patterns of descriptive representation
4 Know the public policy options that shape political representation and how these policies can or cannot facilitate the selection of representatives from different social groups

KEY TERMS

descriptive representation   a facet of political representation that refers to which social groups are represented in the legislature; also known as *mirror representation*

district   the territorial area that an elected official represents in the legislature; also called a *constituency* or *riding*

district magnitude   the number of seats available in the electoral district; abbreviated as the letter "m"

electoral rules   the laws that set forth how voters choose their elected representatives and how votes are turned into seats in the national legislature

ethnic quotas   a quota law that applies to candidates or elected representatives from specific racial, ethnic, linguistic, ethno-linguistic, religious, or ethno-religious groups

gender parity   when the gender quota mandates half men and half women

gender quotas   a quota law that applies to candidates or elected representatives who are women

plurality   referring to the most, not the majority; in single-member districts, candidates win with the *most* votes

political representation   a multifaceted concept describing who is present in a national legislature and what they do

substantive representation   a facet of political representation that refers to which interests are manifested during the lawmaking process as well as the extent to which voters' policy preferences and interests are promoted by their representatives

symbolic representation   a facet of political representation that refers to how citizens' and voters' behaviors and attitudes change in response to descriptive representation

WHAT IS REPRESENTATION?

Citizens do not govern directly. Instead, they choose representatives who govern on their behalf, in lawmaking bodies called legislatures or parliaments. (The difference between legislatures and parliaments is reviewed in Chapter 8. This chapter uses *legislatures* as the generic term for both.) Even semi-democracies or non-democracies can have legislatures, though elections might be less free and less fair than in established democracies, and the policymaking powers of the legislature may be limited. The set of rules through which citizens choose their elected representatives are called **electoral rules**, and the entirety of these electoral rules comprise a country's electoral system. Countries lay out their electoral systems in their constitutions and statutes, which govern everything from who is eligible to vote to how political parties form, operate, and choose candidates.

Electoral rules are extremely important. They vary across countries, and these variations produce different outcomes: Depending on the rules, different social groups within the population end up with more or less representation in the legislature. Consequently, electoral rules determine **political representation**, a multifaceted concept that refers to

1 *who* is represented (called **descriptive representation**);
2 *which interests* are represented (**substantive representation**); and
3 *how citizens respond* to their representatives (**symbolic representation**).

These facets exist in different cause-and-effect relationships.[1] This chapter focuses primarily on how variations in electoral rules produce variations in the descriptive representation of social groups. Descriptive representation is also called *mirror representation,* because the concept shows whether the composition of the legislature mirrors, or reflects, the composition of the country. The chapter also explores the relationship between descriptive representation and symbolic representation. (Substantive representation is reviewed in Chapter 9.)

The facets of political representation allow political scientists to ask big-picture questions about how the inclusion or exclusion of certain groups shapes the quality of democracy and of government. For instance, citizens who perceive that their representatives do not look like them (descriptive representation) are more likely to distrust their government (symbolic representation). Distrust can further erode the legitimacy of the political system. In the United States, people are more likely to agree with a legislature's policy decisions and more likely to perceive the legislature to be trustworthy and fair when women and men hold an equal number of seats, as compared to when men hold all the seats.[2] The finding that citizens prefer gender-balanced legislatures seems straightforward – except this preference is far from being a reality. Globally, men hold 76 per cent of seats in the lower or single houses of the world's legislatures. The United States and Canada are no exception: In 2019, men monopolized 76 and 73 per cent of the lower house seats, respectively. As shown in Figure 6.1, women remain dramatically underrepresented across global regions.

Members of minority groups are also underrepresented relative to their share in the population. In this chapter, *minority* refers to social groups that face systematic disadvantage in a given country, and *majority* refers to a country's dominant social group. Groups can face systematic disadvantage even when their numerical presence is large, such as Black Americans, who comprise numerical majorities in several US states but experience severe social and legal discrimination throughout the country. Data on minority representation are difficult to collect and compare cross-nationally, but recent estimates found that *majority* men comprise just 39 per cent of the population of a typical country but hold 72 per cent of seats in that country's legislature.[3] Minority women are even more underrepresented; because they are disadvantaged by their gender *and* by their other marginalized identities, minority women hold just 2 per cent of seats in a typical legislature.[4]

Figure 6.1. Women's Descriptive Representation in Legislatures

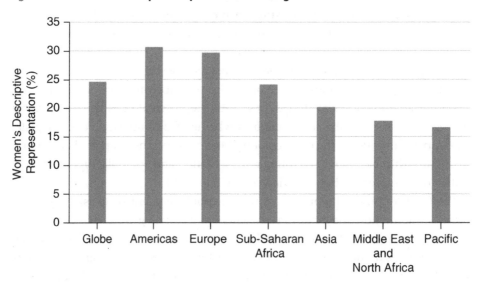

Source: Data from the Inter-Parliamentary Union, 2020.
Notes: Single or lower chamber. Asia includes Central and East Asia. The Pacific includes Australia and New Zealand. The Americas include North and South America and the Caribbean.

To understand how electoral rules shape political representation, this chapter focuses on the building blocks of electoral systems and explains the key differences among them. The chapter explains how this variation produces more or less descriptive representation, meaning legislatures that are more diverse or less diverse. The chapter then turns to mechanisms designed to ensure the descriptive representation of women, racial and ethnic minorities, and youth: quota laws. These laws are *positive action* for candidates from social groups that are traditionally underrepresented in elected office (see Box 6.1) and constitute the most popular electoral reform of the late twentieth and early twenty-first centuries. Finally, the chapter returns to the core question of why political representation matters, showing that greater descriptive representation leads to a more engaged and trusting citizenry.

BOX 6.1: AFFIRMATIVE/POSITIVE ACTION
Anglo-American students are likely familiar with the term *affirmative action*, another term for positive action. For political scientists, *positive action* describes a policy or law through which governments take steps to ensure that a certain social group receives a benefit or has a right protected. Political scientists use the

term to objectively explain how policies work, not subjectively evaluate whether the policies are "good" or "bad." To understand how affirmative action describes rather than judges, it is helpful to understand what political scientists mean by "positive" versus "negative" (again, it's not "good" and "bad"). Positive refers to the presence of an action, whereas negative refers to the absence of one. When the government takes a negative action, *it does nothing.* For example, in the United States, the freedom of religion is often understood as requiring negative action: The government cannot impede the exercise of religion, so it cannot place constraints on worship. An example of the government protecting freedom of religion by *not* doing something is *not* requiring a religious test for elected office. By contrast, when the government takes a positive action, it *does something.* Rather than not placing constraints, the government facilitates an outcome. Creating holidays on days of religious significance can be construed as a positive action: In mandating the holidays by law, the government assists citizens of certain faiths in their religious observances. Similarly, laws or policies that require employers, political parties, universities, or other entities to take steps that recruit members of certain groups is a positive action. Affirmative action or positive action simply refers to the government's decision to do something that helps members of social groups, as opposed to doing nothing.

BUILDING BLOCKS OF ELECTION SYSTEMS

Electoral rules cover two main aspects of choosing representatives: the basis of representation and the mechanics of counting votes and allocating legislative seats to candidates. Decisions about whether representatives are drawn from territories or social groups, as well as decisions about how votes are counted, have consequences for which citizens receive greater opportunities to exercise their political rights, particularly their right to represent and be represented.

Basis of Representation

Traditionally, most representatives are elected on a territorial basis, called the **district**, and representatives are understood to come from and speak for that district. Districts vary in their geographic size and population. Apportionment refers to the ratio between the number of residents in the district and the number of representatives in the legislature: The more this ratio varies across the country, the more *malapportioned* the legislative body. For instance, all US states elect two senators, but their populations are not equal. North Dakota has 760,000 residents and California has 39.5 million residents, but the Senate gives Californians and North Dakotans an equal voice in policy decisions. The US Senate is among the more malapportioned upper chambers worldwide, ranking in the top five alongside Argentina, Bolivia, Brazil, and the Dominican Republic.[5]

Territorially based representation assumes that voters share interests based on where they live. Place does matter – after all, the point of a malapportioned senate in countries like the United States and Argentina is to ensure that more populous, urban states or provinces (like California or Buenos Aires) cannot trample the interests of less populous, rural states or provinces (like North Dakota or Patagonia). Yet not all interests are territorial. Countries experience internal conflict and even civil war because of cleavages among social groups, meaning groups organized on the basis of economic status, race/ethnicity, religion, language, or another identity. Social groups may coincide with territorial divisions, such as Canada's French-speaking province of Quebec, or different social groups may live in close proximity to each other throughout the territory, such as Catholics and Protestants in Northern Ireland. *Power sharing* refers to institutional arrangements designed to ensure the participation of different social groups in government. Power-sharing institutions can take many forms – for instance, the peace accords in El Salvador created a new security force that integrated combatants from both factions in the civil war. A common type of power sharing ensures political representation based not on territory but on social group membership.

Constitutions and peace agreements often reserve seats in the national legislature for representatives from minority social groups. These *reserved seats* are found worldwide, from the Pacific to Western Europe.[6] Reserved seats exemplify the concept of positive action (or affirmative action) discussed in Box 6.1: In establishing reserved seats, governments act affirmatively to ensure social groups' descriptive representation. In many former colonies, reserved seats date back to the nineteenth century, as in India and New Zealand. Reserved seats also became more popular after World War II, as attention to the rights of social groups greatly expanded. World War II raised the world's consciousness about genocide, but decolonization in the decades after World War II saw further ethnic conflict. As new democracies struggled to make peace and old democracies became more concerned with ending persistent exclusion, the popularity of power-sharing arrangements, including reserved seats, expanded.

Reserved seats operate differently depending on their design. India has the most complex case, with about 20 per cent of lower house seats set aside for members from the Scheduled Castes and Tribes. In most other contexts, the percentage of reserved seats is much smaller. For instance, the 1991 Colombian Constitution reserves one seat in the lower house and two seats in the senate for Indigenous communities, and the 1999 Venezuelan Constitution creates three special districts, each of which elects an Indigenous representative to the country's single chamber. To become a candidate, individuals must demonstrate their group membership: In both countries, they must have held a leadership position in an Indigenous community or organization, and in Venezuela they must also speak an Indigenous language and have acted to benefit the community. In both countries, any citizen may vote for the Indigenous candidates, but they must choose between voting for the reserved seat/special district or voting in the "regular" district where they live.

This latter feature may seem counterintuitive: How can Indigenous legislators represent Indigenous peoples if potentially non-Indigenous people vote for them? However, this design makes sense given both countries' history – and given the objectives of having reserved seats to address legacies of mistreatment. The Colombian and Venezuelan states previously classified Indigenous peoples to subject them to discrimination and even genocide. The new constitutions adopted reserved seats precisely to compensate for these past wrongs. Righting these wrongs meant ensuring that the state would *not* determine which citizens were or were not Indigenous. Instead, Colombia and Venezuela let voters choose for themselves. Other countries allow voters to self-identify, but they *do* keep records: In New Zealand, voters must register as Maori to vote for the Maori candidates. Another variation appears in Pakistan, where seats are reserved for religious minorities. There, parties choose the candidates, and voters do not elect the candidates directly. Instead, the seats are allocated to parties after the election, with parties receiving a portion of the reserved seats comparable to their portion of the popular vote.

No matter the institutional design, the presence of reserved seats encourages political parties to form along ethnic lines.[7] Policymakers and researchers also identify the importance of social groups' descriptive representation even in contexts not characterized by colonial legacies, ethnic strife, or civil war. These heightened concerns about whether or not legislatures mirror their populations also benefit women.

In 1998, political theorist Anne Phillips assessed the overrepresentation of men in the world's legislatures, writing "there is no argument from justice that can defend the current state of affairs."[8] Phillips argued that men could claim no special or innate talent that justified their near-monopoly on running for office, writing laws, and leading government. With this argument, Phillips defended a *politics of presence*, describing the underrepresentation of women in national legislatures as a political problem that required political remedies. She wrote during an era when women held only 11 per cent of the legislative seats across the globe. About the same time, the Inter-Parliamentary Union, an international non-governmental organization dedicated to transparency and professionalism in legislatures, began documenting women's access to the world's legislatures. Women's descriptive representation – meaning the proportion of women in the national legislature – became used to assess "how well" countries were doing at ending discrimination against women. Today, women's descriptive representation enters into nearly every index that international organizations have devised to measure the depth of a country's economic and political development, as well as the quality of a country's democracy.

Ideas about the basis of representation thus have evolved in the contemporary era: Territory still matters, but so does identity. Dozens of international and regional treaties have called for women's equal representation in national legislatures. For instance, the 2007 Quito Consensus, signed by countries in Latin America and the Caribbean, committed all signatories to gender parity in government. The International Labour Organization's 1991 Indigenous and Tribal Peoples Convention recognizes the rights of Indigenous peoples to fully participate in government and in the articulation of all policies that affect their well-being. The 1992 United Nations Declaration on the Rights of Persons Belonging to National or Ethnic, Religious and Linguistic Minorities recognizes the same rights for these groups. International norms emphasizing the importance of LGBTQ+ inclusion have gained prominence more recently (and are more contested), but the United Nations Office of the High Commissioner for Human Rights has repeatedly underscored LGBTQ+ peoples' human rights, including their political rights.[9] Civil society organizations also target the underrepresentation of other social groups: In the United States, for instance, Run for Something encourages young people to become candidates, and the National Council for Independent Living prepares people with disabilities to run for office.

These calls for better mirror representation recognize that legislatures not composed of diverse individuals cannot govern on behalf of diverse polities. At the same time, these initiatives largely have unfolded in their siloes: Policymakers and advocates concerned with women's descriptive representation rarely talk about *minority* women, and policymakers and advocates concerned with ethnic minorities rarely talk about ethnic *women*.[10] Attention to the underrepresentation of intersectional identities should improve in the future, as international norms about the importance of diverse legislatures become stronger.

Transforming Votes into Seats

Why *do* men from each country's dominant social group hold the most seats in their country's legislature? Asked another way, why are women – especially minority women – and minority men less likely to be represented? Resources and opportunities matter. As Chapter 5 discussed, women and minorities are less likely to be members of political parties; they also face more barriers to receiving nominations from parties and encounter more voter bias. Electoral systems also shape patterns of descriptive representation in the legislature, as different sets of rules create systems that are more or less inclusive.

Electoral Systems

Two basic differences exist in how countries choose their national legislatures. The first is single-member districts (also called a first-past-the-post system), which includes majoritarian and plurality systems. Second is proportional representation, which includes a variety of systems.

PLURALITY AND MAJORITARIAN SYSTEMS

Single-member districts are familiar to many Anglo-Americans: Each district has one seat in the legislature, so each district elects one representative. (Districts are also called *constituencies* or *ridings*.) In these single-member districts (SMDs), the candidate who receives the most votes wins. The *most* votes means a **plurality**, which is not the same as a majority. If three candidates are running, and Candidate A receives 40 per cent of the votes and Candidates B and C receive 30 per cent each, then Candidate A wins the seat because they got the *most* votes, but not the majority of the votes. For this reason, electoral systems using SMDs are called *plurality systems* or *first-past-the-post (FPTP) systems*. In these systems, the winner takes all. Note that the SMD label applies when the district elects one representative *per election*. For example, even though each US state is represented by two senators, the senators' terms are staggered, and voters do not elect both senators at once. The US Senate districts are therefore also SMDs because voters only choose one senator in a given election. The United States, many countries of the British Commonwealth (also called the Westminster democracies), and some countries in Oceania and Sub-Saharan Africa have plurality systems.

PROPORTIONAL REPRESENTATION SYSTEMS

In a *proportional representation (PR)* system, the number of seats available in a district – known as **district magnitude** and often abbreviated using the letter "m" – is greater than one. (In an SMD system, m equals one.) *Multimember districts (MMDs)* create incentives for more candidates to enter the race, as there are more electoral spoils to go around. Some districts can be very large: The city of São Paulo in Brazil, for instance, elects 70 members to the lower house, and 1,502 candidates ran to represent this mega-city in the Brazilian congress in 2018! Many districts have more modest magnitudes – usually between two and seven – but voters still face high barriers to knowing all the candidates, especially when all parties are likely to field the same number of candidates as seats.

PR therefore uses a more efficient way of translating votes into seats, as follows:

1　Voters choose parties rather than candidates.
2　At the district level, the votes are allocated to the party.
3　Each party then receives a number of seats from that district that is proportional to the number of votes the party received.
4　The party then distributes the seats among the candidates from the district.

For example, if Party A and Party B compete in a 10-seat district, and if Party A receives 20 per cent of the total votes cast in that district and Party B receives 80 per cent, Party A will elect two representatives and Party B will elect eight. Of course, the math is much more complicated in practice, for a few reasons. First, many countries impose *thresholds*, requiring that parties receive some minimum per cent of the district's vote to qualify for a seat (usually between 2 and 5 per cent). Second, there are different formulas available that overcome computational problems – like what to do when the division results in fractions, since parties cannot send a fraction of a person to the legislature. This stylized example nonetheless captures the basic idea of how PR works.

PR translates votes into seats, but how do parties determine which candidates actually go to the legislature? There are two main methods by which parties allocate seats to candidates: closed lists and open lists. In *closed-list proportional representation (CLPR)*, parties draw up lists of candidates, and these lists are presented to voters in their entirety. When a voter casts their vote for the party, they accept the party's list as presented. From a candidate's perspective, the positions at the top of the list are better than the positions at the bottom. Take the example above: Assume that Party A won 20 per cent of the district's vote in the previous election, which translates into two seats. Candidates one and two thus feel confident they will enter the legislature: So long as the party performs as well as it did before, it will win two seats and candidates one and two will enter the legislature. Candidate three is optimistic, since they will win a seat if the party performs slightly better; candidates four and five are doubtful, as they only enter if the party performs *much* better; and candidates six and higher know they stand no chance. Many candidates thus occupy unelected or *ornamental spots* on the list. In *open-list proportional representation (OLPR)*, parties still present voters with lists, but voters can cast a *preference vote* for individual candidates, moving them up or down the list. CLPR is more common worldwide, found throughout Latin America and much of Europe, Asia, the Middle East, and Africa.

Plurality systems with SMDs and PR systems with MMDs capture the basic differences in how votes are transformed into seats. Of course, some countries make life complicated. *Block voting* occurs when countries have MMDs and voters cast a single vote for the party list, but the electoral rule is winner take all. In other words, the party with the most votes gets *all* the seats in the district, thus electing their entire list. Countries using block voting include Lebanon, Laos, and Mauritius.

In *ranked-choice voting*, also sometimes called *single transferable vote*, candidates compete in single-member districts, but voters rank candidates in their order of preference rather than simply choosing one. A candidate wins if they receive more than half of every voter's first-choice votes. If not, the candidate with the fewest votes is eliminated, and voters who picked this candidate as their first choice then get their second choice counted. This process continues until one candidate emerges victorious. Countries using ranked-choice voting include Ireland and Australia. Ranked-choice voting is thought to produce winners who enjoy more widespread support than winners in a pure plurality contest. Many US states use ranked-choice voting in local elections – an important reminder that many countries use different electoral rules at the national level than they do at the subnational level.

PR systems favor candidates who are party loyalists. When votes are allocated to parties, the party brand matters more than the individual brand. And in CLPR, parties control candidates' rank-order placement on the ballot, which gives parties much greater control over politicians' careers. Parties can punish individuals by awarding them lower rankings (or no rankings) in the next election, which creates incentives for elected officials to follow the party line once in office and to support the party platform when on the campaign trail. Candidates usually build their careers within the parties and have little incentive to cultivate personal followings (except in OLPR, where candidates receive a preference vote). In PR systems, electing minority and women candidates depends on parties' commitments to diversity, discussed in more detail in Chapter 5.

MIXED-MEMBER SYSTEMS

A third, less common, variant of electoral systems are *mixed-member systems*, where some districts are elected using one set of rules and other districts are elected using a different set of rules. Most commonly, countries combine the standard building blocks: single-member districts elected via plurality rules, and multimember districts elected via proportional rules. (Indeed, students can assume that, unless specified otherwise, plurality means the country has SMDs, and proportional representation means MMDs.) For national elections, mixed-member systems combining plurality and PR are found in Germany, Italy, Mexico, New Zealand, and South Korea, among others. Mexico provides a clear illustration. The lower house is elected using 300 single-member districts and 200 CLPR districts, the latter comprising five regions with a district magnitude of 40. Each Mexican citizen casts two votes for the lower house: one in their constituency (their SMD) and one in their region (the PR list).

Mixed-member systems allow countries to capture the best of both worlds, since plurality systems and proportional representation systems produce different outcomes. Critically, plurality systems are *candidate centered*, because votes are allocated to individual candidates, whereas proportional representation systems are *party centered*, because votes are allocated to parties. Plurality systems favor candidates who distinguish themselves as individuals. True, in plurality systems, candidates run under party labels, and many voters simply vote for the candidate based on their party. Nonetheless, the candidate's individual brand and personal style matter enormously, leading to an entrepreneurial and personalistic style of politics. Electing women and minority candidates consequently depends largely on how voters respond to such candidates.

Electoral Rules and Representational Outcomes

Countries often design their electoral rules to obtain certain representational outcomes. PR favors strong parties, and FPTP favors entrepreneurial candidates. Additionally, the choice between FPTP and PR constitutes a *tradeoff between efficiency and representativeness*, which also has consequences for the over- or underrepresentation of different groups in the legislature. Understanding this tradeoff requires first understanding how district magnitude shapes the number of political parties, a concept known as *Duverger's law* (which was introduced in Chapter 5).

In a plurality system where the winner takes all, district magnitude equals one, so the real competition is between the top-two candidates. Imagine a three-way race in which candidates are polling as follows: candidate X at 45 per cent, candidate Y at 35 per cent, and candidate Z at 20 per cent. *Rational voters* will not wish to throw their vote away: Their vote cannot help candidate Z because they are too far behind, but their vote *could* ensure victory for X or help Y close the gap. Voters who prefer Z thus face incentives to abandon Z and choose X or Y. For this reason, most plurality systems are *two-party systems* (thus following Duverger's m + 1 rule, because district magnitude in plurality systems equals one, so the effective number of parties is two). FPTP systems often lack strong third parties not because of government conspiracy but because millions of individual voters behave rationally.

Yet two-party systems can frustrate these same voters, who often feel like neither X nor Y truly "gets" them. FPTP systems technically allow for more than two candidates (remember that candidates can win with a plurality, not a majority), but practically tend toward just two candidates, meaning someone wins with a majority or near-majority. And that means the candidate – and thus their party – needs to appeal to *many* voters in the district, not just a narrow slice. Political parties in plurality systems consequently behave like catch-all parties. Such parties are ideological big tents – they try to forge distinct identities from each other, while keeping their disparate internal factions happy. The problem becomes exacerbated as votes translate into seats. Since only two parties compete in all or most districts, one party usually ends up with a majority of the seats in the legislature, allowing that party to handily pass whatever laws it wants. On the one hand, the ease of lawmaking makes two-party systems efficient. On the other hand, the party may not fully represent the preferences of all voters. Voters who share some but not all of the winning party's objectives may have supported that party at the polls, but not agree with all its decisions in the legislature. And supporters of the losing party, who could be nearly half the population, will consistently have their preferences denied as the majority party runs the agenda during their term in the legislature. People who voted for the minority party may often feel like they have wasted their vote, since they receive no policy representation.

These same incentives toward rational voting do not apply in multimember districts. Voters do not need to coordinate on the top-two contenders when each district can elect more than one candidate. Consider the above example, but this time with proportional rules. Imagine the district has five seats. The contenders are polling as before (at 45 per cent, 35 per cent, and 20 per cent), except because the system is PR and not plurality, the contenders are now parties, not candidates. In this scenario, the party polling at 20 per cent is *not* doomed, because 20 per cent of the vote in a five-seat district would give the party one seat. Voters thus do not need to abandon party Z under PR rules the way they abandoned candidate Z under SMD rules, because PR gives party Z a chance. Voters for party Z will not waste their vote. Consequently, parties in PR systems do not need to behave like big tents; they can specialize and still win (at least some) seats.

PR systems thus tend toward *multiparty systems*, allowing voters to choose parties that better match their preferences. (Recall that Duverger posited that the exact number of parties in each system would vary based on the district magnitude, following the m + 1 rule.) For this reason, PR systems are thought to be more representative. However, they are not necessarily efficient. If more parties can win seats, then elections can result in legislatures where no party controls a majority of the seats. Parties then have to govern in coalition (discussed in Chapter 8), which means that passing laws requires constant bargaining to keep all coalition partners happy. Writing laws based on compromise may allow for greater policy representation, but the process is slower and thus not efficient.

Since PR systems are seen as representative but not efficient (whereas plurality systems are seen as efficient but not representative), PR itself is a form of power sharing. PR, like reserved seats, encourages the formation of political parties that represent specific ethnic, ethno-religious, or ethno-linguist groups. These ethnic parties exist throughout the world, from Southeast Asia to Sub-Saharan Africa to Eastern Europe. However, not all ethnic parties are successful. From the standpoint of electoral system design, one factor affecting ethnic parties' success is the threshold. Recall that the threshold is the minimum proportion of votes a party must win in the district to qualify for at least one of the district's seats. In Israel, the threshold is 1.5 per cent of the vote, whereas in Turkey it is 10 per cent. Niche parties – including ethnic or ethno-religious parties – thus have greater electoral success in Israel than in Turkey.[11] Some countries circumvent this problem by eliminating the threshold requirement for ethnic parties: In Poland, for instance, parties representing the German minority do not have to meet the 5 per cent threshold.

More generally, multimember districts provide parties with more opportunities to diversify their candidate slates than do single-member districts. MMDs give parties more spoils (candidacies) to distribute, and parties can thus "afford" to nominate candidates from underrepresented groups, namely women and minorities. The diversification of PR lists is called *ticket balancing*. These benefits are recognized not just by political scientists, but by policymakers (see Box 6.2).

BOX 6.2: NEW ZEALAND'S ELECTORAL SYSTEM SWITCH

New Zealand switched from a plurality system to a mixed-member system in the 1990s. In the 1970s and 1980s, citizens had become increasingly dissatisfied with the winner-take-all nature of the plurality system. In 1985, a Royal Commission was convened to analyze alternatives. The Royal Commission on the Electoral System recommended a mixed system. In its criteria for judging the most appropriate electoral system, the commission wrote that the design should ensure "effective representation of minority and special interest groups" and that membership in the legislature "should not only be proportional to the level of party support but should also reflect other significant characteristics of the electorate, such as gender, ethnicity, socio-economic class, locality and age."[12] The question of whether New Zealand should switch to a mixed system, which combined plurality SMDs with PR MMDs, was put to voters in 1992, and the referendum passed. Voters chose the mixed system more out of dissatisfaction with majority governments and a desire to have more parties in the legislature, and were not necessarily expressly motivated by PR's promise of greater diversity.[13] Nonetheless, the adoption of PR in New Zealand did contribute to greater ethnic and gender diversity in Parliament. For example, between 1996 and 2014, the descriptive representation of European-origin legislators declined from 85 per cent to 68 per cent, whereas the representation of Asian-origin legislators climbed from 0 to 4 per cent.[14] Unlike the Maori, Asian-origin legislators do not benefit from reserved seats, and though their presence in the New Zealand Parliament (4 per cent) is less than their presence in the population (12 per cent), they gained representation. All five of the Asian members of Parliament in 2014 were women.[15]

How much diversity a PR system yields largely depends on district magnitude. Minority groups attain the highest levels of representation in CLPR systems with large districts, as in many Western European countries. For example, in 2006, six different parties elected minority candidates to the Dutch Parliament, amounting to 15 out of 150 members (10 per cent).[16] Large-magnitude CLPR systems benefit minority women in particular.[17] Generally, scholars have identified a multiple identity advantage for minority women candidates: Whereas stereotypes attached to minority men often cast them as dangerous and threatening, stereotypes attached to minority women often cast them as community oriented and nurturing. Nominating ethnic minority women further allows party leaders to diversify their candidate lists by killing two birds with one stone. Ethnic minority women are better represented than ethnic minority men in the Netherlands and also in Belgium, Spain, and Sweden.[18] That said, the benevolent stereotypes that benefit some minority women's election are still stereotypes, and minority women still face persistent underrepresentation across the globe.

In contrast to PR systems, SMD systems have design features that work against underrepresented groups' access to elected office. SMD systems are more competitive, because there is only one seat per district. Heightened competition combined with candidate-centered elections means that contenders will face more pressure to fit conventional images of a typical politician, who is usually a majority man.

Candidates in SMD systems need to prove they are up to the job, and women and minority candidates are more likely to have their credentials and their fitness doubted. For members of underrepresented groups, the mere act of running for office counters popular beliefs about how members of those groups "should" behave. For instance, women candidates across the globe report that parties and voters perceive a conflict between their candidacy and their prescribed social roles as wives and mothers. A former woman legislator from Nigeria (an SMD system) captured the experiences of many women candidates, no matter their country of origin, when she recalled, "A married woman was penalized for neglecting her husband and family. A woman who was 'unattached' was put to task to prove that she was not a *malaya* (prostitute)."[19]

Campaigns' frenetic pace also poses barriers. For example, women across the globe struggle to balance domestic responsibilities with long hours on the campaign trail. People with disabilities face extra hurdles in just traveling to and physically accessing campaign spaces.[20] In many places, candidates from minority groups face not just structural and cultural barriers, but harassment and even violence. These hurdles exist in all electoral systems, but the stakes are especially high under plurality rules.

MANDATING INCLUSION VIA QUOTAS

The electoral rules discussed so far are not designed to guarantee the descriptive representation of different social groups, but they create conditions that tend toward more or less descriptive representation. For instance, PR does not require parties to balance their tickets, but MMDs provide more opportunities for parties to diversify their candidates, relative to SMDs. The exception is reserved seats, which are designed to guarantee a minimum descriptive representation for certain social groups. Reserved seats are often categorized as a type of *quota law*, referring to statutes or constitutional provisions that create electoral opportunities based on social group membership. The most common quota laws (also called *legal quotas*) are *candidate quotas*, which require that political parties nominate a certain proportion of social group members. Political parties may establish candidate quotas within the parties, but these are not required by law, explaining why *party quotas* are also called *voluntary quotas*. Party quotas were discussed in more depth in Chapter 5. In this chapter, *quota* refers to a legal mandate, so *quota* and *quota law* are used interchangeably in the discussion.

Types of Quota Laws

Quota laws typically target women and ethnic minorities, though a handful of countries have youth quotas, which target citizens under the ages of 40 or 35. Quota laws, especially candidate quotas, often apply to national and subnational elections. Counting both reserved seats and candidate quotas, **gender quotas** for women candidates are found in over 70 countries across the globe,[21] and **ethnic quotas** are found in about 30 countries.[22] Gender quotas commonly take the form of candidate quotas, whereas ethnic quotas commonly take the form of reserved seats. Ethnic quotas can apply to racial, ethnic, religious, linguistic, or ethno-religious groups, with *ethnic quotas* as the generic name.

Gender quotas and ethnic quotas have similar aims – to improve the descriptive representation of the target group – but are adopted for different reasons.[23] As noted in the earlier discussion of reserved seats, ethnic quotas emerge from countries' historic and contemporary efforts to manage conflict. The earliest ethnic quotas date to the colonial periods of the nineteenth or early twentieth centuries, while more recent quota laws were adopted as part of a country's independence or peace settlements. Choices about ethnic quotas are deeply political. For instance, the peace settlement in Bosnia created reservations for Serbs, Croats, and Bosniacs – but not the Roma. The choice about which groups receive the reservations depend on which ethnic groups are seen as important to the country's stability and its future (with "important" often framed in political rather than normative terms).

The consideration for women is different. Women comprise 50 per cent of the population no matter their other identities, so gender quotas do not affect policymakers' calculations about power sharing among ethnic groups.[24] Gender quotas are therefore less tied to political stability but are still contested due to stereotypical conceptions about women's "proper" domestic and private roles. Quotas for women candidates are largely a contemporary phenomenon, grounded in evolving international norms linking women's descriptive representation to development and democracy.

Countries do adopt both ethnic quotas and gender quotas, though usually at different times, following the different causal logics (though see Box 6.3). When countries do end up with both ethnic quotas and gender quotas, they have *nested quotas* (also called *tandem quotas*). On the one hand, nested quotas can benefit ethnic minority women. If the quota laws permit one candidate to be counted as filling both the ethnic quota and the gender quota, then the "two birds with one stone" logic applies. Burundi permits such double counting, and Tutsi women are consequently overrepresented relative to their share in the population.[25] On the other hand, because nested quotas are not nested by design, they can sideline minority women.[26] This sidelining usually occurs when the ethnic quota takes the form of a reserved seat: Ethnic *men* become the beneficiaries of the reservations, while women fill the candidate quotas. For instance, Taiwan reserves six seats for Indigenous peoples and applies a gender quota at 30 per cent, but Indigenous women's representation has declined in recent years.[27]

Gender quotas typically set the threshold percentages between 30 and 50 per cent. A 50 per cent quota is called **gender parity**. Youth quotas are usually around 15 or 20 per cent. The thresholds for ethnic quotas vary more widely, depending

---

BOX 6.3: NESTED QUOTAS

As noted, countries end up with nested quotas by happenstance, because they adopt gender quotas and ethnic quotas at different times for different reasons. However, Melanie Hughes defines nested quotas more narrowly.[28] She argues that "true" nested quotas only occur when gender quotas and ethnic quotas are adopted together, with explicit provisions for how ethnic minority women will benefit. Using this narrower definition, Hughes identifies four instances worldwide of true nested quotas: Afghanistan, Jordan, Nepal, and Bolivia.

Afghanistan and Jordan have reserved seats for women and ethnic minorities. The Afghan Constitution reserves a minimum of two seats per province for women (gender quota) and ten seats per province for Kuchis (ethnic quota). Three Kuchi seats must go to Kuchi women (nested quota). In Jordan, which reserves seats for multiple ethnic groups, the reservations for Christians and for Circassians/Chechens need *not* include women, whereas the reservations for other ethnic groups *must* include women, making Jordan's gender quota only partially nested.

Nepal has ethnic quotas for candidate lists, and 50 per cent of all the candidates must be women. For instance, parties must run 40 per cent Indigenous candidates, and half must be Indigenous women. Bolivia has gender parity for candidates and reserved seats for Indigenous peoples, both adopted in 2009. The reserved seat candidates must reflect gender parity. About 62 per cent of the Bolivian population is Indigenous: They are a numerical majority, but a structural minority given colonial legacies of exploitation and genocide. In 2014, with the nested quotas in place, women made up 51 per cent of Bolivia's lower house; Indigenous peoples 40 per cent; and Indigenous women 19 per cent.[29] These numbers do not precisely mirror Indigenous peoples' and Indigenous women's population percentages, but they constitute dramatic increases relative to before the quotas' adoption.

on that ethnic group's size in the population. Taiwan's six seats for Indigenous peoples amounts to about 5 per cent of the legislature. Singapore's ethnic quota requires that candidate lists in the MMDs – which range in magnitude from four to six and are elected via block vote – contain at least one Malay or Indian candidate. Singapore's ethnic quota thus ranges from 25 per cent (1 in 4) to 16 per cent (1 in 6), but since they have a mixed-member system, the quota only applies in the MMDs. The quota ultimately affects about 17 per cent of Singapore's unicameral legislature.[30] As discussed in more detail below, thresholds and other details about where and how quotas are implemented create almost endless variations in quota design, with different effects on descriptive representation.

Further, quota laws are not clustered in any particular global region. Gender, ethnic, and youth quotas are found in the Global North and the Global South and in established democracies, emerging democracies, and even non-democracies. Given the link between women's descriptive representation and a country's political development, some think that gender quota laws are found in young democracies that wish to demonstrate their commitment to international norms. Gender quotas do appear in recently democratizing countries such as Afghanistan, Mexico, Kenya, and South Korea, but they also appear in advanced industrialized democracies like France and Belgium. At the same time, certain regions excel at adopting candidate quotas, mostly because activists in neighboring countries learn from each other. Sixteen of Latin America's 18 democratic countries have gender quota laws, for instance, explaining why Latin America has the highest women's descriptive representation of any world region – women compose 30 per cent of the region's legislatures.[31]

How Candidate Quotas Work

Both reserved seats and candidate quotas are forms of affirmative action for groups traditionally underrepresented in politics but with an important distinction: Reserved seats affect the final composition of the legislature, whereas candidate quotas affect the composition of the candidates. These candidates must still win their elections. However, candidate quotas often result in electing greater proportions of the target group than reserved seats. Understanding this paradox requires first understanding the finer points of candidate quotas' design.

Recall that most candidate quotas apply to women. The initial gender quota laws were weak. Many laws *recommended* that parties nominate the desired percentage of women rather than required that parties achieve this percentage. Another loophole entailed making the quota a requirement but not including sanctions if parties flouted the law, thus rendering the statute toothless. Most

Figure 6.2. Placement Mandates for a 30 Per Cent Gender Quota in a PR System

Format A	Format B	Format C
1. Man	1. Man	1. Woman
2. Man	2. Woman	2. Man
3. Woman	3. Man	3. Man
4. Man	4. Man	4. Woman
5. Man	5. Woman	5. Man
6. Woman	6. Man	6. Man

commonly, the laws did not stipulate how parties had to distribute the nominations. Parties could, for instance, fill the quota by nominating women in districts where the party usually lost – the equivalent of the US Democratic Party, which usually loses in the south, running all its women candidates in Mississippi, and the US Republican Party, which usually loses on the coasts, running all its women candidates in California. In PR systems, the absence of rules about distributing nominations meant parties could cluster women's names at the bottom of the candidate lists, in the ornamental spots. These weak design features meant that many gender quotas did not, in the beginning, significantly increase the proportion of women elected.

Proponents then pushed legislatures to adopt new gender quota laws, ones that eliminated many of these loopholes. Nearly a third of countries that adopted gender quotas made at least one reform, nearly always to strengthen the law, as gender quota repeals are very rare.[32] These revisions contained many important changes. Countries elevated gender quotas from recommendations to requirements and established sanctions for non-compliant parties (typically, parties are barred from entering the election until the gender quota is filled).

Most significantly, countries established *placement mandates* for PR lists. Placement mandates dictate where on the list women's names must appear, thus preventing parties from concentrating women in the ornamental spots. For example, a typical placement mandate for a 30 per cent quota requires that one woman's name appear in every three places. A candidate list for a six-seat district complies with the quota if the list appears in any of the three formats shown in Figure 6.2. Of course, parties across the globe pursue strategies of *minimal compliance* with placement mandates, choosing format A. Parties consistently nominate men to the first position; women infrequently head lists. Minimal compliance led to another popular quota reform: raising the thresholds from 30 per cent to 40 and 50 per cent. With gender parity, for instance, the placement mandate requires that men's and women's names alternate down the list (known as *vertical parity*), which ranks women higher overall. The lowest list position a woman candidate will obtain under gender parity is position 2, compared to position 3 under a 30 per cent quota.

Placement mandates combined with high thresholds therefore improve how parties rank women candidates *within* the district, but do not address discrimination against women as list-headers. Parties' reluctance to cede the top list position to women especially prejudices women's election in small magnitude districts or highly competitive districts, because parties in these districts are likely to win just one seat. Consequently, some countries have adopted *horizontal parity*, where parties must alternate men's and women's position as list-headers across the entirety of the districts. The combination of vertical and horizontal parity has strong numerical effects. In Costa Rica, for instance, vertical parity applied in 2014, but because most parties ran men in the top list position, women won only 33.3 per cent of seats in the legislative assembly. In 2018, when vertical *and* horizontal parity applied, women won 45.6 per cent of the seats.

Placement mandates can also apply to candidate quotas adopted in plurality systems. Though candidate quotas seem to fit with PR systems' MMDs better than with plurality systems' SMDs, candidate quotas work in any system where political parties control *ballot access*, meaning parties control who becomes a candidate. Many readers are familiar with the US system, where political parties do *not* control ballot access. In the United States, any individual can assign themself a party label; so long as this individual gathers enough signatures, they can register with their local election board and become a candidate for the party of their choosing. In the vast majority of countries outside the United States, however, *parties* choose candidates and *parties* register candidates. So long as parties register candidates, countries can mandate how parties choose them. A candidate quota in a plurality system works similar to horizontal parity: Across the entirety of the districts in which the party will field candidates, the party must nominate the target percentage of group members.

Mexico's gender parity law illustrates how candidate quotas can work in plurality systems. Recall that Mexico uses a mixed-member system, electing its lower house via 300 SMD districts and 200 PR seats. Mexico's gender parity law applies to both district types. For the SMDs, parties must nominate half men and half women: If a party fields candidates in all 300 constituencies, they must nominate 150 men and 150 women. The law further stipulates that parties cannot "exclusively" nominate women in the constituencies it expects to lose. Though "exclusively" does not say exactly how many women parties must assign to winning districts, Mexico's National Electoral Institute evaluates parties' candidate registries to see if parties follow the spirit of the law. First, the National Electoral Institute uses the previous election results to divide the districts into three categories: safe, competitive, and losing. This analysis is performed separately for every party, as one party's safe seat is another party's losing seat. Second, they ask whether each party respected parity in each category. Did the party nominate half men and half women to its safe districts, to its competitive districts, and to its losing districts? This evaluative method keeps parties honest, encouraging them to send women to districts where they can win.[33] Consequently, Mexico elected 49.2 per cent women to the lower house in 2018.

Overall, how candidate quotas are designed matters enormously for their effects on descriptive representation. The fine print matters. Japan just adopted a gender parity law – but the statute is non-binding, meaning parties face no penalty for non-compliance. By contrast, Uruguay has a 33 per cent gender quota with a placement mandate and a sanction (non-compliant parties cannot participate in the election). If one were to judge on threshold alone, one would assume that Japan elects more women than Uruguay – and they would be wrong. This same logic explains why candidate quotas can elect more descriptive representatives than reserved seats. Reserved seats guarantee the spot, but the proportion of the legislature they set aside is usually small, as noted for Taiwan. The same is true for the Latin America examples discussed earlier. Take Colombia: The senate reserves two seats for Indigenous peoples, but has 105 seats overall, so the ethnic quota comprises just 2 per cent of the upper chamber. Colombia also has a 30 per cent candidate quota for women, and even without a placement mandate, women won 21 per cent of senate seats in the 2018 elections. Consequently, advocates of greater descriptive representation argue that candidate quotas generate better results than reserved seats.

Myths and Truths about Quota Laws

Quota laws can raise the descriptive representation of women and minority groups. Well-designed quotas often exponentially increase a group's access to the legislature from one election to the next. Yet some criticize quota laws for privileging group membership over territory as the basis of political representation and for bringing unqualified individuals into legislatures. The first criticism presumes that identity does *not* matter for how representatives govern. However, this contention ignores arguments about the politics of presence. Political theorists further argue that identity shapes the exercise of political power in fundamental ways, determining which citizens enjoy the good life – and which do not (see Chapter 2). Researchers also find considerable evidence that descriptive representation significantly improves substantive representation (see Chapter 9). In fact, most experts studying ethnic quotas make the opposite critique: that the measures, especially reserved seats, do not provide minorities with *enough* descriptive representation.

The second criticism, that quota candidates are unqualified, also receives no empirical support. A vast body of scholarship comparing legislators' career paths finds that women legislators elected using quotas are either as qualified as or *more* qualified than their male colleagues.[34] In fact, gender quotas may weed out the mediocre men: Since the implementation of gender quotas will require that some men step down to make way for some women, incumbent men must justify why *they* – and not another man – should get to stay.[35] Moreover, how legislators carry out their representative duties once in the legislature depends on factors ranging from party discipline to whether individual legislators can even introduce bills (see Chapter 9). These factors, more than whether a legislator occupies a quota spot, will affect how political representation unfolds.

Quota laws do pose some challenges, however. How gender quotas, especially gender parity, will affect the candidacies of non-binary individuals (those individuals who identify as neither male nor female) remains unknown. Yet this question has not moved to the forefront of policy debates. Persistent discrimination, harassment, and violence severely limit the political participation not just of non-binary individuals but all LGBTQ+ individuals. In the United States, only seven openly lesbian, gay, or bisexual individuals have served in the House of Representatives. Worldwide as of 2016, only three openly transgendered candidates have ever served in national legislatures.[36] These trends indicate that LGBTQ+ people face severe underrepresentation, which also explains why a tension between gender quotas and aspirants who identify neither as "male" nor as "female" has not yet appeared. Yet worries about this tension reflect broader concerns that gender quotas lock citizens into identifying as either "male" or "female," meaning that quotas reinforce a binary notion of gender.

A similar concern appears with ethnic quotas: In making ethnicity the basis of representation, some worry that ethnic quotas make identity *too* salient in people's lives. These concerns especially matter in countries that have experienced ethnic strife. That rewarding ethnic identities will entrench rather than diffuse conflict is a common critique of power-sharing arrangements more broadly.[37] Yet again, these fears are not typically realized in practice. Recall that reserved seats of the kind found in Colombia and Venezuela facilitate the formation of ethnic parties – but the reservations amount to small percentages of the legislature. In these contexts, ethnic parties will have to ally with "mainstream" parties to attain policy influence. This design favors cooperation among the majority and minority group, but also risks having the minority group's interests co-opted by the majority. Both outcomes (cooperation or co-optation) reduce the overall influence of ethnicity.

Ethnic quotas can also work against the formation of ethnic parties, especially when they are candidate quotas rather than reserved seats. Consider the Singapore case, described above. Parties must include at least one Malay or Indian candidate on their MMD list, but elections are decided via a block vote. Since the electoral rule is winner take all, voters are unlikely to choose an ethnic party presenting an all-minority ticket, and they are more likely to choose a mainstream party that minimally complies with the quota and has just one minority candidate.

In summary, quota laws are the tools of their creators. The political calculations entailed in their creation, adoption, and implementation provide lawmakers with numerous opportunities to manipulate their effects on descriptive representation. Women's increased presence in legislatures breaks men's monopoly on political power, explaining why initial gender quota laws were often designed to be weak. At the same time, women's presence in legislatures neither creates nor fuels the kinds of social divisions that lead to conflict and civil war. The same logic applies to youth. By contrast, social groups defined on racial, ethnic, linguistic, ethno-linguistic, or ethno-religious lines often reflect deep cleavages in society. The way ethnic quotas negotiate these cleavages is less shaped by ethnic groups' inherent traits or characteristics and more by the quota laws' design and interface with the electoral system.

THE SYMBOLIC EFFECTS OF REPRESENTATIVE DIVERSITY

This chapter has examined how different electoral rules, including quota laws, affect the descriptive representation of different social groups. The descriptive representation of women and marginalized groups matters in and of itself, for reasons of justice: The right to stand for election is a political right, so a distribution of legislative seats that favors certain groups over others suggests that political rights themselves are not evenly protected. Descriptive representation also matters for consequential reasons, because who has political representation affects how the polity feels about their government. Descriptive representation has *audience effects*, known as symbolic representation. Symbolic effects can accrue not just to the social group that is over- or underrepresented, but also to the broader polity.

A large body of scholarship in political science has shown that higher levels of women's descriptive representation lead women citizens to evaluate politics more positively and to participate in politics more.[38] When more women hold seats in the national legislature, women – but also men – express more trust in democracy and the government. They also express more interest in politics and are more likely to contact their representatives and to vote. They also become more likely to run for office themselves. The descriptive representation of ethnic groups has similar effects. For instance, Black voters in the United States are more likely to contact their representative when that person is also Black.[39] The higher the descriptive representation of Black Americans, the more likely Black citizens perceive policy decisions as fair.[40]

Ultimately, descriptive representation might erode the very beliefs that perpetuate the underrepresentation of certain groups in the first place. In countries where women have higher levels of descriptive representation, women citizens are more likely to believe they have the skills necessary to govern.[41] The Indian case receives particular attention from researchers and policymakers. India is a federal country, and some states have adopted gender quotas for municipal elections. Importantly, these states apply the quota randomly: A lottery selects which municipalities will follow the quota. This randomization creates a natural experiment, with a control group (non-quota municipalities) and a treatment group (quota municipalities). Consequently, when scholars compare the quota municipalities with the non-quota municipalities, they are confident that any differences in outcomes result from the quota itself. And they find that, in villages governed by women, men *and* women express less sexism and less gender bias than in villages governed by men.[42] Descriptive representation facilitates long-term processes of attitudinal and ultimately social and cultural change.

The fundamental importance of descriptive representation underscores why political scientists care about electoral rules. Variations in electoral rules produce real differences in descriptive representation, with consequences for the quality of democracy and of government. Decisions about the basis of representation, the mechanics for translating votes into seats, and the adoption of quotas shape which social groups are present in the legislature and which are not. This chapter has largely focused on the descriptive representation of women and racial and ethnic minorities, as these are the groups that, until now, have most benefited from policymakers' efforts to diversify political representation. Global norms repeatedly emphasize the importance of inclusion, which should generate attention to intersectional identities as well as to other groups that face persistent exclusion, such as LGBTQ+ individuals and people with disabilities. As this chapter has shown, those designing electoral rules can make conscious choices that affect whether or not national legislatures mirror the polities over which they govern.

SUMMARY

- Being represented in the legislature is a political right.
- Descriptive representation (also called mirror representation) captures whether legislatures are composed of individuals who, in their entirety, reflect the diversity of the polity.

- Variations in electoral rules affect descriptive representation:
  - Greater representative diversity typically occurs in multimember districts elected using proportional representation.
  - Generally, proportional representation systems are thought to be more representative but less efficient, whereas plurality systems are thought to be more efficient but less representative.
- Quota laws are the most popular electoral reform of the past 50 years.
- Quotas are designed to ensure the descriptive representation of women and ethnic minorities.
- Quota laws take the form of reserved seats or candidate quotas.
- Common myths associated with quota laws, such as the belief that quota laws facilitate the access of unqualified candidates to the legislature, are not supported by empirical research.

CONCLUDING QUESTIONS

1 Why do political scientists, policymakers, and everyday citizens and voters care about descriptive representation?
2 Identify how the design of an electoral system affects descriptive representation. Pick a country, research its electoral system, and find information about the diversity of groups represented in its legislature. Does your research match what you learned in this chapter? Explain.
3 If you wanted to make a plurality system like the United States or Canada more representative of different social groups, what reforms would you recommend and why? Would you recommend different reforms depending on whether you were targeting women or ethnic minorities? Why or why not?
4 Quota laws are forms of affirmative action. How does political science approach the idea of positive action and how does this approach resemble or differ from your previous encounters with the term?

NOTES

1 Leslie A. Schwindt-Bayer and William Mishler, "An Integrated Model of Women's Representation," *Journal of Politics* 67, no. 2 (2005): 407–28.
2 Amanda Clayton, Diana Z. O'Brien, and Jennifer M. Piscopo, "All Male Panels? Representation and Democratic Legitimacy," *American Journal of Political Science* 63, no. 1 (2019): 113–29.

3 Melanie M. Hughes, "The Intersection of Gender and Minority Status in National Leg-islatures: The Minority Women Legislative Index," *Legislative Studies Quarterly* 38, no. 4 (2013): 489–516.

4 Hughes, "The Intersection of Gender."

5 David Samuels and Richard Snyder, "The Value of a Vote: Malapportionment in Com-parative Perspective," *British Journal of Political Science* 31, no. 4 (2001): 651–71.

6 Andrew Reynolds, "Electoral Systems and the Protection and Participation of Minorities," Minority Rights Group International, 2006, https://minorityrights.org/wp-content/uploads/old-site-downloads/download-161-Electoral-systems-and-the-protection-and-participation-of-minorities.pdf.

7 Mala Htun, "Is Gender Like Ethnicity? The Political Representation of Identity Groups," *Perspectives on Politics* 2, no. 3 (2004): 439–58.

8 Anne Phillips, "Democracy and Representation: Or, Why Should It Matter Who Our Representatives Are?," in *Feminism and Politics*, ed. Anne Phillips, 224–40 (1998), 232.

9 UNHCR, *Born Free and Equal: Sexual Orientation and Gender Identity in International Hu-man Rights Law* (Geneva: United Nations Office of the High Commissioner for Human Rights, 2012), 45.

10 Karen Bird, "Intersections of Exclusion: The Institutional Dynamics of Combined Gen-der and Ethnic Quota Systems," *Politics, Groups, and Identities* 4, no. 2 (2016): 284–306; Melanie M. Hughes, "The Combination of Gender and Ethnic Quotas in Politics," in *Gender Parity and Multicultural Feminism: Towards a New Synthesis*, eds. Ruth Rubio-Marín and Will Kymlicka (New York: Oxford University Press, 2018).

11 Reynolds, "Electoral Systems."

12 New Zealand Royal Commission on the Electoral System, *Report of the Royal Commis-sion on the Electoral System: Towards a Better Democracy* (1986).

13 Jonathan Boston, Stephen Levine, Elizabeth McLeay, and Nigel S. Roberts, "Why Did New Zealand Adopt German-Style Proportional Representation?," *Representation* 33, no. 4 (1996): 134–40.

14 Fiona Barker and Hilde Coffé, "Representing Diversity in Mixed Electoral Systems: The Case of New Zealand," *Parliamentary Affairs* 71, no. 3 (2017): 603–32.

15 Barker and Coffé, "Representing Diversity," 618.

16 Reynolds, "Electoral Systems," 14.

17 Melanie M. Hughes, "Electoral Systems and the Legislative Representation of Muslim Ethnic Minority Women in the West, 2000–2010," *Parliamentary Affairs* 69, no. 3 (2016): 548–68.

18 Liza M. Mügge, Daphne J. van der Pas, and Marc van de Wardt, "Representing Their Own? Ethnic Minority Women in the Dutch Parliament," *West European Politics* 42, no. 4 (2019): 705–27.

19 Ayisha Osori, *Love Does Not Win Elections* (Lagos: Narrative Landscape Press, 2017).

20 Elizabeth Evans and Stefanie Reher, "Disability and Political Representation: Ana-lysing the Obstacles to Elected Office," *International Political Science Review* (2020), https://journals.sagepub.com/doi/full/10.1177/0192512120947458.

21 Hughes, "The Combination of Gender and Ethnic Quotas in Politics."

22 Karen Bird, "Ethnic Quotas and Ethnic Representation Worldwide," *International Politi-cal Science Review* 35, no. 1 (2014): 12–26.

23 Hughes, "The Combination of Gender and Ethnic Quotas in Politics."

24 Htun, "Is Gender Like Ethnicity?"

25 Hughes, "The Combination of Gender and Ethnic Quotas in Politics," 107.

26 Bird, "Intersections of Exclusion."

27 Chang-Ling Huang, "Falling through the Cracks? Indigenous Women's Political Participation in Taiwan," APSA 2012 Annual Meeting Paper (2012).

28 Hughes, "The Combination of Gender and Ethnic Quotas in Politics."

29 Stéphanie Rousseau and Christina Ewig, "Latin America's Left-Turn and the Political Empowerment of Indigenous Women," *Social Politics: International Studies in Gender, State & Society* 24, no. 4 (2017): 439.

30 Netina Tan, "Ethnic Quotas and Unintended Effects on Women's Political Representation in Singapore," *International Political Science Review* 35, no. 1 (2014): 27–40.

31 Inter-Parliamentary Union, "Global and Regional Averages of Women in National Parliaments," 2020, https://data.ipu.org/women-averages.

32 Melanie M. Hughes, Pamela Paxton, Amanda B. Clayton, and Pär Zetterberg, "Global Gender Quota Adoption, Implementation, and Reform," *Comparative Politics* 51, no. 2 (2019): 219–38; Jennifer M. Piscopo, "States as Gender Equality Activists: The Evolution of Quota Laws in Latin America," *Latin American Politics and Society* 57, no. 3 (2015): 27–49.

33 Jennifer M. Piscopo, "When Informality Advantages Women: Quota Networks, Electoral Rules and Candidate Selection in Mexico," *Government and Opposition* 51, no. 3 (2016): 487–512.

34 For an overview, see Diana Z. O'Brien and Jennifer M. Piscopo, "The Impact of Women in Parliament," in *The Palgrave Handbook of Women's Political Rights*, eds. Susan Franceschet, Mona Lena Krook, and Netina Tan, 53–72 (Basingstoke, UK: Palgrave Macmillan, 2019).

35 Timothy Besley, Olle Folke, Torsten Persson, and Johanna Rickne, "Gender Quotas and the Crisis of the Mediocre Man: Theory and Evidence from Sweden," *American Economic Review* 107, no. 8 (2017): 2204–42.

36 Phillip Ayoub, *When States Come Out* (Cambridge: Cambridge University Press, 2016).

37 Reynolds, "Electoral Systems."

38 For an overview, see O'Brien and Piscopo, "The Impact of Women in Parliament."

39 Claudine Gay, "Spirals of Trust? The Effect of Descriptive Representation on the Relationship between Citizens and Their Government," *American Journal of Political Science* 46, no. 4 (2002): 717–32.

40 Matthew Hayes and Matthew V. Hibbing, "The Symbolic Benefits of Descriptive and Substantive Representation," *Political Behavior* 39, no. 1 (2017): 31–50.

41 Amy C. Alexander, "Change in Women's Descriptive Representation and the Belief in Women's Ability to Govern: A Virtuous Cycle," *Politics & Gender* 8, no. 4 (2012): 437–64.

42 Lori Beaman, Rohini Pande, and Alexandra Cirone, "Politics as a Male Domain and Empowerment in India," in *The Impact of Gender Quotas*, eds. Susan Franceschet, Mona Lena Krook, and Jennifer M. Piscopo (Oxford: Oxford University Press, 2012).

RESOURCES AND SUGGESTIONS FOR FURTHER READING

Bird, Karen. "Ethnic Quotas and Ethnic Representation Worldwide." *International Political Science Review* 35, no. 1 (2004): 12–26. https://doi.org/10.1177/0192512113507798.

Hughes, Melanie M. "The Combination of Gender and Ethnic Quotas in Politics." In *Gender Parity and Multicultural Feminism: Towards a New Synthesis*, edited by Ruth Rubio-Marín and Will Kymlicka, 97–118. New York: Oxford University Press, 2018.

Hughes, Melanie M., Pamela Paxton, Amanda B. Clayton, and Pär Zetterberg. "Global Gender Quota Adoption, Implementation, and Reform." *Comparative Politics* 51, no. 2 (2019): 219–38. https://doi.org/10.5129/001041519X15647434969795.

Piscopo, Jennifer M. "States as Gender Equality Activists: The Evolution of Quota Laws in Latin America." *Latin American Politics and Society* 57, no. 3 (2015): 27–49. https://doi .org/10.1111/j.1548-2456.2015.00278.x.

PART TWO

Comparative Politics

CHAPTER SEVEN

What Is Comparative Politics?

Dr. Silvia Erzeel   *Dr. Liza Mügge*

LEARNING OBJECTIVES

1   Define what comparative politics is and how the subfield distinguishes itself from other subfields in political science
2   Identify the major merits and pitfalls of comparative political research
3   Distinguish between different research subjects in comparative politics, and discuss both the meaning and relevance of political institutions, political culture, and inequality regimes in the study of comparative politics
4   Describe the comparative method of analysis, in particular the "most different" and "most similar" systems design, and illustrate this method using real-world examples

KEY TERMS

conceptual stretching   a conceptual problem that arises when a concept is applied to a broad set of cases; the meaning of the concept is "stretched" in an attempt to cover all cases, yet it loses meaning or becomes distorted in the process

conceptual traveling   a conceptual challenge faced by comparativists because concepts do not always have the same meaning in different contexts, yet concepts should be able to "travel" to different contexts without losing meaning

cross-sectional research   a research design used to compare different cases at one point in time

cross-temporal research   a research design used to compare one case over a longer period of time

decolonization   the political and economic processes of removing formal colonial governance by Global North countries of Global South countries (also called *decolonialization*); often also refers to transformation in the informal and formal knowledge and education systems so that the formal colonial governing power is not merely replaced with neocolonial exercise of economic power

explanatory unit   the major relevant entity used to explain patterns of results

falsification   the scientific process during which existing theories are tested and revised in light of new empirical evidence

historically marginalized groups   groups whose interests, grievances, and voices risk being overlooked in politics as a result of historical and structural processes of marginalization

inequality regimes   a broad set of political practices, processes, actions, and meanings that (re)produce power hierarchies and social inequalities in relation to social class, gender, race, ethnicity, age, and so on

inference   the process of generalizing characteristics from a set of cases to the entire population (*causal* inference means drawing conclusions on the causal link between characteristics)

observational unit   the major relevant entity used in data collection and analysis

political culture   sets of beliefs and values people have about politics that are related to how they think about politics, the political values they cherish, whether they believe politicians can be trusted, how they relate to the political system, and how they define and express their political identities

unit of analysis   the major relevant entity under study

WHAT IS COMPARATIVE POLITICS?

How does presidential power vary across Latin American countries? Why do Scandinavian countries have strong welfare states? Why do we witness democratic backsliding in some countries? Why are younger women more "left" oriented than older men? Which policies are most successful in tackling climate change? What are the causes of international terrorism?

If you want to answer any of these questions (and many more), comparative politics is the right approach for you. Indeed, comparative politics, as one of the major subfields of political science, engages with everyday real-world questions and offers an impressive set of conceptual and analytical tools to tackle them. In its early days, comparative politics was defined as "the study of politics in *foreign* countries."[1] Hence, doing comparative politics implied that scholars studied politics in countries other than their own. Many comparative political scientists, however, would find that this perspective insufficiently captures what comparative politics is about today. The field of comparative politics has grown increasingly diverse and is nowadays characterized by high levels of theoretical and methodological variation.

This chapter offers an introduction into the field of comparative politics. It starts by describing the contours of this particular subfield: What does it mean to study political science in a "comparative" fashion? What is the distinctive nature of comparative politics? Next, we will discuss why it is useful to study comparative politics: What are the promises of the subfield, and what are some of its shortcomings? This is followed by a broad discussion of "what" to compare in political science: What are the research subjects in comparative politics? Finally, we pay attention to the question of "how" to compare. We describe the most important comparative methods of analysis and suggest ways to understand and evaluate similarities and differences between political phenomena.

DEFINING COMPARATIVE POLITICS

The subfield of comparative politics has grown increasingly diverse over the years, which turns the seemingly easy task of defining the subfield into a rather complicated one. Indeed, there is considerable disagreement among scholars about what comparative politics is or should be. However, using a lowest common denominator, comparative politics can be defined as both a *research subject* and a *method of analysis*.[2]

As a research subject, comparativists concentrate on studying and comparing political phenomena that occur within the broader context of the state.[3] In that sense, comparative politics as a field of study sets itself apart from another major subfield in political science, namely international relations. While international relations scholars study interactions (of cooperation and conflict) *between* states, comparative politics concentrates on studying political phenomena that take place *within* the context of the state.[4] The types of political phenomena (or the "research subjects") studied by comparative political scientists vary greatly nonetheless. Comparativists study phenomena that differ as widely as the opinions and behavior of political actors (e.g., citizens, political elites, social movements, and interest groups), the development of public policies (e.g., climate policy, constitutional change, foreign policy), the functioning of political institutions (e.g., parliaments, executives, and courts), the actions of non-state organizations (e.g., non-governmental organizations, terrorist organizations, the church), and many more. The current field of comparative politics is characterized by its "substantive inclusiveness" and its relative openness to a broad range of research questions, approaches, and methods.[5]

While comparative politics is different from international relations, it would be inaccurate to claim that comparative politics does not or cannot have an international dimension. Comparativists regularly compare political phenomena cross-nationally, which makes comparative politics almost intrinsically international (as in comparing countries across the globe). Comparativists will also investigate how transnational processes like globalization or the spread of international terrorism affect the decisions and policies developed by actors and institutions within states. Especially in relation to these latter examples, the line between comparative politics and international relations is not a hard-dividing line, but rather takes the form of a Venn diagram with overlapping circles.

Comparative politics is not only a research subject but also a method for the study of similarities and differences between political systems. This means that comparative politics is essentially an *empirical* field of study. Its goal is to observe, study, and draw conclusions on the occurrence, features, nature, causes, and consequences of observable phenomena, thereby using political science tools and methods of analysis. By maintaining this empirical outlook, comparative politics sets itself apart from a third major subfield in political science: political theory.[6]

As you learned earlier, political theorists pose mostly normative questions when studying the political world. Normative questions are questions about values, about what is "fair," "good," or "just" in the world. For example, is democracy the best form of government? Is it fair to deny voting rights to children and adolescents? Who deserves to pursue the "good life"? Hence, normative political scientists are not so much concerned with what actually is observed but with what should or ought to be. Comparative political scientists, in contrast, mostly answer empirical questions. Rather than studying whether it is fair to give voting rights to adolescents, comparativists study why voting rights for 16-year-olds have been adopted in Argentina, Brazil, and Ecuador. Which conditions led to their adoption? Why did other South American countries like Chile, Paraguay, or Uruguay not adopt a similar change? And what are the consequences if these countries *were* to lower their voting age?

As a method of analysis, comparative politics relies on the systematic description, explanation, and prediction of similarities and differences between political phenomena.[7] At the most fundamental level, detailed and systematic description improves our understanding of the phenomena under study and our capacity to interpret them. It allows us to know and understand what these phenomena are like. In order to offer descriptions, comparativists need to develop a good understanding of the contextual specificities of the different cases under study and identify elements that make them, in fact, comparable. For some comparative scholars, description is the main or even the end goal of comparative research.[8] They argue that the contextual and historical specificities of each case make it nearly impossible to make well-founded **inferences** (Box 7.1).

BOX 7.1: INFERENCES VERSUS DESCRIPTION

Making an inference is "using facts we know to learn something about facts we do not know."[9] This implies generalizations based on the characteristics from a set of cases to the entire population (e.g., looking at a set of protest movements to determine under what circumstances protests movements are likely to occur). Description involves "evidence without inference": the description of a particular event (say, the 2019–20 Hong Kong protests) without making any larger claims about the occurrence of protest movements in the world.[10]

For other comparativists, however, description is only the first of many stages. Some will furthermore attempt to explain the occurrence of political phenomena by identifying a causal link with other phenomena. The aim is to test whether one political phenomenon leads to or is causally related to another. For instance, if scholars want to explain why we witness democratic backsliding in some countries (see Chapters 1 and 3 in this volume), they might investigate how other related phenomena affect the quality of democracy. Factors that potentially matter because they affect the quality of democracy are increasing corruption, declining government performance, centralization of executive power, rise of ethnic conflicts, or decreasing socioeconomic performance. To understand the relationship between two phenomena, comparativists will need to *operationalize* the phenomena in the form of dependent (outcome) and independent (explanatory) variables and formulate hypotheses on the link between the two that can be empirically tested.

If the link between two variables is solid, it can furthermore allow comparativists to make some predictions on the future occurrence of a particular phenomenon. A comparative study of democratic backsliding in a well-defined set of cases allows comparativists to identify a list of factors that either improve or decrease the quality of democracy. Such a comparison could in turn help to predict (future) occurrences in other cases. Casting predictions in political science, however, is never easy. Comparative politics is not an exact science, and predictions about political phenomena can never be made with absolute certainty.

So far, we have tried to delineate the disciplinary boundaries of comparative politics. At this point, it is worth mentioning that not all comparativists agree that comparative politics *should* be treated as a separate subfield within the broader field of political science. Indeed, some comparativists argue that comparative politics is not markedly different from other subfields or from political science in general (some would argue that *all* political science is comparative). Yet, we argue in this chapter that, for the sake of analytical clarity, it is important to at least try to distinguish among major lines of thought and analysis that exist in the increasingly diverse field of political science. *If* we accept that comparative politics is a distinct subfield in political science, its distinctiveness lies in both its research subject and its method of analysis:

- As a research subject, comparative politics studies a wide variety of political phenomena that are detected mostly within states.
- As a method of analysis, comparative politics aims to describe, understand, explain, and predict differences and similarities between political phenomena across political systems.

WHY DO WE STUDY COMPARATIVE POLITICS?

Now that we've established what comparative politics is, another question arises: *Why* do we draw comparisons in political science? What is the use, and what do we learn from it?

Comparativists are eager to provide you with numerous reasons why comparing political phenomena is both useful and instructive. One obvious, yet important, reason is that it helps us to gain a deeper knowledge and better understanding of political systems and processes in a variety of countries. This is often necessary because political scientists study phenomena that in many cases are not confined to the borders of one's own country. If scholars want to understand the rise of populism, chances are that a focus on one country will not allow them to capture the full story. It is by systematically comparing the rise and spread of populism in multiple countries that scholars get a clearer understanding of the conditions leading to populist support and activism. According to Charles Ragin and Lisa Amoroso, the main advantage of comparative politics is that it actually allows scholars to explore and understand diversity in the broader social and political world.[11] By gaining a better understanding of politics in various countries, scholars are able to see alternative ways to handle specific research topics and solve particular questions.[12]

Comparative politics also enhances scholars' understanding of their own political system. Political scientists studying political processes in their own country might find it useful to compare their findings to those in other countries. They might explicitly choose to compare their own country to another country that is, in terms of institutional design or macro-social context, very similar to their own; or they might decide to compare to countries that are, politically speaking, very different (later in this chapter we will discuss *most similar systems design* versus *most different systems design* in more detail). In both cases, comparing with other countries allows comparativists to draw meaningful conclusions on how to analyze and assess political processes in their own country.

Relatedly, an additional purpose of comparison is that scholars avoid an "ethnocentric bias" in their research.[13] As a discipline that first developed in the United States and Europe, political science has been largely influenced by Western ideals and schools of thought. Political systems in the Western world functioned as standards by which other cases were judged, causing problems of both explicit exclusion and implicit bias. Recent calls to "decolonize political science" (Box 7.2) in various parts of the world have drawn specific attention to this partiality in political science. Although engaging in comparative politics might not be an airtight solution to prevent problems of bias in political science, it can be argued that it does help scholars detect potential biases and ultimately help overcome them.

BOX 7.2: DECOLONIZING POLITICAL SCIENCE

To **decolonize** a subject means "to fundamentally transform knowledge production. It means that the unquestioned value systems that govern what knowledge is, how it is produced and who is allowed to be a knowing and knowledgeable agent must be radically reshaped."[14] Decolonization campaigns criticize knowledge production in political science, in particular the fact that contemporary political science is based on Western values, rendering non-Western academic voices and societal perspectives invisible.[15] They criticize the absence of (female) scholars of color in university classrooms and course curricula, with the aim of increasing the number of scholars of color in higher education and incorporating non-Western knowledge. While national and international political science associations are increasingly monitoring the persistent gender gap among professors in the discipline, data on race is scarce.[16] North American political scientists consistently find that moving up the career ladder is extremely hard for scholars of color and Indigenous scholars.[17] Racialized women may face extra barriers. For instance, there were only 25 Black women employed as full professors across all disciplines in the United Kingdom in 2019.[18]

Comparative politics furthermore also helps to develop, test, and revise theories about how politics works. The development of science relies on a process of **falsification**, during which "old" theories and assumptions are tested and revised in light of new ideas and empirical evidence. Comparative politics contributes to this process: By adding new cases and by testing theories in previously overlooked systems, comparativists are able to falsify and revise existing theories and adjust them to new conditions.

A final argument is that comparison is part and parcel of political research. It is hard to practice empirical political analysis without engaging in some form of implicit or explicit comparative analysis. As written by Swanson, "Thinking without comparison is unthinkable. And in the absence of comparison, so is all scientific thought and scientific research."[19]

Like any other subfield, comparative politics also has its limitations. One important critique is that every country or political system is unique and that drawing comparisons is therefore always misleading and reductionist. Comparison always implies a process of making abstractions and generalizations of systems or phenomena under study, which some scholars would argue is downright impossible because the social world is irreducibly complex.

Another limitation is that comparativists deal with phenomena that are not easily "researchable." Contrary to scholars in the natural or exact sciences, political scientists often cannot control or manipulate political phenomena to study their effects. Every political scientist, comparativist or not, needs to work with the "messiness" that is everyday social life and human behavior.

Finally, comparativists will sometimes struggle to find empirical data when studying some of the phenomena in which they are interested.[20] In some countries, a wealth of data and indicators are systematically stored and available online; in other countries, scholars will be hard-pressed to find any comparable data at all. Comparativists always need to assess how this incompleteness of data might influence the eventual results of their study, and they typically need to build research strategies to work around this limitation.

MAIN FOCI IN COMPARATIVE POLITICS

In the previous sections, we have defined comparative politics in a broad and inclusive manner, and we have argued that many political phenomena are and can be studied in comparative politics. But what makes the subfield of comparative politics intrinsically "comparative"? To what does the subfield owe its comparative name and focus?

To answer that question, we need to consider the unit of analysis in comparative politics. Generally speaking, a **unit of analysis** is the major relevant entity that is analyzed in a particular study. According to Charles Ragin, comparativists usually work with two different types of units of analysis: an **observational unit** and an **explanatory unit**. Whereas the observational unit refers to "the unit used in data collection and data analysis," the explanatory unit relates to "the unit that is used to account for the pattern of results obtained."[21] Imagine that a comparativist wants to explain differences in the electoral success of Green parties in two countries. In order to do so, they will collect and analyze data on Green parties' electoral scores; hence, the observational unit is the political party. However, to explain such differences in electoral scores, the researcher could focus on how different electoral systems shape the electoral success of Green parties. The explanatory unit of analysis becomes the country – or better, the electoral system.

The types of observational units used in comparative politics are quite diverse. In fact, *almost any type of observational unit thinkable* can be compared in comparative politics, including data on individuals, social groups, social interactions, political organizations, sociopolitical processes, political interests, political discourses, public policies, and so on. The choice of observational unit will depend on the research question and what the researcher defines as the "major relevant" entity. In a study of age differences in political participation, a researcher can define individual voters as the main observational unit if they see political participation as an individual act. If researchers consider participating in politics as an act that is shaped by group processes, they will likely consider social groups as observational units and consequently compare the group of younger citizens to the group of older citizens. If scholars see political participation not only as a group process but also as a process that is shaped by intra-group inequalities, they might locate the observational unit at the within-group level. In that case, they might decide to compare older men and older women to younger men and younger women.

Contrary to the observational unit, the scope of the explanatory unit is more narrowly defined. According to Ragin, what ultimately separates comparativists from non-comparativists is the former's focus on *macro-social units* as key explanatory units of analysis.[22] Macro-social units are located at the systemic (rather than individual) level of analysis and include political entities (countries, subnational regions, world regions), economic structures, social processes and value systems. What makes comparative politics "comparative" is that scholars compare two or more macro-social units to describe, understand, explain, or predict patterns in a variety of observational units.

Let's take a closer look at three types of macro-social explanatory units that are quite common in comparative political research. We label them (1) political institutions, (2) political culture, and (3) inequality regimes and briefly consider each below.

Political Institutions

Political institutions can be defined as sets of rules that make up the political game (Box 7.3). Comparativists analyze both the rules themselves and the many ways in which rules shape the political behavior of individual actors (ordinary citizens, political leaders) and collective actors (political parties, social movements, social groups). Institutions operate as both sticks and carrots: They reward certain types of behavior and sanction others. A good example is found in studies of legislators' voting records, which show that legislators in parliamentary democracies often remain "loyal" to the programs and policies of their party leaders when casting a vote (see Chapter 8 for a discussion of parliamentary and presidential systems). This is the result of the informal rule of party discipline. In parliamentary democracies, legislators who stick closely to the party line are rewarded by their party leaders and given opportunities to climb up the party hierarchy (reward); those who do not get punished by not receiving a winnable seat at the next election (sanction). This rule is not enshrined in any written document, but it is shared among and understood by the actors involved.

BOX 7.3: POLITICAL INSTITUTIONS

Political institutions are sets of rules that "structure social interaction by constraining and enabling actors' behavior."[23] Institutions can be either formal or informal. Formal institutions are the formal or written rules of the political game that are enshrined in written documents like constitutions, laws, party statutes, and so on. Informal institutions are unwritten rules that are nevertheless socially shared.[24] They can be seen as "the hidden life" of institutions: They are difficult to perceive and are often taken for granted by actors operating under them. For instance, a study on ethnic minority candidates in Belgium and the Netherlands finds that ethnic minority women have an advantage over ethnic minority men. Gender quotas – the formal institution – appear to play a lesser role than strategies of party leadership – the informal institution. Parties aim to diversify for electoral gains. By placing an ethnic minority woman in a winnable position, they kill two birds with one stone.[25]

Rules, however, are followed not only because they lead to rewards or sanctions, but also because they are seen as "natural," "rightful," or "legitimate."[26] As such, institutions produce a "logic of appropriateness": They convey messages on what constitutes acceptable behavior and offer spoken or unspoken guidelines to individuals about how they ought to behave.[27] If we use the example of party discipline once more, we could say that legislators follow their party line not because they expect rewards or sanctions but because they believe the rule is "rightful" and do not think it is appropriate to dissent.

Institutions do not shape the behavior of various actors in *similar* ways. The experiences of actors in institutions vary substantially based on, among other things, their seniority, age, gender, race, ethnicity, social class, or the interaction of two or more of these features – as the example in Box 7.3 illustrates.[28] The logic of appropriateness is also *not bias free*. Rules and norms surrounding the executive office, for instance, tend to reflect the values of the previous officeholders. If executive officeholders traditionally are white, male, and middle-aged, chances are that both the institution of the executive and the outcomes produced by it will reflect the interests of those groups (see Chapter 8). Due to this tendency toward a preservation of the status quo, institutions are sometimes said to be resilient to change. However, institutions are not made of stone and can change.[29] External shocks, like political crises, can change what counts as "acceptable" behavior. Actors within institutions can also change those institutions. Comparative studies around the world have shown that the influx of larger amounts of women and ethnic minorities in political office have changed how legislatures and executives operate and the types of outcomes they produce (see Chapters 8 and 9).

Political Culture

Politics is not only organized based on institutions and rules. It is also shaped by how people think about politics, the values they cherish, and their beliefs about fundamental questions like whether they think politicians can be trusted, how they relate as citizens to the political system, and how they define and express their multiple political identities. The concept of **political culture** is often used to refer to this broad set of beliefs and values people have about politics.[30] Although beliefs and values are often expressed by individuals, they are also macro-social phenomena in the sense that we see commonalities in the otherwise unique ways in which individuals operating in one specific context or belonging to one sociopolitical group think and act politically.

Since the 1960s, comparative political scientists have invested considerable time and effort in "tracking" differences and changes in political culture across the globe. These attempts have been supported by (and are manifested in) the development of large-N surveys such as the World Values Survey,[31] the European Values Study,[32] and the European Social Survey,[33] which have documented the (long-term) political beliefs and orientations of citizens in a number of countries in different parts of the world.

One of the best documented trends in recent scholarship on political culture has been the rise and spread of "emancipative" or "self-expression" values. In his work *The Silent Revolution*, Ronald Inglehart describes how the transition from industrial to post-industrial societies has brought about a shift in the cultural values of people.[34] Material values and concerns among the population (like social order, authority, and traditional family values) have gradually and silently been replaced by post-material values emphasizing personal freedom, self-expression, quality of life, community participation, women's emancipation, and racial equality.

Such changes in political culture have also transformed notions of citizenship and patterns of political engagement. Citizens have become increasingly "critical" or "assertive" in their stance toward democratic politics.[35] In countries where emancipative values are high, people generally demonstrate lower levels of confidence in political institutions like parliaments and political parties, and are more distrustful of traditional authority like the police force and the military.[36] They are furthermore more likely to engage in new and elite-challenging forms of political behavior, including direct action, protest politics, and grassroots movements. A central question in recent years has been whether the existence of emancipative values renders citizens less supportive of (liberal) democracy. Research is still ongoing and inconclusive. Some studies present hopeful signs that despite the fact that citizens in established democracies are increasingly critical in their assessment of the functioning of democracy in practice, they do not become less supportive of the basic principles of liberal democracy.[37] Other studies are less optimistic and present evidence of a widespread democratic disconnect, especially among younger citizens.[38]

Inequality Regimes

A third type of macro-social explanation are **inequality regimes**, which refer to a broad set of "loosely interrelated practices, processes, actions, and meanings that result in and maintain class, gender, and racial inequalities within particular organizations."[39] Inequality regimes come in many forms, but what they have in common is that they create thresholds for **historically marginalized groups** (Box 7.4) such as women; blue-collar workers; ethnic, racial, and religious minorities; lower-educated people; and so on in politics.

BOX 7.4: HISTORICALLY MARGINALIZED GROUPS

Historically marginalized groups are groups whose interests and concerns risk being overlooked in politics as a result of historical and structural processes of marginalization.[40] Historically marginalized groups had no voting rights in the past. For instance, in many countries around the world women only received voting rights sometime in the last 100 years. In Canada, it was not until the 1960s that voting rights were granted to Registered Indians, while there were reserved seats for Maori men in New Zealand since 1867.[41]

Some of these barriers present themselves in a tangible and visible manner. In a variety of countries, migrants face legal barriers in politics in their country of residence because voting rights are only granted to nationals of that country. Because participation in political life requires that citizens have material resources such as money and time, political opportunities are more limited for people facing financial insecurity or precariousness.

But thresholds can just as easily work in less visible or less observable ways. Inequalities that exist in the private sphere (e.g., the fact that women more often than men combine paid work with larger care responsibilities) go more unnoticed, but they can (and do) prevent women from moving into a political career. Moreover, a variety of studies show that subtle and less subtle processes of marginalization, including stereotyping and silencing, keep some groups from expressing their views in politics and having their voices heard in the political process (see Box 7.5). In some cases, thresholds also come in the form of physical or verbal violence against members of particular social groups.[42]

BOX 7.5: MARGINALIZATION THROUGH "RACED–GENDERED" PRACTICES

Intersectionality scholars have been among the first to document the pervasive practices of "racing–gendering" that have hindered women of color's access to and positional power in politics.[43] In a study of Congresswomen of color reports in the 103rd and 104th US Congress, Mary Hawkesworth describes the ongoing racing–gendering in Congress as processes through which organizational practices and "standard operating procedures" created and reproduced gender and race inequalities.[44] Congresswomen of color in particular encountered both racial and gender discrimination. They were silenced and stereotyped during floor debates, and they were treated as "others" and as less than equals in interpersonal interactions. Their legislative achievements were made invisible, and they were frequently challenged in their authority as Congresswomen. These practices worked against the legislative success of Congresswomen of color and the opportunities they had to represent the substantive interests of their constituent groups.

As the above examples make clear, inequality regimes are largely shaped by power hierarchies and inequalities, which can take at least three different forms or "faces."[45] The first face – power as decision making – is related to people's ability to make political decisions. Power inequalities arise when some groups are systematically excluded from influencing political decisions and are underrepresented among those calling the shots. The numerical underrepresentation of women, ethnic minorities, and lower-educated groups in many elected assemblies and executives worldwide is an example of the first face of power inequalities. The second face entails agenda-setting power, which occurs when actors are able to prevent political decisions from being made at all by controlling the political agenda and by deciding which issues are being discussed and which are kept off the table. The example in Box 7.5 offers a good illustration of how power as agenda setting operates to keep the voices and interests of women of color from being considered in the democratic process. A third face is even more subtle and sees power as thought control. Sometimes power becomes so elusive that it is exerted through the influence and control over the thoughts, minds, and beliefs of others. Power takes the form of "hegemonic power," which legitimizes inequalities (either purposely or not) and keeps them in place through mechanisms of control and compliance.[46]

At this point it is important to mention that inequality regimes, and the processes of power and exclusion that are associated with them, often work in an intersectional manner.[47] The experiences of Congresswomen of color in Box 7.5 again illustrate this: Their exclusion does not arise from either racial or gender discrimination, but from a complex combination of both.

Inequality regimes can be challenged and changed, but attempts to do so are often met with resistance. Especially where change has been sudden or drastic, this also has triggered new power struggles, sometimes increasing opposition to further attempts to change the status quo.[48]

COMPARATIVE METHODS OF ANALYSIS

Diversification in the research subjects of comparative politics also goes hand in hand with methodological diversity.[49] Indeed, many comparativists would argue that there is no single way to do comparative research. Whereas some studies compare a few cases (2 to 5; *small-N* analysis), others use tens (*intermediate-N*) or even hundreds or thousands of cases (*large-N*). Different research designs and strategies are moreover possible and workable. Some scholars compare different cases at one point in time (i.e., **cross-sectional research**). Other studies compare one case over a longer period of time (i.e., *longitudinal* or **cross-temporal research**).

Even though comparative research can take many different forms, researchers do not generally draw comparisons out of thin air. Every comparison is guided by some general principles that allow the researcher to draw reliable and valid conclusions. First, any choice of comparison is primarily informed by the research question that needs to be answered. It is the research question that guides the selection of comparable cases, methods, and strategies, not the other way around.

Second, the comparison of cases should allow you to conclude something meaningful about the occurrence of a particular political outcome. In order to draw such meaningful conclusions, we can use two well-known strategies of comparative research: the *most similar systems design* and the *most different systems design*.[50] Both provide guidelines on how to select cases for comparative research and allow scholars to assess whether a specific set of (macro-social) factors affects a particular political outcome.

The most similar systems design (MSSD) is based on the principle that the researcher selects two or more political systems (or cases) which share a lot of similarities but also exhibit a few important differences. Scholars will typically opt for such a design if they want to explain why two similar systems in the end produce different political outcomes. In an MSSD, the (many) similarities that exist between the two systems can be eliminated as potential explanations for the differences in outcome. After all, these similarities are "held constant" in both systems and can therefore not account for any differences in outcome. Instead, a focus on the (few) features that *are* different in both systems help scholars shed light on why differences in outcome might exist.

To clarify, consider the comparison of the United States and Australia in Table 7.1. The question is why Australia presents much higher voter turnout rates compared to the United States. The difference in voter turnout is remarkable, because both countries exhibit many similarities on many variables that are known to influence voter turnout: the electoral system that is in play (both are majoritarian systems), the presence of bicameralism, and the socioeconomic development of the country (comparable levels of GDP per capita and similarities in size).[51] Yet both countries exhibit one crucial difference: Australia has a system of compulsory voting and the United States does not. This difference in compulsory voting can account for the different outcomes in voter turnout.

The most different systems design (MDSD) applies a reverse logic. In an MDSD, two systems with considerable systemic differences and few similarities

Table 7.1. Most Similar Systems Design in the United States and Australia

	Case 1: United States	Case 2: Australia	Similar or different
Outcome:			
• Voter turnout 2016	65.4%	91.0%	Different
• Voter turnout 2013/14	42.5%	93.2%	Different
Major differences:			
• Compulsory voting	No	Yes	Different
Systemic similarities:			
• Electoral system	Majoritarian	Majoritarian	Similar
• Uni/bicameralism	Bicameral	Bicameral	Similar
• GDP per capita	> 50.000 USD	> 50.000 USD	Similar
• Size of country	Large	Large	Similar

Sources: André Blais, "What Affects Voter Turnout?," *Annual Review of Political Science* 9 (2006): 111–25; André Blais, Louis Massicotte, and Agnieszka Dobrzynska, *Why Is Turnout Higher in Some Countries Than in Others?* (Ottawa, ON: Environment Canada, 2003); IDEA, "International IDEA Annual Report 2013: A Record of Actions" (2014); IDEA, "International IDEA Annual Results Report 2014" (2015); IDEA, "International IDEA Annual Results Report 2016" (2017); World Bank Group, *World Development Report 2019: The Changing Nature of Work* (Washington, DC: World Bank, 2019).

are compared, with the goal to explain similarities in political outcome. The idea is that under these circumstances, the similarities between otherwise dissimilar systems should be able to account for similarities in political outcomes. Hence, it might help the researcher to show that the causal relationship between a particular condition and outcome variable holds in a variety of settings. In order to illustrate this design, we compare Australia to Luxembourg in Table 7.2. Both countries present similar and high levels of voter turnout (close to 90 per cent in both cases). Yet both countries are very different systems overall. Luxembourg has adopted a proportional representation electoral system and unicameralism. It is a relatively small country but with a very high GDP per capita. Australia, on the other hand, has a majoritarian electoral system and bicameralism. It is a large country with a GDP per capita that is lower than in Luxembourg. Because these differences in systems cannot explain similarities in the outcome variable, they can be eliminated as possible causes for voter turnout. One systemic similarity, on the other hand, might account for similarities in voter turnout – compulsory voting.

In the examples in Tables 7.1 and 7.2, two countries are compared. However, the "systems" compared in an MSSD or MDSD do not have to be situated at the country level. Consider the example of an MSSD in Table 7.3, where the voting turnout of two groups of women are compared based on Bernadette Hayes's study of voter turnout in post-conflict Northern Ireland.[52] From 1998 onward, voter turnout for different elections has been significantly lower for Protestant women than for

Table 7.2. **Most Different Systems Design in Australia and Luxembourg**

	Case 1: Australia	Case 2: Luxembourg	Similar or different
Outcome:			
• Voter turnout 2016/18	91.0%	89.7%	Similar
• Voter turnout 2013	93.2%	91.2%	Similar
Major similarities:			
• Compulsory voting	Yes	Yes	Similar
Systemic differences:			
• Electoral system	Majoritarian	PR	Different
• Uni/bicameralism	Bicameral	Unicameral	Different
• GDP per capita	> 50.000 USD	> 100.000 USD	Different
• Size of country	Large	Small	Different

Sources: André Blais, "What Affects Voter Turnout?," *Annual Review of Political Science* 9 (2006): 111–25; André Blais, Louis Massicotte, and Agnieszka Dobrzynska, *Why Is Turnout Higher in Some Countries Than in Others?* (Ottawa, ON: Environment Canada, 2003); IDEA, "International IDEA Annual Report 2013: A Record of Actions" (2014); IDEA, "International IDEA Annual Results Report 2014" (2015); IDEA, "International IDEA Annual Results Report 2016" (2017); World Bank Group, *World Development Report 2019: The Changing Nature of Work* (Washington, DC: World Bank, 2019).

Catholic women. In 2015, 55 per cent of Protestant women voted in the Westminster elections, compared to 70 per cent of Catholic women. Because the study takes place in one country, many institutional factors are held constant (after all, both groups of women operate in the same electoral, political, and socioeconomic context in Northern Ireland). Hence, differences can only be explained by looking at differences in political culture. When comparing the two religious groups of women, Hayes comes to the conclusion that two key factors – party engagement and trust in political leaders – were crucial in accounting for differences in turnout. Compared to Catholic women, Protestant women showed higher levels of antipathy against political parties and political leaders, which accounted for their lower turnout rates.

At this point, you might intuitively feel that comparing cases is never straightforward. Surely, several problems arise when scholars start comparing political systems in practice.

One problem is that most systems, even "most similar" ones, still differ in a thousand different ways. Most comparativists will therefore identify the need to conduct historically located and "situated" comparisons, which pay attention to the complex manners in which macro-political and historical processes interact, are informed by particular contexts, and play out differently in different contexts.[53] But even situating cases in their political, social, and historical context might in some instances prove insufficient to account for the unique sequence of events that are found in each case.

Table 7.3. **Most Similar Systems Design in Northern Ireland**

	Case 1: Catholic women	Case 2: Protestant women	Similar or different
Outcome:			
• Voter turnout 2015	70%	55%	Different
Major differences:			
• Party engagement	Rather high	Rather low	Different
• Trust in political leaders	Rather high	Rather low	Different
Systemic similarities:			
• Compulsory voting	No	No	Similar
• Political context	Post-conflict	Post-conflict	Similar
• Socioeconomic development	Similar	Similar	Similar

Source: Bernadette C. Hayes, "Religious Differences in Electoral Turnout among Women in Northern Ireland," *Parliamentary Affairs* 70, no. 2 (2016): 322–43.

A second issue relates to conceptual problems that might arise in comparative studies. Comparativists will often apply relatively abstract concepts (like "democracy," "welfare states," "social movements," "equality," etc.) to a wide variety of cases and systems. During that process, they risk encountering two specific problems: **conceptual traveling** and **conceptual stretching**.[54] Conceptual traveling refers to the idea that comparativists need to use concepts and analytical categories that can "travel" to different contexts without losing meaning. This is a potentially challenging task, as many of the vocabularies of political science have been developed in relation to a predefined set of cases and might not be equally relevant in other (un)related cases. Does *populism* have the same meaning in Latin America and North America? How do you use the term in a comparative study of populist leaders in both regions of the world? How to use the terms *left* and *right* in studies of the European Union, taking into account the different ideological legacies of Western and Eastern Europe? Conceptual traveling might lead to conceptual stretching, when the meaning of a particular concept becomes too vague or when it no longer provides a good "fit" with the cases under study.[55] For obvious reasons, this should be avoided.

SUMMARY

This chapter provided a short introduction into the field of comparative politics. The following points offer a summary of the major issues discussed above:

- Comparative politics can be defined as both a research subject and method of analysis. As a research subject, it studies a variety of political phenomena that are detected mostly within states. As a method of analysis, it aims to describe, understand, explain, and predict differences and similarities among political phenomena across political systems.

- Comparative politics has many merits: It encourages us to learn from other countries, it enhances our understanding of our own political system, it encourages us to look for ethnocentric biases in research, and it helps to falsify existing theories. However, comparative politics also has its limitations: Comparative data are not always available, and drawing comparisons can be difficult, reductionist, and messy.
- Comparativists usually work with two units of analysis: an observational unit and an explanatory unit. The observational units in comparative politics are quite diverse, but the explanatory units usually focus on the macro-social level of analysis.
- Three types of macro-social explanations are common in comparative politics: political institutions, political culture, and inequality regimes. Political institutions focus on the formal and informal rules that structure politics. Political culture relates to the sets of beliefs and values that influence people. Inequality regimes refer to practices, processes, actions, and meanings that (re)produce social inequalities in politics.
- Two well-known strategies in comparative research are the most similar systems design (MSSD) and the most different systems design (MDSD). An MSSD is used to explain differences in political outcomes between two otherwise similar systems. An MDSD is used to explain similarities in outcomes between two otherwise different systems.
- Remember, at the end of this book there is an appendix with ideas for how you can get involved and safeguard against democratic backsliding.

CONCLUDING QUESTIONS

1 What sets comparative politics apart from other subfields in political science?
2 Briefly explain the following concepts:
    a. Cross-sectional and cross-temporal analysis
    b. Historically marginalized groups
    c. Macro-social unit
3 What is *conceptual traveling*, and why is it often a problem in comparative politics?
4 Can you develop a comparative research question with a micro-level observational unit of analysis and a macro-level explanatory unit of analysis? Why or why not?

NOTES

1 Nikolaos Zahariadis, *Theory, Case, and Method in Comparative Politics* (Belmont, CA: Wadsworth, 1996), 2 [cited in Timothy C. Lim, *Doing Comparative Politics: An Introduction to Approaches and Issues* (Boulder, CO: Lynne Rienner Publishers, 2006), 4].

2 Daniele Caramani, *Comparative Politics* (Oxford: Oxford University Press, 2017); Lim, *Doing Comparative Politics*.

3 Caramani, *Comparative Politics*; Lim, *Doing Comparative Politics*.

4 Caramani, *Comparative Politics*; Lim, *Doing Comparative Politics*.

5 Karen Beckwith, "A Comparative Politics of Gender Symposium Introduction: Comparative Politics and the Logics of a Comparative Politics of Gender," *Perspectives on Politics* 8, no. 1 (2010): 161.

6 Caramani, *Comparative Politics*.

7 Caramani, *Comparative Politics*, 4; Lim, *Doing Comparative Politics*.

8 Leslie McCall, "The Complexity of Intersectionality," *Signs* 30, no. 3 (2005): 1771–1800.

9 Gary King et al., *Designing Social Inquiry* (Princeton, NJ: Princeton University Press, 1994), 119 [cited in Todd Landman, *Issues and Methods in Comparative Politics* (London: Routledge, 2003), 12].

10 Gabriel Almond, "Political Science: The History of the Discipline," in *The New Handbook of Political Science*, eds. Robert E. Goodin and Hans-Dieter Klingemann (Oxford: Oxford University Press, 1996), 52.

11 Charles C. Ragin and Lisa M. Amoroso, *Constructing Social Research: The Unity and Diversity of Method* (Thousand Oaks, CA: Pine Forge Press, 2019).

12 Ragin and Amoroso, *Constructing Social Research*, 39.

13 Lim, *Doing Comparative Politics*, 7.

14 Akwugo Emejulu, "Can Political Science Decolonise? A Response to Neema Begum and Rima Saini," *Political Studies Review* 17, no. 2 (2019): 204; see also Neema Begum and Rima Saini, "Decolonising the Curriculum," *Political Studies Review* 17, no. 2 (2019): 196–201.

15 Peace A. Medie and Alice J. Kang, "Power, Knowledge and the Politics of Gender in the Global South," *European Journal of Politics and Gender* 1, no. 1–2 (2018): 37–53.

16 Isabelle Engeli and Liza M. Mügge, "Patterns of Gender Inequality in European Political Science," in *Political Science in Europe: Achievements, Challenges, Prospects*, eds. Thibaud Boncourt, Isabelle Engeli, and Diego Garzia (London: Rowman & Littlefield ECPR Press, 2020), 179–98.

17 Yasmeen Abu-Laban, "Representing a Diverse Canada in Political Science: Power, Ideas and the Emergent Challenge of Reconciliation," *European Political Science* 15, no. 4 (2016): 493–507; Jessica Lavariega Monforti and Melissa R. Michelson, "Diagnosing the Leaky Pipeline: Continuing Barriers to the Retention of Latinas and Latinos in Political Science," *PS: Political Science and Politics* 41, no. 1 (2008): 161–6.

18 Nicola Rollock, *Staying Power: The Career Experiences and Strategies of UK Black Female Professors* (London: University and College Union, 2019).

19 Guy Swanson, "Frameworks for Comparative Research: Structural Anthropology and the Theory of Action," in *Comparative Methods in Sociology: Essays on Trends and Applications*, ed. Ivan Vallier, 141–202 (Berkeley: University of California Press, 1971), 145.

20 Kenneth Newton and Jan W. van Deth, *Foundations of Comparative Politics: Democracies of the Modern World* (Cambridge: Cambridge University Press, 2016).

21 Charles C. Ragin, *The Comparative Method: Moving Beyond Qualitative and Quantitative Strategies* (Berkeley: University of California Press, 1987), 8–9.

22 Ragin, *The Comparative Method*; Ragin and Amoroso, *Constructing Social Research*; Charles C. Ragin and Benoît Rihoux, "Qualitative Comparative Analysis (Qca): State of the Art and Prospects," *Qualitative Methods* 2, no. 2 (2004), 3.

23 Gretchen Helmke and Steven Levitsky, "Informal Institutions and Comparative Politics: A Research Agenda," *Perspectives on Politics* 2, no. 4 (2004): 725–40.

24 Helmke and Levitsky, "Informal Institutions"; Georgina Waylen, *Gender and Informal Institutions* (London: Rowman & Littlefield International, 2017).

25 Karen Celis, Silvia Erzeel, Liza Mügge, and Alyt Damstra, "Quotas and Intersectionality: Ethnicity and Gender in Candidate Selection," *International Political Science Review* 35, no. 1 (2014): 41–54.

26 James G. March and Johan P. Olsen, "The Logic of Appropriateness," in *The Oxford Handbook of Political Science*, ed. Robert E. Goodin (Oxford: Oxford University Press, 2011), 478.

27 Louise Chappell, "Comparing Political Institutions: Revealing the Gendered 'Logic of Appropriateness,'" *Politics & Gender* 2, no. 2 (2006): 223–35; March and Olsen, "The Logic of Appropriateness."

28 Ange-Marie Hancock, *Intersectionality: An Intellectual History* (Oxford: Oxford University Press, 2016); Kimberlé Crenshaw, "Mapping the Margins: Intersectionality, Identity Politics, and Violence against Women of Color," *Stanford Law Review* 43, no. 6 (1990): 1241–99.

29 Waylen, *Gender and Informal Institutions*; Meryl Kenny, *Gender and Political Recruitment: Theorizing Institutional Change* (New York: Springer, 2013).

30 Newton and van Deth, *Foundations of Comparative Politics*, 175.

31 World Values Survey, http://www.worldvaluessurvey.org/wvs.jsp.

32 European Values Study, https://europeanvaluesstudy.eu.

33 European Social Survey, https://www.europeansocialsurvey.org.

34 Ronald Inglehart, *The Silent Revolution: Changing Values and Political Styles among Western Publics* (Princeton, NJ: Princeton University Press, 1977).

35 Pippa Norris, *Critical Citizens: Global Support for Democratic Government* (Oxford: Oxford University Press, 1999); Russell J. Dalton and Christian Welzel, *The Civic Culture Transformed: From Allegiant to Assertive Citizens* (Cambridge: Cambridge University Press, 2014).

36 Russell J. Dalton and Martin P. Wattenberg, *Parties without Partisans: Political Change in Advanced Industrial Democracies* (Oxford: Oxford University Press, 2002).

37 Dalton and Welzel, *The Civic Culture Transformed*.

38 Roberto Stefan Foa and Yascha Mounk, "The Danger of Deconsolidation: The Democratic Disconnect," *Journal of Democracy* 27, no. 3 (2016): 5–17.

39 Joan Acker, "Inequality Regimes: Gender, Class, and Race in Organizations," *Gender & Society* 20, no. 4 (2006): 443.

40 Melissa S. Williams, *Voice, Trust, and Memory: Marginalized Groups and the Failings of Liberal Representation* (Princeton, NJ: Princeton University Press, 1998).

41 Jennifer E. Dalton, "Alienation and Nationalism: Is It Possible to Increase First Nations Voter Turnout in Ontario?," *Canadian Journal of Native Studies* 27, no. 2 (2007); Augie Fleras, "From Social Control Towards Political Self-Determination? Maori Seats and the Politics of Separate Maori Representation in New Zealand," *Canadian Journal of Political Science* 18, no. 3 (1985): 551–76.

42 Mona L. Krook, *Violence against Women in Politics* (Oxford: Oxford University Press, 2020).

43 For an overview, see Liza Mügge, Celeste Montoya, Akwugo Emejulu, and S. Laurel Weldon, "Intersectionality and the Politics of Knowledge Production," *European Journal of Politics and Gender* 1, no. 1–2 (2018): 17–36.

44 Mary Hawkesworth, "Congressional Enactments of Race–Gender: Toward a Theory of Raced–Gendered Institutions," *American Political Science Review* 97, no. 4 (2003): 529–50.

45 Steven Lukes, *Power, a Radical View* (Basingstoke, UK: Palgrave Macmillan, 2005).

46 Joan Acker, "From Glass Ceiling to Inequality Regimes," *Sociologie du travail* 51, no. 2 (2009): 211–12.

47 Rita Kaur Dhamoon, "Considerations on Mainstreaming Intersectionality," *Political Research Quarterly* 64, no. 1 (2011): 230–43; Hancock, *Intersectionality*.

48 Mieke Verloo, *Varieties of Opposition to Gender Equality in Europe* (London: Routledge, 2018).

49 Beckwith, "A Comparative Politics of Gender," 161.

50 Adam Przeworski and Henry Teune, *The Logic of Comparative Social Inquiry* (New York: Wiley-Interscience, 1970).

51 André Blais, "What Affects Voter Turnout?," *Annual Review of Political Science* 9 (2006): 111–25; André Blais, Louis Massicotte, and Agnieszka Dobrzynska, *Why Is Turnout Higher in Some Countries Than in Others?* (Ottawa: Environment Canada, 2003).

52 Bernadette C. Hayes, "Religious Differences in Electoral Turnout among Women in Northern Ireland," *Parliamentary Affairs* 70, no. 2 (2016): 322–43.

53 Dhamoon, "Considerations on Mainstreaming Intersectionality"; McCall, "The Complexity of Intersectionality."

54 Giovanni Sartori, "Concept Misformation in Comparative Politics," *American Political Science Review* 64, no. 4 (1970): 1033–53.

55 David Collier and James E. Mahon, "Conceptual 'Stretching' Revisited: Adapting Categories in Comparative Analysis," *American Political Science Review* 87, no. 4 (1993): 845–55.

RESOURCES AND SUGGESTIONS FOR FURTHER READING

Bassel, Leah, and Akwugo Emejulu. *Minority Women and Austerity: Survival and Resistance in France and Britain.* Bristol, UK: Policy Press, 2018.

Beckwith, Karen, ed. "A Comparative Politics of Gender Symposium," *Perspectives on Politics* 8, no. 1 (2010): 159–240.

Caramani, Daniele, ed. *Comparative Politics.* Oxford: Oxford University Press, 2017.

Givens, Terri E., and Rahsaan Maxwell, eds. *Immigrant Politics: Race and Representation in Western Europe.* Boulder, CO: Lynne Rienner, 2012.

Hinojosa, Magda. *Selecting Women, Electing Women: Political Representation and Candidate Selection in Latin America*. Philadelphia: Temple University Press, 2012.

Newton, Kenneth, and Jan W. van Deth. *Foundations of Comparative Politics*. Cambridge: Cambridge University Press, 2016.

Ragin, Charles, and Lisa M. Amoroso. *Constructing Social Research: The Unity and Diversity of Method*. London: Sage, 2019.

Wilkinson, Richard, and Kate Pickett. *The Spirit Level: Why Greater Equality Makes Societies Stronger*. New York: Bloomsbury Press, 2010.

CHAPTER EIGHT

Executives

Dr. Pedro A.G. dos Santos   *Dr. Farida Jalalzai*

LEARNING OBJECTIVES

1 Differentiate between and define common types of executive systems and executive positions worldwide
2 Understand the key components of parliamentary, presidential, and semi-presidential systems
3 Analyze differences in roles and powers available in executive positions and systems
4 Evaluate diversity among leading actors in executive positions and systems and why this matters
5 Understand the role of bureaucracies in the political process

KEY TERMS

bureaucracy   a subsidiary of the executive, tasked with implementing and executing the laws of the state
cabinet   the set of appointed officials (often referred to as secretaries or ministers) in a government who oversee specific policies such as healthcare, defense, and the like
coalition   a partnership between parties who agree to govern together because neither party has a majority on its own

competitive authoritarianism   political regimes where democratic institutions are put in place but authoritarian political leaders consistently undermine these institutions to stay in power

executive   the branch of governments tasked with implementing and executing the laws and policies in a state

head of government   oversees the day-to-day functions of the government

head of state   the country's symbolic representative

one-party rule   one party possesses overwhelming control over the political process; in general, other parties do exist, but they have limited power and are kept in check by the dominant party

parliamentary system   a government system where the head of government is chosen from the legislature by the ruling party and also serves as the head of state

president   the chief executive in a presidential democracy; serves as both the head of state and the head of government

presidential system   a government system where the legislative and executive branch have separation of powers; unlike in parliamentary systems, the legislature is unable to remove the government

prime minister   the chief executive in a parliamentary democracy; serves as head of state and typically is also head of the largest party in parliament

semi-presidential system   a mix between pure parliamentary and pure presidential systems. The legislature elects the head of government and has the ability to remove the government from office, but there is also a popularly elected head of state.

separation of powers   a system in which different branches of the government possess separate and independent powers, so no specific political institution has too much power; this is also known as checks and balances and is typically divided into three branches: the legislative, the executive, and the judiciary

vote of (no) confidence   constitutionally mandated authority to remove the government through a vote of the legislature

WHAT ARE POLITICAL EXECUTIVES?

In 2007, Pratibha Patil became the first woman to hold the Indian presidency. India's parliamentary system provides prime ministers with much more power than presidents. It is worth noting that India had already seen a woman – Indira Gandhi – crack the executive glass ceiling as prime minister in 1966. At the end of 2018, Annegret Kramp-Karrenbauer was elected the successor to Angela Merkel as the leader of Germany's Christian Democratic Union party (CDU). The change in leadership in the CDU likely puts Kramp-Karrenbauer on track to succeed Merkel as chancellor of Germany, meaning the first woman chancellor (who initially came to power in 2005) may be followed by another woman. Germany is also a parliamentary system, so it has both a chancellor (essentially the same position as a prime minister) and a president; as is typically the case in parliamentary systems, the chancellor is very influential while the president is substantially weaker. This makes the possible continuation of a woman in the chancellorship especially noteworthy.

We have also seen increased diversity among leaders of presidential systems. In 1994, South Africa elected its first Black president, Nelson Mandela, after the end of apartheid. Evo Morales, widely considered to be the world's first Indigenous president, was the president of Bolivia between 2006 and 2019. Barack Obama made history by becoming the first Black president in the United States in 2008, staying in power for eight years. And 2010 was a banner year in Latin America, with women presidents in four states: Dilma Rousseff (Brazil), Laura Chinchilla (Costa Rica), Christina Fernandez de Kirchner (Argentina), and Michelle Bachelet (Chile). The wave of "firsts" elected or appointed to national executive positions in the end of the twentieth century and beginning of the twenty-first century indicate that we are seeing more leaders from previously marginalized groups reaching what in many countries is seen as the most powerful political position. This is a big deal, but why?

Chancellors, prime ministers, and presidents are often the most well-known politicians in a country, domestically and internationally. Politics and policymaking are associated with these positions and the people occupying them (the Obama administration did this, Merkel's coalition supported that). The way each executive system is organized directly influences how these well-known officeholders lead. These executives all wield wide-ranging powers in their respective countries, but the extent of such powers and the dynamics between them and other political actors vary greatly from country to country. In this chapter we explain how and why executive powers differ around the world and the ways power relations between the executive and other branches of government influence policy and policymaking. In doing so, we highlight the role of diversity among officeholders and how this may shape outcomes.

EXECUTIVE GOVERNMENT: THE BASICS

Modern political systems tend to work under a clear **separation of powers**, where different branches of the government possess separate and independent powers so no specific political institution has too much power. This is also known as checks and balances and is typically divided into three branches: the legislative, the executive, and the judiciary. The **executive** is the branch of governments tasked with implementing and executing the laws and policies in a state. Often comprising one leader (unified executive) or two leaders (dual executive), the executive consists of complex institutions, including the **bureaucracy**, that require a multitude of actors beyond presidents and prime ministers to function properly. Nevertheless, the heads of executive offices (also known as chief executives) are extremely important in setting national agendas, developing and implementing foreign policy, waging wars, among other key influences. Chief executive roles are often divided into two distinct types: **head of state** and **head of government**. The head of state is the country's symbolic representative, while the head of government is tasked with formulating and implementing policies and oversees the day-to-day functions of the government.

Government type directly affects who does what in the executive. Generally, **parliamentary systems** separate the head of government (prime ministers) and the head of state (some symbolic positions such as ceremonial president, queen, king, emperor, governor general) while **presidential systems** combine these two roles into the presidency. Things get more complicated when you add **semi-presidential systems** and other hybrid government types (more on this later in the chapter), but regardless of the government and leadership structure, chief executives are often the most prestigious positions sought after by political elites.

Here are a few examples of chief executives around the world to help contextualize these differences:

- Brazil has a traditional presidential system. The president plays the role of head of state and head of government, as well as commander in chief of the armed forces.[1] This leadership model is used in most presidential systems.
- Japan, a constitutional monarchy, divides executive roles between the prime minister (head of government and commander in chief of the Japanese Self Defense Forces) and the emperor (head of state, or "the symbol of the state and of the unity of the people," as written in Japan's constitution). In the case of Japan, the emperor, selected from members of the imperial family through a clear law of succession, has the important ceremonial power of appointing the prime minister (and the power to designate the person they deem fit for the position).
- Ukraine is a semi-presidential system that has both an influential president and prime minister, but the president holds a lot more power, is elected, and is the head of state and commander of chief.

These differences are procedural, but in many ways they represent historical legacies that helped shape the government structures we see throughout the world today.

THE MODERN EXECUTIVE: HOW DID WE GET HERE?

With over 190 recognized countries in existence today, government type and consequently executive structures vary. Executive systems can be divided roughly into three categories: presidentialism, parliamentarism, and hybrid government types[2] (semi-presidentialism and other "in-between" types). It is important to note that even countries with similar government structures on paper will operate differently in practice depending on several factors, including but not limited to geography, regional history, pre-colonial and colonial past, post-colonial dynamics, federal or unitary structures, previous political institutions, history of conflicts, political party dynamics, and the involvement of elites in the political process. Even within the same country, being mindful of how powers and procedures described on paper may diverge, particularly over time, is important. Major changes in political institutions within countries can occur over time that affect the executive.

When thinking about these government types, specific country cases that exemplify each tend to readily come to mind: The United States as a presidential system, the United Kingdom as a parliamentary system, and France or Russia as the semi-presidential/hybrid examples. These cases are important when thinking about modern government (and the modern executive) for various reasons, but there is one key factor that is important in understanding how we got to the contemporary executive: colonialism.[3]

Broadly, we can think about the impact of colonialism in three ways. First, after independence, the United States (a former British colony) established its system of checks and balances (and the presidency) in direct response to what it saw as abuse from the British crown. As other colonies (especially in Latin America) sought independence in the eighteenth and nineteenth centuries, the US model was emulated (in some instances directly copied) by many of the newly formed countries. Second, the decolonization of Africa and Asia following World War II saw the independence of dozens of countries (UN membership went from 32 states in 1946 to 127 in 1970). Many of these former colonies of Great Britain and France (as well as other European states) sought to establish governments that would be deemed "modern" by the United States and Western Europe. Finally, the fall of the Soviet Union at the end of the twentieth century caused political restructuring of countries in Eastern Europe and the Caucasus region, leading to decades of institutional changes in these areas.

Today, colonial legacies help us understand one of the reasons for the predominance of one government type over others in specific regions. In the Americas we see mostly presidential systems, often featuring a strong president with vast executive powers. Many Caribbean states and countries in Oceania use variations of the Westminster parliamentary system, a legacy of British colonialism. African states have moved toward presidential systems, with the preponderance of powers exercised by the president, even where a prime minister also governs. Western and Central European states feature mostly parliamentary systems (including several constitutional monarchies), while in Eastern Europe (former Soviet Bloc countries) we have seen an increase in semi-presidential systems. Asia defies simple categorization as executive structures vary considerably, including all three main system types as well as military dictatorships and absolute monarchies. Absolute monarchies in the Middle East continue to dominate executive structures. Exceptions exist, with several being hybrid government types with dominant presidents, but we also see parliamentary forms taking hold. With all these government types and the variations that can come within each type, we focus first on the three most popular systems (presidentialism, parliamentarism, and semi-presidentialism) and then we move on to specific types of non-democratic executives.

PRESIDENTIALISM, PARLIAMENTARISM, AND SEMI-PRESIDENTIALISM

Most countries in the world operate along the presidential and parliamentary spectrum, with hybrid systems like semi-presidentialism being somewhere in the middle. We cannot emphasize enough that even countries with similar government types on paper may have very different manifestations of these systems, including similar types operating under democracies and under dictatorial regimes. Here we will talk about some of the most common characteristics of the democratic versions of each of the three prevailing government forms; these are summed up in Table 8.1.

Typically, presidential systems concentrate power in an executive – the **president** – who serves as both the head of state and head of government. As stated, while the head of state symbolizes the country and its citizenry, the head of government performs more substantive executive duties. In parliamentary systems, though a **prime minister** may govern alongside a president (if it is a dual executive), the president serves as a symbolic head of state while the prime minister (who holds a seat in the legislature) is the head of government. Where the parliamentary system has a unified executive, the head of state function is often performed by a

Table 8.1. Characteristics of Presidential, Parliamentary, and Semi-Presidential Governments

	Presidentialism	Parliamentarism	Semi-Presidential
Chief Executive Roles	President is head of state and head of government	Head of government (prime minister, chancellor, etc.) is separate from head of state (president, monarch, governor general, etc.)	Head of government is separate from head of state; powers are delineated according to a country's specific dual executive structure
Elections	Elected directly by the citizenry	Elected indirectly by the legislature	Two separate positions, one elected directly by the citizenry, one elected indirectly by the legislature
Terms	Fixed terms according to the country's election rules	Terms are not fixed; elections can be called by the executive or the legislature	There is more variation, and different positions may have different rules
Executive Governance	Executive is separate from legislative power	Executive and legislative power are more closely connected; chief executive comes from the legislative branch	Executive is separate from legislative power, but the dynamics can be different from a full presidential system
Coalition Formation	Not required, but an important element of executive–legislative relations	Required if a party does not hold a majority of seats in the legislature	There are more variations depending on the powers and roles of the executive roles

figurehead, commonly by a hereditary monarch or a representative of a monarch like a governor general. Finally, semi-presidential systems employ dual executive structures and empower both a president (usually elected) and a prime minister (appointed from the legislature), with government roles (head of state, head of government, commander in chief powers) clearly delineated between the two positions in accordance with the country's laws. Currently, roughly one-third of countries are semi-presidential.

The type of government directly influences executive governance, meaning that the dynamics of who gets what, when, and how will be different depending on the way the executive is set up. One of the most important differences between executive system types relates to the extent to which executive and legislative powers are separated or united. In presidential systems, a clear distinction exists between the executive and the legislative branches. Rather than concentrate power, this separation of powers is meant to provide checks on legislative and executive authorities. For example, in many presidential systems the president nominates individuals for key positions (such as Supreme Court justices), but the legislature votes to accept the nomination. In the United States, a total of 30 nominations have been rejected or withdrawn before a vote because of the likelihood of rejection. In many presidential systems the governmental budget also requires a proposal originating in one branch with the other branch approving or rejecting it. To ensure this separation, the legislative and executive are elected independently to serve fixed terms. In contrast, parliamentary systems combine executive and legislative functions and the prime minister is selected as a result of party performance in parliamentary elections, but the election procedures may vary. **Coalition** governments complicate matters even more when no party attains a parliamentary majority; prime ministers emerge when governing partners reach a consensus.

Another related factor distinguishing these systems centers on whether the executive is accountable to a parliamentary majority through some sort of **vote of (no) confidence**. In parliamentary systems, prime ministers require majority support in parliament to remain in power. If they do not reach this threshold of support (in other words, if they lose a confidence vote), they will be dismissed from their position as prime minister. An ordinary vote of confidence simply requires a majority vote of members of parliament against the prime minister for dismissal; the constructive form (only used in a small minority of parliamentary systems, including Germany) requires parliament to select a new prime minister beforehand. Election timing in parliamentary systems is usually not fixed given that votes of confidence can trigger snap elections. In addition, prime ministers can also call elections and usually try to do so when they think their party has a strong chance of winning (but see Box 8.1 for how this strategy can sometimes backfire). This prime ministerial authority of being able to schedule elections is usually viewed as a necessary counterweight to their removal and meant to foster cooperation between the executive and legislature. Prime ministerial terms are thus flexible and potentially tenuous.

BOX 8.1: SNAP ELECTION BACKFIRES!

We said that prime ministers can call an election when they *think* they have a strong chance of winning parliamentary elections. But this can also backfire. In 2017, UK Prime Minister Theresa May of the Conservative Party called for snap elections to try to expand her party's majority. Opinion polls prior to the call for a snap election showed strong support for the Conservative Party and a likely seat gain if an election were called. Given the contentious Brexit negotiations happening in parliament, a stronger majority would help May's party in pushing a Brexit deal in line with their interests. The election, held June 8, led to the Conservative Party losing 13 seats and therefore losing its clear majority in parliament. Worst of all (for May and the Conservatives), the Labor Party (their

biggest opposition) won 30 seats. This loss of seats meant that after the election
the Conservative Party had to build a coalition to govern, something that under-
mined their Brexit deal objectives and led to the eventual resignation of Theresa
May as prime minister.

In contrast, presidents in presidential systems are not directly accountable to
the legislature (through a confidence relationship) and lack the power to dismiss
the legislature. Presidential terms are defined by a specific number of years and
clear expectations of when the next elections will be held. Presidents may be removed by the legislature before their terms end via an impeachment process, but
this tends to be difficult and only used in cases where presidents have committed
egregious abuses of power or other impeachable offenses. If this does happen, constitutions usually outline how power will be transferred until the next regularly
scheduled election. For example, the vice-president may then temporarily assume
the presidency.

The **cabinet**, or the set of appointed officials (often referred to as secretaries or
ministers) in a government, oversee specific policies such as healthcare, defense,
and the like. The respective role of the cabinet in each system also differs. Cabinets
in presidential systems usually wield less power than those in parliamentary systems – cabinets execute policy while the president ultimately steers their preferred
course of action. In contrast, cabinets in parliamentary systems are vested with
more autonomy, though their work is still overseen by the prime minister. We will
talk about diversity in cabinets later in this chapter.

In semi-presidential systems, the president can be removed by impeachment
but is otherwise insulated from untimely removal, while the prime minister is
responsible to the parliament and is subject to a confidence vote as previously
outlined. Even though, again, a great deal of variation exists, we can identify two
main types of semi-presidential systems. *President-parliamentarism* is a system in
which the prime minister and cabinet are together responsible to the legislature
and the president. We can see how this would equip the president with a greater
degree of influence compared to *premier-presidentialism*, when the prime minister
and cabinet are both responsible only to the legislature *and not* the president. During periods of cohabitation – when the president and prime minister are from opposing parties – the cabinet does not have members of the president's party.

Presidents in presidential systems can leverage popular support through their
visibility as symbols, substantive policy relevance, and mode of entrance (usually from a form of direct, popular election). Though invested with a great deal

of authority, their ability to amass accomplishments depends a great deal on their relationship with the legislature. Since it is quite common for the president and the parliament to not be controlled by the same party, this can produce policy stalemate. The essence of parliamentary politics is usually considered to rest on collaboration. To achieve their policy agendas, prime ministers also heavily depend on parliamentary cooperation. We see that presidential, parliamentary, and semi-presidential systems may have legislatures where no party possesses a majority, also highlighting the importance of establishing cooperative relationships and coalitions.

NON-DEMOCRATIC GOVERNMENTS AND THE EXECUTIVE

As noted earlier, thus far we have talked only about democratic executives, yet non-democratic regimes may also be set up – at least nominally – as parliamentary, presidential, or semi-presidential systems. It is important to note that executive power and political dynamics differ greatly between democratic regimes and non-democratic regimes. Here we briefly discuss two non-democratic political regimes that may look like presidential, parliamentary, or semi-presidential systems: **one-party rule** and **competitive-authoritarian** regimes.

One-party rule means exactly that: One party possesses overwhelming control over the political process. In general, other parties do exist, but they have limited power and are kept in check by the dominant party. This model is prevalent among the remaining communist states (China and Cuba are the most known examples), but is also present in political systems that in theory fit the three government types we have been learning about but in reality are led by one group that controls both the executive and legislative (which likely leads to control of the judiciary). Examples include the *Partido Revolucionario Institucional* in Mexico's presidential system between 1929 and 2000, and the Kenya African National Union's control of Kenyan politics between 1963 and 2000.

Competitive authoritarianism represents hybrid regimes (not to be confused with hybrid government types!), or political regimes where democratic institutions are put in place but political leaders consistently undermine these institutions to stay in power, also known as *democratic backsliding* (see also Chapters 1, 3, and 7).[4] In these regimes, various aspects of a "normal" democratic regime exists, such as elections and explicit separation of powers (on paper). The executive exists in one of the forms we discussed above, but the power resides in the hands of one powerful leader or a group of influential politicians. This is a common experience in former Soviet states and countries in Africa. The most recent popular

Table 8.2. **Sample of Countries by Government Type**

Regions	Presidentialism	Parliamentarism	Mixed/Hybrid
African Continent	Angola Benin Ghana Kenya Nigeria	Botswana Ethiopia Mauritius Somalia South Africa	Algeria Cape Verde Mali Niger São Tomé e Príncipe
Americas	Argentina Brazil Mexico United States Venezuela	Bahamas Belize Canada Jamaica Suriname	Haiti
Asia and Oceania	Indonesia Maldives Philippines Seychelles South Korea	Australia India Japan Malaysia Thailand	East Timor Mongolia Taiwan
Europe and Post-Soviet Countries	Belarus Cyprus Kazakhstan Turkmenistan Uzbekistan	Albania Germany Norway Slovakia United Kingdom	Azerbaijan France Lithuania Russia Ukraine
Middle East and North Africa	Turkey South Sudan	Iraq Israel Lebanon	Egypt Palestine Tunisia

example is Russia, where the semi-presidential system has allowed Putin to stay in power even as he alternates between president and prime minister in Russia's semi-presidential system. Table 8.2 provides a number of examples of countries with the various types of government we've discussed.

POWER, POLITICS, AND EXECUTIVES: WHO GETS TO BE A CHIEF EXECUTIVE?

Historically, people in executive positions were among the most privileged in society. This elite subset benefited from access to education and financial resources. Monarchical systems transferred power through the bloodline and through sons. Monarchical political institutions established and maintained a family's political dominance. These systems connected such monarchs to divine figures and texts that helped justify their continued leadership and wealth. Monarchies were strong across regions of the world, including Asia, where social stratification in caste-based dynastic systems preserved wealth among families of the same economic, geographic, and social type and prevented upward mobility of others. As access to education and political participation expanded across world regions, so too did the notion that a broader array of the population possessed natural rights, abilities, and resources to lead. These societal changes created opportunities to diversify executive systems of governance and potentially broaden the pool of political executives – that is, prime ministers and presidents.

As you learned in Chapters 2 and 3, *liberal democratic theory* emphasizes the protection of civil liberties and human rights and public participation in the decision-making process. Accountability also proves critical; public officials are answerable to their electorate at regular intervals via elections, and voters should be provided a meaningful choice. With these conditions satisfied, a political system could be considered democratic. Yet this ignores the demographics related to those in office, specifically the degree to which elites are drawn from a narrow subsample of the larger population. That's when thinking intersectionally matters: If chief executives are mostly men drawn from a country's dominant racial/ethnic group and from the socioeconomic elite, what does that say about democracy? Why does being a woman, a racial/ethnic minority, a religious minority, or a member of the working class (among other identities) make it harder for someone to lead the country?

Being part of elite networks presents various resource advantages, including wealth and education as well as access to financial donors. Families can essentially transfer such benefits to future generations forging political careers. Belonging to a political family in which multiple generations have wielded political power (essentially democratic political dynasties) can provide particular advantages, including name recognition, access to powerful political alliances, and the like. The ability to observe a family member in politics also provides important socialization experiences unavailable to others. Worldwide, we see that belonging to a political family is still relevant. On average 12 per cent of executives worldwide come from political families. This is true in democracies (such as the United States, Canada, and Japan) and countries that have struggled with democratic governance (such as Bangladesh, Angola, and Nicaragua). Recall that earlier in this chapter we outlined the influence that the emperor of Japan has on selecting the prime minister. Japan is one of the most notorious countries in the democratic world where members of political dynasties (to this point – only men) regularly come to power as prime ministers.

Another observation we offer is that as of 2019, women make up less than 10 per cent of all political executives worldwide. This is particularly important because the last two decades represent a high point for women in executive office. This means that despite these record highs, almost all executives are still men! Linking to our previous point about political families, to get into high office women still often must be members of political families to rise to the highest levels of power.[5] They do so at greater rates than their male counterparts: nearly one-third of women presidents or prime ministers possess familial connections, while only about 10 per cent of men share this characteristic. Women's links are particularly direct and powerful in Asia; almost all women invested with high levels of executive power still tend to have followed the family path. Some may call this an unfair advantage for women, but men have the privilege of taking many paths to political executive office, including through family connections.

Another important area of exploration related to executive demographics is education. Do executives come from the most elite educational backgrounds, assessed by number of years of education, and have they obtained their degrees abroad? Unsurprisingly, the answer to both questions is yes. About half of all executives in power in 2011 obtained at least a graduate degree, and only 5 per cent had a high school degree or less. Nearly half of all executives in power during this time frame were educated outside of their home countries, most in universities in Western Europe and the United States.

Worldwide, the average education level is just over seven years of schooling. African executives, many of whose countries were part of colonial empires during their youths, are among the most likely to obtain degrees outside of their home countries. The Caribbean and Latin America show a low preponderance of this pattern. Education of elites outside their home countries signals whether executives hail from wealthier families. The implication of this as a common pathway to power is that it would suggest that those from more modest backgrounds would be at a disadvantage compared to those from more privileged upbringings, perpetuating the dominance of a select group (upper-class and highly educated men) of executives worldwide. While a high level of education may empower leaders with the skills for the job, when the perceived eligibility pool excludes substantial numbers of people (many of whom lack the resources to obtain prestigious educations), this may consequently keep some high-quality leaders out of the running.

CABINETS AND INTERSECTIONALITY

When Justin Trudeau was sworn in as Canada's prime minister in 2015, attention focused on the diversity of his cabinet choices (see Box 8.2). As he introduced his cabinet at a press conference he stated, "It's an incredible pleasure for me to be before you today ... to present a cabinet that looks like Canada." The cabinet consisted of 15 men and 15 women. When asked by a reporter about what prompted his decision to appoint Canada's first ever gender-parity cabinet, he made international waves by offering this simple explanation: "Because it's 2015."[6] Several of his cabinet picks were from minority ethnic groups, including two Indigenous members of parliament (both women) and others of Indian and Afghan descent, to name a few. Three cabinet ministers were also of the minority Sikh religion.

BOX 8.2: DIVERSE CABINETS: THE CANADIAN CASE

Though Prime Minister Trudeau's cabinet remains diverse, some key cabinet ministers no longer continue to serve. This includes Jody Wilson-Raybould of the We Wai Kai Nation, who was Canada's first Indigenous justice minister and attorney general. Her selection sent a message about the importance of equality more generally and a focus on justice and reconciliation for Indigenous groups more specifically. However, in 2019 she was moved to the Veterans' Affairs portfolio, which represented a significant demotion. While cabinet shuffles are common, this decision was widely criticized. Wilson-Raybould was a highly regarded and effective cabinet minister. This demotion was seemingly linked to her standing firm on a decision to not lessen the punishment of a company engaging in fraud and corruption, against the wishes of the prime minister's office. She resigned from the cabinet altogether one month after she started serving in this cabinet post. Jane Philpott, another cabinet member who had been promoted and a rising star in the Liberal Party, also soon left the cabinet, in solidarity with Wilson-Raybould. The resignations of two ministers – both recognized as strong members of the cabinet and noted for their commitment to inclusion and empowerment of disadvantaged groups – sent a strong message about the importance of principled stances. As one member of an opposition party stated: "Trudeau came out and asked for strong women, and he got them." These developments led some to question Trudeau's commitment to cabinet diversity beyond creating a picture-worthy moment.

Trudeau's comments align with the idea that representation matters. In simple terms, who is in power matters because these individuals' experiences will inform their decisions in various ways, including who they select to work with them, policy priorities, and language used in policies, among others. If those in power stem from a homogenous and dominant group, they are less likely to think about minorities when discussing nominations and policymaking. Therefore, having individuals from known underrepresented groups in power matters because they will provide important differing viewpoints on what the government should do, something unlikely to happen (or likely to happen less often) if only established groups have a say on the political process.[7] For example, research shows that when there are more women in cabinet, there is a higher likelihood of better parental leave and more women-friendly policies.[8]

Worldwide, gender-parity cabinets are on the rise and have taken hold in diverse regions in recent years. Some examples include Western Europe (Finland, France, Spain, and Sweden), Eastern Europe (Bulgaria and Slovenia), Latin America (Chile, Nicaragua, Costa Rica, and Colombia), and Africa (Cape Verde, Rwanda, Seychelles, and Ethiopia). More recently, South African President Cyril Ramaphosa announced a cabinet comprising half men and half women. While these developments appear promising, we note that gender-parity governments constitute only a handful of countries, and women's average cabinet membership is still less than 20 per cent worldwide. If we add minority groups in the various country contexts, we also see a limited number of minority group members represented in cabinets around the world.

Several factors shape cabinet choices made by executives. Some executives select nominees, while other actors or institutions formally accept or reject these candidates, as in the US system. In Latin America, in contrast, presidents can, in theory, freely appoint their ministers. In parliamentary systems like Canada or the United Kingdom, the cabinet usually consists of people who currently hold seats in the legislature. This is not the case in presidential systems. Therefore, whether the prime minister can even appoint a diverse cabinet in the first place often depends on whether members of these groups have been elected to parliament. At the same time, prospective cabinet appointees in presidential systems may gain the notice of selectors if they have established legislative careers. Worldwide, legislatures with fewer women are associated with smaller quantities of women ministers. The same is true about other marginalized groups in different countries.

Coalition governance means the executive can independently appoint their preferred cabinet officials, but they must pay attention to the interests of other parties in the coalition. In coalitions, the governing party will reserve a certain number of ministerial posts to their partners that are from different parties, likely negotiating cabinet positions that other parties have a direct interest in leading. By keeping coalition parties happy with key cabinet nominations, the executive uses coalitions to offset the governance problems that arise when a party does not have the majority. This process ends up placing important constraints on the executive in terms of cabinet selection, policy priority, and policymaking. Coalitions also may inhibit cabinet diversity compared to unified cabinets. This may be due to the increased intra-party competition for cabinet portfolios, which makes it more likely that people from a narrow subset of backgrounds (such as upper-class men from the dominant ethnic group) will be selected.

We do note, however, that national executives have been increasingly expected to govern with diverse cabinets. That relatively few individuals make up cabinets enables presidents and prime ministers to achieve a fairly high level of cabinet diversity, if they view this as important. We also note that cabinet membership changes, and this effects diversity. At the starts of their terms, executives may enjoy more public support and goodwill. Those driven to diversify their cabinets may seize this opportunity during such honeymoon periods. Increased attention also generates a heightened symbolic impact of diversifying their governments. They, may, however, appoint fewer members of underrepresented groups as their terms progress.

Though the inclusion of diverse groups is increasingly seen as an important objective and cabinets are generally becoming more diverse compared to prior decades, we can identify important exceptions. While Trudeau's cabinet in 2015 sent traditional and social media ablaze in its picture of equality and representativeness, one year later, Brazilian Interim President Michel Temer's decision to not appoint any women (where women are 51 per cent of the population) or persons of African descent (in a country where a majority self-identify as Black or being of African heritage) sent shockwaves throughout the world. This proved even more unnerving given that his predecessor, impeached President Dilma Rousseff (the country's first woman president), had the most diverse cabinet in Brazilian history.[9]

BUREAUCRACIES AND INTERSECTIONALITY

The executive is tasked with implementing and executing the laws of the state, but when it comes to the nitty gritty, the president or prime minister will not be the one personally rolling out a new healthcare policy or explaining to educators the local impacts of new education policies. Members of the executive, including the chief executive and those appointed by the chief executive, are a small fraction of the personnel needed to fully implement and execute laws and policies. In most countries this task is conducted by bureaucrats, civil servants working inside governmental bureaucratic structures who are mostly invisible in public debates about politics and policymaking but are essential for carrying out laws and policies.

A government's bureaucratic structure is characterized by a clear hierarchy with specific roles and functions, fixed rules and procedures, and strict adherence to the impartial execution of said rules and procedures. Bureaucrats working inside these structures are expected to be highly specialized and impartial.

Government structures need individuals able and willing to fully implement, execute, and provide oversight over laws and policies. There are several reasons why a bureaucratic structure may be desirable. Well-organized bureaucracies can help the government implement laws and policies effectively and efficiently, possibly serving as a check against corruption and government overreach. More importantly, the impartial execution of rules and procedures should, in an ideal situation, provide for fair and equitable implementation and execution of the laws and policies established by the executive.

The ideas proposed in the paragraph above are in one way or another connected to sociologist Max Weber's ideas of *rationalization*. These ideas, popularized in the 1940s, provide a blueprint for the ideal-type bureaucracy: a rational and efficient administrative system developed to pursue clear organizational goals. While bureaucracies have changed considerably since then, the ideas of rationality and efficiency are still paramount to the theory and practice of bureaucracies. One key aspect with distinct implications to an intersectional understanding of the executive is the idea of impartiality (or neutrality) of bureaucracies.

Thinking about politics with an intersectional lens allows us to question the idea of impartiality. The rationality and impartiality proposed by a bureaucratic model assumes that the political system can be impartial, that there are no biases in the laws and policies and in the individuals enforcing these laws. But intersectionality teaches us to look for the complex ways in which individual and group identities shape structures and behaviors. Politics, including bureaucratic politics, is about power. As Collins and Bilge put it, "power operates by disciplining people in ways that put people's lives on paths that make some options seem viable and others out of reach."[10] In what ways do bureaucracies discipline people and dictate the viable options?

Feminist and intersectional scholars have been calling for deeper discussion about institutions that are deemed "neutral," "rational," and "impartial." Feminists emphasize the importance of looking at gender as a social construct, especially when thinking about political institutions that directly shape individual behaviors. One can argue that no one can escape bureaucracy in modern political systems. If we assume such institutions are not gendered, we are assuming that this rationality and impartiality may be a reality. Intersectionality scholars go one step further and encourage us to look beyond gender and into the intersections between gender, race, ethnic identity, social class, and any other important category that may influence the impartial behavior of bureaucrats and bureaucracies. If the rules are set to standardize procedures but procedures are created (consciously or unconsciously) with, for example, white middle-class men in mind, then the rationality (and impartiality) of these institutions is not universal.

Beyond the design of bureaucratic structures, another main issue relates to *who* are the bureaucrats in a society. Research on representative bureaucracy has grown considerably in the last decades, and a lot of what is discussed by these scholars have direct impact on our understanding of intersectionality and representation in politics.[11] Most of the discussions about representation in bureaucracies is divided into two groups. *Passive representation* examines if those working in the bureaucratic structures share identity traits with those who seek the services provided by specific bureaucratic institutions. For example, do the people employed by the local Department of Motor Vehicles share demographic traits with those who seek the services of that branch of the department? *Active representation* examines if bureaucrats share values and attitudes with their clients (those they serve) and if these values affect their decisions. For example, does a worker for the Social Security Administration share the values of those seeking their services, and if they do (or do not), do these values affect the kind of service this bureaucrat provides? Research on both areas overwhelmingly shows that women and minorities are underrepresented in many bureaucratic structures, something that has negative consequences (sometimes severely negative) to the services these groups receive.[12]

In sum, executive leaders rely on bureaucrats to carry out the laws and policies implemented by their governments. In an ideal world, these bureaucrats would be impartial and would carry out these laws and policies exactly how executive leaders intended them to be carried out. But the reality is one that undermines women and minorities, arguably twice in the process. Most times, intersectional identities that are not shared by political elites are excluded from the development of laws and policies. They are then doubly excluded when bureaucrats also do not share their identities and values in the implementation of laws and policies.

WHY INTERSECTIONAL IDENTITIES MATTER FOR EXECUTIVE POLITICS

Our last section touches briefly on why it is important to have more inclusive executive structures. We focus on the potential political empowerment of marginalized groups, including the importance of symbols and the substantive policy impacts that occur when members of marginalized groups gain a seat at the political table, whether as cabinet ministers, presidents, prime ministers, or bureaucrats. We will begin with the importance of symbols.

When the executive is from a demographic group, or multiple groups, that departs from the established norm, we see important opportunities for advancing those groups' political empowerment. The presence of excluded groups in the highest political offices (especially those that are placed in the most visible and powerful positions, like presidents and prime ministers) can positively shape attitudinal and behavioral responses among the public (see Box 8.3). They are more likely to challenge traditional norms limiting the political roles of minorities. This can potentially transform citizens' acceptance of their political participation and leadership. Generally, when members of excluded and marginalized groups occupy political offices, they send strong signals to the public regarding their group. Role models can positively affect perceptions of members of excluded groups' abilities to hold these positions. When few role models exist, some may deem them as unfit for office. The extent to which members of marginalized groups gain a foothold as political leaders will cue citizens about the openness and responsiveness of the system to diverse political interests. Members of that group in the larger society may especially be inspired by seeing political trailblazers, propel their own political engagement, and improve the general public's opinions about the presidency, minorities in political power, and democratic governance.

BOX 8.3: "CAN BOYS ALSO GROW UP TO BE PRESIDENTS?"

This was a question a young boy asked Vigdis Finnbogadottir, the first democratically elected female president in the world. She came to power in 1980 in Iceland and held the position for 16 years. That a woman held this position of power affected the way this boy conceived the presidency. Women positioned as visible symbols may challenge long-standing associations of executive positions as being a male-only domain. Furthermore, women and girls may be inspired to become politically engaged, some deciding to run for office one day.

This was the case for Halla Tómasdóttir, an entrepreneur and business woman who can recount the impact of seeing the first woman president come to power while she was growing up: "I remember on the day – on the morning when the votes were in. I will never forget this picture when she steps out on the balcony of her own home with her daughter by her side … it was so different from every other exhibition I had seen of power and leadership."

Thirty-six years later, Tómasdóttir ran for the presidency herself. While she did not win, she may run again. Iceland has had two women prime ministers. Together, these visible symbols of women leaders can inspire future generations of women like Tómasdóttir, changing the gendered political landscape.

While thus far we have not focused much attention on symbolic presidents, it is important to mention the potential ways even these more ceremonial officeholders may break down barriers related to historically oppressed groups gaining political positions. India is a country that is characterized as having extreme ethnic, religious, and caste divisions. It has a prime minister that exercises significant powers in a parliamentary system and a president who has substantially fewer authorities. The president is not directly elected and is expected to renounce their partisanship upon taking office. In recent years, political minorities including women (Pratibha Patil), Muslims (Abdul Kalam), and Dalits (K.R. Narayanan) have served as presidents. While we noted at the beginning of the chapter that India also had a woman prime minister, Indira Gandhi, she was the daughter of India's first leader post-independence, Prime Minister Jawaharlal Nehru. While there are limits of influence when members of politically marginalized groups are only invested with limited powers and have narrow pathways to power, ceremonial leaders also provide societies with important symbols. For example, the selection of a president who is from the Dalit caste (formerly called "untouchables") sends a signal that politics is open to all groups.

Prime ministers and presidents may exercise significant legislative authority in some regions, including Latin America and Africa; this may provide them a high degree of policy latitude, sometimes empowering minorities.[13] Cabinet members also influence the policies they are charged with overseeing. Finally, bureaucrats have an important role in overseeing the day-to-day implementation of policy. Another compelling benefit to having a more inclusive executive involves greater responsiveness to political interests that might otherwise be ignored. When members of marginalized groups achieve policy influence, their social status may hasten their greater awareness of the inequities faced in society at large. As such, they may be more likely to promote policies advancing equality.

SUMMARY

This chapter provided an overview of what executives are, what they do, and why they are important. The following points provide an overview of the major issues discussed:

- Prime ministers, chancellors, and presidents are often the face of a country. The powers that emanate from these executive positions vary greatly from country to country, but they all have considerable power, even if sometimes it is merely symbolic.

- Who holds these executive positions matters. The people who help these leaders execute the law (cabinets and bureaucrats) matter. Next time you pay your taxes, register to vote, or go renew your driver's license or government identification, think about the people who crafted the laws influencing these activities: Do they look like you? Do you think they have your best interests in mind? Thinking about government structures through intersectional lenses will show you that these questions are important ones to ask.
- There are deeper historical legacies influencing the type of government used. Colonial legacies are a good starting point to understanding why a country uses presidential, parliamentary, or a hybrid system to organize their executive government structures.
- The powerful elites, different in each country, tend to hold executive power. Sociocultural changes and pressure from other groups have led researchers and the population to pay closer attention to who holds positions of power. While these elites still dominate most executive posts in most countries, efforts to bring more diverse voices have spread throughout the world.
- The different types of executives lead to different strategies for governance. Coalition formation is important since most executive leaders in the world do not hold a clear majority of seats in parliament to carry out their policies. Coalition negotiations have recently become more inclusive (at least in theory), but the politicians holding these positions still tend to come from elite networks.
- Bureaucracies carry on most of the day-to-day operations laid out by executives. Diversity in these institutions also matters, and discussions about how to make bureaucracies more responsive to all citizens in a country is an important area of research.
- Remember, at the end of this book there is an appendix with more information on how you can get involved and safeguard against democratic backsliding.

CONCLUDING QUESTIONS

1 What are the biggest differences between presidential, parliamentary, and hybrid systems? In your opinion, which one is likely to better represent minority groups and why?
2 Do ceremonial roles matter? Why or why not?
3 Explain the role of colonialism in the development of government types around the world.
4 Who tends to be elected to executive positions? Which individual characteristics matter the most when thinking about those elected to those positions? Are

there regional differences in the kind of person likely getting elected to executive positions?

5 What is the role of cabinets in executive governance? How can we think about
cabinets and cabinet appointments from an intersectional perspective?

6 Explain the importance of Max Weber's ideas in the study of bureaucracies.
How do some of the ideas connected to him (such as rationalization) relate to
the intersectional understanding of how a government should work?

NOTES

1 Pedro G. dos Santos and Farida Jalalzai, "The Mother of Brazil: Gender Roles, Campaign Strategy, and the Election of Brazil's First Female President," in *Women in Politics
and Media: Perspectives from Nations in Transition*, eds. Maria Raicheva-Stover and Elza
Ibroscheva, 167 (London: Bloomsbury, 2014).

2 Not to be confused with hybrid regimes, which indicate a system that combines democratic and non-democratic elements, though they largely fail to uphold key features of
democracy.

3 Ola Olsson, "On the Democratic Legacy of Colonialism," *Journal of Comparative Economics* 37, no. 4 (2009): 534–51.

4 Mikael Wigell, "Mapping 'Hybrid Regimes': Regime Types and Concepts in Comparative Politics," *Democratisation* 15, no. 2 (2008): 230–50.

5 Farida Jalalzai, *Women Presidents of Latin America: Beyond Family Ties?* (New York: Routledge, 2015); Farida Jalalzai and Meg Rincker, "Blood Is Thicker Than Water: Family
Ties to Political Power Worldwide," *Historical Social Research* 43, no. 4 (2018): 54–72.

6 Rachel Browne, "'Because It's 2015': Why Justin Trudeau Pushed for Gender Parity in
His Cabinet," *Vice News*, November 4, 2015, https://news.vice.com/en_us/article
/d39ykv/because-its-2015-why-justin-trudeau-pushed-for-gender-parity-in-his-cabinet.

7 Maria C. Escobar-Lemmon and Michelle M. Taylor-Robinson, *Women in Presidential
Cabinets: Power Players or Abundant Tokens?* (Oxford: Oxford University Press, 2016).

8 Amy Atchison and Ian Down, "Women Cabinet Ministers and Female-Friendly Social
Policy," *Poverty & Public Policy* 1, no. 2 (2009): 1–23; Christina Bergqvist, "The Nordic
Countries," in *Women in Executive Power*, eds. Gretchen Bauer and Manon Tremblay
(New York: Routledge, 2011).

9 Pedro A.G. dos Santos and Farida Jalalzai. *Women's Empowerment and Disempowerment
in Brazil: The Rise and Fall of President Dilma Rousseff* (Philadelphia: Temple University
Press, 2021).

10 Patricia Hill Collins and Sirma Bilge, *Intersectionality* (Hoboken, NJ: John Wiley & Sons,
2016), 9.

11 Kenneth J. Meier, "Theoretical Frontiers in Representative Bureaucracy: New Directions for Research," *Perspectives on Public Management and Governance* 2, no. 1 (2018):
39–56.

12 Carl Dahlström, Victor Lapuente, and Jan Teorell, "The Merit of Meritocratization: Politics, Bureaucracy, and the Institutional Deterrents of Corruption," *Political Research Quarterly* 65, no. 3 (2012): 656–68; Imran Rasul and Daniel Rogger, "The Impact of Ethnic Diversity in Bureaucracies: Evidence from the Nigerian Civil Service," *American Economic Review* 105, no. 5 (2015): 457–61.

13 Octavio Amorim Neto, "The Presidential Calculus: Executive Policy Making and Cabinet Formation in the Americas," *Comparative Political Studies* 39, no. 4 (2006): 415–40.

RESOURCES AND SUGGESTIONS FOR FURTHER READING

Bauer, Gretchen, and Manon Tremblay, eds. *Women in Executive Power: A Global Overview.* Abingdon, UK: Routledge, 2011.

Celis, Karen, and Joni Lovenduski. "Power Struggles: Gender Equality in Political Representation." *European Journal of Politics and Gender* 1, no. 1–2 (2018): 149–66. https://doi.org/10.1332/251510818X15272520831085.

Escobar-Lemmon, Maria, and Michelle M. Taylor-Robinson. "Getting to the Top: Career Paths of Women in Latin American Cabinets." *Political Research Quarterly* 62, no. 4 (2009): 685–99.

Escobar-Lemmon, Maria C., and Michelle M. Taylor-Robinson. *Women in Presidential Cabinets: Power Players or Abundant Tokens?* Oxford: Oxford University Press, 2016.

Jalalzai, Farida. *Women Presidents of Latin America: Beyond Family Ties?* New York: Routledge, 2015.

Jalalzai, Farida, and Meg Rincker. "Blood Is Thicker than Water: Family Ties to Political Power Worldwide." *Historical Social Research* 43, no. 4 (2018): 54–72.

Krook, Mona Lena, and Diana Z. O'Brien. "All the President's Men? The Appointment of Female Cabinet Ministers Worldwide." *Journal of Politics* 74, no. 3 (2012): 840–55. https://doi.org/10.1017/s0022381612000382.

Meier, Kenneth J. "Theoretical Frontiers in Representative Bureaucracy: New Directions for Research." *Perspectives on Public Management and Governance* 2, no. 1 (2019): 39–56. https://doi.org/10.1093/ppmgov/gvy004.

Reyes-Housholder, Catherine. "Presidentas Rise: Consequences for Women in Cabinets?," *Latin American Politics and Society* 58, no. 3 (July 1, 2016): 3–25. https://doi.org/10.1111/j.1548-2456.2016.00316.x.

CHAPTER NINE

Legislatures

Dr. Tiffany D. Barnes *Victoria Beall*

LEARNING OBJECTIVES

1 Recognize the role the legislature plays in the policymaking process
2 See how the variation in legislatures across the globe matters for the policymaking process and for representation
3 Appreciate why a diverse legislature is important for the policymaking process and for representation more generally
4 Understand whose interests get represented in the policymaking process and whose don't

KEY TERMS

bicameral legislature   legislative branches with two chambers as opposed to a unicameral legislature, where there is only one chamber

constituency service   services a legislator provides to constituents who are seeking assistance, such as helping them navigate bureaucratic processes; also known as casework

gatekeeping authority   the authority to block legislation from advancing to the chamber floor

legislative agenda   what bills will be heard on the chamber floor, when they will be discussed, and if they will come before the chamber for a vote

legislators   the individuals elected to hold office in the legislature

legislature   "a body created to approve measures that will form the law of the land"[1]

malapportionment   apportionment is the ratio between the number of residents in the district and the number of representatives from that district in the legislature; malapportionment happens when the votes of voters in some territorial sectors count more than others – that is, when the ratio between the residents and representatives is significantly different from district to district (as is the case in the US Senate)

negative agenda control   the ability to prevent bills from being heard on the chamber floor, typically because they are blocked in the committee process

seniority   legislators who have served the most terms in office are said to have legislative seniority

unicameral legislature   legislative branches with only one chamber as opposed to a bicameral legislature, where there are two chambers

WHAT ARE LEGISLATURES?

A **legislature** can be defined as "a body created to approve measures that will form the law of the land."[2] Legislatures play an important role in the policymaking process and they are the most important political institution for democratic representation. **Legislators** are the individuals elected to hold office in the legislature. Legislators are frequently referred to as representatives, members of congress, parliamentarians, or deputies.

Legislators are expected to represent their constituents by identifying problems, designing and approving policy solutions, and engaging in bureaucratic oversight to ensure that legislation is implemented in a transparent and timely manner that is consistent with the legislative intent. Legislators are also responsible for **constituency service**. In particular, legislators seek to establish trust and a relationship with constituents; they are responsible for the allocation of state resources to their constituents, and they provide a link between their district and the government.

That said, legislatures vary in terms of who gets elected to office, who has power once they are elected, and the incentives legislators have to represent different groups' interests. These factors are important for understanding who gets represented. Although in theory legislatures are often believed to be representative of the majority of citizens, in practice legislators are drawn from a narrow set of elites, as representatives tend to be men from the dominate racial and ethnic class who are much wealthier than the average citizen. In contrast, groups that have been historically excluded from politics (e.g., women, racial and ethnic minorities, the poor, the young, and people with disabilities) remain underrepresented in most legislatures across the globe today. Who has access to office is important because descriptive representatives – that is, lawmakers from politically marginalized groups such as women, racial and ethnic minorities, and working-class representatives – are more likely to represent these groups' policy interests.

In this chapter, we introduce you to the most common types of legislatures as well as the different ways legislatures are organized internally. Afterward we discuss a fundamental role of legislatures: representation. You will learn about the policymaking process in legislatures and the different types of policies representatives promote as well as how these policies may affect some groups in society more than others. Finally, we will explain why access to leadership within the chamber gives some legislators more influence over policy outcomes than others. We will explain who has access to power and how this shapes policymaking. As you will see, access to key positions of power is limited, and as a result some groups are better represented in the policymaking process than others.

TYPES OF LEGISLATURES AND LEGISLATIVE ORGANIZATION

Though all legislatures are charged with representing citizens and passing laws, there are different types of legislatures. Most notably, in a cross-national context there is an important distinction between presidential systems (such as democracies in the United States and most of Latin America, Central and southern West Africa, and in Central Asia), parliamentary systems (including United Kingdom, Australia, and most of Western Europe), and semi-presidential systems (most commonly found in Eastern Europe and the former Soviet republics).

Additionally, in more than half of the worlds' legislatures, legislative authority is concentrated into one chamber. These **unicameral legislatures** are common in Nordic countries and are scattered throughout Europe, Africa, the Middle East, and Asia. In **bicameral legislatures**, by contrast, legislative power is distributed between two chambers. Bicameral legislatures are common in North and South America, parts of Western Europe, and most former British, French, and Spanish colonies. These distinctions are important for understanding the amount of power any single chamber has and whose interests are represented in the policymaking process. In this section, we first explain the differences in parliamentary, presidential, and semi-presidential systems, and then we turn to a comparison of unicameral and bicameral systems.

Parliamentary, Semi-Presidential, and Presidential Systems

Recall from Chapter 8 that democracies can be categorized based on the relationship between the government and legislative branch. The government is defined as those holding cabinet portfolios – in most countries, the prime minister/president and cabinet ministers.[3] There are three main types of democracies: parliamentary, presidential, and semi-presidential. Two characteristics determine which category a democracy falls into: (1) a head of state, elected by popular elections, and (2) whether the legislature has a constitutionally granted power to remove the government from office. As the topic of this chapter is the legislature, we will focus on its role in these systems.

First, in parliamentary systems the head of government is chosen from the legislature by the ruling party and also serves as the head of state. The legislature has a constitutionally mandated authority to remove the government through what is commonly known as a vote of no confidence. So, how does this work? A vote of no confidence allows the legislature to remove the government from office if a majority of the members of the legislature are dissatisfied with the leadership and agree it is time to replace the prime minister and their cabinet. For example, in 2019 Austrian Chancellor Sebastian Kurz was removed from office after the Austrian parliament called a vote of no confidence. After the 2019 elections, however, he was returned to power. When the government loses a vote of no confidence, either elections are held immediately or a "caretaker" government serves until the next election.

An exception to this procedure is that some countries offer a *constructive vote of no confidence*. In this case, when a majority of the legislature agrees to remove the government from power, the legislature must also provide a replacement government rather than calling for a new election.

Second, in presidential systems, the executive and legislative branches are separate institutions. The legislature is unable to remove the government (in presidential systems, the government is the president and their cabinet) from office. Because the head of government is elected separately from the legislature, sometimes the government and legislature are led by two different majority parties. This can make it difficult for the two branches of government to reach agreements to pass proposed legislation into law.

Third, semi-presidential systems are a mix between pure parliamentary and pure presidential systems. As with parliamentary systems, the legislature elects

Table 9.1. **Presidential, Parliamentary, and Semi-Presidential Systems in Democracies**

Type of System	Is the head of state elected through popular elections?	Is the head of government chosen through the legislature?	Can the legislature remove the head of government from office?
Presidential	Yes	Yes	No
Semi-Presidential	Yes	Yes	Yes
Parliamentary	No	Yes	Yes

the head of government and has the ability to remove the government from office. As with presidential systems, it has a popularly elected head of state. Table 9.1 provides a summary of the differences among the three types of democratic systems.

Bicameralism versus Unicameralism

Legislatures also differ according to whether the legislature is composed of a single (unicameral) legislative chamber or two (bicameral) chambers that share power and responsibilities. Importantly, legislatures with two chambers can provide representation that targets different constituencies. For example, some chambers are designed to represent different geographical regions, whereas others offer representation for various ethnic, religious, territorial, and other factions. As of 2018, 79 countries have a bicameral legislature and 113 have a unicameral legislature.[4]

Not all bicameral systems are designed exactly the same. The variation in bicameral systems can be thought of in terms of *congruence* and *symmetry*.[5] Congruence refers to the constituencies each chamber represents and how they are elected; in essence, the political structure of each chamber. Whether or not the two chambers are congruent depends on how representatives are elected. A legislature is considered congruent when the legislators in both chambers represent the same constituencies. The lower chamber is typically elected via direct elections, but the same is not always true for the upper chamber, where legislators come to power through a variety of means: appointments by the current government or monarch; indirect elections or direct elections by citizens; and historically (though not in modern times) hereditary inheritance.

Congruence is also influenced by each chambers' constituency. Most lower house members are elected under the principle of equal representation for all citizens. This simply means that each legislator represents an equal share of citizens. In the upper chamber, by contrast, there are many examples where key segments of society are overrepresented. Upper chambers are commonly used to represent key subnational territories. This often results in **malapportionment**, where voters in some territorial sectors count more than others, as is the case in the US Senate. When both chambers are elected through similar means and represent the same groups of individuals in society, the chambers are argued to be politically congruent and hold similar preferences.

Symmetry in bicameral systems refers to the allocation of power between the two chambers. When bicameralism is symmetrical, both chambers hold the same or similar power. In practice, symmetrical bicameralism is rare. The United States represents one of four countries where the chambers hold symmetrical powers. Asymmetry is more common, where the chambers have power differentials, and the lower chambers hold more power.

Internal Legislative Structures

Now that we have explored the most common types of legislatures, let's take a look at how legislatures are organized. Legislative organization is key for determining who has power within the policymaking process and how policies get made. Legislatures are generally organized to include chamber-wide leadership positions, legislative committees, and committee leadership posts.

CHAMBER-WIDE LEADERSHIP

Legislatures are typically organized to include a speaker (this position is also referred to as the president of the chamber), vice-president/vice-speaker, and secretaries. The speaker of the house is the most influential member of the chamber, because they have the authority to set the **legislative agenda**. That is, the speaker decides what bills will be heard on the chamber floor, when they will be discussed, and if they will come before the chamber for a vote. Since a bill cannot be passed into law if it is not heard on the chamber floor, these agenda-setting powers give the speaker immense influence over the fate of legislation. The speaker also presides over the chamber, moderates floor debates, and recognizes members to speak. The speaker of the house may be a member of the legislature, or in some presidential systems, such as the US Senate and the Argentine Senate, the vice-president of the country serves as the speaker of the chamber.

The vice-speaker of the chamber has far less power than the chamber speaker. Still, this leadership position is prestigious and desirable. If the speaker cannot attend the session, the vice-speaker may preside over the chamber. In cases where the vice-president of the country presides over the chamber, the first vice-speaker of the chamber is usually the party leader from the governing party and is regarded as the most powerful member of the legislature. If the vice-president of

Figure 9.1. Key Positions of Power in the Chamber

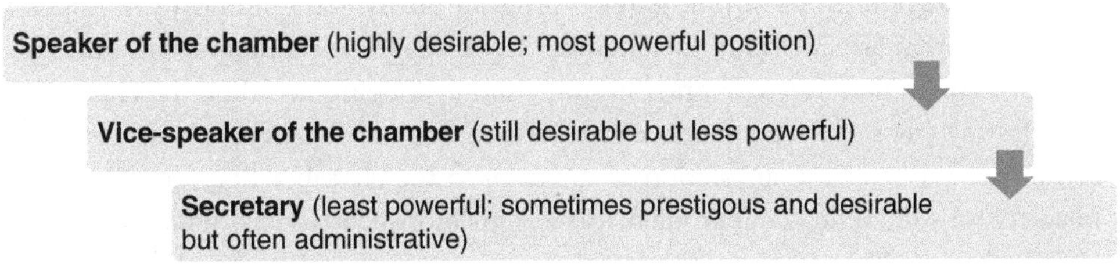

Speaker of the chamber (highly desirable; most powerful position)

Vice-speaker of the chamber (still desirable but less powerful)

Secretary (least powerful; sometimes prestigous and desirable but often administrative)

the country does not preside over the chamber, the vice-speaker of the chamber is often the leader of the opposition party.

In some countries a legislator holds the secretary position. In such cases, the secretary is viewed as a prestigious leadership role – but their powers and privileges pale in comparison to the speaker's. In other countries, the secretary position is administrative and not occupied by an elected official. The hierarchy of power for speakers, vice-speakers, and secretaries is shown in Figure 9.1.

LEGISLATIVE COMMITTEES

The workload in the legislature is divided among committees. Committees are responsible for drafting, examining, and amending legislation; hearing expert legislative testimony; and providing the chamber with a recommendation that the legislation either be considered on the chamber floor or tabled.[6] Given their influence over the policymaking process, some committees are very powerful. But the power and prestige of committees varies both within and across chambers.[7]

Within legislative chambers, committees are often organized around different policy areas. For example, there could be an education committee for handling education policy, an agriculture committee for addressing agriculture legislation, and so on. In most chambers the budget committee is the most powerful and prestigious because this committee oversees government expenditures – typically, any legislation that requires government funding must be approved by this committee. Since most important legislation passes through the budget committee, holding a seat on this committee grants legislators disproportionate influence over the policymaking process, allows committee members to increase their visibility among their colleagues and constituents, and even facilitates opportunities to earmark funds for their own legislative projects. For these reasons, committee appointments are a clear indicator of how powerful legislators are.

Committee power also varies across chambers. Most importantly, some legislators give committees strong **gatekeeping authority** – the authority to block legislation from advancing to the chamber floor.[8] In some chambers, committees are powerful in that they can prevent bills from ever being heard on the chamber floor (known as **negative agenda control**). If representatives who are not on the committee wish for the legislation to advance to the chamber floor, an absolute majority (or sometimes a super majority) of legislators have to pass what is known as a *discharge petition* to allow the legislation to advance to the chamber floor. In chambers with relatively weak committee systems, by contrast, a simple majority in the legislature can discharge legislation from the committee.

COMMITTEE LEADERSHIP

Legislators who are appointed to committee leadership have more authority than rank-and-file committee members. Though the structure of committees may vary, committee leadership often includes a committee chair (or president), vice-chair, and secretary. The chair is the most powerful position. The chair is charged with setting the committee agenda and deciding what legislation the committee will hear. Agenda setting gives the chair unparalleled influence over the fate of legislation – indeed, if the chair decides not to schedule legislation for a committee hearing, they can usually prevent the legislation from ever advancing to the chamber floor. Further, the chair determines the order in which amendments to legislation are taken up during committee hearings, giving them the ability to shape the final content of the legislation.

Still, there are limits to the chair's power, particularly if they are not supported by a majority of the committee. Chairs from the minority party are not able to unilaterally advance their legislative agenda because for a bill to be passed out of committee it needs a consensus. Despite this limitation, it is clear that leadership posts give some legislators disproportionate power in the chamber.

The committee vice-chair and secretary have less power than the chair. The vice-chair presides over the committee in the absence of the chair. The secretary is responsible for keeping minutes. Although they are viewed as largely ceremonial and less prestigious positions than the chair post, the vice-chair and secretary posts are viewed as valuable – particularly those from powerful committees.

To recap, in this section you learned how positions of power in the legislature not only vary in terms of the power they hold but also in terms of who has the ability to hold these important positions and who does not. Below, we will discuss how access to these different positions has implications for who holds power and influence in the legislative chamber.

WHO HAS POWER AND INFLUENCE?

Throughout this chapter we have discussed different types of legislatures, how legislatures are organized, and how and why legislators represent different groups in society. But how do legislators gain access to powerful positions within the chamber? The answer to this question is important, because access to power enhances legislators' ability to represent their constituents.

Access to Chamber-Wide Legislative Leadership

Members from the governing party typically hold the most important and prestigious positions in the chamber – namely, speaker of the house. Still, members from the opposition have access to leadership appointments in some chambers, such as the vice-speaker position. In particular, the governing party is more likely to grant authority to the opposition party when they foresee being in the opposition themselves in the near future or when they anticipate needing support from other parties to form a majority to pass their legislation.[9] But even when the opposition has little or no access to formal positions of power, they provide important checks on the governments' power.[10]

An exception to this power structure is the speaker of the house in Westminster parliamentary systems – that is, those parliaments modeled after the United Kingdom. In the United Kingdom, the speaker is to remain non-partisan. In order to remain impartial, the speaker is asked to renounce their partisan affiliation. The speaker does not participate in debates or cast votes. In Westminster parliamentary systems, the speaker is viewed more as an administrative role than a powerful position for the largest political party.

In thinking about who gains access to chamber-wide positions of power, scholars have only recently started thinking about representatives with multiple marginalized groups in society, such as Indigenous women. Yet there is a large body of research exploring women's and racial and ethnic minorities' access to power. Women, for instance, are less likely to preside over the chamber or to hold top party-wide leadership posts.[11] And although women are increasingly likely to be members of the government in parliamentary systems, they are less likely than men to hold the most powerful and prestigious posts, such as the minister of finance, defense, or foreign affairs.[12]

Though we know less about racial, ethnic, and religious minorities' access to leadership, they also tend to have limited access.[13] In Estonia, for example, whereas Estonians (the dominate ethnic group) have historically controlled all leadership positions in the Riigikogu (the national parliament), national minorities remain excluded from legislative leadership.[14] When minority legislators are elected into office through smaller political parties that organized to represent the interests of racial or ethnic minorities, they are far less likely than minority legislators from larger political parties to gain access to legislative leadership. This is because legislators from small parties rarely gain leadership appointments.

Exclusion from Legislative Committees

As we discussed, legislative power is also allocated via committee appointments. Since committees are an extension of a political party's power, party leaders are primarily responsible for deciding committee appointments. Legislators who want to be appointed to the most powerful post must have a good reputation among the party leadership. A combination of legislative networks, political capital, and legislators' reputation for policy expertise all influence committee appointments.

Formal rules also govern the appointment process. In some chambers, committee appointments are distributed to political parties in proportion to their seat share in the legislature. In such circumstances, political party leaders (in consultation with the party delegation) are charged with deciding which legislators from the party will be assigned to each committee. In other chambers, the speaker of the house may have disproportionate influence over committee appointments. In such circumstances the speaker's party may seek to gain disproportionate control over the legislative agenda by "party stacking" – appointing an overrepresentation of the majority party to important legislative committees.[15] In some chambers with high re-election rates (such as the US Congress, where most legislators run for and win re-election), **seniority** is regarded as important for appointments to powerful posts. Legislators who have served the most terms in office are said to have legislative seniority, and they are most likely to be appointed to powerful committees.

In addition to members of the majority party and legislators with seniority, research demonstrates that some politicians have more access to powerful committee posts than others. In Latin America, despite having high levels of numeric representation as a group and comparable levels of seniority as individuals, women are less likely than men to be appointed to the most powerful committees, such as the economic and budget committees (see Box 9.1).[16] Instead, women are more likely to serve on social issues, women's issues, and family issues committees. Notably, this is not because women are less likely than men to desire powerful committee appointments and is more appropriately attributed to discrimination or gender bias in the committee appointment process.[17]

> **BOX 9.1: WHY DOES WOMEN'S UNDERREPRESENTATION ON POWERFUL COMMITTEES MATTER?**
>
> In Argentina, as in many legislatures throughout the world, women are less likely to gain access to the budget committee. A woman legislator from Buenos Aires explains why women's underrepresentation on budget committees matters for the policy representation of women: "[The budget committee] is where everything is defined. With money, a lot is defined. You decide what others can decide. It is the mother of all committees." The power of the budget committee to "decide what others can decide" comes from the fact that any legislation that requires state funding must be approved by the budget committee. Consequently, access to the legislative budget is important for legislators' abilities to represent their constituents more generally and to advance women's rights.
>
> She explains that the state needs financial resources to address a number of problems women face in society: "When it comes to violence, if there are any women's centers in the city, there aren't enough workers. And this happens all over the country. Then there is labor discrimination against women; women are the ones who have the worst jobs – without social benefits." Improving the quality of life for women in Argentina requires more resources, and female legislators' limited access to the committees that control these resources makes it difficult for them to successfully promote and advance women's rights.[18]

In the United States, Black and Latinx legislators are more likely than white legislators to serve on lower prestige and less powerful committees, thus limiting their influence over major policy reforms.[19] But Latinx have been slightly more likely to be appointed to committees that allow them to target government spending at their constituency.[20] In the Netherlands, ethnic minority women are more likely to serve on committees that address issues facing ethnic minority women than ethnic minority men or ethnic majority women.[21] This is in part because women and ethnic minorities are often underrepresented on powerful committees and overrepresented on social committees targeting women's and ethnic minorities' interests.[22] The interests of ethnic minority women are not fully represented without the presence of ethnic minority women representatives because of their greater likelihood to work on committees that directly address these interests.

Attaining Committee Leadership

Party leaders have substantial influence over who receives committee leadership posts. If legislators want to be appointed to top committee posts, they need to have a good rapport with the party leader. Thus, party loyalty, an individual's political clout, professional networks, and perceptions about individuals' expertise and ability to govern all work together to determine who will be appointed to these valuable posts. As previously mentioned, in countries with strong seniority systems, seniority also influences leadership appointments.

In systems with strong seniority, women are about as likely as men to climb the party ranks and be appointed to prestigious posts when they attain seniority. But in systems where seniority is not the primary factor that governs leadership appointments – as is the case across most of Latin America, for instance – women are less likely than men to be appointed to preside over committees.[23]

Outcomes for minority legislators are similarly mixed. On the one hand, minority legislators who get elected to office through large political parties may have similar opportunities to gain access to leadership appointments. Black Americans elected into the Democratic Party in the United States, for example, sometimes advance to leadership positions in subcommittees more quickly than white and Latinx legislators in the Democratic Party, though the same is not true for Latinx in the United States.[24] But in circumstances where minority legislators are elected into office through smaller political parties, institutional rules that disproportionately distribute leadership posts to large political parties may preclude minority members from committee leadership appointments.

All of this is important because access to positions of power in the chamber influences the ability of legislatures to perform its central function: political representation, which we discuss next.

REPRESENTATION AND LEGISLATURES

Legislatures are designed to provide representation through policymaking, constituency service, and legislative oversight. Here we provide a brief description of the policymaking process, then we consider how policymaking varies across different institutions and constituencies. Finally, we explain how legislators can use constituency service and legislative oversight to provide representation.

But first, it is important to briefly remind you of descriptive representation and the role the legislature plays. As you learned in Chapter 6, women and minority groups are often underrepresented in the political process, with the legislature being no different. Progress has been made with the introduction of electoral rules such as gender and minority quotas, but work remains to be done. Indeed, other marginal groups, such as those at the intersection of sexual identity and gender identity, are only recently attaining political representation in legislatures worldwide.[25]

Figure 9.2. **The Policymaking Process in Bicameral Presidential Systems**

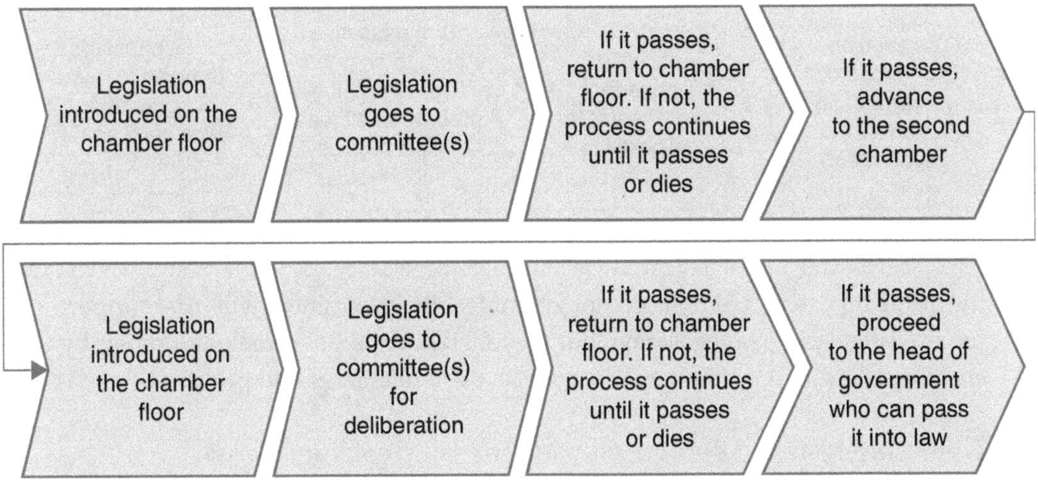

Legislation introduced on the chamber floor	Legislation goes to committee(s)	If it passes, return to chamber floor. If not, the process continues until it passes or dies	If it passes, advance to the second chamber

Legislation introduced on the chamber floor	Legislation goes to committee(s) for deliberation	If it passes, return to chamber floor. If not, the process continues until it passes or dies	If it passes, proceed to the head of government who can pass it into law

The Policymaking Process

Legislatures are charged with passing laws. The policymaking process varies across legislatures, but generally the process plays out over multiple stages. A bill is typically introduced on the chamber floor, where it may next advance to one or more committees for consideration, then back to the chamber floor where it may be approved by the chamber. If the legislature is a bicameral chamber, the bill must next advance through the same steps in the other chamber (see Figure 9.2).

In presidential systems, bills are typically introduced by an individual legislator or a group of legislators. Although legislation introduced by the majority party is most likely to be passed into law, in many legislatures no single political party holds a majority of seats. In this case, legislators must work within their own political party and across party lines to cultivate support for their legislation.

Some groups are more successful at advancing their legislation than others. Women legislators, for example, are more likely than men to collaborate with colleagues when developing legislation,[26] and in US state legislatures, such collaboration is shown to increase the likelihood that women's bills are passed into law.[27]

In parliamentary systems, bills are most often presented by the government – that is, the prime minster and cabinet ministers.[28] This process is shown in Figure 9.3. Although individual legislators can introduce legislation, it is highly unlikely that a bill will pass into law if the government does not approve it. When no party holds a majority of seats in the legislature, parties typically coordinate, establishing a formal coalition where cabinet ministers from more than one party agree to support

Figure 9.3. The Policymaking Process in Parliamentary Legislatures

Legislation introduced on the chamber floor (often by the government)	Legislation goes to committee(s) for deliberation	If it passes, return to chamber floor. If not, the process continues until it passes or dies	If it passes, proceed to head of government who can pass it into law

the prime minister. Coalitions do not guarantee the government will have support for any single piece of legislation, but they facilitate the policymaking process by enabling coordination among parties' legislative preferences and priorities.

Whose Interests Get Represented in the Policymaking Process?

Ideally, legislatures are designed to represent the entire population. But in reality some legislators' have incentives to represent a broad constituency base whereas others have incentives to prioritize subsets of constituents within society.[29] This is because representatives are motivated by political ambition – the desire to either win re-election or advance to a new political post (e.g., become mayor of a big city, be appointed to a cabinet position). If a legislator wants to run for president, they may have an incentive to pass legislation that is good for the entire country, since everyone will vote in the presidential election. But if they want to win re-election in a small rural district, they will be better served by passing legislation that chiefly benefits the constituents in their district (even if it is not good for people in other districts) because only their district will have influence over their re-election. Thus, political ambition drives legislators' behavior. Yet the rules of the game that shape how legislators get re-elected or climb the political ladder are different everywhere. To understand why legislators pass the policies they do, we have to understand the rules of the game.

In Chapter 6 you learned about electoral systems and some of the ways they can influence political representation. In this section we will revisit some of these electoral systems and discuss how they influence the different types of policies representatives promote.

Whereas some institutions are designed to represent a plurality of interests, others prioritize the will of the majority to the exclusion of the minority. When representatives promote policies designed to affect large segments of society and a plurality of interests, these policies are known as programmatic policies. In contrast, targeted policies can be public or private goods designed to target a specific constituency or group in society.[30] Finally, clientelist policies are similar to targeted policies in that they target a specific group in society but are different in that a representative promotes this policy in exchange for that group's support during election time.[31] For example, a national education policy is considered a programmatic policy, while a policy that brings a new school to a single territory in exchange for that territory's vote is considered a clientelist policy. An example of a targeted policy is bringing education resources to a specific territory in a country but not in explicit exchange for electoral support. Here we will consider how different institutional arrangements and the composition of the electorate influence the type of policies representatives promote.

ELECTORAL SYSTEMS AND REPRESENTATION

How representatives are elected into office is a key factor that influences whether legislators have an incentive to promote programmatic, targeted, or clientelistic policies. Representatives are less likely to promote programmatic policies in electoral systems with low district magnitude. As you learned in Chapter 6, single-member district systems are those in which a single candidate can win a seat in a given district. In these systems, personal reputation is more important than the party's reputation.

In general, representatives are more likely to propose programmatic policies under closed-list proportional representation systems. As you learned previously, candidates' personal reputations are far less important for winning election under these systems. In these systems, legislators rely on the party's reputation to win election as voters cast their ballot for political parties and not individual candidates. Thus, representatives are unlikely to improve their chances of winning re-election by promoting targeted policies for a specific voting bloc in society. Instead, representatives are more likely to promote policies that align with their party's values and policy platforms, with the goal of improving the party's reputation.

The opposite can be said for open-list proportional representation systems. In these systems, legislators compete against a number of other candidates both from the same party and from different parties. Voters cast their vote for individual candidates. As a result, representatives have an incentive to make a name for themselves and stand out against competition from within and outside their own party. One way to develop their own personal reputation is to propose targeted or clientelistic policies that (1) the legislator can explicitly claim credit for and (2) that target voters in their district so they can garner support at the polls.

CONSTITUENCIES AND POLICY TYPES

The composition of the electorate can also influence the types of policies representatives promote. Two ways the composition of the electorate can influence whether representatives have an incentive to promote programmatic, targeted, or clientelist policies is the territorial distribution of the voting population and the extent to which social cleavages are cross-cutting or reinforcing (as discussed in Chapter 5). When different social groups are concentrated in territorial sectors, representatives have an incentive to target the territories with the largest social groups to ensure they receive their votes.

Social cleavages are divisions in which society is organized based on one or more social identity groups. These groups are formed around one or more attributes, such as skin color, language, or location. Some of the most common cleavages found in societies around the world include the secular–religious, class, urban–rural, and ethnic, racial and, linguistic cleavages. When different attributes such as region and language are highly correlated, these cleavages are reinforcing. For example, if a large proportion of Indigenous voters lived in the north while non-Indigenous voters primarily lived in the south, we would say region and ethnicity are reinforcing cleavages.

Social cleavages are cross-cutting when these different attributes are not correlated. Keeping with our previous example, the cleavages would be cross-cutting if the population of Indigenous and non-Indigenous voters were evenly distributed in the north and south. Reinforcing cleavages can disincentivize representatives to promote programmatic policies because representatives can target one social group or territory and increase their chances of winning an election. When cleavages are cross-cutting, representatives must engage with multiple segments of society to win elections.

Additionally, the composition of the district or voting base that elects a representative can also constrain representatives' behavior. For example, when a racial minority representative is elected through voters who are primarily in a racially dominant social group, then the representative faces the tradeoff between ensuring their re-election by providing policies that impact all of their constituents or promoting targeted policies for a small subset of their voters.

SUBSTANTIVE REPRESENTATION

Beyond institutional and constituency factors that affect representation, a growing body of research also shows that descriptive characteristics of legislators also influence their policy priorities and preferences. In this section we discuss how representatives' gender, racial and ethnic background, and class can influence the likelihood different groups in society will experience substantive representation.

Substantive representation refers to the extent to which voters' policy preferences and interests are promoted by their representatives. Substantive representation is conceptualized in two ways: as a process and as an outcome.[32] When referring to substantive representation as an outcome, we mean passing legislation or making tangible differences in politics and society. For example, research in Argentina shows that women are more likely to pass legislation on women's rights, and research in Western Europe shows that more women in cabinet is associated with increases in policies of particular interest to women.[33]

Substantive representation as a process occurs when representatives are able to effectively make changes to the policy agenda, advocating for specific issues and introducing legislation and issues into the legislature even when they do not succeed in passing bills into law. For example, research from the UK shows working-class legislators use their time in legislative speeches to advocate for policies that benefit working-class voters.[34] Substantive representation is important because it has critical implications for political legitimacy, the quality of democracy, and the daily lives of voters.

When women's presence in politics increases, so does women's substantive representation (see Box 9.2). One of the central reasons for this relationship is that women as a social identity group experience similar gender socialization through childhood and continuing through adulthood. These shared experiences among women are not available to men, giving women a unique position and expertise to create legislation that promotes the interests of women. Women's shared experiences and gender identity also make them more likely to prioritize women's interests and issues. For example, research demonstrates how increased women's representation in politics influences whether or not countries have maternity leave policies. Countries across Europe with increased women's representation in the legislature not only have higher-quality maternity leave policies (i.e., longer periods of time off and paid leave provisions), but also had better implementation rates for these policies than did countries with lower numbers of women in the legislature.[35]

BOX 9.2: SPEAKING OUT ON BEHALF OF WOMEN AS A TRANSGENDER WOMAN IN POLAND: ANNA GRODZKA

In 2011, Anna Grodzka became the first Polish transgender legislator (and the world's third). As a transgender woman, she has used her unique position as both a transgender person and a woman to advocate for both women's and transgender rights in Poland. An excerpt of her speech illustrates how the intersection of sexual and gender identity has been overlooked in the political process in Poland:

> Alas, we are still living in societies where there exists systems of social segregation based on gender and sexual norms. Such systems are a source of

suffering and violence … The system of gender segregation affects transsexual people as well. In my country none of the stages of sex reassignment procedures are refunded. Transsexual people fall victims to violence and hatred. Trans people have until recently been largely absent in social awareness and they are still invisible in the body of Polish law.[36]

A similar story emerges when we consider the experience and preferences of different racial and ethnic groups in the legislature.[37] In the same way that women representatives share a direct link between them and their female constituents, positioning them as experts on women's issues, individuals who share a racial or ethnic social identity also share experiences that are not necessarily shared with members of other racial or ethnic groups. This is especially the case in instances of racial and ethnic discrimination (see Box 9.3). As a result, voters from different racial and ethnic groups are more likely to have their own interests and preferences prioritized and promoted by representatives who share the same racial or ethnic social identity.

BOX 9.3: UNDERSTANDING INTERSECTIONALITY: THE CASE OF ETHNIC MINORITY WOMEN IN BOLIVIA

In Bolivia, Indigenous women representatives worked together with various actors in society to make sure *all* forms of discrimination were identified in new legislation prohibiting racial discrimination.[38] The reason for explicitly identifying each form of discrimination, including gender discrimination, is that Indigenous women in Bolivia face ethnic stereotyping and violence as a result of their ethnic identity. Without the representation of Indigenous women in politics, these issues may have gone overlooked.

Another policy that changed as a result of taking the intersectional interests of Indigenous women into account is the gender quota law in Bolivia.[39] Originally, the proposed gender quota was for 30 per cent. However, this was conceived by feminist and urban women, with rural Indigenous women's viewpoints largely left out. Indigenous women conceptualized women's roles in society differently from that of feminist women, specifically with the concept known as *chacha-warmi*. *Chacha-warmi* emphasized parity and equality between a couple: Men and women had distinct roles, but they were equally distributed and valued.

The concept of *chacha-warmi* forced women from the urban centers, including conventional feminists, to reconsider their conceptions of gender relations. As a result, gender parity was included along with other laws that alternated men and women candidates largely because of the advocacy of Indigenous women in public and in the legislature.[40]

Legislators' occupational backgrounds likewise structure their policy preferences and priorities. Whereas career politicians are more likely to advance policy for strategic reasons, working-class representatives are more likely to introduce progressive economic proposals such as welfare reform and to advocate for labor and employment-related legislation.[41] In Latin America, representatives who hold labor union affiliations are more likely to propose legislation that targets union members and workers more generally.[42] The intersection of legislators' occupation and gender influence policy outcomes in unique ways. For instance, the presence of women state legislators from women-dominated working-class jobs (also known as pink-collar jobs) such as education, healthcare support, and social services is associated with larger state budgets in education, healthcare, and social services.[43]

Even though copious research demonstrates that descriptive representation of politically marginalized groups is associated with substantive representation, representatives still operate within a political context. Representatives face constraints from parties, lacking access to positions of power in the legislature, and constraints from ideology. As a result, legislators from marginalized groups are more likely to be effective when they have access to and hold positions of political power and influence. Further, they are more likely to be influential when working within political parties that are sympathetic to their group's interests.

SUMMARY

This chapter provided an introduction to the study of legislatures in political science. You learned about the different types of legislatures, how legislatures provide political representation, and how legislatures vary in terms of who has access to office and positions of power in the chamber. Finally, we discussed how varying levels of access to these positions of power have implications for which legislators (and the groups they represent) are able to influence political outcomes and which are not. Below we summarize the key points covered in this chapter:

- Legislatures can be categorized by several aspects:
  - The number of chambers
  - The ability to remove the government from office
  - The internal political composition and distribution of power between chambers in bicameral legislatures
- Legislatures vary on how positions of power are distributed in the chamber(s). Chamber-wide leadership positions, legislative committees, and committee leadership posts play critical roles for deciding who has power within the policymaking process and how policies get made.
- Legislators from politically marginalized groups tend to have limited access to powerful posts in the legislature. This in turn results in these legislators having limited influence and power in promoting their group interests and policies.
- Although all legislatures share the function and goal of policymaking, the types of policies legislators promote varies considerably. Different institutional settings can incentivize representatives to promote programmatic policies that target society as a whole over targeted or clientelist policies aimed at specific blocks of voters.
- In addition, the characteristics of legislators matter for the policies they promote. Jane Mansbridge summarized it nicely: "Black legislators do a better job than Whites of representing Black constituents, women legislators do a better job than men of representing female constituents and legislators from working-class backgrounds do a better job than others of representing working-class constituents."[44]
  - Individuals are connected to their representatives through a unique set of shared experiences. These representatives in turn are the best suited to advocate for specific policies that most impact their group.

CONCLUDING QUESTIONS

1 Thinking about the country where you live, imagine that women, racial and ethnic minorities, and minority women were represented in the legislature in equal proportions to the population. How do you think policy outcomes, constituency service, and legislative oversight would be different than it is today?

2 What are the pros and cons of the different types of legislatures: presidential systems, parliamentary systems, and semi-presidential systems? Do you think

one type of legislature is better positioned to represent the policy interests of politically underrepresented groups in society?

3 Thinking about substantive representation, why does intersectionality matter? Are there some interests that you can think of where any legislator can provide quality substantive representation? Which policy interests and issues do you think intersectionality matters more?

4 In this chapter, you learned about three different types of policy outcomes legislatures produce: programmatic, targeted, and clientelistic. Which of these policy types is most ideal for society? Why might groups in society want different types of policies? What factors must legislators take into account when deciding what type of policy to promote?

NOTES

1 Philip Norton, *Parliament in British Politics* (London: Macmillan International Higher Education, 2013), 1.

2 Norton, *Parliament in British Politics*, 1.

3 Michael Laver and Kenneth A. Shepsle, "Ministrables and Government Formation: Munchkins, Players and Big Beasts of the Jungle," *Journal of Theoretical Politics* 12, no. 1 (2000): 113–24.

4 IPU, "Compare Data on Parliaments," 2019, https://data.ipu.org/compare?field =country%3A%3Afield_structure_of_parliament#map.

5 Arend Lijphart, *Patterns of Democracy: Government Forms and Performance in Thirty-Six Countries* (New Haven, CT: Yale University Press, 1999).

6 Ernesto Calvo, *Legislator Success in Fragmented Congresses in Argentina: Plurality Cartels, Minority Presidents, and Lawmaking* (Cambridge: Cambridge University Press, 2014); Keith Krehbiel, Kenneth A. Shepsle, and Barry R. Weingast, "Why Are Congressional Committees Powerful?," *American Political Science Review* 81, no. 3 (1987): 929–45.

7 Gary W. Cox and Mathew D. McCubbins, *Setting the Agenda: Responsible Party Government in the US House of Representatives* (New York: Cambridge University Press, 2005); Roseanna Michelle Heath, Leslie A. Schwindt-Bayer, and Michelle M. Taylor-Robinson, "Women on the Sidelines: Women's Representation on Committees in Latin American Legislatures," *American Journal of Political Science* 49, no. 2 (2005): 420–36.

8 Ernesto Calvo and Iñaki Sagarzazu, "Legislator Success in Committee: Gatekeeping Authority and the Loss of Majority Control," *American Journal of Political Science* 55, no. 1 (2011): 1–15.

9 Sarah A. Binder, "The Partisan Basis of Procedural Choice: Allocating Parliamentary Rights in the House, 1789–1990," *American Political Science Review* 90, no. 1 (1996): 8–20; Malcolm E. Jewell, "State Legislative Elections: What We Know and Don't Know," *American Politics Quarterly* 22, no. 4 (1994): 483–509.

10 Betul Demirkaya, "What Is Opposition Good For?," *Journal of Theoretical Politics* 31 (2019): 260–80.

11 Tiffany D. Barnes, *Gendering Legislative Behavior: Institutional Constraints and Collaboration* (New York: Cambridge University Press, 2016); Leslie A. Schwindt-Bayer, *Political Power and Women's Representation in Latin America* (Oxford: Oxford University Press, 2010); Diana Z. O'Brien, "Rising to the Top: Gender, Political Performance, and Party Leadership in Parliamentary Democracies," *American Journal of Political Science* 59, no. 4 (2015): 1022–39.

12 Tiffany D. Barnes and Diana Z. O'Brien, "Defending the Realm: The Appointment of Female Defense Ministers Worldwide," *American Journal of Political Science* 62, no. 2 (2018): 355–68; Tiffany D. Barnes and Michelle M. Taylor-Robinson, "Women Cabinet Ministers in Highly Visible Posts and Empowerment of Women: Are the Two Related?," in *Measuring Women's Political Empowerment across the Globe*, eds. Amy C. Alexander, Catherine Bolzendahl, and Farida Jalalzai, 229–55 (Basingstoke, UK: Palgrave Macmillan, 2018); Mona Lena Krook and Diana Z. O'Brien, "All the President's Men? The Appointment of Female Cabinet Ministers Worldwide," *Journal of Politics* 74, no. 3 (2012): 840–55.

13 Oleh Protsky, *Promoting Inclusive Parliaments: The Represenation of Minorities in Indigenous Peoples in Parliament* (New York: Inter-Parliamentary Union and United Nations Development Programme, 2010).

14 William E. Crowther and Irmina Matonyte, "Parliamentary Elites as a Democratic Thermometer: Estonia, Lithuania and Moldova Compared," *Communist and Post-Communist Studies* 40, no. 3 (2007): 281–99.

15 Gary W. Cox and Mathew D. McCubbins, *Legislative Leviathan: Party Government in the House California Series on Social Choice and Political Economy* (Berkeley: University of California Press, 1993), 23.

16 Tiffany D. Barnes, "Women's Representation and Legislative Committee Appointments: The Case of the Argentine Provinces," *Revista Uruguaya de Ciencia Política* 23, no. 2 (2014): 135–63; Heath, Schwindt-Bayer, and Taylor-Robinson, "Women on the Sidelines"; Marwa Shalaby and Laila Eliman, "Arab Women in the Legislative Process," Sada – Carnegie Endowment for International Peace, April 26, 2017, https://carnegieendowment.org/sada/68780.

17 Barnes, *Gendering Legislative Behavior*; Scott A. Frisch and Sean Q. Kelly, "A Place at the Table: Women's Committee Requests and Women's Committee Assignments in the US House," *Women & Politics* 25, no. 3 (2003): 1–26, Schwindt-Bayer, *Political Power and Women's Representation in Latin America*.

18 Barnes, *Gendering Legislative Behavior*.

19 Michael S. Rocca, Gabriel R. Sanchez, and Jason L. Morin, "The Institutional Mobility of Minority Members of Congress," *Political Research Quarterly* 64, no. 4 (2011): 897–909; Katherine Tate, "Political Incorporation and Critical Transformations of Black Public Opinion," *Du Bois Review: Social Science Research on Race* 1, no. 2 (2004): 345–59.

20 Walter Clark Wilson, *From Inclusion to Influence: Latino Representation in Congress and Latino Political Incorporation in America* (Ann Arbor: University of Michigan Press, 2017).

21 Liza M. Mügge, Daphne J. van der Pas, and Marc van de Wardt, "Representing Their Own? Ethnic Minority Women in the Dutch Parliament," *West European Politics* 42, no. 4 (2019): 705–27.

22 Jorge Fernandes, Jeremy Dodeigne, and Laura Morales, "Access to Positions of Influence in the Parliamentary Arena: Are MPs of Immigrant Origin Disadvantaged?," in *Pathways to Power: The Political Representation of Citizens of Immigrant Origin in Seven European Democracies*, eds. Laura Morales and Thomas Saalfeld (Oxford: Oxford University Press, 2017).

23 Barnes, *Gendering Legislative Behavior*; Schwindt-Bayer, *Political Power and Women's Representation in Latin America*.

24 Rocca, Sanchez, and Morin, "The Institutional Mobility of Minority Members of Congress."

25 Melanie M. Hughes, "Intersectionality, Quotas, and Minority Women's Political Representation Worldwide," *American Political Science Review* 105, no. 3 (2011): 604–20.

26 Barnes, *Gendering Legislative Behavior*.

27 Barnes, *Gendering Legislative Behavior*; Mirya R. Holman and Anna Mitchell Mahoney, "The Choice Is Yours: Caucus Typologies and Collaboration in US State Legislatures," *Representation* 55, no. 1 (2019): 47–63. See also Anna Mitchell Mahoney and Christopher J. Clark, "When and Where Do Women's Legislative Caucuses Emerge?," *Politics & Gender* 15, no. 4 (2019): 671–94.

28 Laver and Shepsle, "Ministrables and Government Formation."

29 Brian F. Crisp, Betul Demirkaya, Leslie A. Schwindt-Bayer, and Courtney Millian, "The Role of Rules in Representation: Group Membership and Electoral Incentives," *British Journal of Political Science* 48 no. 1 (2018): 47–67.

30 Gary Cox and Mathew D. McCubbins, "The Institutional Determinants of Economic Policy Outcomes," in *Presidents, Parliaments, and Policy*, eds. Stephan Haggard, Mathew D. McCubbins, and Randall Calvert (Cambridge: Cambridge University Press, 2019).

31 Ernesto Calvo and Maria Victoria Murillo, *Non-Policy Politics: Rich Voters, Poor Voters, and the Diversification of Electoral Strategies* (New York: Cambridge University Press, 2019).

32 Susan Franceschet and Jennifer M. Piscopo, "Gender Quotas and Women's Substantive Representation: Lessons from Argentina," *Politics & Gender* 4, no. 3 (2008): 393–425.

33 Amy L. Atchison, "The Impact of Female Cabinet Ministers on a Female-Friendly Labor Environment," *Journal of Women, Politics & Policy* 36, no. 4 (2015): 388–414; Amy L. Atchison and Ian Down, "The Effects of Women Officeholders on Environmental Policy," *Review of Policy Research* 36, no. 6 (2019): 805–34; Jennifer M. Piscopo, "Rethinking Descriptive Representation: Rendering Women in Legislative Debates," *Parliamentary Affairs* 64, no. 3 (2011): 448–72.

34 Tom O'Grady, "Careerists versus Coal-Miners: Welfare Reforms and the Substantive Representation of Social Groups in the British Labour Party," *Comparative Political Studies* 52, no. 4 (2019): 544–78.

35 Miki Caul Kittilson, "Representing Women: The Adoption of Family Leave in Comparative Perspective," *Journal of Politics* 70, no. 2 (2008): 323–34. But see also Atchison and Down, "The Effects of Women Officeholders on Environmental Policy"; Atchison "The Impact of Female Cabinet Ministers."

36 *Kaleidoscope Trust* (2013), quoted in Pamela Paxton, Melanie M. Hughes, and Tiffany Barnes, *Women, Politics, and Power: A Global Perspective*, 4th ed. (New York: Rowman & Littlefield, 2020).

37 Nadia E. Brown, *Sisters in the Statehouse: Black Women and Legislative Decision Making* (New York: Oxford University Press, 2014); Danielle Casarez Lemi, "Identity and Co-alitions in a Multiracial Era: How State Legislators Navigate Race and Ethnicity," *Politics, Groups, and Identities* 6 no. 4 (2018): 725–42; Christopher J. Clark, *Gaining Voice: The Causes and Consequences of Black Representation in the American States* (New York: Oxford University Press, 2019); Michael D. Minta and Nadia E. Brown. "Intersecting Interests: Gender, Race, and Congressional Attention to Women's Issues," *Du Bois Review: Social Science Research on Race* 11 no. 2 (2014): 253–72; Crisp et al., "The Role of Rules in Representation."

38 Christina Ewig, "Forging Women's Substantive Representation: Intersectional Interests, Political Parity, and Pensions in Bolivia," *Politics & Gender* 14, no. 3 (2018): 433–59.

39 Ewig, "Forging Women's Substantive Representation."

40 Mala Htun and Juan Pablo Ossa, "Political Inclusion of Marginalized Groups: Indigenous Reservations and Gender Parity in Bolivia," *Politics, Groups, and Identities* 1, no. 1 (2013): 4–25.

41 O'Grady, "Careerists versus Coal-Miners."

42 Juan Pablo Micozzi, "Division or Union of Labor? Analyzing Workers' Representation in the Argentine Congress," *Latin American Politics and Society* 60, no. 4 (2018): 93–112.

43 Tiffany D. Barnes, Victoria Beall, and Mirya Holman, "Pink-Collar Representation and Budgetary Outcomes in US States," *Legislative Studies Quarterly* (2020).

44 Jane Mansbridge, "Should Workers Represent Workers?," *Swiss Political Science Review* 21, no. 2 (2015): 261.

RESOURCES AND SUGGESTIONS FOR FURTHER READING

Barnes, Tiffany D. *Gendering Legislative Behavior*. Cambridge: Cambridge University Press, 2016.

Brown, Nadia E. *Sisters in the Statehouse: Black Women and Legislative Decision Making*. New York: Oxford University Press, 2014.

Davidson-Schmich, Louise K., ed. *Gender, Intersections, and Institutions: Intersectional Groups Building Alliances and Gaining Voice in Germany*. Ann Arbor: University of Michigan Press, 2017.

Hardy-Fanta, Carol, ed. *Intersectionality and Politics: Recent Research on Gender, Race, and Political Representation in the United States*. Binghamton, NY: Haworth Press, 2007.

Severs, Eline, Karen Celis, and Silvia Erzeel. "Power, Privilege and Disadvantage: Intersectionality Theory and Political Representation." *Politics* 36, no. 4 (2016): 346–54. doi:10.1177/0263395716630987.

CHAPTER TEN

Courts and the Law

*Dr. Kimberly
P. Fields*

LEARNING OBJECTIVES

1 Examine typical judicial structures and arrangements
2 Understand different legal traditions
3 Learn the traditional functions of and roles the judiciary plays in states throughout
the world
4 Explore the conceptual and practical relationships between the judiciary, constitutions, and the most common types of legal systems across the globe

KEY TERMS

appellate jurisdiction   when higher courts have the authority to hear appeals from
lower-level courts
civil law   a legal system in which the law is a strongly constructed, detailed entity
created by a legislature or other lawmaking political institution. Judges apply the
law rather than interpreting it. Civil law is the most common legal system around
the world.
collegial politics   how judges interact with their colleagues
common law   a legal system in which the laws are less detailed and in which judges
have considerable room for interpreting the law. Most Anglo-American states have
common law systems.

constitutional courts   in many states, these are the only courts that have the power of judicial review.

constitutionalism   a system in which constitutions place limitations on government power

illiberal   freedom restricting

judicial independence   the idea that courts should not be subject to improper influence from the other branches of government or from private or partisan interests

judicial review   the power of a court to declare an act of government (or action of a government official) unconstitutional

original jurisdiction   a court's power to hear and decide a case before any appellate review

religious law   a legal system in which the law is derived from the sacred texts of religious traditions and in most cases claims to cover all aspects of life. At present, found mainly in Muslim-majority states and Vatican City.

statutory interpretation   the process of determining what a particular statute means so that a court may apply it accurately

WHAT IS THE JUDICIARY?

The judiciary is perhaps the most confusing and controversial of the major branches of modern government. Legislatures, executives, and bureaucracies are commonly understood to be tasked with the creation, enforcement, and implementation of policies consistent with citizen and national interests. The judiciary, on the other hand, occupies a fundamentally distinct role and decides differently. Unlike the other branches, the judiciary's decisions are expected to be grounded in a state's constitution and legal system; they are also expected to be fair and objective interpretations of what existing laws mean – not ideology, politics, or judgments about which policy alternative is most practical or popular. As a result, and in sharp contrast to other political institutions (such as legislatures), courts are often respected because their decisions are viewed as being principled rather than motivated by self-interest or partisanship. To the extent that courts are perceived as legitimate by their constituents, their decisions – including their unpopular ones – are respected, obeyed, and accepted.

However, courts are inherently political institutions. They are created and continually shaped by political processes (e.g., constitutional conventions, court-curbing legislation, elections, and appointments). As a result, they reflect the preferences of their creators and dominant governing coalitions. In many cases this means the values, preferences, and interests of some segments of a society disproportionately shape and are reflected in the judiciary's structure, operation, composition, and outputs more than others. Such circumstances, particularly when persistent and pervasive, challenge judicial institutions' credibility, which can spell disaster for a country's ability to keep the peace.

To earn and maintain legitimacy, judicial institutions must produce decisions that carefully balance legal analysis, political and social pressures, and judges' personal preferences. To do so they must pay attention to the ways in which the intersections of politically constructed categories of identities render some citizens by virtue of their assignment to those categories more vulnerable to abuse in ways not visible to or adequately addressed by the "blind," "impartial," or "objective" application of the law. Failure to strike such a balance can threaten a nation's domestic stability and the judiciary's reputation, authority, and influence, which may lead to ignoring court decisions or violent opposition to those decisions. In some countries, unpopular rulings have resulted in riots (Bulgaria); court buildings have been attacked and burned (Pakistan); judges have been intimidated and removed from office (Zimbabwe), assassinated (Uganda), or reassigned to courts in the hinterland (Japan); courts have been stripped of their jurisdiction (United States); and, in the most extreme cases, judicial institutions have been suspended (United States) or abolished (Russia).

While no two judicial systems are exactly the same, the history of colonization and the processes associated with globalization and international trade have contributed to the homogenization of judiciaries and legal systems throughout the world. As a result, this chapter begins from the premise that, for most states in the modern context, the judiciary's decisions are supposed to be fair and objective assessments of the state's constitution and laws. Therefore, before we can tackle the courts, we first need to tackle constitutions and the law. Once we have established that foundation, we will turn to the courts.

CONSTITUTIONS

Almost every country in the world has a constitution. While they share some characteristics and content, no two are likely to be the same. Some are written down (codified) and contained in a single physical document. Others refer to sets of laws, judicial decisions, and other foundational documents that spell out how the state is structured and how it should function. Some provide universal healthcare (e.g., Denmark, Belarus, Malta); others extend rights and protections to animals and plants (Ecuador). Some set up monarchies (e.g., Cambodia, Jordan, Belgium), while others establish presidencies (e.g., Mexico, Angola, Indonesia) or arrange for a seven-member Federal Council (Switzerland). Many are short and general, but others are long, detailed, and try to specify the kind of society and political system they aspire to – for example, Rwanda's constitution mandates that 30 per cent of its parliamentary seats be reserved for women, and Malta's provides for universal healthcare and gives constitutional rights to people regardless of their sexual orientation and gender identity. Such variations contribute to significantly different political, social, environmental, and economic outcomes, particularly for women and minority populations.

In recent years there has been renewed attention to constitutions by policymakers, academics, and citizens. This is not surprising considering constitutions provide the underpinning for government in nearly every society across the world. They simultaneously establish, authorize, and constrain the institutions that govern society. As a result, they are closely linked to the distribution and acquisition of public goods, resources, and services. Outcomes, like democracy, economic performance, and human rights protection, are all associated with the contents of countries' constitutions. This chapter examines the nature and purpose of constitutions – what they are, why we have them, and whether they promote and protect equality.

What Is a Constitution?

Despite the significance and ubiquitousness of constitutions in both scholarship and practice, there is some confusion about the precise definition of a constitution. In general, constitutions are typically defined and understood in two ways – as a written, physical document and as a basic set of laws and practices that establish the shape and form of a state's structure and operations. Constitutions are, in essence, the fundamental laws of each country; they are special types of laws – uberlaws – that regulate the way a country is run. They lay out a state's most important institutions and positions, and they define their scope, powers, responsibilities, and limitations. They are often referred to and understood to be the supreme law of the land, taking precedence over all others. Additionally, they define how all the other laws should be made. Furthermore, they outline the proper relations between institutions and offices of the state, as well as between the government and its citizens. This is probably a constitution's most crucial role because it allocates powers and functions to government and specifies the rights and duties of both governments and citizens – who can do what, to whom, and under what circumstances.

Purpose of a Constitution

Constitutions serve several purposes simultaneously. Preventing tyranny and abuse of power, defining the state and its values, and establishing government and offices and defining their powers are the traditional purposes of constitutions. Let's take each of these in turn.

PREVENTING TYRANNY AND ABUSE OF POWER

A central idea here is that, in democratic states, constitutions place limitations on government power. Constitutions create a set of uninfringeable principles and more specific provisions to which future law and government activity more generally must conform. This function, commonly called **constitutionalism**, is integral to the working of democracy. Absent the constraints on power and commitment to higher authority elites, powerful interests and majorities can use the state for their short-term benefit to the detriment of minorities and the historically, socially, politically, and economically disadvantaged – who may then deem it necessary to turn to extra-constitutional means (e.g., riots, civil disobedience, terrorism) of securing power. By limiting the scope of government and mandating politicians to respect certain limits, constitutions help make government possible. In so doing, constitutions contribute to a country's stability by providing an enduring structure for politics, setting expectations about outcomes, and facilitating predictability. As such, constitutions are important because they can impact how politics unfolds, particularly who gets what and when.

DEFINING THE STATE'S GOALS AND VALUES

A second function that constitutions serve is the symbolic one of defining the state and its goals. In principle, constitutions are assumed to enshrine a society's vision of itself, including its primary values. In other words, looking at a state's constitution should provide a glimpse into what a society considers important and wants for itself. In this conception, the constitution functions not just as a set of rules, but also as an ongoing set of practices grounded in values, principles, and beliefs that define the political unit. In theory, constitutions should facilitate the emergence or solidification of a national identity. Whether or not these national identities are inclusive and tolerant depends on the substance of the beliefs, values, and principles they rest upon. See Box 10.1 for examples.

BOX 10.1: HARMFUL VERSUS HELPFUL CONSTITUTIONAL PROVISIONS: THE UNITED STATES AND INDIA

Some constitutions reflect customs and traditions that are hostile to particular segments of the country's population or exclude certain people from full participation or citizenship. The US Constitution's inclusion of the 3/5 clause is an example where a constitutional text reflected, enshrined, and supported a system of exploitation and abuse of its Black population. Also sometimes called the 3/5 Compromise, this clause allowed states to count enslaved persons as part of the population for the purposes of seat apportionment in the US Congress (the more people a state has, the more seats it gets in the House of Representatives).

However, since enslaved persons were treated as property rather than people, some members of the Constitution Convention argued that they should not be counted at all. The compromise was that for the purposes of apportionment, the population would be counted as "the whole Number of free persons ... and three fifths of all other [enslaved] persons." Its inclusion in the founding document and centrality to the political system's decision-making processes and governing institutions sent clear messages to its citizens and the rest of the world about the values and beliefs the country and its government rested upon.

Other constitutions reflect the hope that society can rectify the harms that have been done to marginalized people. The Indian Constitution, for example, specifically protects the rights of India's Dalit population. The Dalits were traditionally the lowest-status group in India's 3,000-year-old caste system, a rigid hierarchy that specified the status of each group in Indian society. Dalits were thought to be so lowly that people of higher castes literally would not touch them, hence they were once called *untouchables*. The practice of untouchability meant that Dalits were regularly subjected to abuse for which they had no recourse under the law. The highly unequal caste system was incompatible with democratic governance, so the system was (technically) abolished in India's post-independence constitution. Dalits were given special constitutional protections that ban the perpetuation of untouchability, meaning that Dalits cannot be denied employment or education on the basis of their caste. Unfortunately, constitutional protections cannot force people to change their views, so the protections have not ended discrimination against Dalits; they still face widespread abuse and exclusion. However, they now have constitutionally guaranteed legal recourse.

In thinking about the values that states enshrine in their constitutions, it's also important to think about how difficult most states make it to amend their constitutions. Thus, when you have constitutionally mandated systems of oppression, as with the 3/5 clause, it takes tremendous effort (the United States had a civil war) to reverse those oppressive systems. However, it is also true that it would take tremendous effort to remove the constitutionally guaranteed rights specific to the historically oppressed, as with the Dalits.

ESTABLISHING GOVERNMENT INSTITUTIONS AND DEFINING THEIR POWERS

A third and very practical function of constitutions is that they define patterns of authority and set up government institutions. Pragmatically speaking, constitutions also lay out who can vote, who can run for and hold office, what powers they are to have, and the rights and duties of citizens. This function differs from the constitutionalist function of limiting government. Although the mere process of defining an institution involves some constraints on its behavior, these organizational maps and procedural rules and requirements are conceptually distinct, albeit subtly, from the substantive and entrenched limits on government action incorporated into the notion of constitutionalism.

Parts of a Constitution

In spite of their huge variety, most written constitutions have four main parts: preamble, list of fundamental rights, description of main government institutions and offices along with duties and powers, and amendment procedures.

Preambles typically mention important historical events and moments of national pride. They may also include declarations about national aspirations and make reference to national symbols. Constitutions' preambles tend to be inspirational rather than prescriptive or descriptive.

Constitutions vary in what they choose to provide, but certainly one of the most common elements is a set of rights. Most constitutions contain a list of civil and political rights and statements about the limits of government powers on those rights. Some constitutions refer also to economic, social, and cultural goods and services the government is required to provide its citizens (e.g., healthcare, education, housing). Such guarantees are known as *positive rights* and are contrasted with *negative rights*, which refer to restrictions placed on government from interfering with a citizen's ability to do or pursue certain activities or behave in particular ways (e.g., speak freely, associate with whom one wants, practice one's preferred religion).

Additionally, most constitutions include descriptions of the main structures or institutions of government along with their powers and duties. Typically, this includes the executive, legislative, and judicial branches of national government, and sometimes lower levels of government as well. Also commonly included are the procedures to be followed in amending the constitution.

To What Extent Do Constitutions Shape Political Practice?

While constitutions are important documents, perhaps supremely important, their influence on a nation's political and social environments is not a given but depends on various factors – both internal and external to the constitution itself. In some countries, the constitution may be mainly symbolic and hence practically insignificant. Many authoritarian regimes, run by dictators or military juntas, have constitutions espousing democratic values and principles that politicians ignore, disregard, or circumvent. Relatedly, constitutions can lack credibility because they do not reflect the citizens' lived experiences in their country, and as a result these constitutions lack the ability to inform or influence political practice.

Some constitutions fail to address significant social issues or inadequately spell out important offices, procedures, and the structure of crucial political institutions. They can be too vague and as such neglect to cover exceptional or specific circumstances. What's more, constitutions can develop and change through formal and informal processes, even if the documents themselves do not. For example, at its inception the US Constitution was not understood to have given the Supreme Court the sole authority to interpret the constitution. The Supreme Court, in 1803, through one of its own decisions (*Marbury v. Madison*) gave itself the power of judicial review, which we will discuss at length below. These circumstances reveal that a state's constitution, no matter how well constructed, cannot guarantee particular outcomes.

As you saw in the example from India, achieving a constitution's goals requires both citizen and elites' acceptance of the values enshrined in it and commitment to putting them into practice. This suggests that constitutions are like guidelines or instructional manuals for the main institutions of government but actual operations may differ – even differ radically – from the legal documents. These observations undergird and inform the debate about how important institutions are and to what extent they actually determine the operations of a political system and the behavior of political actors within it.

THE COURTS

There are many elements that need to be considered when we study the courts. Their structure, functions, and powers are all important to how courts work in practice.

Court Structure and Organization

Hierarchy is a feature of nearly all judicial institutions. Practically all political systems have multiple tiers of the judiciary – and some courts are explicitly subordinate to others. For example, in the United States there are 94 district courts in the first tier, 13 courts of appeal in the second tier, and the Supreme Court at the top. This simple three-tier judicial system has been widely adopted around the world, although the size of the tiers varies across countries. The most important distinction among the tiers is between the lowest courts and all the others. Trial courts are the courts that exercise **original jurisdiction**, which means they are the first to hear a case. The trial courts are the first line of action and where the lion's share of judicial activity occurs. Trial courts are where the facts of the case are introduced. They are also responsible for keeping a record of the proceedings. In the trial court, the "finder of fact" is either a judge or a jury, which means the judge or the jury must determine the credibility of the witnesses, discuss and assess the facts presented, and determine the winner.

Higher courts, known as appellate courts, exercise **appellate jurisdiction**, which means they review the records from trial courts. Normally, they do not hear or consider new facts or evidence but reserve their time to evaluate the application of the law and procedures followed in the lower court(s). They are limited to decisions on matters of law and process. As such, appellate courts focus on determining whether the trial court(s) applied the appropriate laws, followed established procedures, and made the correct interpretation of applicable laws. Because most cases are not appealed, there are fewer appellate courts than district courts. Generally, there is a right to appeal to an intermediate appellate court from a decision or a judgment of a trial court. Typically, the intermediate appellate court must accept the case if there is a right to appeal. This is called an "appeal as of right." The appeals court cannot reject the case unless there has been a valid waiver of the right to appeal.

Some countries allow for appeals of appellate court rulings, too. In the United States, this occurs at the level of the Supreme Court. However, there is generally no right to appeal to a Supreme Court. In most instances, the highest appellate courts have the authority to reject any case they do not want to decide. This is because those appellate courts are courts of discretionary jurisdiction. They have the discretion to pick and choose which cases to take and which to reject. The cases those courts take on are usually limited to cases of great importance that will impact many others or decide unsettled legal issues to provide uniformity of the law in the entire state.

The hierarchy of the judiciary has two important benefits. First, it provides for an effective check on biased, corrupt, incompetent, arbitrary, or irresponsible judicial decisions. If a trial court excludes or improperly considers evidence, if a prosecutor fails to follow proper procedures, if a judge gives biased jury instructions, or if an abnormal criminal sentence or monetary award is given, the appeals court may reverse the decision, modify it, or call for a new trial. Second, a system of appellate courts creates the possibility of consistent interpretation of the law. Without a system of superior appellate courts, new interpretations of the law would apply only in the jurisdictions where the trial courts created the interpretation. When the highest appellate courts interpret the law, the law means the same thing throughout the system.

Despite these benefits, appellate courts do present some issues as well. Unlike trial courts, where often one judge or a jury makes the decisions, many appellate courts use panels of judges to review cases. This can introduce other factors outside the law and the legal procedures appellate courts are tasked with focusing on that influence decision making. Legal scholar Jonathan Kastellec found that the US judiciary's hierarchical structure shaped the **collegial politics** (how judges interact with their colleagues) in ways that influenced how judges voted on cases and case outcomes.[1] Kastellec's study found that when three-judge appellate court panels had a single judge from an opposing political party as the other two judges on the same panel – but aligned with the Supreme Court – the single judge was able to influence the decisions of their colleagues. As such, this interaction increases the Supreme Court's control of the judicial hierarchy.

The Role and Functions of the Judiciary

Courts play an important role in society. Scholars throughout history have found that the practice of looking for a neutral third party to resolve conflict between two people is so basic that almost every society employs it. However, the functions of courts goes well beyond the resolution of private disputes between individuals. Judicial institutions and the decisions they render shape and are shaped by the societies in which they are embedded. Moreover, because they are culturally bound political institutions, how the courts operate and the outputs they produce disproportionately reflect the interests and preferences of the society's most powerful forces and dominant governing coalitions. As such, they are essential to the maintenance and reproduction of societies' norms, values, practices, and power arrangements including illiberal, classist, racist, and sexist ones. This means that regardless of the type of government that exists, the amount of freedom citizens possess, or the level of inequality between them, it is nevertheless true that the courts are going to enforce the state's dominant, basic rules. For example, if the state is a *theocracy* the courts' treatment of non-adherents will send a message to those who may question the tenets of the country's official religion. Similarly, if the society is racist and sexist, the court's treatment of women assigned to marginalized and vilified racial categories will be harsher than its treatment of women in privileged racial categories.

The judiciary is the branch of modern government most people expect to be the great leveler in society – the arena in which citizens are all equal before the law regardless of race, class, gender, or creed. However, courts can also be understood as political institutions that, through their decision making, function to preserve a society's preferred or dominant status quo. As durable institutions expected to reproduce consistent and predictable outcomes over time, some courts become captured by the powerful elites within the political system. This can mean that courts may be used to entrench inequality, existing power dynamics, and elites' preferences.

As many legal analysts, critical race scholars like Kimberlé Crenshaw and Derrick Bell, as well as citizens involved in the justice system point out, the outcomes courts produce vary in ways that reflect states' social, political, and economic divisions.[2] Their decisions and the cumulative impact of those decisions reveal that the intersection of socially constructed identities around race, gender, and class provide some citizens with less legal protection and support than others and ultimately render them fundamentally less free. When these types of disparities are present and persistent, citizens question the legitimacy of the judiciary and its ability to fulfill its role to pursue equality in society.[3]

If a state is a democracy where a significant proportion of its voting population embrace **illiberal** (freedom-restricting) traditions – those that include or tolerate discrimination based on constructed categories of race or gender – the judiciary will reflect those traditions in both composition of the judiciary and its decisions. Additionally, the courts' decisions regarding discrimination toward those categories of people reinforce the societies' racial or gender power relationships. Additionally, they will convey messages about the acceptability of disparities between citizens and the mechanisms of marginalization. When the US Supreme Court decided in 2007 that the Seattle school district's bus plan to integrate its racially segregated schools was unconstitutional because there was no history of *de jure* (in law) segregation and that *de facto* (in fact) segregation resulting from individual preferences or "white flight" were permissible, the court was also reinforcing the norms of the nation.

The judiciary also plays more functional roles. First, judicial institutions' primary function is to resolve conflict. In this role courts provide societies with a predictable form of dispute resolution. Where they are perceived as legitimate, courts resolve conflicts citizens would not resolve on their own. For this reason, judicial institutions can be said to help maintain social control, preventing civil unrest and domestic discord. To the degree that the courts are considered reliable and fair, most citizens feel comfortable complying with their decisions. As such, courts can also be said to help legitimize the state. Second, like other political institutions, courts make policy. They not only participate in applying and interpreting the law, but they shape policy and laws as well. Third, courts also function as monitors of other branches of government. In this role they ensure government entities and actors act within the scope of their jurisdictions and fulfill their obligations and responsibilities. Additionally, they determine the appropriate punishment for government actors who breach the law.

Finally, judicial institutions have been credited with performing the function of protecting minority rights, especially in democracies where the executive and legislative branches are responsive to majority preferences through voting in elections. Courts have the ability to hear the cases of numerical minorities who would, because of their small numbers or marginalization, have difficulty influencing the other branches of government to reflect their interests in policies. However, legal scholars and citizens argue that judicial protection of minorities is inconsistent, at best, and often inadequate. Depending on the ideological composition of the court and the interactions between citizens and states, judicial institutions can interpret the law in ways that restrict minority rights and at other times protect minority rights; a good example of the latter comes from Canada's *Persons Case*, discussed in Box 10.2.

BOX 10.2: ARE WOMEN PEOPLE UNDER THE LAW?

In 1927, five women (known as The Famous Five) approached Canada's governor general with a simple question: Are women "persons" under Canadian law? The question stemmed from the government's interpretation of the Constitution Act of 1867, which stated that only "qualified persons" could be appointed to the Canadian Senate. Because women had few rights in 1867, the government determined that "qualified persons" clearly meant *men*; therefore women could not be appointed to the Senate. However, by 1927 Canadian women could vote and stand for election in most provinces, thus the women wanted the Supreme Court to rule on whether it was constitutional for Parliament to amend the law to allow women to serve in the Senate. *Edwards v. Canada*, often referred to as the *Persons Case*, was decided in 1928; the court ruled that it was not, in fact, unconstitutional. Because women were not considered "persons" in 1867, they could not be considered "persons" in 1928. The women had one more appeal to make. Canada was still technically part of the British Empire, thus the women appealed to the Judicial Committee of the Privy Council in England. In 1929, the Privy Council ruled that women were, in fact, persons under the law.

DISPUTE RESOLUTION

Without the arena that courts provide for citizens and entities to resolve conflicts, societies might resort to vigilantism and descend into chaos. As such, perhaps the most important role courts play is that of dispute resolution. In this role courts resolve disputes peaceably through formal proceedings. By performing this function, courts provide citizens with an avenue to settle their disputes in an orderly, organized, predictable, and authoritatively controlled way. If in a criminal case the defendant (one charged with a crime) denies committing the acts charged against them, the court must choose between the defendant's version of the facts and that presented by the prosecution. If the defendant asserts that their actions did not constitute criminal behavior, the court (often aided by a jury) must decide whether the defendant's view of the law and facts or the prosecution's is correct. In a civil case, if the defendant disputes the plaintiff's account of what happened between them – for example, whether they entered into a certain contract or agreement – or if they dispute the plaintiff's view of the legal significance of whatever occurred – for example, whether the agreement was legally binding – the court again must choose between the claims of the parties. The issues presented to and decided by the court may be either factual or legal, or both.

Courts do not, however, spend all their time resolving disputes between opposing parties. Many cases brought before the courts are not contested (e.g., a "no-fault" divorce or a routine debt collection case). As no dispute exists over the facts or the law, the court's role in such cases is more administrative than adjudicatory. Moreover, the mere existence of a court may render the frequent exercise of its powers unnecessary. The fact that courts operate by known rules and with reasonably predictable results leads many of those who might otherwise engage in legal action to reach a compromise, because people are typically unwilling to incur the expense of going to court if they believe there is a good chance they will lose.

Judicial institutions also settle disputes informally by setting the context for common practices within the judicial process. For example, in common law systems (discussed in the next section, but familiar to most students in Anglo-American states), when sentencing those convicted of crimes, judges send messages about punishment expectations – thus shaping what attorneys advise and negotiate with respect to plea bargaining. This is also true in *civil lawsuits* where courts and juries determine whether entities or individuals committed wrongdoing and are responsible for repairing any resulting damage. In common law systems, courts' past decisions set the expectations for future relations between plaintiffs (those suing) and defendants (those being sued). Based on courts' past decisions, litigants (those involved in lawsuits) can decide which available option is best. Additionally, attorneys base their advice to clients on past court decisions.

MONITORING GOVERNMENT

Courts also have the task of monitoring the actions of the government or government officials to ensure they follow the prescribed rules and procedures, including the ones that check the behavior of others. Courts also monitor government actions through the prosecution of corrupt or otherwise criminal government officials. By holding government officials to the same rules as everyone else, courts send the message to citizens that no one is above the law. In this way the judiciary plays a role in legitimizing government. It also functions as an informal peacekeeping mechanism by letting people know government officials are being held accountable to the laws of the land. In the United States, even sitting presidents have been required to testify in court.

In some states, courts exercise a power called **judicial review**. This power enables the judiciary to review the state's laws as well as the actions of government officials to determine their constitutionality or whether they violate some other aspect of the state's legal structure. Judicial review allows the courts to directly monitor the actions of the government. Courts have the power of judicial review in the United States, Italy, Canada, Germany, Japan, India, the Republic of Ireland, Australia, Norway, and some two dozen other countries.

There are two forms of judicial review. The first is concrete and the second is abstract. *Concrete judicial review*, sometimes called the American model, means that for a case to be reviewed for constitutionality by the courts, there must be an actual (concrete) case in which a person has suffered some sort of (legal) harm and has brought suit against a government agency or official. This is called the American model because it comes from *Marbury v. Madison*, the case mentioned earlier, in which the US Supreme Court gave the courts the power to review acts of government or officials. In the concrete model, any court can consider constitutionality, but the Supreme Court (or highest court) has the final say on what is and is not constitutional.

The second form of judicial review is *abstract*, meaning that the court can rule on the constitutionality of a law that has not yet been implemented. If the law has not yet been implemented, no one has (yet) been harmed, and thus the case is abstract – the question is *will* this cause unconstitutional harm rather than *has* this caused unconstitutional harm. Abstract review is sometimes thought of as the European model, because after World War II several European states adopted **constitutional courts**, and in these states only the constitutional court can rule on constitutionality. Some systems blend the two, as you can see in Box 10.3.

BOX 10.3: IRISH JUDICIAL DISCRETION

The Republic of Ireland makes for an interesting case because, although the Irish legal system evolved from the British legal system, Ireland's judicial review provisions look far different than anything found in the United Kingdom. The UK has weak judicial review that grew out of the Human Rights Act of 1998.[4] In contrast, judicial review is detailed in Articles 26 and 34 of the Irish Constitution of 1937.[5] Article 26 establishes abstract review, specifying that the president[6] "may, after consultation with the Council of State, refer any Bill to which this Article applies to the Supreme Court for a decision on the question as to whether such Bill or any specified provision or provisions of such Bill is or are repugnant to this Constitution or to any provision thereof." Article 34 establishes that the courts have jurisdiction over "the question of the validity of any law having regard to the provisions of this Constitution." Original jurisdiction for constitutional cases belongs to the Irish High Court, while the Supreme Court is the court of final jurisdiction.

In states with federal government systems (like the United States, Canada, Australia, and India), which have multiple levels of government (like the local, state, and federal government in the United States), judicial review also allows the judiciary to settle conflicts between different levels of government. In such systems there are conflicts over which level of government is responsible for providing some specific service or enacting a particular piece of legislation and whether state or federal law should be followed.

Judicial review is also at work when the courts strike down laws that violate the constitutional rights of groups or individuals. Courts are often asked to determine whether laws violate citizens' voting, privacy, or religious rights. When a court says that the state may not conduct white-only voting primaries, ban abortions, or create local zoning ordinances that prevent unpopular religious groups from practicing its sacraments, the courts are monitoring government behavior. In the United States the courts get a lot of credit for protecting citizens' rights. However, even this aspect of the courts is subject to the reality that because judicial institutions do not have enforcement powers, their decisions must be supported and implemented by other actors.

As a result, some of their decisions may be circumvented or ignored. Just because a court declares a practice unconstitutional doesn't mean everything changes. For example, the US Supreme Court declared in *Roe v. Wade* (1973) that the US Constitution provides a fundamental "right to privacy" that protects a pregnant woman's liberty to choose whether or not to have an abortion. Thus, state bans on abortions were deemed constitutionally impermissible. Yet 46 years after the landmark decision, women across the country, particularly in southern states like Alabama, continue to face challenges getting access to abortions because of onerous regulations effectively functioning as a ban. The US Supreme Court regularly hears related cases but has not, as of this writing, made a decisive ruling on the constitutionality of many of these restrictions.

Courts also determine whether government officials are operating within the sphere of their authority and jurisdiction. For example, in 2019 members of the United Kingdom's Parliament asked the courts to review Prime Minister Boris Johnson's decision to suspend (prorogue) Parliament in the lead up to the UK's exit from the European Union. The MPs believed Johnson's actions to be unlawful interference in the duties of Parliament. The UK's Supreme Court (established in 2009) sided with the MPs and declared the prime minister's suspension of Parliament unlawful.

The thing to keep in mind is that, although we want them to be the great equalizers in society, courts are majoritarian institutions. This means that their policies tend to coincide with the preferences of policymakers in the other branches of government and those of the country as a whole. This tendency results from several different processes, including the appointments of judges, pressures on the courts from both the legislative and executive branches of government, and the effects of societal developments on the judges' thinking.

POLICYMAKING

The types of decisions judicial institutions make distinguish them from other branches of government. However, it is when courts' decisions require government officials to act or refrain from acting that the judiciary operates the most like other political institutions. When operating in this capacity, courts are said to be engaged in policymaking. In most political systems, citizens agree on the need for an independent judiciary in cases that have no significant impact on policy, such as criminal cases; the ebbs and flows of public opinion should not influence a court's decision to uphold an armed robbery conviction. But when judicial decisions involve policy – such as those affecting legal counsel for the indigent, sexual harassment, or pollution – the question of **judicial independence** (the idea that courts should not be subject to improper influence from the other branches of government or from private or partisan interests) becomes far more controversial. Officially, courts are not supposed to engage in policymaking – they are only supposed to resolve the disputes others have over policy. Officially, judges are supposed to use the constitution or laws of the state to find appropriate solutions to disputes between the policymaking branches of government. However, when hearing and deciding cases involving policy disputes, the courts are making policy.

Many court cases require more than a determination of the facts; they also raise questions of legal interpretation. As such, policymaking also occurs when courts are involved in **statutory interpretation** – the process of determining what a particular statute means so that a court may apply it accurately. By defining how laws can and cannot be interpreted, courts are making policy. The precise meaning of the law is often uncertain due to unforeseen circumstances or to legislators seeking to avoid the politically painful process of spelling out the particular applications of the law. As a result, many laws are vaguely or ambiguously worded and thus open to multiple interpretations. In these instances, courts must determine whether these laws are meant to be applied narrowly to specific circumstances or litigants. The application of laws requires specificity, so courts must interpret what particular statutes mean precisely. As soon as they engage in this interpretation by "filling in the gaps," they are making policy, as shown in Box 10.4.

BOX 10.4: JUDICIAL POLICYMAKING: THE CASE OF COLOMBIA'S DISPLACED PERSONS

Due primarily to the escalation of internal armed conflict, Colombia has an enormous displaced population. During the Uribe administration, "return to home" policies were promoted as the principle response to Colombia's internal displacement crisis. At various away times, the Uribe administration focused on limiting or redirecting[7] resources and assistance from displaced persons, whom the administration referred to as "economic migrants," suggesting that directing assistance to internally displaced persons discriminated against other poor Colombians. In 2004, the Colombian Constitutional Court responded to several *tutela* (legal actions requesting protection of constitutional rights) filed by displaced persons that called for the national and local authorities to protect their fundamental rights.

The facts of the cases were relatively simple. Actions were filed by 1,150 family groups located in departmental capitals and municipalities throughout Colombia, all of them belonging to the internally displaced population, with an average of four persons per family and primarily composed of women caretakers, elderly persons, and minors, as well as a number of Indigenous persons. They claimed that the municipal and departmental administrations in charge of the jurisdictions where the families were located were not complying with their legal duty to protect the displaced population because there was a lack of an effective administrative process and response to the displaced persons petitions for housing, access to work and training, healthcare, education, and humanitarian aid.[8]

The Constitutional Court determined that because of the conditions of extreme vulnerability of the displaced population, as well as the inconsistency and precarious nature of state policy implementation and administrative practices concerning forced displacement, the rights of the displaced population to a dignified life, personal integrity, equality, petition, work, health, social security, education, minimum subsistence income, and special protection for elderly persons, women caretakers, and children had all been violated.[9] The court went on to elaborate that the aforementioned violations had been taking place in a massive, protracted, and reiterative manner and were the result of a structural problem that affects the entire assistance policy designed by the state because of the insufficiency of the resources allocated to finance such policy and the precarious institutional capacity to implement it.

The court determined that the situation required the national and territorial entities in charge of assisting the displaced population to allocate the resources required to secure the displaced persons' rights to life, dignity, integrity (physical, psychological, and moral), family unity, urgent and basic healthcare, protection from discriminatory practices based on the condition of displacement, and education of displaced children under 15 years of age. Additionally, the decision demanded that these entities, in an effective and timely manner, adopt any and all corrective measures required to resolve the unconstitutional state of affairs.

By resolving the case, the court established a set of social welfare policies and programs of action regarding socioeconomic stabilization following forced internal displacement. A decision on other grounds would have had more far-reaching implications for intergovernmental relations than strict reliance on the interpretation of the duties of local governments to develop and implement policies and procedures that protect the rights and facilitate the stabilization of internally displaced persons.

Even well-written laws are open to the kind of judicial policymaking seen in the Colombian case. Because a non-discrimination law intended to ensure Black Americans can live in any neighborhood in a city says that all citizens must be treated equally, that law can be interpreted to mean that Ku Klux Klan members can march in the city's annual parade. A law intended to keep gang-related clothing out of public school classrooms can be interpreted to give school boards the ability to require see-through backpacks or ban afros and braids as part of setting a minimum standard of dress and appearance.

The point here is that judicial lawmaking is inevitable. It is clear that the courts make policy through interpretation, and the court's understanding of the law will remain until the legislature passes a specific law that changes that interpretation. Courts cannot limit the impact of their decisions to the parties before them. The interpretation of law changes policies and programs, sometimes altering decisions previously considered political or managerial matters.

Note: This discussion of courts is primarily about the role of courts in the common law tradition, which is discussed in the next section. This book is, after all, targeted at students in the Anglo-American states, all of which have primarily (but not purely) common law legal systems.

LEGAL SYSTEMS

When appellate courts review the actions of lower courts, or when the judicial system reviews the constitutionality of laws passed, they are not doing so in a bubble or a vacuum. Every judicial action undertaken in a state is informed and shaped by that nation's legal system, which is the processes and procedures a society constructs for interpreting and enforcing its laws. It is based on a basic understanding of how the law is created and how it functions. In the modern world, three kinds of legal systems are commonly used. The first of these is the **religious law** system; this type of system is currently most commonly found in Islamic nations. The second is the **civil law** or code law system; this is the most widely used type system in the world. Third is the **common law** system, which began in and is primarily used in Britain and its former colonies/dependencies.

Religious Law

The first major type of legal system in the world is the religious legal system. This type of legal system differs from other legal systems in significant ways. While many states have religious law, it is most common today in Islamic countries, where it is based on sharia or Islamic law. Religious law is derived from the sacred texts of religious traditions and in most cases claims to cover all aspects of life. Religion for law must be defined broadly, but unlike in civil and common law systems, the comprehensiveness and value of the religious laws' truth need not, and ought not, be addressed, and it governs every aspect of religious and secular life. Sharia and other religious law systems, like Halakha in Judaism, both of which denote the "path to follow," are derived primarily from the religions' sacred texts – the Koran and Torah, respectively – as well as other related legal sources. Generally speaking, the understanding and development of the religious law is the responsibility of scholars who are authorities on the religion. For example, in countries following sharia, it is the *qadi*'s responsibility to resolve disputes by finding the appropriate, relevant law. A *mufti* (an expert on Islamic law) may assist a *qadi* to issue legal opinions called *fatwas*. However, this can cause conflict because different muftis can offer different fatwas.

While some states' legal systems, like Iran and Saudi Arabia, are based entirely on sharia, most countries where sharia is important have a legal system that is mixed with either civil law (Syria, Kuwait, Morocco, and Egypt) or common law (Singapore, Bahrain, Qatar, Sudan, and Pakistan).

Civil Law

In civil law countries, all judicial decisions are, in theory, based on legislative enactments. Civil law systems begin from the proposition that the law is a codified (an arrangement of information in a logical order that others can follow), constructed entity created by a legislature or other lawmaking political institution. Consequently, the political process of compiling and writing down the law is the central component of the civil law system. The idea is to create a law for governing every conceivable human interaction. Additionally, civil law systems assume undergirding these laws is a coherent moral or legal philosophy informing them, and hence guiding and unifying the state and society.

The history of the modern civil law system is said to have begun in the sixth century when the Byzantine Emperor Justinian codified what had been the law of Rome. The codification enterprise was undertaken for a second time under Napoleon, who incorporated a variety of laws from different countries and spread the system through his conquests. The last major codification update ended in 1900 and was initiated by Germany. Civil law systems are predominant in continental Europe, former French colonies, Quebec, and the US state of Louisiana. Because the civil law systems rely on written law, it tends to be more specific, easier to apply to particular cases, and easier to understand.

In the civil law system judges merely "apply" the law created by the legislature. Practice, however, often departs from theory. Although the civil code adopted in these countries is quite comprehensive, attempting to cover nearly every aspect of human conduct and purporting to supply ready-made answers for all problems that can arise, many of the provisions are exceedingly vague (because they are abstract) and are sometimes almost meaningless until applied to concrete situations, when judicial interpretation gives them specific meaning. Furthermore, the legislative codes cannot anticipate all situations that may arise and come before the courts. The gaps in legislation must be and are filled by judicial decisions, as a court is unlikely to refuse to decide a case merely on the grounds that it has not been told in advance the answers to the questions presented to it.

Civil law systems use an *inquisitorial system*, which requires a rather elaborate pre-trial investigative process where all the courtroom participants take part in the investigation. Information is also shared freely among all participants. The goal of this process is to try to protect the innocent. Because all of the courtroom participants take part in the investigation, the accused has the benefit of multiple perspectives seeking the facts, examining the evidence, and contributing resources and opinions that guide the process. As a result, the inquisitorial system is said to reduce the influence of wealth and other biases within the judicial system and on outcomes.

Common Law

While the goal of the common law system of rendering uniform and predictable outcomes in similar circumstances mirrors the primary objective of civil law systems, the methods of and processes for achieving that goal differ substantially – as do their histories. Beginning in 1066 under William the Conqueror, who commissioned judges to travel the English countryside to enforce the king's law and resolve disputes by basing their decisions on local customs and precedent (past judicial decisions), the common law legal system is characterized by the strong rule of the judge and the importance of precedent. The common law system of creating precedents is sometimes called *stare decisis* (Latin for "let the decision stand" or "to stand by decided matters"). In common law systems, judges are expected to follow earlier decisions to ensure that similar cases are treated similarly. This system of *stare decisis* is sometimes referred to as "judge-made law," as the law (the precedent) is created by the judge, not by a legislature.

One of the chief characteristics of the common law system is the adversarial process. Unlike the civil law systems where the participants work together to uncover and determine the facts, in a common law system the participants battle it out. Also, unlike the civil law system the judge in the common law system is not a participant but functions more as a referee ensuring the participants follow the rules of engagement.

Another distinction between the two legal systems is that judicial lawmaking is more prevalent, acknowledged, and widespread in states with common law systems. In addition to issuing decisions that authoritatively interpret statutes, the decisions in courts in common law states are sometimes not based on any statute or legislation at all because whenever judges are confronted with a dispute where there is no clear statutory answer they make decisions using their own discretion. Subsequent judges follow these rulings, deciding similar cases in the same way but distinguishing earlier cases when dissimilar factors are discovered in the cases before them. All together these judicial decisions make up "the common law."

While there are important distinctions between common law and civil law systems, it should be clear that the divisions between the two are simplistic. Indeed, just as states with a primarily religious legal tradition are frequently mixtures of religious/civil or religious/common law, most common law systems contain elements drawn from civil law and vice versa.

CONCLUSION

In principle, states' constitutions, courts, and legal systems are designed to function together to create and maintain a safe, predictable, and fair society for all of a state's citizens. They are formally and informally connected together by states' constitutions that reflect and express the country's core values, norms, traditions, and customs; set up its government institutions; and lay out their powers and limitations by defining the relevant associated processes and procedures. These priorities and practices are to be upheld, identified, and enforced by the courts that interpret the laws, evaluate and monitor the actions of government, resolve disputes/conflicts, and make policy through decision making. All of these judicial actions are to be executed through a legal system (civil, common, or religious) that uses a defined set of socially constructed processes and procedures for interpreting and enforcing laws.

While in principle the above-mentioned relationships reflect how things are theoretically/conceptually supposed to work (and in some cases things do work this way), in practice the relationship between a state's constitution, courts, and legal system sometimes function much differently than they were designed to. Oftentimes, and in many places, the judiciary functions in ways that are inconsistent with the stated norms and values expressed in constitutions. Marginalized and minority populations throughout the world have less access to justice and often receive disproportionately negative outcomes and treatment by the judiciary than their fellow citizens from majority populations. Indeed, as you can see in the examples in Figure 10.1, in many states minorities are incarcerated at rates far higher than their proportion in the general population.[10] Additionally, well-resourced

Figure 10.1. Disparities in Minority/Majority Incarceration Rates

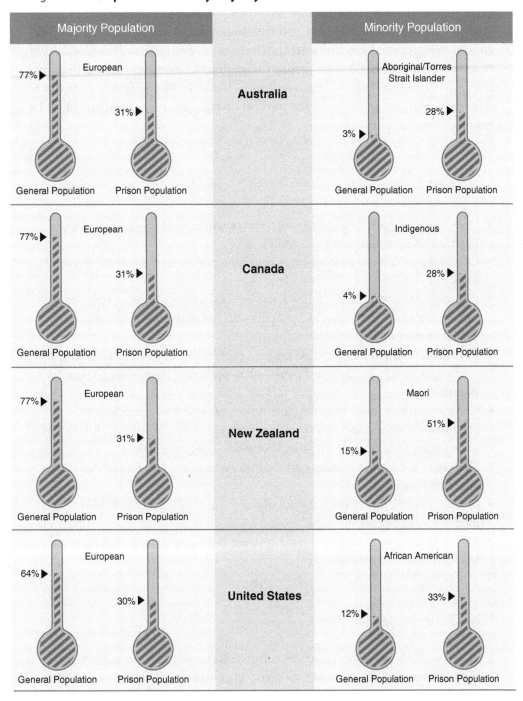

and powerful elites exercise disproportionate influence over the judiciary and receive disproportionate benefits from their courts and legal systems than non-elites.

Despite these disparities and shortcomings, courts are often respected and
considered important governmental institutions necessary to the maintenance of
peaceful, civil societies. While perhaps sometimes considered the most confusing or controversial branch of government, it is clear that judiciaries constitute
a fundamental part of the modern nation-state and are an essential branch of its
government.

SUMMARY

- Once societies grow beyond kinship relationships, most create some type of
  legal/court system to resolve conflicts.
- One of the judiciary's primary roles is to interpret its state's constitution and
  laws.
- Constitutions are typically defined and understood as a written, physical document or a basic set of laws and practices that establish the shape and form of
  a state's structure and operations.
- Constitutions are shaped by and reflect a society's customs and traditions, including those that exclude and marginalize particular segments of a country's
  population.
- Constitutions typically include a list of citizens' rights to government-
  provided goods and services (positive rights) or from government interference
  in engaging in certain practices and behaviors (negative rights).
- Hierarchy is a feature of nearly all judicial institutions. Most have trial courts
  and appellate tiers.
- Courts perform the functional roles of resolving conflicts, making policy, and
  monitoring government.
- There are three major types of legal systems throughout the world: common
  law, civil law, and religious law.

CONCLUDING QUESTIONS

1 What are the basic differences between civil and common law traditions?
2 Why is it important to look at courts and the law through an intersectional
   lens?

3   What are the purposes of a constitution?
4   In a democratic society, courts are theoretically the great leveler in society – the place where everyone is equal before the law. Is that the case in reality in your country? Make a case for your position.

NOTES

1   Jonathan P. Kastellec, "Hierarchical and Collegial Politics on the U.S. Courts of Appeals," SSRN (2010), http://dx.doi.org/10.2139/ssrn.1262940.
2   Kimberlé Crenshaw, "Demarginalizing the Intersection of Race and Sex: A Black Feminist Critique of Antidiscrimination Doctrine, Feminist Theory and Antiracist Politics," *University of Chicago Legal Forum* 1 (1989); Derrick A. Bell, "Who's Afraid of Critical Race Theory?," *University of Illinois Law Review* (1995): 893.
3   Derrick A. Bell, *And We Are Not Saved: The Elusive Quest for Racial Justice* (New York: Basic Books, 2008); Derrick A. Bell, *Faces at the Bottom of the Well: The Permanence of Racism* (New York: Basic Books, 1992); Kimberlé Crenshaw, "Framing Affirmative Action," *Michigan Law Review* 101, no. 1 (2006): 123–33; Kimberlé Crenshaw and Gary Peller, "The Contradictions of Mainstream Constitutional Theory," *UCLA Law Review* 45 (1997): 1683.
4   Séamus Ó. Tuama, "Judicial Review under the Irish Constitution: More American Than Commonwealth," *Electronic Journal of Comparative Law* 12, no. 2 (2008).
5   Aisling O'Sullivan and Phil C.W. Chan, "Judicial Review in Ireland and the Relationship between the Irish Constitution and Natural Law," *Nottingham Law Journal* 15 (2006): 18.
6   Note that Ireland is a parliamentary republic; therefore the president is the head of *state*, not the head of *government*, so this is one of the more important duties of the Irish president.
7   Rodrigo Uprimny Yepes, "Judicialization of Politics in Colombia: Cases, Merits and Risks," *Sur-Revista Internacional de Direitos Humanos* 3, no. SE (2007): 52–69.
8   Yepes, "Judicialization of Politics in Colombia."
9   Yepes, "Judicialization of Politics in Colombia."
10 ABS, "Estimates of Aboriginal and Torres Strait Islander Australians," Australian Bureau of Statistics, 2018, https://www.abs.gov.au/ausstats/abs@.nsf/mf/3238.0.55.001; ABS, "Aboriginal and Torres Strait Islander Prisoner Characteristics," Australian Bureau of Statistics, 2018, https://www.abs.gov.au/ausstats/abs@.nsf/Lookup/by%20Subject/4517.0~2019~Main%20Features~Aboriginal%20and%20Torres%20Strait%20Islander%20prisoner%20characteristics%20~13; Government of Canada, "Percentage of Inmates by Race," Office of the Correctional Investigator, 2017, https://www.oci-bec.gc.ca/cnt/comm/presentations/longdesc/presentations20171031-eng.aspx?texthighlight=race; Elese B. Dowden, "Colonial Mind, Colonised Body: Structural Violence and Incarceration in Aotearoa," *Parrhesia* 30 (2019): 88–102; John Gramlich, "The Gap between the Number of Blacks and Whites in Prison Is Shrinking," Pew

Research Center, April 30, 2019, https://www.pewresearch.org/fact-tank/2019/04/30
/shrinking-gap-between-number-of-blacks-and-whites-in-prison.

RESOURCES AND SUGGESTIONS FOR FURTHER READING

Böckenförde, Markus, Nora Hedling, and Winluck Wahiu. "A Practical Guide to
    Constitution Building." International IDEA, December 15, 2011. https://www.idea
    .int/publications/catalogue/practical-guide-constitution-building.
Dreisinger, Baz. *Incarceration Nations: A Journey to Justice in Prisons around the World.* New
    York: Other Press, 2016.
International Institute for Democracy and Electoral Assistance (IDEA) Constitution
    Building Module. https://www.idea.int/our-work/what-we-do/constitution-building.
Juriglobe. www.juriglobe.ca. *Juriglobe is a research project, run by members of the Faculty of
    Law at the University of Ottawa, that focuses on the world's legal systems.*
The Marshall Project. www.themarshallproject.org. *The Marshall Project provides non-profit
    journalism about criminal justice.*
Prison Policy Initiative. www.prisonpolicy.org. *The Prison Policy Initiative is a non-profit,
    non-partisan US-based research and advocacy organization.*
Reynolds, Andrew. *The Architecture of Democracy: Constitutional Design, Conflict
    Management, and Democracy.* New York: Oxford University Press, 2002.

CHAPTER ELEVEN

Public Policy through an Intersectional Lens

*Dr. Raul
Pacheco-Vega*

LEARNING OBJECTIVES

1 Define public policy
2 Understand the policy process
3 Learn why an intersectional lens is vital to understanding public policy

KEY TERMS

empirical validity refers to whether our explanation works in the real world

interdisciplinary relating to more than one branch of knowledge or academic discipline

methodology the processes, strategies, and tactics we follow to investigate or study a phenomenon

policy analysis the process by which experts identify and analyze potential solutions to public issues (social problems, public health concerns, national security, etc.); often focused on the economic ramifications of policy solutions

policy evaluation a comprehensive analysis of a specific policy; its target populations; the resources spent in creating, designing, and implementing the program; and the costs and benefits that these programs may have generated

poverty   a socioeconomic status in which the person or community lacks the financial resources to meet a minimum standard of living

regime   a group of concepts that, taken collectively, help explain phenomena

target population   a group of individuals whose public affairs are important and should be tackled and solved

WHAT IS POLICY STUDIES?

In this chapter, my objective is to bring forth a discussion centered on why an intersectional lens is useful for public policy analysts, scholars, and practitioners. Generally, public policy scholarship (or policy studies, as it is often called) is considered highly **interdisciplinary**, which helps when we introduce considerations regarding intersectionality. Considering different disciplinary viewpoints enables policy analysts to broaden their view and become more open to considering how a multiplicity of factors may negatively affect people of different ethnic backgrounds, social class, gender, economic strata, and so on.

This chapter maps out an examination of intersectionality in public policy by first defining what public policy is, what policy instruments are, and how a policy cycle framework can help us understand how policies are designed, implemented, and evaluated. Second, I explain how a policy cycle can be seen through the intersectionality lens. I offer the view that, given policy analysts' role as "clinical professionals,"[1] they're perfectly suited to using intersectionality as an analytical tool to understand how policies and policy instruments may have compounding negative effects and to understand **target populations**. I also discuss how intersectionality is a proscriptive (normative/values-based) framework that can be used to design better tools to better serve the communities they're focused in. I then discuss how we can combine the policy regime framework with an intersectionality framework to provide a richer, fuller, and more powerful view of policy problems than we would have if we used traditional tools.

This discussion is a prelude to a series of two examples I provide to showcase what intersectional public policy looks like. Whether trying to understand how homeless individuals experience vulnerability to disasters, examining the politics of aging in an intersectional way, or observing how gay men experience health issues, intersectionality can offer public policy analysts an extraordinarily powerful set of tools to better discern negative impacts of individual factors, which are then compounded depending on the characteristics of each group. Finally, I conclude with a few reflections on what an intersectional public policy body of scholarship would look like, particularly for comparative politics.

DEFINITIONS AND CONCEPTS: WHAT IS PUBLIC POLICY?

Public policymaking is a process that involves engaging with (1) actors who have their own interests, (2) ideas held by participants in those groups, and (3) the institutions, rules, and norms created through the routinization of different activities related to tracking and solving public affairs. This means that when we refer to public policies, we mean the actions that governments undertake to solve a problem that has been identified as "public."[2] In turn, before anything else happens, we need to determine who the public is and which types of issues are public.

Governments have limited resources, and for that reason they are unable to solve every problem that the public brings forth. Therefore, their duty is to design policies that are beneficial for as many people as possible within the sometimes restrictive budgetary and resource constraints they face. Public policy is, therefore, as political scientist Harold Lasswell often said, the study of who gets to do what with whom under which circumstances and constraints.[3] Public policy is, in the end, the study of how governments can solve public problems while under multiple constraints (like budget, time, and availability of human capital). But it is also important to note that private organizations can and do tackle issues that should be in the purview of governments. For example, many migrant support groups do much work that could potentially be considered part of what government should be doing. Support for elderly people is often provided by religious organizations or through altruistic voluntary groups. This is a challenge for those of us who study public policy: Who should be responsible for solving societal problems? Are all public issues the duty of government?

We study public policy because we are interested in the reasons behind governmental decision making, on the one hand, but also to help them design better policy instruments and make sounder decisions. We are particularly interested in ensuring that policies are designed with the best possible evidence.[4] But it is important that we use the best technical approaches to policy design and implementation, as well as the most sound and robust models for policy evaluation, both quantitative (based on numbers) and qualitative (based on text). We should also consider the possibility of including spatial (maps) and network (connectivity) information to our studies.

THE POLICY CYCLE: UNDERSTANDING HOW POLICIES ARE MADE

When an issue raises concerns at a community, regional, or societal level, citizens may be able to bring it to the fore by reaching out to local or regional government through their respective councils or at the national level through elected representatives (in some countries these are called deputies or senators). However, not all problems can be solved in the same way, nor does the government have enough money to address all issues. Therefore, it is imperative that bureaucratic agencies and politicians choose which problems they can and will be willing to address within the budgetary and resource constraints within which they operate. Then, once a list of issues is decided upon, it is fundamental that technical teams design potential options to solve each problem. These options are carefully analyzed to determine which programs can really be implemented and which ones should be phased out temporarily or permanently. Implementing solutions is challenging in and of itself, but once a specific course of action has been chosen, public agencies should be able to determine how this implementation process should take place. Finally, in the same analytical way as each of the previous stages, governments need to evaluate to what extent the programs, policies, instruments, and techniques have been successful and which ones did not live up to expectations.

The process I have just described is what in policy studies we call the *policy cycle*. An iterative problem-solving process has a direct parallel with how policies are designed, implemented, and evaluated. The policy cycle as a framework of analysis was established to discern a systematic process that scholars could follow to understand how public affairs are solved. While different authors have discussed the policy cycle as having multiple stages, most scholars have settled on five.[5] I've listed them here, using examples drawn from work on homelessness:

1 Agenda setting (Would homelessness be considered a problem worthy of public action by the government? Why or why not?)
2 Policy formulation (What kinds of programs, strategies, instruments, or plans can a government agency implement to tackle homelessness? Which ones get omitted?)
3 Decision making and instrument choice (Which one of the different suggestions we have made to the government will be implemented and why? Will homeless individuals be part of the decision-making process?)
4 Implementation (What is the best strategy and timing to implement the chosen program/plan/policy instrument to tackle homelessness?)
5 Evaluation (Did the program we chose manage to reduce homelessness? By how much? Is the reduction in number of homeless people the right metric /measure?)

Let's have a look at the five stages of the policy cycle in more detail.

Agenda Setting

Agenda setting refers to the process by which different stakeholders define and discern which problems the government can realistically and efficiently solve. This is one of the most important parts of the policy cycle, and one that is often misunderstood. No government is capable of tackling, let alone solving, every single issue that requires attention. There are several budgetary, human resources, infrastructure, and political resources constraints that establish relatively clear limits on what governments can do. Agenda setting is, of course, political and not just a technical process, and this is something we need to understand from the outset since it's also why intersectional considerations are important in the field.

One of the most popular models of thinking about these issues is the notion of a government agenda and a public agenda. The *public agenda* refers to the gamut of all possible public problems that require attention and problem solving. The *government agenda* establishes a subset of issues from the public agenda as those that it intends to solve. The literature on public policy offers specific processes that help us discern which issues from the public agenda can or should be tackled by government. It is important to clarify that not every issue on the public agenda has a technically feasible, economically viable policy solution. Some problems exist within the purview of consecutive governments, meaning they're ongoing over several governments or administrations, without ever being solved. The perfect example is **poverty**, which is a societal problem that affects so many people that it is really hard to solve the problem within the time period that an elected government will remain in power.

As you may remember from Chapter 9, who gets the chance to set the agenda and whose issues get to reach the governmental agenda are both issues that should be analyzed with an intersectional lens. Race, gender, ethnicity, and sexual representation are all elements that have an impact on whether an issue is considered important enough to be tackled by a government. Representation is precisely at the core of intersectionality discussions. Who is part of a target population and how are they represented? Which issues are considered most relevant for decision making and problem solving? To what extent are issues in neighborhoods that are clearly populated more by minorities less likely to reach a governmental agenda? How do different representations collide, and how are politicians less inclined to tackle issues affecting marginalized populations? Why are there fewer women politicians, and how does this lack of participation in public life and political decision making negatively affect how public policies are made and whether these policies really solve problems affecting women? All these questions can and should be tackled with an intersectional lens. Doing so would clearly shine light on the various ways in which governments could be able to tackle policy problems. When government agencies are able to understand how the various groups' characteristics and individual identities could potentially combine to face compounded negative effects, they can design better policies.

One important consideration for practice is that moving issues through the agenda may depend on which venue we are using to negotiate advancement. Seen through an intersectional lens, we may be able to push forward an issue to be included in the decision agenda by suggesting the various (intersectional) ways in which a specific issue broadly affects multiple communities (and identities). This venue shopping is not uncommon and has been successfully used in issues such as Canadian pesticide policy decision making and forest policy design.[6] Intersectional activists may choose to shop for venues where considerations of the intersection of multiple vulnerabilities and challenges are part of the policymaking process.

Policy Formulation and Policy Design

The policy formation stage includes proposing programs, suggesting strategies, encouraging practices, and the interrelated sets of activities that make those work, all in order to tackle public problems.[7] Peter John indicated that instruments are "the tools of government" – the programs, regulations, systems, practices that were used to tackle those societal needs that require government intervention, although there is now wide variation in the types of tools we can use.[8]

Most of the literature we associate with the concept of policy design deals with which target populations are served through which tools or instruments. An intersectional lens to policy design would be well-suited to consider race, gender, ethnicity, dis/ability, and other factors in the creation of specific policy tools. Intersectionality would also help us better understand why some instruments work and others don't when considering issues at the intersection of various groups' characteristics. It also helps us to understand why policies often have different outcomes for different groups.

Decision Making and Instrument Choice

Who decides which policy instruments are used and which populations will be served? This is one of the key considerations in public policymaking. One of the first things we should do as policy analysts is to determine which target populations we are trying to serve.[9] This process should be carried out in tandem with choosing which issues will reach the governmental (decision) agenda. As scholars of public policy, we may not serve as policy advisors and, therefore, in our capacity as researchers we should be able to discern how governments choose which problems are relevant and which target populations are being served (or not).

Theoretically, if we followed the work of Schneider and Ingram on aligning policy tools to the actual characteristics of target populations,[10] designing proper policies and implementing them should be relatively easy, because alignment enables policy designers to establish which tools work better for which populations. Yet this is often not the case. An intersectionality analysis would help us better align policy tools to target populations through a consideration of the different intersections of race, class, gender, ethnicity, and how these could potentially transform the definition of a target population. We cannot talk about the potential vulnerabilities that elderly people face without considering, for example, their ethnicity, sexual orientation, economic status, and so on. The same considerations should be given to other populations as well.

Implementation

Implementation is considered the least studied of the five stages of the policy cycle, particularly because it involves so much beyond what one would normally think of as the responsibility of governments.[11] Implementing public policy depends on many factors, not only the efficient design of a policy instrument but also on the local conditions of the country, region, community, or neighborhood where a specific program will be carried out. Implementation theory focuses on the successful execution of policy programs, strategies, and plans within the constraints of resource allocation. Street-level bureaucrats are usually at the heart of policy implementation, and their own group characteristics may also be relevant to explore through an intersectional lens, as implementers themselves may face specific challenges depending on their identity. Bureaucratic discretion – the ability of an appointed official or a bureaucrat to make decisions based on their own judgment – is an important component of implementation. How policies are implemented is frequently the result of street-level bureaucrats' decision-making processes.

From a scholarly viewpoint, one of the best strategies for us to ensure successful implementation is to engage in participatory action implementation research.[12] Participatory action research is modeled after the notion that researchers themselves may be able to better understand a phenomenon by actively participating in the activities they are supposed to be studying. Participatory implementation research therefore encourages participation both from researchers and government actors in the implementation of policy programs and plans. I would argue that scholars trained in intersectionality theory or having what the literature calls an "intersectional sensibility" would be better positioned to implement policy tools in contexts where individual groups' characteristics interact and potentially generate negative compounded effects.

Evaluation

Evaluating public policy is much more than the economic assessment of whether a public policy was efficient or whether it achieved its goal. Evaluation involves a comprehensive analysis of a policy; its target populations; the resources spent in creating, designing, and implementing the program; and the costs and benefits that these programs may have generated. This is not the same as policy analysis (see Box 11.1).

> **BOX 11.1: COMPARING POLICY EVALUATION AND POLICY ANALYSIS**
> Contrary to common belief, **policy analysis** and **policy evaluation** are not the same! As Geva-May and Pal show, values and politics are both present in evaluation, particularly because goals and objectives of evaluation studies are established by those who decide to engage consultants or analysts to undertake it.[13] There are many different and competing views of who a specific policy tool should target and to what extent a program should continue or be terminated. As Hanberger notes, where a policy is made and implemented in multi-actor contexts, the various stakeholders frequently view problems and solutions differently, and some will try to influence the aim and direction of a policy all the way through the policy process.[14]

Considering intersectionality in policy evaluation requires us to understand all different viewpoints from stakeholders. These may or may not collide with the global set of objectives guiding a public policy, and evaluators should be ready to determine to what extent policy objectives clash with societal values of ethics, justice, equity, and equality. While most studies of policy evaluation are ex-ante (done before the policy has been implemented), there are fewer analyses of ex-post evaluations.[15] An intersectional ex-post evaluation of public policies is therefore fertile ground for future scholarly research.

Policy Termination

While there are five official stages in the policy cycle, I should make a brief note on the often unspoken of and invisible sixth stage of the policy cycle process: policy termination.

Some scholars point out that when policies don't seem to be working out they should be terminated.[16] Why spend money, human capital, and infrastructure on stuff that is not useful or is not having the desired or needed impact? This is an important question to ask, and one that most governments face at various points during their tenure, depending on the specific jurisdictional responsibilities they have and how stringent their budgetary and resource constraints are. The literature on policy termination is scant, yet in a context of increasing austerity, budgetary cuts, and government shrinkage it may experience a resurgence.

I make an explicit reference to policy termination even though I do not cover it in much detail through the chapter precisely because an intersectional lens could help us uncover the politics of policy termination when we look at the identity and group characteristics of individuals affected by a specific public policy. Why would governments want to terminate a policy that partially or collaterally supports LGBTQ+ individuals? Which types of policies are terminated, and which groups does this termination affect more disproportionately? These are questions that we can grapple with more clearly once we apply an intersectional lens to public policy.

WHAT DOES THE POLICY CYCLE AS SEEN THROUGH AN INTERSECTIONALITY LENS LOOK LIKE?

The public policy cycle is an extraordinarily versatile framework for understanding how policies are made; how policy instruments are formulated, chosen, and implemented; and how their effects are evaluated through time. This framework (also dubbed the *policy process* in many academic circles) has the advantage of having feedback loops throughout the process. While it can be seen as a conceptual and analytical model that requires both the analyst as well as all actors participating in the political and policy process to be rational,[17] there is also a tacit assumption that sometimes, particularly when constrained by institutional architectures, actors may not engage in such economical, self-interested thinking.

Why is it important for public policy analysts to consider intersectionality or to use an intersectional lens in their analytical considerations? Let me offer an example directly from Mexico. The literature on homeless people in Mexico is rather sparse, as are public policies designed to explore, analyze, and help solve the kinds of problems that these highly vulnerable individuals face daily. Individuals experiencing homelessness also face a broad range of other difficulties. Some of them may be struggling with mental health issues; others may not speak the same language as the host community or have disabilities or special needs that should be taken into account when designing public policies. Many of these struggles may or may not have public policies that are specifically designed to be solved in a systematically integrated manner.

If we are remiss in seeking to understand the disaggregated demography of chronically homeless individuals (race, ethnicity, gender, health disparities, etc.), we are also not engaging in what Geva-May calls the most important role of a public policy analyst: a clinical examiner.[18] Undertaking public policy analysis, design, and implementation with a clinical approach also helps us comprehend and highlights the need for intersectionality and intersectional thinking as lenses. The intersectional paradigm is helpful in diagnosing which factors may potentially contribute to further marginalization of vulnerable populations and to what extent these factors cancel each other or exacerbate their individual effects when considered globally. For example, women who experience homelessness may be at higher risk of being assaulted. Furthermore, if these women are Indigenous, they may also experience stigma and racism.

Designing public policies with an intersectional lens requires us to think about the composite results of multiple differences across populations and degrees of marginalization and how the individual effects of these oppressions are compounded. Intersectionality theory is, therefore, helpful in identifying potential sources of disparity, marginalization, and oppression that need to be considered in the design of public policy interventions.

Crenshaw focused her initial work on "the race and gender dimensions of violence against women of color."[19] We ought to consider Black, Asian, Hispanic, or any other non-white racial groups as people of color for this kind of analysis to hold validity across different categories. This distinction is important because, even though feminist thought certainly highlights the wide variation in access to public policy options between women and men, Crenshaw's work brings an additional layer of complexity to the analysis by focusing on the racial dimension in addition to the gender one. This means that women may disproportionately be burdened by specific public policies, but women of color will face additional marginalizations precisely because of their race.

Critiques of Intersectionality and Intersectional Thinking and Their Relationship to Public Policy

No conceptual framework is without its critics, and advancing social science requires us to be willing to listen to and engage with these critiques in a thoughtful, analytically convincing manner. Critiques of intersectionality bring to the fore the importance of not taking any individual paradigm before examining the potential areas for further growth of said paradigm. Nash offers a critique that highlights four tensions, in her own words: "the lack of a defined intersectional methodology; the use of black women as quintessential intersectional subjects; the vague definition of intersectionality; and the empirical validity of intersectionality."[20]

In this chapter, I tackle Nash's first and fourth criticisms (the lack of a defined intersectional **methodology** and the question of whether intersectionality has **empirical validity**) by applying an intersectional lens to several public policy questions that, were it not for intersectional thinking, would definitely be lacking depth and applicability in their development. The first question of whether there is an intersectionality methodology (or, the way I understand Nash's question, a social science research method that is inherently intersectional) can be easily tackled in the policy sciences by reminding ourselves that problem definition, instrument design and choice, analysis of policy proposals, and target population identification are all activities that require us to consider all potential outcomes for various groups.

If we fail at identifying potentially compounding factors that could lead to composite negative effects, we are not doing policy analysis very well. This is not an opinion – this is a methodological tenet. To do public policy analysis well, we need to consider how different policy options may negatively affect specific populations. These groups may face challenges that are a direct result of their membership in a marginalized group, such as women of color. Denying the potentially marginalizing effects of race and gender in public policy design therefore leads to poorer policies being implemented, and potentially exacerbating or making challenges already facing those communities at the margins worse.

Furthermore, as I have shown throughout this chapter, it is easy to demonstrate that public policy is inherently intersectional (or should be, at least). The very inspiration for the design of proper policies and policy instruments is the desire to solve public problems with the best tools available and extend their benefits to all populations possible. Public policy should be done considering all potential sources of problems and using a broad vision.

Analyzing Public Policy Change through an Intersectional Policy Regime Framework

Generally, we are interested in two types of scholarly treatments of public policy: Why and how do governments create policies, and how do these policies evolve through time, space, location, jurisdiction, and so on. To study the first part, we use a framework developed originally by Peter DeLeon called the policy cycle, as we've discussed in earlier parts of this chapter. To answer the second question, I propose that we use the policy **regime** framework as posited by George Hoberg (see Figure 11.1).[21]

Figure 11.1. Hoberg's Policy Regime Framework

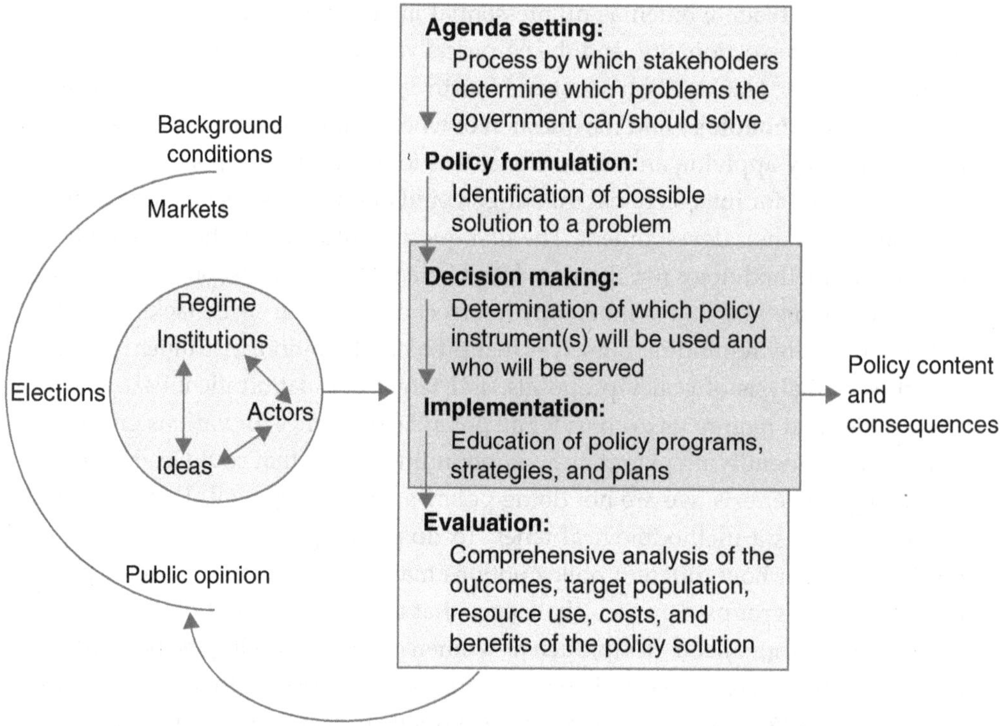

Source: Adapted from George Hoberg, "Policy Cycles and Policy Regimes: A Framework for Studying Policy Change," in *In Search of Sustainability: British Columbia Forest Policy in the 1990s,* eds. Benjamin Cashore, George Hoberg, Michael Howlett, Jeremy Rayner, and Jeremy Wilson, 3–30 (Vancouver: UBC Press, 2001).

The policy regime framework allows us to understand how ideas, interests, and institutions combine to influence how policies evolve and change. Most scholars who analyze political phenomena manifest an interest in the role of actors (interests), ideologies (ideas), and rules and norms (institutions), albeit it was Hoberg who articulated how these may form a regime that is constituted around and influenced by markets, public opinion, and elections. While I have limited space to discuss all of the policy regime framework, I do want to address how intersectionality can help strengthen it by asking thoughtful questions on how policies change and evolve.[22]

When analyzing interests (actors) it is particularly important to remember that there are various types of actors: those in government, non-governmental organizations, business interests, unions and syndicates, and so on. Each of those groups may have a diverse composition, but in the end, as a group they represent specific interests. Therefore, it is important that we discern whether these interests are aligned with specific causes or against them. Because intersectionality is so strongly focused on tackling inequalities and challenging oppressive groups, it is indispensable that interests are seen through an intersectional lens.

Ideas refer to two types of beliefs: causal and principled. Causal beliefs refer to matter-of-fact assessments of reality. For example, a causal belief would be "excessive rain can cause flooding." A principled belief is an evaluation of right or wrong. A principled belief would express "racism is wrong." Here is where intersectionality can help us understand how specific policy choices are made and how policies may or may not change through time. If the principled beliefs of certain policymakers included that "we have achieved racial equality" or "we are no longer a society where gender inequality exists," advancing intersectional policy objectives would be incredibly hard.

Institutions refer to the rules and norms that govern the relationships between actors. There are two main types of institutions: formal (encoded in rules, regulations, code books, etc.) and informal (not physically or digitally encoded but known as a result of customary practices, routines, and repetition). A formal rule would be a legal document that established whether cars should be driven on the right-hand side of the road. A set of informal rules governs the interaction of, for example, gangs and other types of organized crime groups. While institutions do not encode groups' identities, institutions may run the risk of sustaining certain oppressions against vulnerable populations by limiting access to governmental actors.

Examples of Intersectional Policy Analysis

The role of a policy analyst is in many ways similar to what a clinician does, and therefore should be considered as a clinical profession.[23] A physician will examine a patient, consider all the symptoms that they present with, ponder the potential causes and mechanisms through which a disease might have been contracted, discern treatment trajectories, select the proper medication and consumption/delivery schedule, as well as evaluate (diagnose) how the patient is evolving and whether the illness has been fully addressed and the patient given a bill of clean health. In a similar fashion, a policy analyst should be able to detect issues that are relevant to the public and determine whether it is worthy of being included in the governmental agenda.

Perhaps the best clinical analogy to intersectionality in public policy is that the same way clinicians choose medications and evaluate the potential side effects of each one as well as determine the negative interactions that these pharmaceutical products may have, public policy scholars who use an intersectional lens should be able to evaluate specific public policy instruments and discern whether their usage and implementation may have potentially deleterious effects that, once we consider the specificities of each target population, could potentially be compounding one another.

There are plenty of types of policies and issue areas that we could discuss in this chapter. I have chosen two examples that I believe will highlight how an intersectional lens can help policy analysts and policymakers in general design and implement better policies. One of the most important elements to remember is that intersectionality is a lens that can help evaluate each element of the policy cycle. I believe that we ought to focus on policy design, instrument choice, and policy evaluation as the three stages where we explore how the intersection of race, class, and gender can have an impact on target populations.

The first public policy example I have chosen is the vulnerability of homeless populations to disasters.[24] One could think that all populations are approximately equally vulnerable to storms, flooding, earthquakes, and so on. However, the degrees of vulnerability vary by population, and specifically across different races in countries where races are less homogeneous. Moreover, as is the case with water and sanitation, how much a particular population is affected varies by gender. It has been well documented that women bear the brunt of water collection efforts in households around the world, but even more so in the Global South.[25] Therefore, when we consider the plight of individuals facing homelessness, we should also consider their group characteristics to evaluate which policy approach would work best. This approach would therefore work well with an intersectional lens, as Vickery outlines.

The second public policy example I have chosen is the intersectional vulnerabilities of LGBTQ+ individuals regarding housing options. While all elderly people experience a high degree of vulnerability and risk for physical and emotional harm as they age, older persons who belong to groups that have traditionally been marginalized, such as LGBTQ+, Black or communities of color, disabled, and Indigenous, face intersectional challenges as all of these individual characteristics collide with each other. The potential negative effects of urban segregation could be even more pernicious in a context where already marginalized elderly individuals may be housed in neighborhoods that do not offer any sense of belonging nor support services. These same issues may also impact how and whether gay teens engage in suicidal ideation.[26]

These are all important public policy issues, but not the only ones, and it is critical that we consider intersectionality as a framework of analysis and as a normative approach to designing and implementing policies across the board. I mention this because, from the examples I have presented, a perception could emerge that intersectionality is only ripe or useful as an analytical tool for environmental problems. This is certainly not the case. In the Hankivsky and Jordan-Zachery edited volume we can find more than a dozen different examples of policy issues where intersectionality generates a richer approach to designing, choosing, implementing, and evaluating policy problems, and in studying how these problems reached the agenda in the first place. Tobacco control (Douglas), education policy in South Africa (Schmidt and Mestry), and rural health policy in Ukraine (Vorobyova) are but three examples of the different policy areas that intersectional public policy scholars have examined.[27]

Before I sum up, I want to make a few points on three important areas: mainstreaming intersectionality in public policy, the comparative turn in intersectional public policy thinking, and how positionality affects intersectional policy studies.

Mainstreaming Intersectionality: Making Public Policy Sensitive to Intersectional Challenges?

One of the most important elements of intersectionality as a paradigm, in my view, is the integrative, cross-cutting, and holistic consideration of different modes of oppression and marginalization. Considering how various factors (gender, race, caste, difference in bodily ability) may potentially interact and impact the design and implementation of the same public policies across populations is key to determining whether those policies will effectively serve the publics they intend. Therefore, mainstreaming intersectionality would be important to consider across widely diverging policy areas.

The idea of mainstreaming intersectionality is relatively new, even though the main theoretical framework has been around for a while now. Emanating from feminist Black scholar Kimberlé Crenshaw, intersectionality has slowly been gaining ground as an analytical lens, although we are still far from having made intersectional public policy "a thing."[28] Crenshaw makes it clear that the intersection component is fundamental:

> Where systems of race, gender, and class domination converge, as they do in the experiences of battered women of color, intervention strategies based solely on the experiences of women who do not share the same class or race backgrounds will be of limited help to women who because of race and class face different obstacles.[29]

Even if we were to apply a feminist lens that looked at public policy interventions that were sensitive to the challenges women face, we must consider the intersection of race, gender, and class domination because otherwise we fail to recognize that these other additional group characteristics of identity may have negative and compounding effects precisely due to their belonging to these groups. Tiffany Manuel aptly stated:

> [p]olicy scholars have not ignored the context in which people make choices, but the analytical frameworks commonly used in public policy tend to view identity characteristics like race, class, and gender as linear, static, unconnected phenomena rather than multifaceted, fluid, and intersectional.[30]

In this chapter, I showcased a few ways in which public policy scholarship may benefit from applying an intersectional lens to offer a more integrated analysis, in response to Manuel's suggestion that we move beyond the disconnectedness of groups' identity characteristics.

The Comparative Politics Turn in Intersectional Public Policy

One may wonder to what extent the frameworks I discussed in this chapter apply in different contexts. This chapter is, after all, in a section on comparative politics. I chose not to discuss comparative public policy per se (i.e., specific methodological innovations associated with how we examine policy problems from a comparative perspective, or comparative policy analysis as a separate subfield of policy studies' scholarship) because the concepts I presented here are inherently comparative, and therefore a comparative political perspective would permeate through regardless of whether I discuss the methods within comparative politics (for more on methods in comparative politics, see Chapter 7).

One important caveat, though, is that as intersectionality theory shows us, there are different ways in which populations' characteristics define how negatively they might be affected and whether these impacts will be compounded. To determine these negative interactions and the extent to which they occur and the degree of impact they may have on already marginalized populations, we need to consider that across cities, countries, regions, and towns, intersectionality will operate differently because each population is different. This means that, for example, in countries where homosexuality is relatively well accepted within the general population, the degree of oppression a gay person may face and perceive will be different than someone who lives in a highly homophobic country. This is not a small issue to consider, and this is the reason why I encourage policy analysts and comparative politics scholars to reflect on cross-city, country, or region variations and their potential impacts.

The Positionality Component within Intersectional Public Policy Studies

One of the elements I wanted to discuss that I consider very important, but that at the same time I have purposefully left to the end of the chapter, is how our (as policy analysts) positionality affects our public policy analysis. You may wonder, What is positionality and how does it relate to public policymaking? *Positionality* refers to a self-reflective stance in social science analytical thinking that requires us to consider who we are, how we self-identify, and what our individual backgrounds, life experiences, and stages bring to the analysis of public and societal problems. While originally the concept and definitions of positionality come from anthropologists and the discipline and practice of anthropology, other fields in social science have adopted it as an important mode of self-reflection that asks us to consider how our own individual characteristics and identities may color which issues we analyze and the paradigms and conceptual lenses we use to discuss them.[31]

As I discussed in earlier sections of this chapter, our problem definition may be influenced by which issues we consider most important, and how we rank these is necessarily a process that is influenced by our positionality. In my case, I am a single, gay, Mexican male who was trained in Mexico, the United Kingdom, and Canada and who has held faculty positions in Canada, Mexico, and France. My PhD is from a Canadian university, and I was trained in a multidisciplinary setting in a very liberal, welcoming environment that has also had their historical challenges with how they have dealt with Indigenous peoples and with land claims from these communities.

Writing about intersectionality from a relatively privileged position as a tenure-track faculty member at a higher education institution in Mexico that functions, essentially, like an R1 (research 1, the top tier of universities) in the United States or Canada is very challenging, not only intellectually but also personally. The kinds of oppressions that Kimberlé Crenshaw identifies in her foundational work on intersectionality, particularly against Black women in the United States, are substantially distinct from those experienced by male queer Latino scholars from the Global South like myself.

As a scholar of public policy, I am keenly attuned to the need to consider all possible solutions to a public problem. As a qualitative methods practitioner, I am firmly on the side of declaring my positionality and the different privileges that accompany me in undertaking the work I do.[32] And as a scholar committed to global justice and to shrinking the gap between the marginalized and the privileged, I am keen to engage with the topic of intersectionality and with the need to use an intersectional lens in the study of public policy. In this chapter, I combine my experiences as a male queer Latino professor based in the Global South with my expertise in comparative public policy to discuss the importance of considering intersectionality as a lens to examine how we conduct public policy.

As I noted above, I have experienced intersectional challenges such as bullying and marginalization as I grew up, but I am not from Indigenous blood nor am I Black, and my family upbringing is decidedly middle class. Therefore, I do have some intersectional sensibility and experience with how different individual characteristics are disproportionately affected in a compounded negative way, but I am more attuned now as a faculty member, particularly after having taught in Canada and France. This is important to describe and assert as I write a chapter on intersectionality in public policy. I also suggest that being able to consider their own positionality is an important element for policy analysts and designers to consider when undertaking their work.

SUMMARY

In this chapter, I have tried to provide a modest contribution to the study of public policy and of comparative politics of public policy by examining how intersectionality applies across all five stages of the policy cycle.

- Intersectional thinking allows us to provide a fuller, richer, and more robust foundation to any public policy we analyze and design, and policy implementation can be strengthened through intersectional thinking.
- The policy regime framework can be interwoven with an intersectional sensibility to help explain how policies change and how these changes may be triggered by the control or participation suppression of specific groups to disproportionately affect already marginalized communities.
- The chapter offered two examples of public policies that could be strengthened either through intersectional thinking or where intersectionality was brought into the analysis.
- Finally, additional thoughts on three important areas were offered: mainstreaming intersectionality in public policy, the comparative turn in intersectional public policy thinking, and how positionality affects intersectional policy studies.

CONCLUDING QUESTIONS

1 How is public policy inherently intersectional?

2 What is positionality and why is it important that policy analysts consider their own positionality when analyzing public policy?

3 This chapter detailed multiple reasons that an intersectional lens is important to the study of public policy. Why do you think the intersectional approach to public policy is not yet a fully mainstream approach?

4 What are some of the criticisms of intersectionality in policy analysis? How might one rebut those criticisms?

NOTES

1 Iris Geva-May, *Thinking Like a Policy Analyst: Policy Analysis as a Clinical Profession* (Houndmills, UK: Palgrave Macmillan, 2005).

2 Michael Howlett and Ben Cashore, "Conceptualizing Public Policy," *Comparative Policy Studies: Conceptual and Methodological Challenges* (2014): 17–33.

3 Douglas Torgerson, "Contextual Orientation in Policy Analysis: The Contribution of Harold D. Lasswell," *Policy Sciences* 18(1985): 241–61.

4 Paul Cairney, *Understanding Public Policy* (Houndmills, UK: Palgrave Macmillan, 2012); Paul Cairney, *The Politics of Evidence-Based Policy Making* (Basingstoke, UK: Springer – Palgrave Macmillan, 2016).

5 Werner Jann and Kai Wegrich, "Theories of the Policy Cycle," in *Handbook of Public Policy Analysis*, eds. Frank Fischer and Gerald J. Miller, 43–62 (Abingdon, UK: Taylor & Francis, 2006).

6 Sarah Pralle, "The 'Mouse That Roared': Agenda Setting in Canadian Pesticides Politics," *Policy Studies Journal* 34, no. 2 (2006): 171–94; Sarah Pralle, "Venue Shopping, Political Strategy, and Policy Change: The Intenationalization of Canadian Forest Advocacy," *Journal of Public Policy* 23, no. 3 (2003): 233–60.

7 Michael Howlett and Ishani Mukherjee, "Policy Formulation: Where Knowledge Meets Power in the Policy Process," in *Handbook of Policy Formulation*, eds. Michael Howlett and Ishani Mukherjee, 3–22 (Cheltenham, UK: Edward Elgar, 2017); Andrew J. Jordan, John R. Turnpenny, and Tim Rayner, "The Tools of Policy Formulation: New Perspectives and New Challenges," in *The Tools of Policy Formulation: Actors, Capacities, Venues and Effects*, eds. Andrew Jordan and John Turnpenny, 267–94 (Cheltenham, UK: Edward Elgar, 2011).

8 Peter John, "All Tools Are Informational Now: How Information and Persuasion Define the Tools of Government," *Policy and Politics* 41, no. 4 (2013): 605–20.

9 Anne Schneider and Helen Ingram, "Social Construction of Target Populations: Implications for Politics and Policy," *American Political Science Review* 87, no. 2 (1993): 334–47.

10 Anne Schneider and Helen Ingram, "Systematically Pinching Ideas: A Comparative Approach to Policy Design," *Journal of Public Policy* 8, no. 1 (1988): 61–80; Anne Schneider and Helen Ingram, "Behavioral Assumptions of Policy Tools," *Journal of Politics* 52, no. 2 (1990): 510–29; Schneider and Ingram, "Social Construction of Target Populations."

11 Jill Schofield and Charlotte Sausman, "Symposium on Implementing Public Policy: Learning from Theory and Practice," *Public Administration* 82, no. 2 (2004): 235–48.

12 Pamela A. Mischen and Thomas A.P. Sinclair, "Making Implementation More Democratic through Action Implementation Research," *Journal of Public Administration Research and Theory* 19, no. 1 (2009): 145–64.

13 Iris Geva-May and Leslie A. Pal, "Good Fences Make Good Neighbours: Policy Evaluation and Policy Analysis: Exploring the Differences," *Evaluation* 5, no. 3 (1999): 259–77.

14 Anders Hanberger, "What Is the Policy Problem? Methodological Challenges in Policy Evaluation," *Evaluation* 7, no. 1 (2001): 45–62.

15 Lhawang Ugyel and Janine O'Flynn, "Measuring Policy Success: Evaluating Public Sector Reform in Bhutan," *International Journal of Public Administration* 40, no. 2 (2017): 115–25.

16 David Dery, "Evaluation and Termination in the Policy Cycle," *Policy Sciences* 17 (1984): 13–26; Geva-May and Pal, "Good Fences Make Good Neighbours."

17 Sophia Everett, "The Policy Cycle: Democratic Process or Rational Paradigm Revisited?," *Australian Journal of Public Administration* 62, no. 2 (2003): 65–70.

18 Geva-May, *Thinking Like a Policy Analyst.*

19 Kimberlé Crenshaw, "Mapping the Margins: Intersectionality, Identity Politics, and Violence against Women of Color," *Stanford Law Review* 43 (1991): 1242.

20 Jennifer C. Nash, "Re-Thinking Intersectionality," *Feminist Review* 1 (2008): 1–15.

21 George Hoberg, "Policy Cycles and Policy Regimes: A Framework for Studying Policy Change," in *In Search of Sustainability: British Columbia Forest Policy in the 1990s*, eds. Benjamin Cashore, George Hoberg, Michael Howlett, Jeremy Rayner, and Jeremy Wilson, 3–30 (Vancouver: UBC Press, 2001).

22 Hoberg, "Policy Cycles and Policy Regimes."

23 Geva-May, *Thinking Like a Policy Analyst.*

24 Jamie Vickery, "Using an Intersectional Approach to Advance Understanding of Homeless Persons' Vulnerability to Disaster," *Environmental Sociology* 4, no. 1 (2018): 136–47.

25 Farhana Sultana, "Fluid Lives: Subjectivities, Gender and Water in Rural Bangladesh," *Gender, Place and Culture* 16, no. 4 (2009): 427–44.

26 Olivier Ferlatte, Travis Salway, Olena Hankivsky, Terry Trussler, John L. Oliffe, and Rick Marchand, "Recent Suicide Attempts across Multiple Social Identities among Gay and Bisexual Men: An Intersectionality Analysis," *Journal of Homosexuality* 65, no. 11 (2018): 1507–26.

27 Olena Hankivsky and J.S. Jordan-Zachery, eds., *The Palgrave Handbook of Intersectionality in Public Policy* (Cham, Switzerland: Palgrave Macmillan, 2019).

28 Hankivsky and Jordan-Zachery, eds., *The Palgrave Handbook of Intersectionality in Public Policy.*

29 Crenshaw, "Mapping the Margins," 1246.

30 Tiffany Manuel, "Envisioning the Possibilities for a Good Life: Exploring the Public Policy Implications of Intersectionality Theory," *Journal of Women, Politics & Policy* 28, no. 3–4 (2006): 175.

31 Cindi Katz, "Playing the Field: Questions of Fieldwork in Geography," *The Professional Geographer* 46, no. 1 (1994): 67–72; Beverley Mullings, "Insider or Outsider, Both or Neither: Some Dilemmas of Interviewing in a Cross-Cultural Setting," *Geoforum* 30, no. 4 (1999): 337–50; Raul Pacheco-Vega and Kate Parizeau, "Doubly Engaged Ethnography: Opportunities and Challenges When Working with Vulnerable Communities," *International Journal of Qualitative Methods* 17, no. 1 (2018): 1–13.

32 Pacheco-Vega and Parizeau, "Doubly Engaged Ethnography."

RESOURCES AND SUGGESTIONS FOR FURTHER READING

In addition to the works cited in this chapter, it is important that scholars of comparative politics and public policy consider the following as key works in this field:

Hankivsky, O., and J.S. Jordan-Zachery, eds. *The Palgrave Handbook of Intersectionality in Public Policy.* Cham, Switzerland: Palgrave Macmillan, 2019. https://doi.org /10.1007/978-3-319-98473-5. *The entire book is great, but readers may find the empirical chapters particularly useful.*

Manuel, Tiffany. "Envisioning the Possibilities for a Good Life: Exploring the Public Policy Implications of Intersectionality Theory." *Journal of Women, Politics & Policy* 28, no. 3–4 (2007): 173–203.

Schneider, Anne, and Helen Ingram. "Social Construction of Target Populations: Implications for Politics and Policy." *American Political Science Review* 87, no. 2 (1993): 334–47.

PART THREE

International Relations

CHAPTER TWELVE

What Is International Relations?

*Dr. Brooke
Ackerly*

*Anna
Carella*

LEARNING OBJECTIVES

1 Identify diverse intellectual approaches to international relations and distinguish the concerns with international politics raised by each
2 Identify the international political problems that each theory either helps illuminate or does not predict well
3 Question the role of funding and other forms of privilege and power in determining what gets studied and taught in the field of international relations
4 Identify three ways to study international relations without privileging the histories and experiences of certain states, cultures, identities, peoples, and viewpoints while marginalizing others

KEY TERMS

Bretton Woods institutions   the collective name given to the international financial institutions set up as World War II ended. These institutions, the World Bank and the International Monetary Fund, were set up by agreement of 43 countries at a conference in Bretton Woods, New Hampshire, in 1944.

Cold War   A conflict between the two largest military powers in the world after World War II, the United States with its allies and the United Soviet Socialist Republics and its allies. The conflict was militarized in that both sides invested heavily in military power aimed at the other, but the conflict was "cold" because, despite a few incidents in which threat of use of force seemed imminent, neither side pulled the trigger.

empirical   having to do with observation, data, or experience rather than theory or logic

epistemology   a branch of philosophy concerned with asking questions about why and how we know what we know, and how we distinguish "fact" from "opinion" and "objectivity" from "subjectivity"

Global North   those countries of Europe, North America, Australia, New Zealand, and Japan that were the first part of the world to industrialize in the nineteenth century and where economic and political power relied on the raw materials of countries from the Global South. May also refer to those parts of a political economy *within* a country that experience economic growth by relying on the labor and raw materials of others.

Global South   those countries that were either legally or economically colonized by countries of the Global North, resulting in economic and political positions in the global political economy whereby they have marginalized voices in influencing the terms of international institutions, including trade, finance, climate, and security. May also refer to those parts of a political economy *within* a country that experience economic stagnation or decline even when other parts of that same economy grow, often because they provide labor and raw materials.

international relations   an interdisciplinary field of study blending political science, law, history, anthropology, economics, linguistics, geography, philosophy, women's studies, environmental science, and more that takes up questions of international, transnational, regional, and global politics and how these are influenced by and affect national and local politics

positivism   in international relations, an epistemology that holds that knowledge is the result of empirical data interpreted through reason and logic, as it might be in the natural sciences and math

racialize   a process of constructing a political and social hierarchy by ascribing racial identities and political meaning to difference, often reified in social and political policies and institutions

sovereignty   a state's control of their own affairs both domestically (internal sovereignty) and externally (over foreign policy)

structural violence   ways in which social structures or institutions systematically harm or disadvantage certain groups of people

WHAT IS INTERNATIONAL RELATIONS AND WHY DO WE STUDY IT?

> [R]ather than searching for one universal history, we need to uncover stories about forgotten spaces that respect difference, show tolerance and compassion, and are skeptical about absolute truths. Such stories can help us build a more inclusionary, more open minded, and more reflexive International Relations that transcends the structures of domination that all of us still carry within ourselves from the past.
>
> – J. Ann Tickner[1]

International relations is an interdisciplinary field of study blending political science, law, history, anthropology, economics, linguistics, geography, philosophy, gender studies, critical race studies, environmental science, and more that takes up questions of international, transnational, regional, and global politics and how these are influenced by and affect national and local politics.[2] It is a field of study for the curious among us with a broad, and ever-broadening, worldview. It is the study of the world and all its peoples, of cultures and ways of organizing ourselves politically, socially, and economically. International relations studies conflict and violence, sustainable peace and human rights, international institutions and law, and transnational social movements.

We study international relations (IR) to understand the world. Therefore, scholars study different kinds of global political questions depending on their view of the world and the puzzles about it that intrigue them. The discipline has often been characterized as focused narrowly on issues of interstate conflict and global trade – but IR has always been studied by those who considered it as much more than that.[3]

Some scholars study IR to understand the global ethics around the use of violence and strategies for peace (see Chapter 4 on social movements and Chapter 14 on security and conflict). Some study IR to understand the political implications for the global economy of international, global, and local structures, institutions, and their decisions (see Chapter 13 on international political economy and Chapter 16 on international organizations). Some study IR because being aware of the suffering of others compels them to take action to make conditions better and more just (see Chapter 2 on theory, Chapter 3 on ideology, and Chapter 15 on international law and human rights). Some want to know how political and social change happens and how much power is involved in maintaining things as they are. Some want to know why global problems such as poverty persist (see Chapter 13 on international political economy). Some want to understand why promoting human rights is a generalizable and effective tool for redressing injustice, yet at the same time a discursive tool that can be used to mask injustice as justice (see Chapter 15 on international law and human rights).

We study IR because we have questions. How does a global trade agreement affect the conditions of domestic workers, nurses, and others in the global care economy? Why does gender-based violence increase at the end of conflict, and can we say that a conflict has ended or that peace is secure if that is the case? What about global politics makes *you* curious?

With different questions come different theoretical lenses to explain what kind of problem a puzzle in global politics poses. Hence, the field of IR is often discussed not so much around questions as around schools of thought or *paradigms*. In this chapter we discuss the principle paradigms around which the discipline of IR – to date a Western-centric discipline – has been taught to generations of Anglo-American students. *Liberalism* and *realism* predominate in US IR; some alternatives (*Marxism, liberal realism, constructivism*) are being taught in the United States and around the world; a third family of theories (*feminism, post-structuralism, post-colonialism, green theory, critical theory*) reveal and resist the ideological underpinnings of those approaches.[4] At this moment of global history, IR taught in English is centered on international relations scholarship that has been written by and for an English-speaking audience. Such a perspective is globally incomplete.

Further, with different questions come different ways of doing **empirical** research. Some use large data sets of conflicts, treaties, or human rights violations by state and across time. Others use qualitative data, historical analysis, or discourse analysis.

If we look historically, culturally, politically, socially, and even economically at the field of IR, we come to understand what is at stake. In fact, arguably the field of IR is itself a terrain of global politics, as we will show in the coming pages.[5]

HOW HAS IR AS A DISCIPLINE EVOLVED?

It is important to draw a distinction between international relations the *discipline* and international politics as practiced and lived daily by bureaucrats, political leaders, diplomats, activists, revolutionaries, non-governmental organizations, merchants, traders, multinational corporations, religious leaders, laborers, parents, and everyday people. If a discipline is defined solely by the existence of a faculty and a program of study, then the discipline of IR emerged at the end of World War I when the first Department of International Politics was established at the University College of Wales, Aberystwyth, at the end of 1918.[6]

However, international *politics* existed long before the discipline was established: The Silk Road, the Byzantine Empire, the Mongol Empire, the Chinese explorer Zheng He's voyages via a fleet of ships to India and Africa from 1405–33, Muslim circum-conversion and settlement in Africa and into the Iberian Peninsula, Columbus landing in the Americas in 1492, the intensification of the colonization of Africa by Europe in the 1870s, women's movements criticizing war, and more are all parts of our international political history. But the study of international politics and the establishment of the discipline of IR have lagged far behind international politics in practice.

Doing IR requires articulating your questions in a way that enables you to see the complexity of a global problem and the different ways that policy decisions about it may affect different people differently. However, the focus and theories that have historically dominated IR as a discipline have been greatly, and mostly not self-reflectively, influenced by the politics of the times and by the worldviews of the Western scholars, mostly men, generating theories to explain the world as they saw it while claiming objectivity and universality.[7]

Most Western, mainstream histories of IR cite World War I and the Western political desire to prevent another deadly, interstate war as the key motivation behind the emergence of the discipline. However, at the dawn of the field and the twentieth century, IR in the United States and Europe was also deeply invested in "civilizing" those "underdeveloped" parts of the world we now refer to as the **Global South** and was steeped in racism, colonialism, and white supremacy.[8] In other words, in Western academia there was interest in the study of foreign cultures and politics to learn how to more effectively use the colonial and imperial power of the (white) **Global North** to secure access to the resources in the Global South.

Politicians and IR scholars paternalized, **racialized**, and dehumanized the people of the Global South, referring to them as "backward," uncivilized "barbarians" who were unwilling or unable to secure and efficiently exploit their own natural resources for their benefit. The colonial project was often cast in euphemisms such as advancement, enlightenment, and development (see also Chapter 3 on ideology in this volume). As an example of the large impact colonialism and the racialization of colonial rule had on the establishment of IR, consider the name of the first IR journal in the United States, *Journal of Race Development*, which was founded in 1910, renamed *Foreign Affairs* in 1922, and is still widely read by scholars, policymakers, and others seeking academic analysis of global politics.

Both visions of IR – as a way to prevent interstate war in the post–World War I period and as a way to "civilize" the Global South via colonization – are steeped in Western political theory dating back to the founding of liberal democracy as an idea and as a political practice during the American, French, and Haitian

Revolutions. Liberalism's theoretical roots lie in Western philosophy, with philosophers such as Locke, Rousseau, Kant, and Mill, whose liberalisms were concerned both with how to end conflict and war and with how to "civilize" the people of the Global South as a way to achieve that goal.

As an approach to IR, *liberalism* seeks to understand the institutions and conditions under which states can maximize economic growth and minimize conflict, with particular emphasis on international institutions, interdependence, and democratizations of states (see Box 12.1). Note that "liberalism" in IR and as we are using it here (as you learned in Chapter 2) is a political theory associated with social contract theory and the fundamental equality, freedom, and rights of all people. It should not be confused with a political ideology of "the left" in contemporary US politics or any political party.

BOX 12.1: THE LIBERAL VIEW OF THE WORLD AND WORLD POLITICS
From the liberal perspective:

- A free market provides incentives for states to cooperate.
- Domestic actors influence how states define their foreign policy interests.
- Economic and social issues are as important to understanding state power as military power.
- The important actors in international politics are states, international organizations, and multinational corporations.

Liberalism does not ignore power as a motivation for state behavior; liberals assume that power is important, but not the sole driver of state action.

One of liberalism's primary contributions to the field of IR is the democratic peace theory and research paradigm. It argues that democracies are more peaceful in their foreign relations than non-democracies, particularly with each other, with trading partners, and with those who participate in international institutions. This idea is rooted in Enlightenment philosophy and attributed to Kant's 1795 essay *Perpetual Peace: A Philosophical Sketch*.[9] There has been significant research in IR to test and refine democratic peace theory. There are three main arguments for the mechanism underlying democratic peace. One argument is *institutional*, meaning that the constraints that democratic leaders face, such as being more accountable to their constituencies and facing greater domestic penalties if they go to war and lose, is what causes democracies to be more peaceful. Another argument is *normative*, that democracies share similar values and have similar political cultures and therefore tend to view each other with less hostility. The final argument is *economic*, since democracies tend to be wealthier and have greater economic interdependence, and so are less likely to risk economic prosperity for war.[10]

Grounded in unexamined enlightenment thinking, liberal theory has a dark side that has been used to justify colonialism and imperialism: If democracy is foundational for peace, then spreading democracy by *any means* becomes morally tenable and even necessary. Kant himself saw a duty for every state to fulfill what he saw as nature's plan by using reason to bring all men in harmony, even if against their will, by submitting to the "empire of right."[11]

Similarly, many Enlightenment philosophers explicitly or implicitly supported imperialism. For example, Locke qualified the ability to own private property for only those who "are counted the civilized part of mankind."[12] Rousseau believed that "For nations, as for men, there is a time of maturity which they must reach before they are made subject to law."[13] J.S. Mill, known for his concern with liberty and equality of women, declared "backward states of society" were "still in a state to require being taken care of by others" and "must be protected against their own actions as well as against external injury" as we do with children.[14] He goes on: "Despotism is a legitimate mode of government in dealing with barbarians, provided the end be their improvement."

Responding to the hunger and struggles of people left out of or exploited by the industrialization and colonization of the eighteenth and nineteenth centuries, communists criticized the ideology of liberalism for perpetuating economic tyranny within and across state boundaries even while it challenged political tyranny. As we will see below, Marxism reveals the role of the ideology of liberalism in concealing the exploitative dimensions of capitalism and the economic inequalities that it relies on and exacerbates.

In domestic politics, in response to communists' criticisms, twentieth-century liberalism incorporated features of the welfare state to provide for all citizens. In international politics, liberalism supported state **sovereignty** and international institutions like the League of Nations, founded in 1920, to solve international disputes with diplomacy and thereby discourage states from using violence against other states.

Interestingly, those who date the emergence of the IR discipline to the post–World War I period cite the overtly normative goal of this new field of study for helping ordinary people avoid the horrors of another war.[15] Yet the voices of the people have historically not been prominent as narrators in the discipline, but rather as objects.[16] This is not only an ethical mistake but a practical one. As Enloe explains, a consequence of the norm in IR that "the margins stay marginal, the silent stay voiceless, and ladders are never turned upside down – is that many orthodox analysts of international politics are caught by surprise" – for example, by revolutions, by failed referenda, and other political events that the people at the top cannot predict because of their disconnect from the experiences of ordinary people.[17]

World War II (1939–45) shattered liberalism's dominance in IR and the belief in the power of institutions to constrain aggressive states if the most powerful states were not part of those institutions.[18] The United States, United Kingdom, France, Russia, and China tested the nuclear bomb. Non-Western countries began to challenge the economic and political power of European countries on their soil. In this post–World War II era, Hans Morganthau drew on historical ideas from Thucydides, Machiavelli, and Hobbes to offer the field of IR another paradigm for understanding global politics in which the most individually and militarily powerful nations in global politics were also the most important nations for the field of IR to study. Coined *realism*, this approach explains politics as resulting from an unchanging and destitute human nature motivated by fear (see Box 12.2).

BOX 12.2: THE REALIST VIEW OF THE WORLD AND WORLD POLITICS
From the realist perspective:

- States are the only important actors in international politics, and they are unitary actors, meaning "the state" is the only actor rather than the various people and institutions who make up the state.
- State interests are survival and territorial sovereignty (autonomy, independence).
- State aims are security and the power to achieve these.
- Power is measured by military capabilities, the size of the economy and population, and access to natural resources.

Realists assume that power is the overriding concern and primary motivation of state actors.

Because the realist assumption was that powerful *states* were all important, vibrant movements for decolonization in the Global South were not central themes in the study of IR. These movements were virtually ignored by IR scholars, despite their being central to the lives of most peoples of the world at the time, despite the colonies being important sources of natural resources and economic power for European countries, and despite their decolonizing states being sites of proxy conflicts between the United States and Soviet Union.

The development of the **Cold War** provoked a refined "neo" realism. The main power struggle as perceived by Western scholars shifted from a "multipolar" world of many European states vying for the power to control global resources to a "bipolar" struggle between the United States with its allies and the United Soviet Socialist Republics (USSR) and its allies. This shift led to more interest in the *structure* of the world system – anarchical, bipolar, or multipolar – which, like state power, has explanatory power for state behavior.

The central analytical assumption of the state as a unitary actor with interests and power is the same under realism and neorealism; however, where *neorealism* breaks with realism is in its explanation of state behavior, notably articulated in Kenneth Waltz's *Theory of International Relations* and further developed by twentieth-century Western IR theorists, including John Mearsheimer and Robert Jervis.[19] Under neorealism, state behavior isn't shaped by human nature, but rather by the anarchical structure of the international system, with its lack of an effective central authority and the distribution of power among states. Domestic politics and social movements are not part of the terrain of study; rather, neorealists focus on the balance of power in the international system.

The preceding approaches focus on the state as a unitary actor (domestic politics don't explain state behavior) and attempt to predict international behavior based on the assumptions that states behave "rationally," where rational is understood to mean in their own national interest. Marxism, liberal realism, and constructivism approach questions of international relations by offering alternatives to those simplifying assumptions about international politics. Though many scholars exploring these three alternatives do not themselves explore the importance of domestic politics for international relations, each invites us to think critically about how they might be connected.

Marxism is the view that capital and labor are global and that the inequalities of industrial political economy and the mobility of production around the globe means that, internationally, workers have a common political and economic interest in resisting labor exploitation of all workers, not just themselves. Marxist IR focuses on the political economy of exploitation that can happen across borders in the form of colonialism, imperialism, and economic dependence of less powerful countries on institutions and norms governed by the more powerful ones. These include, significantly, the exploitation of workers by global corporations, which are governed by terms of trade that favor states and corporations over workers globally. Marxists also note the way that the exploitation of some people within states can make them internationally vulnerable, for example by forcing them to migrate for economic or political security.

An intellectual idea centered in the UK and grounded in Cold War politics, *liberal realism* focuses on the other side of that picture. It holds that states construct international societies – groups of states – around common values and that these can be a basis for stability in the international system. The disparate impacts of this international system on different subsets of the population within each state is not central.

Coming into development after the end of the Cold War, *constructivism* notes that the structure of the international system affects what states can do in the international system, but it also notes that states can change the system through their actions. By rethinking their ideas, interests, and norms of behavior, states can change the stability of the international system. Domestic politics affects these ideas and interests. Consider, for example, the impact on the international system of the shift in US policy toward North Korea after the 2016 election. Constructivism argues that identities and interests change and are shaped over time and that states act according to norms, which are shaped by culture, identity, their form of government, history, and prevailing ideas.[20] Identities are relational; actors do not have a conception of self except in relation to and through their relations with others.

The theories of IR offered by liberalism, realism, Marxism, liberal realism, and constructivism have views of state behavior that are conditioned on the politics and economic situation of people within states, but leave all or most of the complex dynamics of exploitative and oppressive politics underexplored.

This inattention to domestic politics and social movements is somewhat shocking given that throughout the development of the discipline decolonization, global exploitation of resources and people, and the unequal effects of global governance on people within countries were a significant part of international politics. The approaches to IR to which we next turn attend to these connections.

THINKING DIFFERENTLY ABOUT IR

International politics were more dynamic than the above characterizations suggest. Moreover, with the exception of Marxism (and as we will see, Marxism misses a lot), those theories are silent on the forms of global injustice supported by the institutions that these international political theories explain and justify. During the Cold War era many countries were undergoing enormous political changes and upheavals. Decolonization movements created new states who might ally with either block. Civil wars divided states. The Non-Aligned Movement sought an alliance among newly independent Asian and African countries, an alliance that would not align with either side in the Cold War. The first World Conference on Women in Mexico City (1975) and women's movements around the world and transnationally sought changes in their own countries and in the international system.

At the same time many of these countries attempted to reap the economic benefits of political autonomy. They took on debt to invest in national infrastructure construction projects. They anticipated being able to repay this debt by mining natural resources, which meant that their ability to repay their debt was subject to global market fluctuations in the prices of these natural resources and exchange rates. Growth of capital investment in Global South countries by corporations headquartered in the Global North was facilitated by terms of trade and taxes that did not result in significantly raising incomes in the Global South. Thus, with two oil shocks in the 1970s, many national recessions, and unfavorable exchange rates, many countries in Latin America, Asia, and Africa experienced persistent poverty and growing national debt.

The **Bretton Woods institutions** like the International Monetary Fund (IMF) negotiated refinancing of national debt with loans from Global North banks, the World Bank, and the IMF that were contingent on "structural adjustment" policies. Structural adjustment policies are policy shifts in how a national government controls its finance system and its national spending. These generally mean cutting government spending on social programs (also known as "fiscal austerity"). In addition, primarily through exchange rates and tariffs, countries were to decrease imports by making these more expensive and increase exports usually of raw materials by making those less expensive to foreigners. These problems and the economic solutions proposed by the IMF in partnership with the World Bank and Global North banks led a group of developing countries, the G77, to follow in the spirit of the Non-Aligned Movement two decades prior and propose a New International Economic Order.

Other global social movements spawned in response to economic and environmental crises locally and transnationally that sought to take on the impact of the global distribution of economic and political power on racialized and marginalized people and on the environment on which so many people in poverty depend for their livelihoods.

The 1990s brought another wave of challenges to rationalist approaches to the study of IR: the fall of the Berlin Wall (1989); the end of the Cold War (1991); the seemingly unexplainable, unilateral relinquishing of power of the USSR by its leader Mikhail Gorbachev; the rise of the anti-apartheid movement as a global movement; the visible role of the United Nations in facilitating globally defining conversations around the environment (1992), human rights (1993), population (1994), and women (1995); the involvement of movements from around the world in these international conversations; the abolishment of apartheid South Africa;

the nationalistic wars in the breakup of the former Yugoslavia; and the ethnic wars in Africa. The events of the last decade of the twentieth century called out (again) for better paradigms in IR. The dawn of the twenty-first century brought a transformation in the IR discipline in which the arguments of critical theories or critical applications of the older theories became increasingly visible in the journals and syllabi of the discipline.

These events, and the growing awareness and persistence of global inequality despite colonial independence and global economic growth, provided the material conditions and political backdrop for the emergence of approaches to IR that both criticized and decentered the conventional approaches to IR discussed in the preceding section. Feminism, post-structuralism, post-colonialism, green theory, and critical theory are strands of IR theory that take up different aspects of how these political events and the conditions that brought them about matter for, and should be part of, the study of IR. We introduce each of these individually, and refer to them collectively as "critical theories" to denote that they are critical of global and local social relations and power dynamics and of theories and worldviews that obfuscate the abuse, exploitation, and oppression in international politics and the affects these have on marginalized peoples.

As noted above, feminism's contribution to IR predates the field. As Tickner and True explain, feminism did not come late to international politics: "Rather, international relations came late to feminism."[21] In its many variants, feminism has made substantive and theoretical contributions to all fields of inquiry in IR by putting people's lives and social movements at the analytical center of global politics.[22] Feminists are particularly attentive to the power of **epistemology** to affect what a discipline characterizes as an important question and of methodologies to shape what can be learned through research. Feminists learn from the theoretical insights of other critical theories as well as critically engaging when even these strands of theory might perpetuate the invisibility of gender inequality. In its twenty-first-century form, feminism is additionally attentive to the observation that the political struggle that precedes all academic inquiry is the struggle for women academics to be recognized by their male colleagues as asking important research questions.

Like feminism, post-structuralism reveals the role of diverse views of politics in shaping ideas. Post-structuralists approach the study of ideas as we are in this chapter, genealogically, paying attention to the relationship between politics and ideas as they both change. Like feminists, these theorists rethink the core concepts of IR (like sovereignty and state power) often using the study of discourse and the flow of ideas to seek empirical evidence for the destabilization of the assumption of the state as a unitary actor (ignoring differences among people within states).

Post-structuralism notes that the story of IR looks different depending on the story a theorist tells about what is important in shaping international politics. World War I is important for liberals. The Cold War is important for realists and liberal realists. Global trade and the institutions for developing and managing the global political economy after World War II are important to Marxists and liberal realists alike, but for very different reasons. Post-structuralists draw our attention to the geopolitics of how we define our terms (e.g., "terrorist" or "freedom fighter") and how we determine which events to make central to international political analysis.

Post-colonialism decenters the intellectual traditions that took shape within colonialism. Post-colonial theorists, like feminists, worry when IR scholars of any approach pay insufficient attention to marginalized perspectives.[23] Like feminists and post-structuralist theorists, post-colonial scholars often study how ideas emerge to better understand their embedded power. As such, post-colonial theory reveals the power of knowledge claims and resists the superiority of those knowledge claims that are embedded in colonialism and scholarship that is inattentive to its colonial roots. In addition, post-colonial scholars invite us to *center* and privilege the ideas and research developed outside the centers of global power.[24]

Green theory has many forms, but the key feature, as the name suggests, is the inclusion of the ecology of the planet in considerations of world politics. The contemporary interest in and growth of these perspectives is due to current environmental crises and their effects on global politics. However, they have roots in other political problems as well. The green analysis enriches a liberal political economy analysis by noting that the economic growth on which peace and cooperation is said to be predicated is not environmentally sustainable. The striving for economic power through resource extraction is an environmentally damaging and conflict-inducing global politics. Further, the use of the military to achieve these ends is environmentally damaging not only because of the exercise of military force, but also because of the environmental impact of the production and maintenance of military power. Whereas for the critical theorists global economic growth is problematically oppressive for many, the greens take that point further and note that it is not sustainable for anyone.

All of these approaches to thinking about IR take seriously Robert Cox's observation that "Theory is always for someone and for some purpose." Seen through perspectives of feminist, post-structural, post-colonial, and green theories, *critical theory* may seem less radical because it emphasizes the role of economics and undermines the role of privilege, exploitation, stereotyping, and discrimination in global politics. Yet it shares with those theorists a criticism of power. Specifically, critical theory – grounded in the thought of Marx, Horkheimer, Adorno, and Gramsci – draws our attention to the material conditions of people and states their influence in international politics. States have differential power in influencing the structure of the global economy whose mechanisms can be exploited to solidify and exploit such differences in power; these have differential impacts on people within states.

The scholarship of the family of critical theorists discussed in this section has been around throughout the development of the field, but it has taken transformation in the power dynamics within the discipline for this scholarship to enter the mainstream of the discipline – to the extent that it has.

INTERNATIONAL POLITICS AND INTERNATIONAL RELATIONS: A MATTER OF PERSPECTIVE

As we see from the preceding discussions, although they were looking at the same global system, scholars from different theoretical perspectives ask *very* different questions and generate correspondingly different knowledge about the world. The IR scholars in the immediately preceding section see an international politics that reflects domestic and global inequality and oppression and develop IR theory to reveal and explain these; scholars in the first two sections see an international politics of sovereign states, treaties, and international institutions and study these.

Only the sociology of the field described above – that is, only differences in the *scholars'* worldviews, empirical assumptions, and normative assumptions – can explain why one school of thought takes up questions of oppression as the central problems of global politics and another looks at that same world and sees the balancing of power or the cooperation among states as the dominant modes of global political engagement (see Chapter 3 on ideologies). Each approach of the last section – feminism, post-structuralism, and post-colonialism, green theory, and critical theory – helps reveal the role of privilege in explaining why scholars can look at the world and see such different international politics.

Consider, for example, the discussion of feminism in *International Studies Quarterly*. Robert Keohane engaged with but was not convinced by feminism. In response to an article by Ann Tickner entitled "You Just Don't Understand: Troubled Engagements between Feminists and IR Theorists," Keohane concludes the following:

> [Q]uestions will not be enough: feminist IR scholars will need to supply answers that will convince others – including those not ideologically predisposed to being convinced. Specifying their propositions, and providing systematically gathered evidence to test these propositions, will be essential: scientific method, in the broadest sense, is the best path toward convincing current nonbelievers

of the validity of the message that feminists are seeking to deliver. We will only "understand" each other if IR scholars are open to the important questions that feminist theories raise, and if feminists are willing to formulate their hypotheses in ways that are testable – and falsifiable – with evidence.[25]

In his view, feminism lacked a clear research program. He suggests that feminism might be incompatible with the scientific method, casting doubt on feminists' legitimacy as knowledge creators. He asserted that feminists lacked testable theories and detailed empirical studies and thus that their claims were impossible to evaluate. What Keohane didn't understand, according to Tickner, is that his concept of social science was itself ideological.[26] In other words, white, Western men like him, whose research and institutions enjoyed financial support from governments (see Box 12.3), had cast their scholarship as "objective" and their theories as universal, but they were actually biased in their view of objectivity by their privileged experience.

BOX 12.3: WHERE ARE THE MONEY AND POLITICS IN IR?
Given the landscape of global politics and the contributions of these critical theories to making visible and making sense of the incredible shifts in power in global politics, it may seem surprising that, particularly in the United States, these approaches did not take hold sooner. The economics and sociology of the power to construct what counts as knowledge in the discipline of international relations in the United States and globally can help us understand why these critical theories were less visible as relevant to IR.

On the economic side, US funding for the study of IR from the 1950s through to the 1970s was generally coming from the US Department of Defense and was significantly in support of centers for international studies to aid in the Cold War.[27] Since the Cold War was framed by Western IR scholars and policymakers within realist and to a lesser extent liberal perspectives on global politics, these approaches had significant economic support. Thus the US centrism of IR as a field and the dominance of realist approaches through the 1950s to 1970s left a global impact on the structure of the field with success of scholars whose research had such funding and the production of graduate students whose introduction to the field was also funded by this research.

In sum, grant by grant, the US Department of Defense created a legacy of dominance of certain theoretical perspectives – namely, liberalism and realism. Moreover, by funding the creation of data sets on countries and conflict, they "helped create the infrastructure necessary for the quantitative study of world politics,"[28] which took off in the hands of the scholars trained in this generation. From a sociological perspective, Waever offers a Eurocentric sociological analysis of the ability of certain theories to thrive in certain European countries, having to do with national variations in the way IR is taught, and those variations are rooted in "societal-political features of the country."[29] His examples include emphasis on peace research in Germany due to its role as aggressor in World War II and a focus on law in France to train bureaucrats.

Since this exchange, the critique of objectivity remains; moreover, feminists have developed scholarship that uses not only hypothesis-testing approaches to theory testing but also a host of methods useful for theory building. This achievement is itself academic *and political*. In the 1990s, these disagreements were not merely ideological, yet ideology was behind the differences in volume and prestige of research that was published. First, in order to have their research funded, feminists needed to convince donors that their questions were not ideological, but rather empirical – having to do with the empirical lived experience of women (not just men). Without an ideological shift in what constituted an interesting question, the funding necessary to generate the data sets needed to do the work Keohane called on feminists to do would not be forthcoming (see Box 12.4). Lack of data makes testing testable critical hypotheses impossible.

BOX 12.4: THE STUDY OF HUMAN RIGHTS

Due to ideological constraints on what constituted an important (fundable) question in IR, the data necessary to test the hypotheses of critical theories had not been collected throughout the decades of growth of neorealist and neoliberal IR. Even when it had been collected (e.g., in the US State Department and Amnesty International national reports on human rights abuses), these reports were incomplete; for example, there were few reports on the human rights abuses of women and Indigenous peoples. Moreover, these reports had not been converted into quantitative data sets on which conventional **positivist** hypothesis-testing techniques could be deployed. Thus, statistical studies of human rights did not take off until the 1990s, when the rich qualitative studies in the US State Department and Amnesty International national reports were re-read and coded for statistical analysis and these sources were critically examined for their incompleteness, resulting in the development of new data sets.

While some might be inclined to think of certain schools of thought as generating testable hypotheses and others not, in fact there is now a rich literature in which critical theories have been used to develop testable hypotheses that have been tested.[30] The debate of the 1990s around whether certain paradigms had "research programs" was a needless distraction from the more important question of what are the important questions for understanding world politics and how do we collect the data necessary to understand them.

This distraction, and the difference in view of what constitutes a global political question, has continued and was amplified by the attack by non-state actors on the United States on September 11, 2001 (9/11). The power of non-state actors to destabilize and reshape international politics demonstrates how fictitious the realist assumptions were. Likewise, evidence for liberal assumptions of a progressive journey toward a world order of secular, modern, liberal states living in peace seemed altogether lacking. The post-9/11 environment has fostered growth in critical theories of IR as well as an interest in international political theory that doesn't revolve around European and Anglo-American worldviews.

Yet, while this moment of US and Western global decline presents an opportunity for continued growth and recognition of scholarship from the margins, and as more research and writing in which European and Anglo-American worldviews are not centered is making its way onto IR syllabi, in the post-9/11 world the politically powerful are once again exerting their influence over the field. Another wave of grants from the US Department of Homeland Security and the Department of Defense post-9/11 has increased support for scholarship using quantitative research within the discipline of IR, and has once again prioritized US foreign policy interests while doing so.[31] Additionally, there has been an effort to restore the state as the primary actor of importance for study in IR, even as the explanatory value of this approach for understanding how non-state actors have shaped global politics is on the wane. A clear example of this is the post-9/11 shift in discourse from "human rights" to "human security."[32] In the 1990s the language of human security had been politically inconsistent with realist framings and therefore mostly on the margins in peace studies, where it had been deployed by those seeking to broaden conflict studies to pay attention to the human side of conflict. However, after 9/11 the "human security" discourse was repurposed as a strategy to continue to center the nation-state while incorporating issues that had long been more important for those outside the West – gender equality, the environment, migration, economic inequality, and so on. In the United States, it displaced human rights language through "securitization," though women's human rights activists have tried to hold onto it.[33] This has had the effect of positioning the state as the actor best positioned to address injustice, even as grassroots movements argue that the state itself is responsible for the greatest injustices felt in their lives.

As we look to the future, there will be increasing demands from the Global South, from previously marginalized voices, and from transnational social movements for justice that does not center on the state.[34] For a student, the most important question is, What do you want to know? The struggle for power will be fought not just in the streets or in state legislatures, but in the discipline itself and in a classroom near you.

THE GLOBALIZATION OF IR

In this chapter, we have treated the field of IR as itself part of global politics. The politics and economics that have been shaping global politics have also been shaping the study of IR. To understand the role of power within the discipline, we need to notice where power lies within the discipline. As we saw in the preceding section, critical theories have not only added to what we study, but have also put up a mirror to *how* we study IR and how the discipline privileges the histories and experiences of certain states, cultures, identities, peoples, and viewpoints.[35] However, from the position of privilege – of reading and writing scholarship about IR – it will always be difficult to see how this is true. Yet we must try.

Acharya and Buzan explain that "IR theory likes to pose as neutral" but in fact ideas about how the world is and how it should be speak for the West and "in the interest of sustaining its power, prosperity and influence."[36] They argue that Western dominance in IR theory is visible in the valorization of theorists from Western countries and the Euro/Anglo-centric historical perspective usually taught in schools. As Steve Smith notes, reflecting back on the decades of IR leading up to 9/11, the discipline of IR has effectively served as handmaiden to Western power and interests.[37]

As a consequence, much of the discipline was taught by omission to ignore other kinds of violence, such as global income inequality, health disparities, poverty, gender inequality, genocide, state violence against its own people, refugees, domestic violence, and civilian casualties of war. These forms of violence are not merely incidents of violence, but also **structural violence**. However, to teach the discipline without these topics misses much of what has made the field of IR flourish with rich diversity, and moreover, it reproduces the inequities and injustices we study. The critical theories discussed above have worked toward decentering the West and amplifying the voices of the margins in the study of IR. We offer three ways to further globalize the field.

The first is to read and study non-Western and queer scholars, particularly those who ground IR in world history rather than Western history, integrate area studies, and recognize other forms of power beyond the material and the state.[38] Consider global theorizing from China, Japan, South Korea, India, Indonesia, a regional study of Southeast Asia, and Islamic IR.[39] Qin challenges unitary and self-interested assumptions about state actors and offers a Chinese "relational theory of world politics" inspired by Confucian cultural communities, and Hui challenges balance of power theory using China as the counterexample.[40] (Be aware that Chinese IR scholars are developing schools of Chinese IR.) Odoom and Andrews offer IR theorizing from Africa, and Tickner offers perspectives from Latin America.[41] Insightful on their own, these theories also challenge the relevance of approaching global politics and the appropriate tools for studying them from within one paradigm. Moreover, they make us critical of the worldviews within approaches to IR that were born in and funded by global powers, calling us to read scholarship from the world, not just about the world.

A second way to amplify the margins is to increase the use of and attention to the concept and study of "positive peace" from peace studies, which focuses on not just the absence of war or a "negative peace" but peace with the integration of human society.[42] Another way to think of this is peace with the absence of structural violence.[43] Or, peace with the presence of justice and an end to state-sanctioned oppression. Increasingly, activists say, "no justice, no peace" arguing that global justice and local justice are essential elements of lasting peace.

How can you make yourself ask "new" questions in IR? One way is to ask questions about how the less powerful experience their everyday world. What are the implications for the study of IR of thinking about justice as essential for peace, not merely as an ideological value? Peace studies center the seven and a half billion people that make up our world, rather than a handful of states and their interests, which are only sometimes and only ever partially able to ensure the human rights of those seven and a half billion people.

As a discipline that from its founding has made the normative commitment to peace over conflict one of its pillars, IR invites us to have rich discussions about what peace is in addition to studying how to achieve it.[44] The importance for this in IR is foundational: If we cannot see the differences in experience, then we underestimate how much power – social power, cultural power, economic power, and political power – is needed to maintain or change the system.[45] Getting at these differences to understand the international system is essential for the study IR. Otherwise, we are studying an incompletely articulated problem with the wrong analytical structure and our research will be irrelevant to people.

A third way to center the margins is to break down the false dichotomy between quantitative research as being in the interests of the powerful and qualitative research as being in the interests of the marginalized, and the ideologically driven hierarchy of quantitative over qualitative research. Quantitative researchers can use critical theory to inform empirical questions.[46] Qualitative researchers can draw on empirical findings to develop theory. IR scholars lose much that we need to understand global politics if we cannot question the foundational assumptions of our theories and expose the biases and politics within the field.

SUMMARY

- International relations is the field of study of global politics.
- International politics is a huge arena of politics. The discipline of IR has not always studied all of it.
- Each approach to international relations has a worldview that determines what questions it finds interesting, what theories it will use to explain and explore international politics, and what data it will rely on for that explanation.
- International politics puzzles are global, and the theories of and for IR will come from around the world.

CONCLUDING QUESTIONS

1 What events in global politics make you curious?
2 Can the questions that interest you about global politics be answered with the approaches outlined in this chapter, or will they require a new approach?
3 Consider two or three schools of thought and their approach to IR. Consider how each might explain state power and global growth.
4 In the chapter, we cite the activist chant "no justice, no peace." What does this mean?
5 What chants have you heard from social movements that seem to make statements about global politics?
6 Look at the list of civic engagement ideas in the appendix at the end of this book. Which of these would help you take on "the structures of domination that all of us still carry within ourselves from the past," as Ann Tickner says in the opening quote?

As you consider the following substantive chapters on international political economy, security and conflict, international law and human rights, and international organizations, think about what kinds of questions different paradigms would ask when considering those topics. When would they ask the same question and come to different answers, and when would they ask different questions?

NOTES

1 J. Ann Tickner, "Retelling IR's Foundational Stories: Some Feminist and Postcolonial Perspectives," *Global Change, Peace & Security* 23, no. 1 (2011): 13.

2 International relations is not always treated everywhere as an interdisciplinary field of study.

3 The Baghava Gita, Ibn Arabi, Machiavelli, Jane Addams, Bertha von Sutter, Ashoka, Kautilya, Sun Tzu, Ibn Khaldun, Bhimrao Ramji Ambedkar, Jawaharlal Nehru, Raul Prebisch, Franz Fanon, C.L.R. James, and so on.

4 Note that this way of describing the schools of thought of IR is itself an artifact of the story that these authors want to tell about the development of the field. For example, people might use different terms such as *neo-Marxists* or *strucuturalist* to describe the ideas we describe as *Marxist*. More significantly, they might divide the field differently. As we will see throughout this chapter, we are arguing that the discipline of IR is constructed in relation to international politics. And we don't all see the same thing when we look at international politics!

5 The field of IR has always taken seriously the philosophy of science – the study of how we know what we know. While a review of the philosophy of science is not within the scope of this brief introduction to the field of IR, we mention it here to emphasize that our approach to outlining the field – one that sees each approach to IR and the dominance of certain approaches to IR in their own political, social, and economic context – is not new to the field of IR, but rather has been a part of the field itself.

6 Ken Booth, "International Relations: The Story So Far," *International Relations* 33, no. 2 (2019): 358–90. On the role of women's pragmatist IR theory, see J. Ann Tickner and Jacqui True, "A Century of International Relations Feminism: From World War I Women's Peace Pragmatism to the Women, Peace and Security Agenda," *International Studies Quarterly* 62, no. 2 (2018): 221–33.

7 The following have offered various ways of "retelling IR's foundational stories": Errol A. Henderson, "Hidden in Plain Sight: Racism in International Relations Theory," *Cambridge Review of International Affairs* 26, no. 1 (2013): 71–92; Ido Oren, "A Sociological Analysis of the Decline of American IR Theory," *International Studies Review* 18, no. 4 (2016): 571–96; Tickner, "Retelling IR's Foundational Stories"; Tickner and True, "A Century of International Relations Feminism"; Ole Waever, "The Sociology of a Not So International Discipline: American and European Developments in International Relations," *International Organization* 52, no. 4 (1998): 687–727.

8 Henderson, "Hidden in Plain Sight"; Robert Vitalis, *White World Order, Black Power Politics: The Birth of American International Relations* (Ithaca, NY: Cornell University Press, 2015).

9 Immanuel Kant, *Perpetual Peace: A Philosophical Essay*, trans. M. Campbell Smith (London: George Allen and Unwin, 1917 [1795]).

10 To read more about the democratic peace theory in IR, see Zeev Maoz and Bruce Rus-sett, "Normative and Structural Causes of Democratic Peace, 1946–1986," *American Political Science Review* 87, no. 3 (1993): 624–38; Andrew Moravcsik, "Taking Preferences Seriously: A Liberal Theory of International Politics," *International Organization* 51, no. 4 (1997): 513–53; James Lee Ray, *Democracy and International Conflict: An Evaluation of the Democratic Peace Proposition* (Columbia: University of South Carolina Press, 1995); Bruce Russett and John R. O'Neal, *Triangulating Peace: Democracy, Interdependence, and International Organizations* (New York: Norton, 2001); Bruce Bueno De Mesquita, Alastair Smith, James D. Morrow, and Randolph M. Siverson, *The Logic of Political Survival* (Cambridge, MA: MIT Press, 2005).

11 Kant, *Perpetual Peace*, 155.

12 John Locke, *Two Treatises of Government* (Cambridge: Cambridge University Press, 1988 [1690]), chap. 5.

13 Jean-Jacques Rousseau, *The Social Contract*, trans. Maurice Cranston (New York: Penguin Books, 2004 [1762]), Book II, chap. 8.

14 John Stuart Mill, "On the Subjugation of Women," in *On Liberty and Other Essays*, ed. Stefan Collini, 117–217 (New York: Oxford University Press, 1998 [1869]), 14.

15 Edward Hallett Carr, *The Twenty Years' Crisis, 1919–1939* (New York: Harper Perennial, 1981 [1939]).

16 Christopher Hill, "'Where Are We Going?' International Relations and the Voice from Below," *Review of International Studies* 25, no. 1 (1999): 107–22; Tickner, "Retelling IR's Foundational Stories."

17 Cynthia Enloe, "Margins, Silences and Bottom Rungs: How to Overcome the Underestimation of Power in the Study of International Relations," in *International Theory: Positivism and Beyond*, eds. Steven M. Smith, Ken Booth, and Marysia Zalewski, 186–202 (Cambridge: Cambridge Univeristy Press, 1996), 189.

18 The United States did not participate in the League of Nations, despite Woodrow Wilson being one of its proponents.

19 Kenneth N. Waltz, *Theory of International Politics* (New York: McGraw-Hill, 1979).

20 See Alexander Wendt, "Anarchy Is What States Make of It: The Social Construction of Power Politics," *International Organization* 46, no. 2 (1992): 391–425.

21 Tickner and True, "A Century of International Relations Feminism," 221.

22 Amrita Basu, "Globalization of the Local/Localization of the Global: Mapping Transnational Women's Movements," *Meridians* 1, no. 1 (2000): 68–84.

23 Lily H.M. Ling, *Postcolonial International Relations: Conquest and Desire between Asia and the West* (New York: Palgrave, 2002).

24 Anna M. Agathangelou and L.H.M. Ling, "The House of IR: From Family Power Politics to the Poisies of Worldism," *International Studies Review* 6, no. 4 (2004): 21–49.

25 Robert O. Keohane, "Beyond Dichotomy: Conversations between International Relations and Feminist Theory," *International Studies Quarterly* 42, no. 1 (1998): 193–97.

26 J. Ann Tickner, "You Just Don't Understand: Troubled Engagements between Feminists and IR Theorists," *International Studies Quarterly* 41, no. 4 (1997): 611–32.

27 Oren, "A Sociological Analysis of the Decline of American IR Theory."

28 Oren, "A Sociological Analysis of the Decline of American IR Theory," 15.

29 Waever, "The Sociology of a Not So International Discipline," 689.

30 See, for example, J.S. Barkin and L. Sjoberg, *Interpretive Quantification: Methodological Explorations for Critical and Constructivist IR* (Ann Arbor: University of Michigan Press, 2017); Mala Htun and S. Laurel Weldon, *The Logics of Gender Justice: State Action on Women's Rights around the World* (Cambridge: Cambridge University Press, 2018).

31 Oren, "A Sociological Analysis of the Decline of American IR Theory."

32 Charlotte Bunch, "Feminism, Peace, Human Rights and Human Security," *Canadian Woman Studies* 22, no. 2 (2003); Roland Paris, "Human Security: Paradigm Shift or Hot Air?," *International Security* 26, no. 2 (2001): 87–102.

33 Anna Carella and Brooke Ackerly, "Ignoring Rights Is Wrong: Re-Politicizing Gender Equality and Development with the Rights-Based Approach," *International Feminist Journal of Politics* 19, no. 2 (2017): 137–52; Rosalind Eyben, "What Is Happening to Donor Support for Women's Rights?," *Contestations: Dialogues on Women's Empowerment* 4 (2011).

34 Kristian S. Gleditsch and Mauricio Rivera, "The Diffusion of Nonviolent Campaigns," *Journal of Conflict Resolution* 61, no. 5 (2017): 1120–45; Timothy Seidel, "'Occupied Territory Is Occupied Territory': James Baldwin, Palestine and the Possibilities of Transnational Solidarity," *Third World Quarterly* 37, no. 9 (2016): 1644–60.

35 Amitav Acharya and Barry Buzan, *Non-Western International Relations Theory: Perspectives on and beyond Asia* (New York: Routledge, 2009); Enloe, "Margins, Silences and Bottom Rungs"; Henderson, "Hidden in Plain Sight"; Chandra Mohanty, "Under Western Eyes: Feminist Scholarship and Colonial Discourses," *Feminist Review* 30, no. 1 (1988): 61–88; Andrew Robinson and Simon Tormey, "Resisting 'Global Justice': Disrupting the Colonial 'Emancipatory' Logic of the West," *Third World Quarterly* 30, no. 8 (2009): 1395–409; Steve Smith, "Singing Our World into Existence: International Relations Theory and September 11," *International Studies Quarterly* 48, no. 3 (2004): 499–515; Gayatri Chakravorty Spivak, "Can the Subaltern Speak?," in *Marxism and the Interpretation of Culture*, eds. Cary Nelson and Lawrence Grossberg, 271–313 (Urbana: University of Illinois Press, 1988); Vitalis, *White World Order, Black Power Politics*.

36 Acharya and Buzan, *Non-Western International Relations Theory*, 3.

37 Smith, "Singing Our World into Existence."

38 Amitav Acharya, "Global International Relations (IR) and Regional Worlds: A New Agenda for International Studies," *International Studies Quarterly* 58, no. 4 (2014): 647–59; Cynthia Weber, *Queer International Relations: Sovereignty, Sexuality and the Will to Knowledge* (Oxford: Oxford University Press, 2016).

39 Acharya and Buzan, *Non-Western International Relations Theory*.

40 Yaqing Qin, "A Relational Theory of World Politics," *International Studies Review* 18, no. 1 (2016): 33–47; Victoria Tin-bor Hui, "Toward a Dynamic Theory of International Politics: Insights from Comparing Ancient China and Early Modern Europe," *International Organization* (2004): 175–205.

41 Isaac Odoom and Nathan Andrews, "What/Who Is Still Missing in International Relations Scholarship? Situating Africa as an Agent in IR Theorising," *Third World Quarterly* 38, no. 1 (2017): 42–60; Arlene B. Tickner, "Hearing Latin American Voices in International Relations Studies," *International Studies Perspectives* 4, no. 4 (2003): 325–50.

42 Johan Galtung, "Violence, Peace, and Peace Research," *Journal of Peace Research* 6, no. 3 (1969): 167–91. No solution is a panacea – peace studies have its own margins. See

Birgit Brock-Utne, "The Relationship of Feminism to Peace and Peace Education," *Bulletin of Peace Proposals* 15, no. 2 (1984): 149–53.

43 Catia C. Confortini, "Galtung, Violence, and Gender: The Case for a Peace Studies/ Feminism Alliance," *Peace & Change* 31, no. 3 (2006): 333–67; Galtung, "Violence, Peace, and Peace Research."

44 Other key conceptual debates about the meaning of democracy (elections versus political participation) and of rights (entitlements or structurally enjoyed) could also provide a basis for globalizing the discipline of IR.

45 Enloe, "Margins, Silences and Bottom Rungs."

46 For examples, see the contributions to Barkin and Sjoberg, *Interpretive Quantification*.

RESOURCES AND SUGGESTIONS FOR FURTHER READING

Enloe, Cynthia. "Margins, Silences and Bottom Rungs: How to Overcome the Underestimation of Power in the Study of International Relations." In *International Theory: Positivism and Beyond*, edited by Steven M. Smith, Ken Booth, and Marysia Zalewski, 186–202. Cambridge: Cambridge University Press, 1996.

Henderson, Errol A. "Hidden in Plain Sight: Racism in International Relations Theory." *Cambridge Review of International Affairs* 26 (2013): 71–92.

Tickner, J. Ann. "Retelling IR's Foundational Stories: Some Feminist and Postcolonial Perspectives." *Global Change, Peace & Security* 23 (2011): 5–13.

Vitalis, Robert. *White World Order, Black Power Politics: The Birth of American International Relations*. Ithaca, NY: Cornell University Press, 2015.

CHAPTER THIRTEEN

International Political Economy

Dr. James Brassett   *Dr. Juanita Elias*   *Dr. Lena Rethel*   *Dr. Ben Richardson*

LEARNING OBJECTIVES

1 Understand the everyday turn in international political economy (IPE)
2 Recognize the inequalities that exist between and within countries
3 Analyze care work, global finance, and resistance using everyday IPE
4 Apply everyday IPE to your own economic experiences

KEY TERMS

commodification   turning something or someone into nothing more than a commodity, an object for sale

commodity fetishism   an understanding of the economy as based on market relationships between commodities rather than social relationships between people

everyday life   daily activities and routines that are subordinated to the imperatives of capitalism and reproduce the status quo in society

exchange rates   the rate at which currency in one denomination (e.g., US dollars) is exchanged for currency in another denomination (e.g., British pounds)

foreign currency   money in a denomination different from your own

gross domestic product   the total measurable output of the national economy, valued in money terms

hierarchies of difference   the stratification of status and wealth along the lines of race, gender, class, nation, and other socially constructed categories, and the normalization of these inequalities

inflation   the increase in price levels without change of the underlying value, often over a short time period

international political economy   the study of power and wealth across countries

market   the physical or virtual site where goods and services are exchanged, but also a way of organizing economic relations

microfinance   loans and savings instruments targeted at individuals and groups with no or little access to banking services

remittance economies   funds that migrant workers send back to households located in their home country

social construction   collective understandings that are the basis for shared assumptions about the world and how it works

social reproduction   the socially necessary work that is central to the production of life itself, including biological reproduction, caring for and maintaining households and intimate relationships, and the reproduction of labor and collective community

WHAT IS INTERNATIONAL POLITICAL ECONOMY?

International political economy (IPE) is the study of power and wealth across countries. But how this should be done is subject to debate. Must you start by finding out why politics and economics tend to be studied separately in the first place? Do you need to know about the contested definitions of "the state" and "the **market**," or can these be taken as self-evident concepts? And are you meant to be solving problems related to the instability and inequality of the global economy, or critiquing the wider structural politics of exploitation and extraction associated with capitalism? Faced with a multitude of options, it can be tempting to adopt a simple "plug-and-play" formula. This tried and tested method of studying IPE requires you to pick one of the theoretical approaches suggested by the course textbook and then apply it to a typical "issue area" with its standard list of debates and defining events. For example, you might try a *realist* approach to the US–China trade war, a *liberal* account of global banking regulation, or a *constructivist* critique of Brexit and economic nationalism. But this way of navigating the disciplinary map of IPE can feel … well, a bit mapped out. The intellectual journeys might be scientifically rigorous and theoretically sophisticated, but somewhat rigid and impersonal, too.

As the chapter on international relations (IR) in this book showed, there are different ways of viewing and understanding how the world works. Many of the existing IPE texts draw on the same kinds of theoretical tools that we find in the study of IR more broadly. What we offer in this chapter is a different kind of orientation – more of a guidebook than a map. It is one that invites you to begin with topics that you are personally familiar with and to learn more about them through the intellectual insights offered by IPE. You might, for example, choose your experience of acquiring this textbook. Did you buy it, rent it, or borrow it from a library? Are you taking this course because it is important to study in its own right, or is it also a way to help sell yourself to potential employers? Who is paying for all these educational resources you need, and what do you need to provide in return? Such questions can kick start inquiries into the relations of consumption, knowledge production, student debt, and more.

Just as the chapter on IR showed, there are different ways of being curious and thinking about the world. We show in this chapter that when it comes to IPE, you don't need to start with the "main" issues and theories. It is equally fruitful to start a journey into IPE through an exploration of everyday objects and daily life experiences. It is an approach that we think you – as a student first encountering the study of IPE – will find useful because it asks you to think about how your own economic practices (what you buy and borrow, how and when you work, etc.) link you to the global economy. Starting with the everyday does not mean you will avoid theory, but it does mean that you can move away from the more standard theoretical toolkit of IPE and its analytical restrictions.

The chapter is organized into four sections. The first section introduces some of the reasons for the turn toward the "everyday" in IPE and the increasing attention paid to non-elite actors and seemingly unimportant daily activities that can – and do – matter to global economic and political processes. It then highlights different ways in which the everyday has been invoked in IPE to provide some conceptual and theoretical guidance for our inquiries, paying particular attention to those approaches concerned with inequality maintained through **hierarchies of difference**.[1] This refers to situations where wealth and status become stratified and normalized along the lines of race, gender, class, nation, and other socially constructed categories. The next three sections each take different entry points into IPE. We have chosen care, finance, and resistance, but really any number of everyday objects or practices can be used – from beer to sisterhood – as you can see for yourself at the International Political Economy of Everyday Life website (http://I-PEEL.org).

THE EVERYDAY TURN IN IPE

In recent years a number of scholars have argued that IPE research has been limited by its conventional macroscopic focus on economic and political elites and should instead be more attentive to the role played by ordinary people, popular culture, and practices of resistance.[2] Foundational to this literature has been the work of scholars such as Cynthia Enloe, whose 1989 book *Bananas, Beaches, and Bases* asked that we think about global politics by first asking the question: "Where are the women?"[3]

Locating women in international politics was important because they were (and largely continue to be) conspicuously absent from the boardrooms of major corporations, meetings of heads of state, or within the diplomatic corps and armed forces. Seeing women meant that we needed to turn to other sites of global politics beyond "high politics." Here we could identify the way women were enrolled as cheap labor on banana plantations and how women were presented as alluring marketing devices for beach resorts or as expendable sex workers around military bases.

Through this analysis of the everyday lives of women around the world, Enloe gave us a route into thinking about international politics, including IPE, that remains deeply influential. Her work shows us that by taking a different starting point, one rooted in everyday life experiences, we can reveal the gendered and racialized structures of oppression that constitute the global economy.

In this vein, everyday IPE scholarship has inquired into the social foundations of issues like trade and finance, asking who makes this economic activity possible and on what basis. For example, in the case of the UK's austerity agenda after the 2008 financial crisis, scholars have argued that government cuts to public spending cannot be understood only by looking at parliamentary voting patterns and fiscal calculations, but must also consider the public discourse through which these policies were mobilized and legitimized.[4] This discourse relied heavily on household analogies of personal restraint and prudent living to convince people that the cuts were actually in their best interest (see Box 13.1).

Everyday IPE has also seen a proliferation in the range of topics used as entry points to the field. Scholars now study the political economy of everything from tourist brochures to the Olympic Games. Importantly, it has also become increasingly permissible to study the lived experiences of previously overlooked subjects like migrants, mortgage defaulters, and Muslim businesswomen.[5] Making the invisible visible in this way carries political and ethical implications, too. If it is only ever the rich and powerful that are studied, there is a risk of naturalizing this hierarchy and reinforcing the positions and views of those at the top. Studying marginalized groups and different people makes an important statement about *whose lives matter* in IPE.

> **BOX 13.1: EVERYDAY ANALOGIES OF AUSTERITY**
>
> "The whole country is having to tighten its belt and save money. So too should their government." – George Osborne, UK shadow chancellor, 2008
>
> "We are asking the British people to reduce the record budget deficit and pay off the national credit card." – George Osborne, UK chancellor, 2011
>
> "The new economy we're building, it's like building a house. The most important part is the part you can't see – the foundations that make it stable. Slowly, but surely, we're laying the foundations for a better future. But this is the crucial point: it will only work if we stick with it." – David Cameron, UK prime minister, 2011

What has so far been neglected in this literature, however, is the educational potential of the everyday: building on the grounded and diverse experiences of economic activity to make IPE meaningful to students. This strikes us as especially important, as the way IPE is practiced in academia is different to the way it is taught. The plurality and vitality of much IPE scholarship tends to be forfeited in the classroom in favor of a reductive Anglocentric story in which positivist "American School" IPE is pitted against normative "British School" IPE – if the different ways of doing IPE are recognized at all.[6] This is another case of forcing an arbitrary theoretical allegiance on students, which quite literally maps the field in terms of geography.[7]

An everyday approach can make the study of IPE not only more interesting but also more urgent. As teachers, we are keen to see students draw on their own lived experiences to reflect upon their own engagements with "the market" and to see how they play a role in shaping (and at times resisting) such processes. For instance: Does your ethnicity affect the kind of advertisements you see or where you tend to spend your money? This mode of thinking can give rise to an understanding of IPE that is far more attuned to the hierarchies of difference that make up the global economy.

Lineages of Everyday IPE

So what does the IPE of everyday life actually consist of? Rather than do away with the diversity that can be found in this scholarship by imposing some uniform definition on it, it is better to instead provide an account of the intellectual lineages that have come to inspire it. Many of these lineages are located outside the immediate field of IPE, in disciplines such as sociology or in the "pre-disciplinary" scholarship that existed before IPE was invented. This should be seen as a strength, a way of renewing our collective ability to recognize urgent questions and take informed positions on them.

It is notable in this regard that Karl Marx – still one of the most widely cited authors in contemporary IPE literature – was himself sharply critical of "political economy," seeing this nascent area of study as a bourgeois rationalization of capitalism in Western Europe.[8] Indeed, some scholars argue that mainstream IPE is still doing the same thing today to the poorer countries of the Global South, where market relations and private property are not yet as entrenched. Presenting foreign investment or export-led growth as positive developments means that the violence and conflicts that frequently accompany these capitalist processes are essentially glossed over.[9]

It is Marx's critique of capitalism that in fact provides our first lineage of everyday IPE. Writing in the 1840s, he and Friedrich Engels argued that the inequalities of capitalism, in particular the class-based division of labor, had been normalized by elites through the habits of social life. This was a lived reality, sustained by an ideological "false consciousness." A higher wage, a free vote, some leisure time, and the appeal to ideals of freedom and progress could all help to distract workers from their underlying exploitation, or even encourage them to accept it. The everyday experience of life under capitalism was thus both real and unreal.[10] An important expression of this is what Marx called **commodity fetishism**. This referred to an understanding of the economy as based on market relationships between commodities rather than social relationships between people. Marx's basic point was that it was increasingly difficult to see that workers were being impoverished not because they happened to work in an unprofitable company or lacked the skills to earn a higher wage, but because they occupied a particular place in the hierarchy of capitalism.

Seeking to expose these underlying social relations in today's global economy, many studies in IPE have traced the journey of familiar commodities to the factories, farms, and mines from whence they came.[11] Take the Apple iPad, for instance. As detailed in one study (see Box 13.2), its *global commodity chain* – the various stages of production that are linked together across national borders to produce a finished good – incorporates underpaid work and unsustainable environmental practices from various territories around the world. By capturing these various cost savings, the study concludes that Apple is not just able to derive a handsome profit for its shareholders but also provide its customers with cheaper products. In other words, consumers in the Global North *benefit at the direct expense of* producers in the Global South.[12]

BOX 13.2: THE GLOBAL COMMODITY CHAIN, IPAD EDITION

The global commodity chain of an Apple iPad includes the following:

1. Low wages paid to the predominantly rural migrants, sometimes illegally so, who work in China's giant Foxconn factories where many Apple products are assembled.
2. Unpaid household labor that maintains this workforce, including by workers themselves in the company dormitories where they are often required to live and by relatives in rural areas who look after the workers' children.
3. Subsistence incomes earned by informal sector laborers used to provide raw materials and components for assembly.
4. Avoidance of any cleanup costs for the air and water pollution caused by factories in its supply chain.[13]

But does revealing the social relations of a commodity mean that we can get past the "fetish" and avoid implicating ourselves in economic acts of social injustice? This is something that Fair Trade labeling initiatives have aimed at, encouraging consumers to pay a little more for products like chocolate or bananas so that extra income can get passed back down the commodity chain to the West African cocoa farmers or Latin American fruit cooperatives. But these remain market niches and are ultimately market oriented, suggesting definite challenges to the task of "de-fetishizing" commodities.[14] The vast majority of the world's cocoa and bananas, in these terms at least, are still unfairly traded. Indeed, some critics of the Fair Trade movement have gone further, suggesting that these attempts to ameliorate injustice are actually a form of recuperation on the part of capital. Facing public disapproval of their sourcing practices, companies respond by **commodifying** the ethical alternative being called for. This internalizes the feeling of "doing good" within their business model and insulates from critique the bigger adverse impacts the company might be having.[15]

Questions about the *cultural legitimation of capitalism*, meaning the normalization of capitalist social relations through popular culture, were taken forward by Antonio Gramsci in the 1930s through his notion of "common sense."[16] Common sense referred to the everyday reality of popular opinion; a collective, if contradictory, set of ideas, which Gramsci thought progressive intellectuals had to engage with if they were to give their redistributive political agendas the necessary emotional force (Gramsci was, after all, a founding member of the Communist Party of Italy and ultimately interested in the overthrow of capitalism).

Common sense has since been used as a conceptual device in IPE to show, among others things, how support for the North American Free Trade Agreement (NAFTA) was built by the business community and its right-wing advocates in the early 1990s. Rather than refer to quantitative economic arguments about job growth and so on, NAFTA was depicted in the popular media as a means of unleashing entrepreneurialism and extending economic liberty – calling on values that would readily appeal to the American public steeped in the discourse of liberal capitalism.[17] An example of where a left-wing agenda engaged the American common sense to *challenge* the prevailing class hierarchy is the Occupy Wall Street movement. The rallying cry of "We are the 99%" was able to put questions of economic inequality front and center by distilling people's varied experiences of diminishing upward mobility and falling real wages into a pithy soundbite.[18] In this lineage, everyday IPE seeks to illuminate the ideological battleground on which class relations are played out, showing how people can be made to conform but also contest the status quo; a tension between power and resistance that runs through this approach to IPE.

The particular phrase **everyday life** is associated with Henri Lefebvre, who conceptualized it not as what people *do* on a day-to-day basis, but *how* daily activities are subordinated to the imperatives of capitalism and made routine and ordinary.[19] Think of the weekend. This can be seen as an example of how the shape and routine of everyday life is "programmed" to pacify workers with leisure time, yet also saturates that time with lots of shopping opportunities – a good example of this is the spectacular retail events in the Anglo-American world: Black Friday! Super Saturday! Lefebvre also suggested that the production of everyday life can be seen as an ongoing process of colonialism, organizing and segregating people into certain ways of living. Writing in France in the 1970s, he gave the example of the location of migrant labor from France's former colonies into "ethnic enclaves" in its major cities as a way in which European colonization has evolved an internal dimension.[20] A contemporary application of this approach can be seen in studies on the global phenomenon of gentrification, whereby inner-city areas are made into "respectable" and profitable real estate by clearing out existing residents and replacing them with higher-paying and racially privileged renters.[21]

As we noted earlier with reference to Enloe's work, a separate lineage of everyday IPE can be found in feminism. A long-standing site of concern for feminists has been the household and how the daily work that goes on there is bracketed out from the formal economy and the public sphere of political debate – work like cooking and cleaning, which is predominantly carried out by women and girls in a gendered division of labor. **Social reproduction** was the academic term coined in the 1980s to make visible this unrecognized work and to reconceptualize it as integral, rather than incidental, to capitalism.[22] At a basic level it referred to the effort required to raise and look after people, to keep things going in other words, and in this sense many feminist writers would argue that social reproduction *is* everyday life.[23]

Intertwining with the Marxist tradition described above, feminist scholars have sought to denaturalize the gendered division of labor and show how it had been **socially constructed**. Arguing against biological determinism and the supposition that because women give birth they should also take on the burden of raising a family and running a household, feminists instead emphasized the role of the state in reinforcing patriarchal and heterosexual families. What is the state's interest in reinforcing this so-called traditional family unit? The answer for these scholars is that it is functionally useful to capital accumulation, which the state depends on for legitimacy.[24]

Paying low wages to workers while getting other people (i.e., women) to pick up the costs of living and the burden of care is good for business. More recent scholarship has made clear that the household is not a static place and that it has been subject to increased commodification and *trans-nationalization*, or the growth of linkages, especially economic ones, across countries and beyond the nation-state.[25] This has been shown in studies of the "maid trade," whereby ethnic minority women undertake paid domestic work as live-in servants or nannies for households in more affluent areas, with their former unpaid responsibilities taken up by other female family members. Where these movements cross national borders they lead to the emergence of "global care chains," a service-based equivalent of the global commodity chain described above.[26]

Studying particular groups of people as a route into everyday IPE resonates with what Enloe dubbed "feminist sense." Different to Gramsci's common sense, this was a methodological call to investigate the workings of masculinities and femininities that shaped international political life from beyond the corridors of power, constantly returning to "women's complex everyday realities" to ensure that "the international" did not become an abstract and sterile sphere of analysis.[27] Echoing Enloe's examples in her book, recent IPE studies have considered the lived realities of Argentine sex workers, Nepalese private security contractors, and Canadian call center workers to name just a few.[28]

Such accounts show how macroscopic global dynamics like foreign investment or mass migration are not disembodied abstract processes, but are created through gendered social relations that people live out in their daily existence. For instance, the growth in international trade in the late twentieth century cannot be understood without appreciating the feminization of the labor force in the major export processing zones – or sweatshops – of Asia and Latin America. This mass mobilization of young rural women into waged work in assembly line production depended both on social renegotiations over where women "belonged" and a recomposition of patriarchal norms from the family home into the workplace.[29]

Studies of women's everyday lived experiences of globalization have also shown how much economic activity still remains *outside* the capitalist sphere of market transactions, wage labor, and profit-oriented companies. This is an important critical insight. Recognizing the continued existence or even reappearance of practices like barter exchange and self-employment can serve to "dislocate the naturalized dominance of the capitalist economy and make a space for new economic becomings."[30] On this view, the varied experiences revealed through a focus on the everyday is not just a litany of overlooked and unjust situations, but a place in which to identify alternative (local) forms of economy and take (global) inspiration.

Extending this line of thinking, Patricia Hill Collins has advocated for standpoint epistemology, in which systematically disadvantaged groups are figured with an intimate understanding of the factors producing those conditions, providing particular ways of knowing the world that can enrich political economy. Writing in the US context, she gives the case of Black American women and their use of intersectionality to understand how "gender, sexuality, race, class and nation … mutually construct one another" as systems of oppression.[31] One example of this intertwining, she argues, can be found in the political economy of the family. Heterosexual intraracial marriage was a powerful cultural norm perpetuating the existence of "white families" and "Black families," which in turn worked to pass racialized inequalities onto the next generation via parental support for educational fees, social connections, and property inheritance. White children have therefore experienced systematically better opportunities than Black children, and thus structural inequality has reproduced itself.

For Collins, there were four domains of power relations through which these intersecting systems of oppression were maintained: a structural domain that organized oppression through social institutions like the family or the labor market; a disciplinary domain that managed oppression through bureaucratic surveillance; a hegemonic domain that justified oppression through school curricula, religious teachings, community cultures, mass media portrayals, and so on; and an interpersonal domain that functioned at "the level of everyday social interaction" through routinized, day-to-day practices of how people treat one another.[32]

As a contribution to IPE, then, this reiterates the everyday as a place where power is exerted from above but also evaded and enacted from below. It also demonstrates that the expressions of power in gender, sexuality, and race that can perhaps be most easily discerned in the interpersonal domain can also provide telling insights into the structures determining the distribution of wealth between *and within* countries. In other words, it insists that the everyday can and should serve as an entry point for IPE.

This section has identified a number of theoretical and conceptual lineages for thinking about everyday IPE. Which ideas do you find insightful? Can these be built on or combined in some way? One temptation might be to try and bring all hierarchies of difference together – including those not yet mentioned, like (dis)ability or faith – in the pursuit of a singular emancipatory vision of IPE. But then doesn't this contradict the importance placed on recognizing different standpoints and risk privileging some interpretations and political agendas over others? For us, it is enough to use the everyday approach to make ambiguous the many elements of IPE that are usually figured as "natural" – money, the nation-state, wages, family, and so on – and to pose telling analytical and ethical questions about the outcomes to which they give rise. In that spirit, we now embark on *our* brief tour of everyday life, and hopefully show how the diversity produced through intersectional study can help make the field of IPE more intellectually fertile and personally engaging.

CARE AND EVERYDAY IPE

Care is not usually studied by IPE scholars. Yet, understood as a particular set of labor practices (i.e., the work involved in caring for others' needs), it can be rendered as a vital aspect of economic life the world over. As we saw above, caring can also be understood as deeply feminized work, one that is conventionally associated with unpaid forms of laboring that occur within the "private sphere" of the household. Nonetheless, care is shaped by political and economic processes.

When state policymakers are designing welfare policies, for example, they typically make assumptions about the extent to which families are able to take on unpaid care work. Or when women relocate for jobs as maids or nannies, it is in part because business managers have helped commodify this "women's work," meaning they have helped transform it into formalized waged labor for profit making (the masculinized household role of gardener or security guard is not immune to this either). But even when women enter the paid labor market, they often do so on an unequal footing compared to men because of their continued responsibilities for unpaid caring. This phenomenon, referred to as the "double burden," is one which reinscribes the public/private divide within an economy.

For many feminist political economists a pressing concern has been how care work is valued. The *undervaluing* of care-related work that takes place in the home was observed in Marilyn Waring's classic study *If Women Counted*.[33] This study looked at how unpaid household labor was, and remains, excluded from systems of national accounting that gives us measures of **gross domestic product** and the like. For Waring, this exclusion creates an incomplete picture of the sources of national economic value and further contributes to the marginalization of women in society more generally.

But of course, care work isn't something that is confined to the household. Many jobs require, indeed demand, appropriate emotional conduct and thus a degree of "affective labor," especially in the service sector. For example, the UK sandwich company Pret a Manger hit the headlines in 2013 when it was revealed that its guidelines to employees included recommendations that they stay happy at all times, touch each other, and never be moody at work. Such instruction can be seen as a deliberate attempt to cultivate displays of caring that improve customer service, and ultimately company profits. The paradox is that such performances in the workplace are assumed to rest on innate characteristics that require no extra effort to enact, meaning that employees are not paid in ways that reflect the market value of their affective labor. Indeed, if you were to think about the kinds of roles that rely on this kind of labor – bar staff, receptionists, college tutors – you might notice a common thread.

One place where the monetary value of caring is more visible is in the ever-growing **remittance economies**.[34] Since the early 1980s, global remittance inflows have increased from US$36 billion to nearly US$700 billion, creating new dependencies (see Figure 13.1). Countries such as the Philippines have promoted the outward migration of female care workers, helping it to become the fourth-largest destination of remittances in the world despite its relatively small population.[35] These women migrate without their families, due in large part to restrictive immigration policies in host countries, and remit most of their earnings back to their families in the Philippines. These remittances have proven essential as a source of **foreign currency** as well as a source of income for both poor and more middle-class families, and which is often spent on consumer goods, education, and housing.

But while the Philippine government might have labeled migrant women as "heroes of the nation," these workers often earn relatively small incomes for the amount of labor they are expected to perform.[36] This is especially the case for those who migrate to take up employment as domestic workers in private homes.[37] It is also notable, given that the Philippines was once a territory of the American empire, that the United States is the major destination for Filipino migrants. As in Lefebvre's argument above, we might thus consider colonialism today to have an important "internal dimension" existing in this case between citizens of different countries subject to unequal treatment *within* the United States.

Figure 13.1. Remittance Inflows, US$ Millions

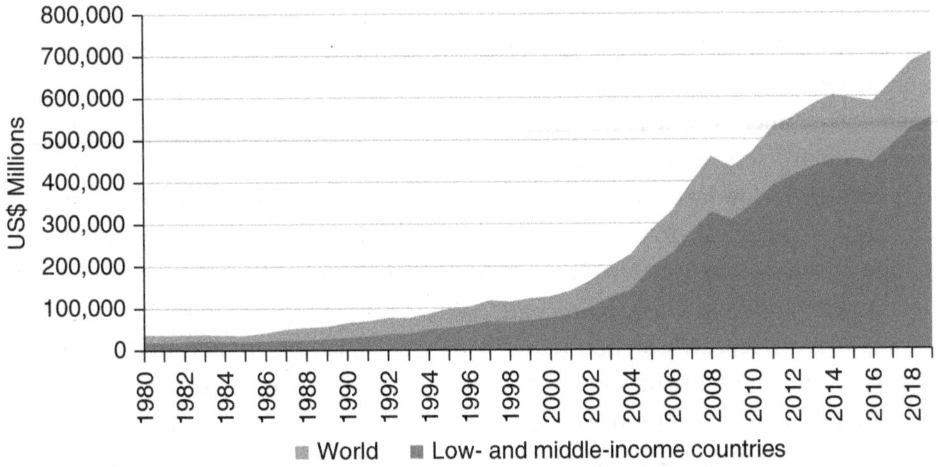

Source: Data from World Bank Group, "Annual Remittances Data (Updated as of April 2019)," World Bank Press Release, 2019, https://www.worldbank.org/en/topic/migrationremittancesdiasporaissues/brief/migration-remittances-data.

Another line of inquiry opened up by the focus on care is how social welfare is governed. An influential typology in this respect was developed by the Danish sociologist Gøsta Esping-Andersen in his book *The Three Worlds of Welfare Capitalism*. This articulated three types of national welfare regimes – liberal, conservative, and social democratic – differentiated on the basis of how care work is distributed among the market, family, and state.[38] It has been criticized by feminist scholars, however, for focusing on the relationship between class forces in determining the type of regime that emerged, thus prioritizing the experience of men.[39] In this view, there was insufficient attention to the way welfare regimes depended on and reproduced gendered norms of care provision.

A focus on welfare regimes from a feminist perspective raises important issues about how care is valued and dominant perceptions regarding the role and position of women within a given society. What if women were supported by the state to work outside of the home through generous welfare state provisions for maternity pay, nursery education, and residential or hospice care? Or if women were supported by the state to stay at home and look after their children and elderly relatives? Or perhaps if care work were seen as something that could be best provided by the private sector, with the tacit assumption that female family members would pick up the pieces if some firms went out of business and left their "customers" bereft of care? Research on the Asian experience has helped highlight the gender biases of Esping-Anderson's tripartite model by pointing to a fourth option, the *anti-welfare state*.[40] This identifies a kind of extreme family-based system of organizing care in which the state supports families (e.g., via marriage guidance and housing policy), but provides no welfare subsidy for unpaid care work at all.

We've seen how care work is systematically undervalued, both economically and socially. This is in large part a reflection of binary gendered assumptions about men and women. But it is not only relations between men and women that are being constructed here. How care work is organized plays an important role in demarcating boundaries *between women*. Low-status domestic work, whether it is undertaken by live-in domestic workers or hourly paid cleaners, is associated with women from lower socioeconomic groupings and frequently with women of a different race/ethnicity, class/caste, nationality, or age group than their employers. In this respect, research on South and Southeast Asia has pointed to the role that the employment of live-in domestic workers plays in the reproduction of an idealized middle-class identity in those regions.[41]

The ability to employ domestic workers in countries such as Malaysia is associated with a set of middle-class aspirations (home, car, university education) in what are increasingly affluent economies. Nonetheless, the common experiences of injustice and exploitation among migrant domestic workers has led to resistance and push back. Female domestic workers themselves, such as those organized by the International Domestic Workers Federation, are pressuring states to recognize them *as employees* so that they are protected by labor law.

In this section we have shown that the everyday practice of care is an intrinsic part of the economy, be it at the household, national, or global scale. While debates over the roles and rewards that should be assigned to men and women were foregrounded, relations of class, race, and nationality were recognized alongside those of gender. By examining how the political arrangements of care provision thus depended on intersections of social difference, we were able to make inroads into questions about how value, development, dependency, and resistance are constituted; that is to say, we could speak to some of the animating questions of IPE. In the next section, we show how the everyday approach is applicable to more traditional "issue areas" in IPE too, in this case global finance.

FINANCE AND EVERYDAY IPE

The global financial crisis of 2008 has been an important moment in the popular imagination of finance.[42] It led to a number of movies focusing on the collapse of major banking institutions in the United States, including *Inside Job*, *Margin Call*, and *The Big Short* to name but a few. These accounts, while critical of the excesses of Wall Street, nevertheless center the experience of finance and its crises around a small elite grouping of privileged white men. In so doing, they erase intersections of gender and race as well as other hierarchies of difference that are crucial to contemporary financial markets. Imagine how different accounts of this crisis would look if they started with the student from a minority ethnic background who fell deeper into debt as the financial markets went into meltdown, the single mother who could no longer afford the interest payments on her mortgage, or the migrant worker dependent on the global financial system for remitting her income to her home country.

Since the 1970s, observers have become both increasingly enthralled by and concerned with footloose international capital and the speculative moves on global financial markets. While for some the liberalization of finance represents new opportunities for making money and generating economic wealth, others highlight the dangers associated with what Susan Strange called "casino capitalism."[43] What both accounts have in common is that in focusing on the high politics of states and markets they tend to ignore the gendered and racialized dynamics of finance that an intersectional approach brings to the fore. As such, rather than reflecting on how the liberalization of financial markets impacts capital flows and the innovation of new financial products, or how states seek to both de- and re-regulate finance, this section explores how people *enact* the economy, including the hierarchies of difference they experience and the forms of power they encounter and exert. In so doing, it focuses on two aspects of finance that are pervasive in everyday life: money and debt.

Money is usually understood as providing three basic functions. First, it is a medium of exchange. If you did buy this textbook, it is likely you paid with money rather than paying "in-kind" with a pound of apples or an offer to cut the cashier's hair. Second, money serves as a unit of account. People and countries use money to measure the value of goods and services and to account for debts. Taken together, these two functions allow for the interchangeability and circulation of the mass of differentiated commodities produced in capitalist economies. A third function of money is that of a store of value. People can keep money in their wallets, hoard money under their mattresses, or put it in their bank vaults and retrieve it at a later stage. Unlike the pound of apples, money does not spoil; and unlike the offer of a haircut, money can more reliably acquire things as and when you need them. An intersectional approach helps highlight some of the problems with these common understandings of money.

Take the role of money as a medium of exchange. This presupposes a stability of money that is not the case for everyone. One reason could be because of rising **inflation**. For example, increases in prices of basic foodstuffs, while wages remain the same, would mean that the relative amount of labor exchanged, let's say for a loaf of bread or bowl of rice, increases. This is the essence of what happened in the global *food* crisis of 2008, which saw riots breaking out across the Middle East and Africa as the world prices of agricultural commodities rose rapidly and people could no longer afford to feed themselves – a change some IPE scholars traced to financial speculation on futures markets in the United States.[44] Another reason for the instability of money is rapidly fluctuating **exchange rates**. This might affect the student going to the United States or United Kingdom for their degree who suddenly finds that their education has become much more costly as their home country currency has devalued against the dollar or pound. International hierarchies in terms of market vulnerabilities – for food or currency, say – shape the extent to which money can play the role of medium of exchange.

The same holds true for money as a means of payment, especially given the many forms that money can take nowadays, including not just banknotes but also digital transfers, mobile payments, and so on. The availability and cost of these payment technologies is very unevenly spread. And while for some hoarding cash is a suitable store of value, for others it generates new individual vulnerabilities, not just due to inflation, but also because of the ease with which it can be taken away through theft and fraud and other means. Even where it comes to the role of money as a unit of account, a more nuanced approach is necessary as not everyone's money is equal. Indeed, the *money itself* might not be equal.[45] How would a homeless person paying with small denominations of coins be treated compared to a businessperson with a gold card? There are also significant hierarchies of difference when it comes to the monetary value of rather similar products, be it the premium women pay for basic items like razors, or the extra cost when shopping for products with a smaller package size that disproportionately impact the poor who cannot afford to buy in bulk.

Another important aspect of finance is debt, a term used to refer to relationships of obligation where one person, institution, or state (i.e., the borrower or debtor) owes something, such as money, to another (i.e., the lender or creditor). These are typically asymmetric relationships working in favor of the latter. Indeed, the strengthening of so-called creditor rights has been one of the cornerstones of the resurgence of global finance in recent decades. It has contributed to inequality in both everyday financial relations as well as at the global level.

Note that both lack of access to credit and forms of overindebtedness share similar root causes. Globally, women are more likely than men to work in the informal economy or irregular hours, making them less "creditworthy." This is compounded by racial segregations in the labor market. It negatively impacts poor women's ability to access credit, in particular in the formal financial system, and is one reason, along with their social construction as "responsible borrowers," why they have been the primary target for **microfinance** lenders in rural South Asia and elsewhere in the Global South.[46]

At the same time, as we have seen above, women often bear greater responsibility in the household, which can extend to providing necessities for their families such as paying for food or medical bills. As a consequence of struggles to make ends meet, women are especially susceptible to predatory forms of debt such as payday lending or loan sharks. Indeed, this is not just restricted to people's daily experiences; we can see here analogies to what happens at the country level. Despite gaining independent statehood, many former colonial territories and other so-called developing countries find it difficult to access credit on international financial markets. And where they do so, they typically have to pay a much higher interest rate and have little say on the terms and conditions of their loans. Moreover, servicing their debt (i.e., paying interest on the loans they have received) takes up a much higher share of their budget, despite overall debt levels usually being significantly lower (less than half) than those of so-called developed countries. Who can raise debt, how much, and at what price are intricately linked to questions of power.

An everyday approach to the dynamics of finance can also provoke us to imagine alternatives to how we engage in finance, and by extension question the contemporary global financial order as a whole. One such alternative that has become more widespread and worth more in the decade since the 2008 crisis is Islamic finance: financial products and services structured so that they comply with the ethico-religious principles that Muslims are expected to follow in daily life. One of these is the prohibition of *riba*, interpreted as the paying and receiving of interest. The underlying thought is that making money from money is unfair and unjust and can lead to exploitation. Modern Islamic finance emerged in the 1970s as a counterpoint to the increasingly speculative and Western-dominated financial order, fueled in part by the reinvestment of "petrodollars" by oil-rich states that were being paid billions in US currency. To avoid *riba*, Islamic financial products can involve the lender taking a stake in the business and being paid in profits from the joint venture rather than interest on the loan. While this may link finance to "real" economic activity in a way that seems to contrast with the de-linked relationship often noted in the West – the different worlds of Wall Street and Main Street, for instance – in its current guise many Islamic financial products closely mirror mainstream finance, making it an alternative in form rather than substance. Nevertheless, it is an evolving approach that retains the potential of more radical forms still to be realized.[47]

So where does this leave our study of global finance? As with the section on care, we outlined how hierarchies of difference are reproduced within financial markets and the intersectional subject-positions to which they give rise. Within the institutionalized daily economic practices of Islam, we also located an alternative form of finance. Like other forms of money such as local currencies, other ways of transacting such as the non-monetary local exchange trading systems, and other responses to indebtedness such as the student debt strikes in the United States, it is perhaps the very characterization of these practices *as* alternatives that makes them so politically interesting. Such possibilities for change from below, latent in the experimental approaches and survival strategies of everyday life, bring us in conclusion to the topic of resistance and the questions of whether, and how, economic and political arrangements might be transformed.

RESISTANCE AND EVERYDAY IPE

It may seem that to look closer at the everyday in IPE is to ignore the "serious" subject matter that IPE conventionally engages with. We see this as a false dichotomy. For us, everyday IPE offers up its own real and serious problematics: Is it trivial that billions of women face systemic gender bias in the expectation that they take on the care work? Does it not matter that ethnic minorities the world over face discriminatory labor and credit markets?

As suggested throughout this chapter, there is also an important critical and normative trajectory for studies in everyday IPE. The argument that markets are not natural and that economic outcomes are politically constructed is also an invitation to imagine them otherwise. By looking at the neglected topic of care, we have sought to raise questions about the gendering of low-paid work, the pressure placed on mobility, and the various valorizations and disarticulations of family life that are deployed to rationalize such provision. By considering global finance in terms of patterns of property ownership that are historically inflected by gendered and racial privileges, we hoped to show that rates of creditworthiness, mortgage default, and bankruptcy in different demographics become less about tracing market dynamics and more about exploring power relations.

This chapter has also shown how to locate moments of resistance that emerge from this focus on (seemingly) marginal groups, be it domestic workers organizing themselves outside the traditional trade unions apparatus or students going on "repayment strike" by refusing to pay off their debts to force reform of the student loan system. How these various empirical examples of resistance might be *theorized* is a somewhat thornier issue. The lineages of everyday IPE that we discussed have all been extended to present accounts of resistance as projects of emancipation, revolution, amelioration, or pluralization. From this point, they then deal with the *politics* of resistance: What is to be done? How is it to be achieved? What understandings of power, rights, and justice will be pursued? While these are all important discussions to be had, they also, at the same time, risk essentializing or downplaying some element of the hierarchies of difference they seek to resist. When it comes to pragmatic choices about who to support in an election or help out in the workplace, the question of whose lives matter is as complicated as it is radically inspiring.

For the purposes of this chapter, it is perhaps just enough to reiterate the point that resistance can be found in everyday life. Resistance is enacted, something we do. Often it is as simple a thing as saying "Enough! *Ya Basta!*" Think of moments when you have said this – inwardly or outwardly. What caused it? Did it lead you to action, or did you conclude you were too insignificant to change things? Perhaps you found significance from joining others? So much of global market life is designed to nurture our individuality, our self-interest, and our own identity or "brand." Think of the endless performances of the self on social media. One theoretical aspect of resistance, then, especially when formed into public protests like Occupy Wall Street or the Arab Spring, is the recognition that it can create – even depend on – a sense of solidarity and hope that emerges from turning a set of individuals into a collective.[48] Political subjectivity transforms as people go from thinking "What can *I* do?" to "What can *we* do?"

The Me Too movement, which you read about in Chapter 3, is another powerful demonstration of how a collective and resistant subjectivity can be formed. By placing the daily violence of sexual harassment of the media and entertainment industries on the news agenda, a credible moment of dialogue, questioning, and action was initiated without the need for "top down" political action. The hashtag #MeToo gave a platform to women beyond the Hollywood circle to identify abuse in their workplaces and reveal the pervasiveness – or "everydayness" – of sexism in the economy. Alongside the countless renegotiations of appropriate standards of conduct within the world of work, this movement also prompted formalized policy proposals for governments and corporations. A petition to prevent sexual harassment being embedded into artificial intelligence, for example, called on its signatories to harness the spirit of Me Too and demand that Apple and Amazon reprogram their digital voice assistants, Siri and Alexa, so as to not respond playfully to gender insults.[49]

In this sense, the mediatized global public sphere that enabled Me Too seems to be intensifying the resistance provided by such fluid social movements. However, in keeping with the intersectional theme of this chapter, it should be noted that Me Too had its biases as well. The movement was largely inaccessible to those excluded from the online world, to those unable to risk reporting sexual harassment, to those whose experiences did not fit into the heteronormative dyad of "male perpetrator/female victim." It must also be acknowledged that such tactics and technologies of resistance are ideologically ambivalent. The mobilization of populist movements like *gilet jaunes* in France and the Five Star movement in Italy along similar lines stands testament to this.

We have selected some examples of resistance here that you might be familiar with, but it would be a mistake to think that it must be high profile to be considered worthy of analysis. In his book *Weapons of the Weak: Everyday Forms of Peasant Resistance*, James C. Scott argues that everyday acts of dissent or refusal like foot dragging, sly civility, gossip, or even jokes were an important element in the social relations of subordinate groups.[50] We might find parallels here with purposeful subversions like "culture jamming," internet memes, and flash mobs, as well as less orchestrated acts such as absenteeism, file sharing, and refusing to pay fines. In and of themselves such things sound irrelevant, but when taken in aggregate or when marshaled to a cause that resonates with a wider public, they can cultivate a collective sense of agency that might lead to something longer lasting. From the daily pressure of everyday life, transformative change can occasionally erupt.

SUMMARY

- International political economy is the study of power and wealth across countries. Everyday IPE seeks to do this by starting with the experiences of daily life, including yours, and drawing attention to hierarchies of difference that sustain global inequalities.
- There are different lineages to everyday IPE, focusing to varying degrees on social relations of class, gender, race, and nationality and how these intersect. What they share is a conviction that economic and political outcomes are not natural but socially constructed in the sphere of the everyday.
- An everyday IPE approach can license the study of different topics. One topic usually overlooked in conventional IPE approaches is care work. The questions of who does this work and for what reward can be illuminated by discussions on the commodification of labor, the trans-nationalization of the household, the gendering of the welfare state, and the racialization of social identities.
- An everyday IPE approach can also provide novel ways of understanding established topics. Finance is typically explored in conventional IPE approaches through the global financial crisis and the perspective of the bankers, regulators, and politicians involved. Looking instead at how the financial economy

is enacted in everyday life revealed the vulnerabilities and prejudices that different groups faced in using money and debt, as well as alternative ways of lending as articulated in Islamic finance.

- Finally, an everyday IPE approach allows us to take the mundane seriously – and for good reason. When it comes to sources of transformation in the global economy, many of these can be traced to everyday acts of resistance and the collective identities and action they made possible.

CONCLUDING QUESTIONS

1 How does the *everyday turn* in IPE contrast with more traditional approaches to IPE?
2 How do practices and objects that are part of your everyday life connect you to the global political economy?
3 How does your area of interest connect to theories and approaches in IPE?
4 How do groups or regions experience the global economy differently? Why?

NOTES

1 V. Spike Peterson, "Getting Real: The Necessity of Critical Poststructuralism in Global Political Economy," in *International Political Economy and Poststructural Politics*, ed. M. de Goede, 119–38 (Basingstoke, UK: Palgrave Macmillan, 2006), 125.
2 Rob Aitken, *Performing Capital: Toward a Cultural Economy of Popular and Global Finance* (Basingstoke, UK: Palgrave Macmillan 2007); Jacqueline Best and Matthew Paterson, *Cultural Political Economy* (New York: Routledge, 2010); James Brassett, *Affective Politics of the Global Event: Trauma and the Resilient Market Subject* (New York: Routledge, 2018); Juanita Elias and Lena Rethel, *The Everyday Political Economy of Southeast Asia* (Cambridge: Cambridge University Press, 2016); Juanita Elias and Adrienne Roberts, "Feminist Global Political Economies of the Everyday: From Bananas to Bingo," *Globalizations* 13, no. 6 (2016): 787–800; John M. Hobson and Leonard Seabrooke, *Everyday Politics of the World Economy* (Cambridge: Cambridge University Press, 2007).
3 Cynthia Enloe, *Bananas, Beaches, and Bases: Making Feminist Sense of International Politics* (Berkeley: University of California Press, 2014).
4 James Brassett and Lena Rethel, "Sexy Money: The Hetero-Normative Politics of Global Finance," *Review of International Studies* 41, no. 3 (2015): 429–49; Liam Stanley, "'We're Reaping What We Sowed': Everyday Crisis Narratives and Acquiescence to the Age of Austerity," *New Political Economy* 19, no. 6 (2014): 895–917.
5 Crystal A. Ennis, "The Gendered Complexities of Promoting Female Entrepreneurship in the Gulf," *New Political Economy* 24, no. 3 (2019): 365–84; Debbie Lisle,

"Humanitarian Travels: Ethical Communication in Lonely Planet Guidebooks," *Review of International Studies* 34, no. S1 (2008): 155–72.

6 Benjamin J. Cohen, "The Transatlantic Divide: Why Are American and British IPE So Different?," *Review of International Political Economy* 14, no. 2 (2007): 197–219.

7 Leonard Seabrooke and Kevin L. Young, "The Networks and Niches of International Political Economy," *Review of International Political Economy* 24, no. 2 (2017): 288–331.

8 Karl Marx, *Capital: Volume 1* (Harmondsworth, UK: Penguin, 1995 [1867]).

9 Heloise Weber, "IPE Just 'Boring,' or Committed to Problematic Meta-Theoretical Assumptions? A Critical Engagement with the Politics of Method," *Contexto Internacional: Journal of Global Connections* 37, no. 3 (2015): 913–44.

10 Ben Highmore, *The Everyday Day Life Reader* (London: Routledge, 2002).

11 Jennifer Bair, "Global Capitalism and Commodity Chains: Looking Back, Going Forward," *Competition & Change* 9, no. 2 (2005): 153–80; Ben Richardson, *Sugar*.

12 Donald A. Clelland, "The Core of the Apple: Degrees of Monopoly and Dark Value in Global Commodity Chains," *Journal of World-Systems Research* 20, no. 1 (2014): 82–111.

13 Clelland, "The Core of the Apple."

14 Laura T. Raynolds, Douglas Murray, and John Wilkinson, *Fair Trade: The Challenges of Transforming Globalization* (New York: Routledge, 2007).

15 Slavoj Žižek, "RSA Animate: First as Tragedy, Then as Farce," The RSA, July 28, 2010, https://www.youtube.com/watch?v=hpAMbpQ8J7g.

16 Antonio Gramsci, *Prison Notebooks*, vol. 1 (New York: Columbia University Press, 1992).

17 Mark E. Rupert, "(Re)Politicizing the Global Economy: Liberal Common Sense and Ideological Struggle in the US NAFTA Debate," *Review of International Political Economy* 2, no. 4 (1995): 658–92.

18 Kate Crehan, *Gramsci's Common Sense: Inequality and Its Narratives* (Durham, NC: Duke University Press, 2016).

19 Henri Lefebvre, *Critique of Everyday Life: The One-Volume Edition* (London: Verso Books, 2014).

20 Matt Davies, "Everyday Life as Critique: Revisiting the Everyday in IPE with Henri Lefebvre and Postcolonialism," *International Political Sociology* 10, no. 1 (2016): 34.

21 Neil Smith, "New Globalism, New Urbanism: Gentrification as Global Urban Strategy," *Antipode* 34, no. 3 (2002): 427–50.

21 Lise Vogel, *Marxism and the Oppression of Women: Toward a Unitary Theory* (New Brunswick, NJ: Rutgers University Press, 1983).

23 Juanita Elias and Shirin Rai, "The Everyday Gendered Political Economy of Violence," *Politics & Gender* 11, no. 2 (2015): 424–29.

24 Susan Ferguson, "Intersectionality and Social-Reproduction Feminisms: Toward an Integrative Ontology," *Historical Materialism* 24, no. 2 (2016): 38–60.

25 Juanita Elias and Samanthi J. Gunawardana, *The Global Political Economy of the Household in Asia* (Basingstoke, UK: Palgrave Macmillan, 2013); Genevieve LeBaron, "The Political Economy of the Household: Neoliberal Restructuring, Enclosures, and Daily Life," *Review of International Political Economy* 17, no. 5 (2010): 889–912.

26 Barbara Ehrenreich, Arlie Russell Hochschild, and Shara Kay, *Global Woman: Nannies, Maids, and Sex Workers in the New Economy* (New York: Henry Holt, 2003).

27 Cynthia Enloe, "Margins, Silences and Bottom Rungs: How to Overcome the Under-estimation of Power in the Study of International Relations," in *International Theory: Positivism and Beyond*, eds. Steve Smith, Ken Booth, and Marysia Zalewski, 186–202 (Cambridge: Cambridge University Press, 1996).

28 Elias and Roberts, "Feminist Global Political Economies of the Everyday."

29 Diane Elson and Ruth Pearson, "'Nimble Fingers Make Cheap Workers': An Analysis of Women's Employment in Third World Export Manufacturing," *Feminist Review* 7, no. 1 (1981): 87–107.

30 J.K. Gibson-Graham, *The End of Capitalism (As We Knew It): A Feminist Critique of Political Economy* (Minneapolis: University of Minnesota Press, 2006), xii.

31 Patricia Hill Collins, "Gender, Black Feminism, and Black Political Economy," *Annals of the American Academy of Political and Social Science* 568, no. 1 (2000): 41–53.

32 Patricia Hill Collins, *Black Feminist Thought: Knowledge, Consciousness, and the Politics of Empowerment* (New York: Routledge, 2000), 277–88.

33 Marilyn Waring, *If Women Counted: A New Feminist Economics* (San Francisco: Harper & Row, 1988).

34 Maliha Safri and Julie Graham, "The Global Household: Toward a Feminist Postcapitalist International Political Economy," *Signs: Journal of Women in Culture and Society* 36, no. 1 (2010): 99–125.

35 World Bank Group, "Record High Remittances Sent Globally in 2018," World Bank Press Release, April 8, 2019, https://www.worldbank.org/en/news/press-release/2019/04/08/record-high-remittances-sent-globally-in-2018.

36 Seth Mydans, "Manila Frets over Export of Its Women," *New York Times*, May 12, 1988, https://www.nytimes.com/1988/05/12/world/manila-frets-over-export-of-its-women.html.

37 Rhacel Salazar Parreñas, *Servants of Globalization: Women, Migration and Domestic Work* (Stanford, CA: Stanford University Press, 2001).

38 Gøsta Esping-Andersen, *The Three Worlds of Welfare Capitalism* (Princeton, NJ: Princeton University Press, 1990).

39 Mary Daly, "Comparing Welfare States: Towards a Gender Friendly Approach," in *Gendering Welfare States*, vol. 35, ed. Diane Sainsbury, 101–17 (Thousand Oaks, CA: Sage Publications, 1994).

40 Marian Baird, Michele Ford, and Elizabeth Hill, *Women, Work and Care in the Asia-Pacific* (Abingdon, UK: Routledge, 2017); You Yenn Teo, "Women Hold Up the Anti-Welfare Regime: How Social Policies Produce Social Difference in Singapore," in *The Global Political Economy of the Household in Asia*, eds. Juanita Elias and Samanthi J. Gunawardana (Basingstoke, UK: Palgrave Macmillan, 2013).

41 Christine B.N. Chin, *In Service and Servitude: Foreign Female Domestic Workers and the Malaysian "Modernity" Project* (New York: Columbia University Press, 1998); Raka Ray and Seemin Qayum, *Cultures of Servitude: Modernity, Domesticity, and Class in India* (Stanford, CA: Stanford University Press, 2009).

42 Brassett, *Affective Politics of the Global Event.*

43 Susan Strange, *Casino Capitalism* (Manchester: Manchester University Press, 1986).

44 Jennifer Clapp, "Food Price Volatility and Vulnerability in the Global South: Considering the Global Economic Context," *Third World Quarterly* 30, no. 6 (2009): 1183–96.

45 Emily Gilbert, "Common Cents: Situating Money in Time and Place," *Economy and Society* 34, no. 3 (2005): 357–88.

46 Marcus Taylor, "The Antinomies of 'Financial Inclusion': Debt, Distress and the Workings of Indian Microfinance," *Journal of Agrarian Change* 12, no. 4 (2012): 601–10.

47 Lena Rethel, "Whose Legitimacy? Islamic Finance and the Global Financial Order," *Review of International Political Economy* 18, no. 1 (2011): 75–98.

48 Chris Rossdale, *Resisting Militarism: Direct Action and the Politics of Subversion* (Edinburgh: Edinburgh University Press, 2019).

49 Mark West, Rebecca Kraut, and Han Ei Chew, "I'd Blush If I Could: Closing Gender Divides in Digital Skills through Education," EQUALS Skill Coalition, 2019, https://docs.wixstatic.com/ugd/04bfff_06ba0716e0604f51a40b4474d4829ba8.pdf, 108.

50 James C. Scott, *Weapons of the Weak: Everyday Forms of Peasant Resistance* (New Haven, CT: Yale University Press, 1985).

RESOURCES AND SUGGESTIONS FOR FURTHER READING

The International Political Economy of Everyday Life (http://I-PEEL.org) is an open-access web-based teaching resource, *created by us*, for use by university students. It pulls together multimedia resources alongside accessible texts written on topics that are likely to interest students.

Brassett, James, and Lena Rethel. "Sexy Money: The Hetero-Normative Politics of Global Finance." *Review of International Studies* 41, no. 3 (2015): 429–49.

Elias, Juanita, and Lena Rethel, eds. *The Everyday Political Economy of Southeast Asia.* Cambridge: Cambridge University Press, 2016.

Enloe, Cynthia. *Bananas, Beaches, and Bases: Making Feminist Sense of International Politics.* Berkeley: University of California Press, 2014.

Peterson, V. Spike. "Getting Real: The Necessity of Critical Poststructuralism in Global Political Economy." In *International Political Economy and Poststructural Politics*, ed. M. de Goede, 119–38. Basingstoke, UK: Palgrave Macmillan, 2006.

Richardson, Ben. *Sugar.* Cambridge: Polity Press, 2015.

CHAPTER FOURTEEN

Security and Conflict

*Dr. Jon
Whooley*

*Dr. Laura
Sjoberg*

LEARNING OBJECTIVES

1 Analyze how intersectionality applies to security
2 Ask whose security "counts" and what concerns "count" as security concerns
3 Look for insecurity in your daily lives and the lives of those around you
4 Cite examples of different sorts of insecurities across global politics

KEY TERMS

environmental (in)security   (lack of) safety from natural disasters, climate events, contaminants, or other environmental factors that may cause humans danger

food (in)security   (lack of) availability of basic food needs, including but not limited to an appropriate number of calories or balanced diet, or (lack of) certainty about where meals will come from and when they will be available

health (in)security   (lack of) health stability or (lack of) access to adequate preventive or treatment mental or physical healthcare, or the (in)ability to protect one's body from damage due to work or living conditions

human security   an understanding that to be "secure" a person or group of people must have their basic needs met, including economic means, nutrition, health resources, environmental safety, personal physical integrity, and a secure community

intersectional security   a broad-based approach to understanding security that takes account of a wide variety of axes on which people are rendered vulnerable or insecure

nation   a group that understands itself to be "inside" of a political organization and understands those that are not included in the group to be "outside" of their political organization

nuclear deterrence   this idea, more frequently discussed during the Cold War than after, is that a state (or non-state actor) can "deter" another state (or non-state actor) from engaging in the use of nuclear weapons by a credible threat of what's called second-strike capacity: Once weapons were used against state/group X by state/group Y, state/group X (or their allies) would still be able to nuke state/group Y; if this is the case, it is assumed that state/group Y will be "deterred" from using the weapons to begin with from fear of the level of retaliatory damage that could be caused.

security/(in)security   the (lack of) ability to be or feel "secure" along a number of dimensions, including but not limited to military security, state security, environmental security, cultural security, gender security, health security, and food security

security narratives   stories that are told or repeated about the ways that people or groups are (in)secure, often told in terms of "the good guys" and "the bad guys" in a way that engenders and escalates conflict while neglecting human security

womenandchildren   written this way, the term *womenandchildren* refers to situations where women and children are grouped into a category understood to be physically or mentally incapable of some activity understood as the purview of men. For example, people often talk about *womenandchildren* as civilians in war – those to be protected. This category betrays gendered assumptions about what women are.

WHAT ARE SECURITY AND CONFLICT?

In 1998 and 1999, Serbian forces fought an ethnic Albanian insurgency in the then-Serbian province of Kosovo. Serbian police, soldiers and paramilitaries deliberately and systematically used rape as a weapon of war, to terrorize the population and aid in ethnic cleansing, according to a report in 2000 by Human Rights Watch (HRW) … No one knows how many women were raped during the conflict …

– Kristen Chick[1]

Peter Bouckaert, emergencies director of Human Rights Watch who investigates war crimes and crimes against humanity, said in an interview the group is collecting data on "what is happening across the border as this ethnic cleansing campaign continues against the Rohingya people" with the intention of prosecuting those responsible for the crimes ... "We're seeing pretty widespread rape and sexual assault on women," Bouckaert explained. "The majority of women who were raped were killed. There is no doubt about that," he said, adding that "racist hatred" is the motivation behind much of the violence.

– Annette Ekin[2]

Similar stories with different details can be found in news magazines, across the internet, and in the research of political scientists. There was a war. In the war, there was sexual violence. That sexual violence was used by one **nation** or one ethnic group against another. There is an estimate of how many women were raped, but no one really knows for sure. These stories are terrible, tragic, horrific – there are no words. Though not all of the victims are women, most of them are. Though not every rape during war or conflict is based on ethnic group membership, many if not most of them are. The victims of sexual violence during war are not all impoverished, but an overwhelming majority of them are. Wartime rape does not take place exclusively in rural areas, but, in many conflicts, the risk of rape is higher the further away from an urban area someone is.

For people who are victimized by conflict sexual violence – or people who fear being victimized by conflict sexual violence – the risks are intersectional. They are higher if you are a woman, if you are a member of a particular ethnic group, if you are poor, and if you live in a rural area. None of those group memberships increase risk randomly. Instead, women are at more risk for conflict sexual violence *because they are women*. This is the case for a number of reasons. Women tend to be more physically vulnerable than men are. Women are also targeted because they are seen as a key part of the opponent's social fabric – as mothers in families and as a foundation for reproducing and educating the nation more generally.

Members of minority groups are often more likely to be targeted because conflict sexual violence often aims at women of a particular group. Poor people are more likely to be raped during conflict because they have less access to resources that might afford them protection, such as secure housing, access to legal systems, or the ability to travel out of insecure areas safely. People who live further from urban areas are often more vulnerable to rape because there are fewer people around to see, prevent, or report the violence.

Conflict sexual violence is a fairly straightforward example of violence that is gendered, sexualized, raced, and classed during war and conflict, but it is nowhere near the only example. Other examples can be found in axes of insecurity as diverse as the environment and nutrition – almost all of the ways that people can be rendered insecure are affected by how people's identities are read and perceived by those around them. As this chapter will show, war, conflict, and **security** cannot be understood without reference to race, class, gender, nationality, sexuality, and their intersection. These and other factors figure into what we think are the key questions of security and conflict: what security means, how security is distributed, how security is experienced, and how it is discussed in policy circles. After briefly discussing our intersectional approach, this chapter will visit all four of those questions, using an intersectional lens to conceptualize and evaluate conflict and security.

INTERSECTIONALITY AND SECURITY

As you may remember from the introduction to this book, Kimberlé Crenshaw first used the term *intersectionality* as a tool to aid in understanding the impact of race, gender, and class within the legal system and society more generally.[3] Crenshaw, in a TED Talk posted online on December 7, 2016, argues that individuals are not simply strands of identity – a sex, a race, a nationality, a class - they are caught within a literal traffic-filled intersection and being impacted by vehicles that are beyond their control to stop or prevent. She argues that intersectional thought moves beyond seeing people as impacted by cars only on the "race road," the "class road," the "ableism road," the "sexual orientation road," or the "gender road," but rather the composite effect of being struck from all sides simultaneously.

The system to remediate these claims – the ambulance, if you will – "arrives" to treat the injured body, but will only treat the injured party if they are injured on one road or another – not at the intersection.[4] But we know that there is not merely one "road" along which traffic collisions occur – it is the intersection of multiple lines of traffic that harms individuals, sometimes lethally. Being intersectional in this sense is not simply being identified, it is being collided with by traffic from many directions, and thus possibly killed because of the intersection one occupies.

The disconnect in the understanding of intersectionality, especially from those who may never be hit by a "car" because their intersection is safer than other intersections, is problematic for security studies. For example, in North America and Europe, the safest "intersection" is white, male, cisgender (identifying as the sex that one was labeled with at birth), and heterosexual (attracted to members of the sex opposite that which one identifies). Security research has long taken place at and been about that intersection. Because theirs is the "mainstream" perspective, the knowledge that white, heterosexual, cisgender men have produced is what is typically taught in international relations classrooms. To move away from that mainstream perspective, it is necessary to think about a wide variety of people's lived experiences and the violences that many people live with regularly.[5] It is from this view that we are interested in an intersectional view of security – one that takes account of the possible roads of and to insecurity and their dangerous intersections. We look to examine how and wherein the lives of people living in busy intersections are routinely impacted, sometimes even fatally, and without an intersectional lens we are literally blind to the impact of living intersectionally.

MEANINGS OF SECURITY

What does it mean to be secure? When students enroll in undergraduate courses on security, they almost always "know" what security means before they arrive – they expect to be taught about the making and fighting of wars. For example, Stephen Walt, a professor at the Kennedy School of Government at Harvard University, declared at the end of the Cold War a "renaissance of Security Studies" where he defines the study of security as being focused on the threat or use of military force.[6] Traditional definitions of security limit it to states and the wars they fight, and people often internalize that interpretation without even realizing it is not the only one available.

Not only are traditional definitions not the only ones available, they are deeply problematic. Security is not limited to the making and fighting of wars, and the story of how some people came to think of it that way is one laced with race, class, and gender blindness. Certainly, wars are a significant cause of insecurity across a wide variety of factors, and it might even be said that the lack of an active war is a precondition to feeling secure. Security, though, is about more than simply physical acts of violation like wartime rape, sexual assault, targeted killing, genocide, and armed conflict. Security is also about food security, environmental security, and health security, among other factors. A look at your own life and the lives of fellow students may help you see how security (or lack thereof) is a part of our everyday lives.

Where do you live? Where do your fellow students live? What resources do you have to get food? Do you know anyone who has trouble finding the resources to get food? Do you have access to healthcare? Do you know anyone who has had trouble finding healthcare? How did you get to class? Do you know anyone who struggles to find transportation to class? On your way to class, did you feel threatened on the street? In your car? On public transit? Are you subject to violence at home? Do you know anyone who is subject to violence at home? Do you experience bullying at school? Do you know anyone who is bullied? The individual without enough to eat, the person without a stable living situation, the refugee, the immigrant, the poor, the person experiencing violence at home – they are all experiencing insecurity, and often multiple insecurities. These insecurities may be in your own life and are definitely in the lives of those around you.

Traditional security scholars may reject these aspects of insecurity because it contrasts starkly with inherited ideas of what security and conflict are, which frequently associates security with militaries and their confrontations. Yuen Foong Khong, another security scholar, suggested that security studies should keep to those narrow boundaries.[7] He argued that thinking about security outside of military clashes meant that we were thinking about safety and not about security – safety is for people, security is for states. What Khong neglected, however, was that the things that make a state secure can directly make people in it insecure, and the security concerns some people have do not even make sense to others, depending on their positions and their experiences. For example, a state may have massive armies that can effectively protect the borders of a state, but still have populations and individuals that feel themselves to be under threat from terrorism, police violence, or sexual assault. The Rohingya minority in Myanmar, for example, is not collectively worried to any great degree about the possibility of a foreign state harming them, but they have been placed in substantial danger and a space of insecurity by the state's security forces, police, and military.

If we took away the weight of traditional military-focused definitions of security and asked people what it meant to *them* to be secure, definitions of security would likely be very different. Some scholars have tried to look at security more broadly and proposed other ways of interpreting the concept, though even these broader definitions have some blinders. For example, Barry Buzan, Ole Waever, and Jaap de Wilde suggest that security is a concept with five sectors: state security, political security, societal security, economic security, and environmental security.[8]

- State security is the sovereignty of the state and its ability to preserve itself in the international arena.
- Political security is people's ability to have a say in their government – essentially, the level of democracy.
- Societal security is the ability to express oneself, socialize with others, and practice cultural and religious rites.
- Economic security is access to nutrition, shelter, running water, healthcare, and other basic needs.
- Environmental security is safety from natural disasters, climate events, contaminants, or other environmental factors that may cause humans danger.

These categories themselves, however, can be defined or applied narrowly or broadly. For example, environmental security can be looked at from the position of preserving the resources that large corporations or wealthy people exploit, or from the position of sustaining the basic needs of people who depend on environmentally vulnerable sources of food or shelter. The self-expression in societal security looks very different if one is weaponizing the "right of self-expression" for hate speech to harm others, or if one is looking to "be oneself" in the face of such violence.

Relatedly, Ken Booth has argued that human emancipation is at the core of the concept of security[9] but does not acknowledge that emancipation looks different for people who are differently situated. Scholars and practitioners who focus on something called **human security** look at whether the basic needs that all people share are met, such that they have adequate economic means, nutrition, health resources, environmental safety, personal physical integrity, and a secure community.[10] Feminist scholars have pointed out that there are security issues, such as sexual violence and bodily vulnerability, that are felt and experienced differently based on sex and gender.[11]

Most of these efforts to define security have looked to broaden and deepen traditional notions of what counts as international security. For the most part, they start by engaging with inherited notions of what security is and how security works. While that is not necessarily a problem, the intersectional approach in this chapter suggests that coming from another direction might shed a different light on what security means and how to understand it. This could be accomplished by problematizing the basic guarantee of physical security that we often presume societies give people when they do not. People who feel threatened when they encounter police officers because of the color of their skin or people who feel threatened walking down a dark street because of their gender know that states do not actually guarantee people physical security. Intersectional approaches to security articulate this *as a security problem.*

From this perspective, we suggest three main components of understanding what security means through an intersectional lens. First, defining security cannot be collective or universal – security is not the same for everyone. Security is not even the same for every wealthy, white, heterosexual, man – much less for people who do not share those identity categories. Certainly, like war or hunger, there are things in global politics that affect everyone's security. But even those things affect real people differently. As we will discuss below, some people live much closer to security threats than others – that is, while everyone would be insecure if they were hungry, some people are actually hungry, some people live with a constant concern about hunger, and other people live without seriously considering the idea that they might ever be hungry.

Further, some security threats are specific to some groups in some situations – for example, in a place where there is ethnic violence toward a minority group, security is experienced differently by members of the minority group than by members of the majority group. Security may even be experienced differently among members of the minority group – some may pass for members of the majority and be able to avoid most risks of violence; some may be able to use money to curry favor; some may be vulnerable to sexual violence while others are not – the possibilities go on. So even "human" security does not capture the needs of every human, because those needs differ in a wide variety of contexts.

Second, then, it is important to think of security in the context of people's daily lives. What needs does each person have to make them secure? What threats exist to each person's security? How are those threats to be read and understood? While there is not a universal answer to these questions, looking at the ways that different insecurities affect different people in different places and different times might provide important, contextualized answers. An intersectional approach to understanding the meaning of security might *end up* sharing significant overlap with other critical approaches, like those discussed in Chapter 12 – describing a security that is broader, deeper, more personal, and less centered on the state and its military than traditional approaches. But an intersectional approach also pays specific attention to the insecurities of intersections – how race, gender, sexuality, class, and other factors *cross* to make different intersectional securities and insecurities.

An intersectional approach to security will ask not only how particular positions in society – those occupied by women, by minorities, by the poor – influence what factors make people secure and insecure, but also what happens at the intersection of those categories. For example, as discussed above, people identified as female are at a higher risk than people identified as male for victimization in conflict sexual violence. But the level of risk cannot be determined by the male/female binary alone. People who fall outside of that binary are often at a higher risk than either side of the binary. Also, within the category of "women," poor women, young women, old women, and minority women are at different (higher) levels of risk than wealthy women who are in a majority group. In addition to affecting the *level of risk*, these categories can also impact *which risks* people feel or which risks people feel more sharply than others.

A rural woman in a place with little income and no military conflict may feel the lack of available nutrition as the greatest security risk to herself or her family. An urban woman in a city being bombed may feel the potential of her home being targeted or hit inadvertently as the greatest security risk to herself or her family. Malnutrition would and could threaten the security of the second woman, as military conflict could threaten the security of the first woman, were they situated differently. Certainly, neither would describe the circumstance of the other as secure. Yet their lived experiences define insecurity (and therefore security) differently.

Finally, then, an intersectional approach to security (and insecurity) defines those concepts with attention to where people live, how people live, and elements of race, class, gender, sexuality, and nationality. A wide variety of different factors can be sources of insecurity, and insecurities can affect people in many different ways. A traditional definition *starting at* security and what it contains, then, seems ill-suited to an intersectional view of security. Rather than suggesting that "security is" a particular inclusive list of things, an intersectional approach might look at how security is distributed, experienced, and framed as a way to understand "what" it is. The remainder of this chapter takes that path.

DISTRIBUTIONS OF SECURITY

The term **food insecurity** is often used to describe a state where a person or persons do not have access to either enough food or food that contains adequate nutrition. The United States Food and Drug Administration, for example, defines "low food security" as "reports of reduced quality, variety, or desirability of diet" and "very low food security" as "reports of multiple indications of disrupted eating patterns and reduced food intake."[12] In other words, people who lack food security either do not get enough to eat or do not get high enough quality food to meet their nutritional needs. We often think of hunger as a problem in poor countries, but it can happen anywhere. For example, more than 12 per cent of residents in the United States are classified as food insecure (see Box 14.1 for a story of one of these people). Unsurprisingly, the risk of food insecurity is higher for those who are in big cities and those who are unemployed, and children, ethnic minorities, women, and disabled people are more likely to be food insecure than their white, male, able-bodied, employed counterparts.[13] MercyCorps suggests that worldwide "one in every nine people goes to bed hungry each night."[14] Figure 14.1 shows the prevalence of food insecurity around the world.

An understanding of food insecurity is closer than most think for many college students. The Swipe Out Hunger program within the University of California system and the California State University system, which allows students to donate unused portions of their meal plans, has been vital to relieving the issue of student hunger on campus. One participant related that "I used to go hungry and that would make it hard to focus in class or study. [The passes] really helped my studying and may have helped me get my GPA up."[15] Going hungry in this instance

Figure 14.1. **Prevalence of Moderate and Severe Food Insecurity in Select Regions**

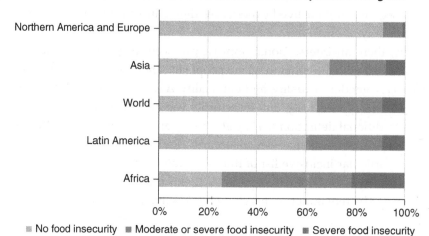

Source: Data from Food & Agriculture Organization of the United Nations, "Prevalence of Moderate and Severe Food Insecurity in the Population," 2019, http://www.fao.org/sustainable-development-goals/indicators/212/en.

BOX 14.1: A FACE OF FOOD INSECURITY

Barbie Izquierdo realized she was food insecure when she was 20. She had two children – one who was two years old, and one who was ten months old. Her home in Philadelphia had no heat, and her younger son was losing his vision. She did not know where she or her children would get their next meal – a combination of food pantries, soup kitchens, income from her job, and public assistance still did not make ends meet. She lived in a "food desert": a place where there were no good grocery stores. The combination of *where* she lived, the lack of access to good food, and the lack of access to knowledge about what counted as good food compounded. The fact that she was a single mother made finding adequate income and, relatedly, adequate nutrition all the more difficult. She and her children suffered serious health consequences as a result of their food insecurity.[16]

is something acutely felt by matriculating students and is not either remote or inaccessible: It simply requires scholars and students to recognize the demographic and intersectional composition of the contemporary student environment.

Across the United States, many college students do not fit the typical mold of a non-working 18-year-old with a middle-class, white upbringing. While that mold is often assumed by universities making decisions about tuition, housing, and activities, many students are instead from poor and largely minority-based communities. For those students, it is possible that dealing with food insecurity is just one of many challenges they face as they enter and maintain their status as matriculating college students. As Katherine Broton explains in an interview with the *Washington Post*, about one in four college students are parents, and about 40 per cent are working. Food insecurity, then, is not just something that affects people "out there" – it affects people around all of us. On the University of California Berkeley campus, "38 percent of undergraduates and 23 percent of graduate students deal with food insecurity at some point in the academic year."[17]

Food insecurity is also present for students in Canada. In a study from 2016 entitled "Hungry for Knowledge," 4,500 students across five Canadian campuses were interviewed about the role of food insecurity and hunger during their time in university.[18] Of those students surveyed, 39 per cent experienced some degree of food insecurity, with 30.7 per cent moderately food insecure and 8.2 per cent severely food insecure. Students who face rising tuition are forced to increasingly rely on stretched paychecks and credit cards to effectively make ends meet. This reality not only affects a student's ability to matriculate effectively but their physical health as well.[19] In one survey, 23.7 per cent reported that their physical health has been impacted by food insecurity, and 49.5 per cent of students responded that they have had to sacrifice buying healthy foods in lieu of purchasing rent, textbooks, or tuition.

Ronnie Cruz, the community services coordinator with the George Brown College Student Association, spoke to the *Toronto Star*, arguing that "this [hunger] problem is visible on campus ... Food bank use is increasing each year because it's getting harder and harder for students to afford to go to school."[20] Even this study may underestimate the level of food insecurity, since individuals who are in their mid-20s, white, and cisgender were much more likely to respond to the survey than students of non-traditional age, members of minority groups, or trans students.[21]

Food insecurity is not the only insecurity that is unevenly distributed among people, either in the United States or across the globe. Instead, many sorts of insecurity are more likely to affect particular segments of populations. Like (and related to) food insecurity, **health insecurity** is much more likely to plague the most marginalized parts of populations, nationally and internationally. HIV/AIDS is a simple example: "the vast majority of people living with HIV are in low- and middle-income countries ... (54%) in eastern and southern Africa, ... (13%) in western and central Africa, ... (15%) in Asia and the Pacific."[22] More than half of the people living with HIV are women, and the likelihood that a woman is infected is significantly higher if she is an adolescent (15–24).[23] Not all citizens of low-income countries are more susceptible to HIV/AIDS, nor are all women more susceptible. At the same time, intersections of location, poverty, sex, gender, race, and sexuality *do* impact one's likelihood of becoming infected with HIV/AIDS *and* the quality of treatment one might receive if infected. We write while the COVID-19 pandemic is still unfolding, but there is strong evidence that this virus has resulted in uneven effects on the basis of race and class.[24]

Linked to both health and food insecurity is **environmental insecurity**. Challenges like deforestation, pollution, lack of access to potable water, and the destruction caused by extreme weather affect people's lives, and their impact on the experiences of the most vulnerable and marginalized people in societies across the globe is only growing. While some think of wars over resources as the only way that the environment can affect security, looking at security intersectionally shows that there is more to environmental in/security. For example, some states within the potential impact of sea level rise, like Federated Micronesia, the San Juan Islands, and parts of the Philippines, are at risk of literally disappearing from the map and their inhabitants being wiped out or displaced. The ability to ignore vulnerable people by limiting security to states erases and silences their diverse health, environmental, and nutritional needs. In terms of intersectionality, this highlights that, like other forms of security, environmental in/security is not experienced equally by all. For those most intersectionally impacted, the ability to create a secure path forward is entirely at risk (see Box 14.2).

BOX 14.2: INTERSECTIONAL ENVIRONMENTAL INSECURITY

Mousuni Island in West Bengal, India, has experienced several serious floods in the last decade. This flooding has a wide range of effects, both anticipated and unanticipated. Anticipated effects include the destruction of homes, businesses, and infrastructure; flood-related displacement; and flood-related injuries. Residents, however, explained that there is more to it – both economically and personally. Economically, a resident explained, "We are born farmers ... We don't have the capacity to do different work. What else can we do? We are surviving barely." Another resident describes the tribulation of displacement: "Many people can understand the pain of a loved one having to move or travel seasonally for work ... Everyone can understand love. Everyone can understand the importance of home – and imagine the trauma of being forcibly displaced from it."[25]

Sea rise and land loss, like student hunger, may be closer than we think here in the Americas. The low-lying areas of the United States are also under substantial threat of subsidence and land erosion, which contributes to a delimited security environment for the people that live there. The residents of Isle de Jean Charles are increasingly facing the possibility that their island may disappear into the Gulf of Mexico or the Mississippi River. The Choctaw Tribe and its chief, Albert Nauin, are currently attempting to build their way out of sea level rise with a $50-million federal grant, which has since been tied up in state politics. "It's kind of hard to imagine that no one's going to be living here," said Billiot, the deputy chief. "But I've watched it erode away."[26] Similar struggles take place in the low-lying areas around the Three Gorges Dam in China, on Ghana's Atlantic Coast, and many other places around the world.

Environmental concerns rarely appear in coverage of "security," whether in newspapers or in textbooks. But a war cannot even happen if there is not land to fight on, and the biggest threats to some people's lives may come from rising seas rather than from the barrel of a gun. This can escape the gaze of many scholars and students of security because the writing of traditional, non-intersectional security narratives reinforces the "systems of power privilege and oppression"[27] that they reflect. An intersectional approach has the capacity to take account of various insecurities more effectively.

Different insecurities matter more or less in different people's lives in different places – that is, who gets security, when, and how varies. That's why context-specific analysis is key to intersectional approaches to security.[28] Insecurity is distributed to different groups in different ways when that insecurity is food insecurity or health insecurity, but also when that insecurity comes from the traditional subjects of security – war and conflict. Wars have many differential impacts on the basis of race, age, class, nationality, and gender. Many wars are ethnic wars, where a person's ethnicity defines one's role and lot in a conflict even when a person is not interested in being involved in that conflict.

It is well documented that men are often expected or even compelled to fight in wars, while women are the overwhelming majority of civilian casualties in every war. People with fewer economic resources are more likely both to be compelled to fight in wars and to be casualties of wars. This is the case because state and non-state militaries tend to recruit from among the poor, and the poor tend to feel like they have very few economically viable alternatives. Both the young and the elderly face special challenges, both from wars directly and from the political/economic changes that come with those wars. For the young, it is often difficult to find adequate nutrition during wars and conflicts. For the elderly, immobility often makes them more susceptible to collateral harm during fighting.

In Laura Conteh's story of the war in Sierra Leone in Box 14.3, she was subject to insecurities only possible because of her age, including not knowing what was going on when the war reached her town and her vulnerability to separation from her family. She also lived through several violations of her security only possible because she was a girl – she was forced to do feminized labor at the camps and was subject to sexual abuse and ultimately forced pregnancy. Laura had experiences with captivity and enslavement that she likely would not have gone through if her family had been well off rather than poor, given that well-off families were more likely to find structures to protect them. Laura struggled with a lack of resources after the war in part because her family's resources were already so limited.

BOX 14.3: DISTRIBUTION OF INSECURITY IN SIERRA LEONE

Laura Conteh was 12 when she started hearing gunshots. Her older sister knew that the rebels had reached their small town in Sierra Leone, and they "just ran" into the bush. She watched her home go up in flames, and then she was separated from her family. She was captured by the Revolutionary United Front (RUF). During her captivity, she cooked and fetched water. She was given a gun and participated in raids where she and other RUF members took food, clothes, and supplies from nearby towns and villages. Almost immediately when she was taken captive, she began being sexually abused, first by different soldiers and then by one man who claimed her as his "bush wife." When she was 14, she had a son. When the war ended, she was simply released, with no resources, no place to live, and no direction for starting her post-war life.[29]

The insecurities that Laura endured in Sierra Leone were distributed on a number of axes of identity and disadvantage, including but not limited to ethnicity, class, gender, and race. Distributions of security and insecurity happen in many contexts across global politics, but no two situations are the same. An intersectional approach to thinking about the distribution of insecurity does not look to have one answer to what security is. Instead, it pays attention to four things:

1 Insecurity is often distributed unevenly among people, both locally and globally.
2 Insecurity is distributed on many axes, but some of the recurring themes include race, gender, class, age, nationality, and disability.
3 It is not possible to understand security without looking at how and why security and insecurity are distributed along those axes.

4 Most importantly, understanding the distribution of insecurity must be done contextually.

No two situations of the distribution of security and insecurity are exactly the same, and conflating them obscures nuance.

EXPERIENCES OF SECURITY

Security and insecurity are not only material things that are distributed. They are also felt, lived, and experienced. We do not often think or talk about what it means to live a secure life, or the sources or impacts of insecurities in individuals' lives, but an intersectional approach identifies *living* insecurity as a key part of security. While there may be "states" or "situations" of security and insecurity, there are also feelings and experiences of security and insecurity. Scholars have acknowledged that "emotions are everywhere in world politics, and deeply embedded in the assumptions of our theories."[30] In addition to being experienced emotionally, Ronni Alexander points out that security and insecurity are sensory experiences – they can be felt, tasted, smelled, seen, and heard:[31]

- Sarah Kruger heard reverberations of the Rwandan genocide in Burundi and described the sounds of war: "The thud of grenades broke the silence, followed by machine-gun fire."[32]
- When asked what war tastes like, a colleague of ours who was a child during World War II in Britain responded without pausing with just one word: "potatoes."
- Besim, who survived the most recent war in Kosovo in a prison camp, discusses the things he felt during the war: hunger, fear, pain.[33]
- Soldiers who fight in wars describe a wide variety of emotions, including but not limited to fear, exhilaration, excitement, companionship, purpose, and homesickness. When soldiers try to reintegrate into normal life, they report struggling with injury, trauma, quiet, and guilt.
- Those who live wars as civilians report similar emotions and physical trials, if in different situations and different contexts.

Whether people live wars and conflicts as soldiers or civilians, understanding that those are things people *live* rather than simply things people *do* or *receive* opens up space to see the emotion, sense, and affect in security and insecurity. Even seeing these things, though, is not enough. Often, people are expected to experience war and conflict in particular ways depending on their (understood) position in social and political life. There is a stereotypical expectation not only of who a soldier *is* (an adult male) but also how that solider lives warfare – war is hell, but the soldier confronts it with a spirit of bravery, self-sacrifice, and loyalty to those he is protecting back home. The stereotypical expectation of who a civilian *is* (someone helpless in the face of war – in Cynthia Enloe's wording, *womenandchildren*[34]) includes an expectation of how she copes with the war – quiet desperation, creative resource allocation, and inspiring soldiers to fight. In other words, even insomuch as it is acknowledged that wars and conflicts are lived, there is a narrow spectrum of feelings that are expected of those who live them.

Often, many of the uglier emotions and feelings involved in living war and conflict (whether it is fear during fighting or injury after) are left out of traditional narratives about war and conflict. Most of the time when emotion and sense during war and conflict are discussed, the stories feature bravery in the face of conflict and joy in prevailing. Very rarely are other emotions discussed, and often the photographs of wars and the narratives of both soldiers and civilians that are made public are sanitized – people see pictures of victorious soldiers rather than dead bodies, and stories of survivors rather than struggles of casualties.

War and conflict are not the only insecurities that people live and feel. People live hunger, infectious diseases, natural disasters, environmental degradation, crime, political instability, discrimination, and all sorts of other violences. Students may feel insecurity in their daily lives – for example, they may experience worries over climate change's impact on their future health or the persistent risk of racially or ethnically motivated violence. People live those violences as victims and sometimes as perpetrators. Bodies and sense, feelings and expressions are involved in the living of security and insecurity, and neither can be understood without reference to those dimensions. Looking at security intersectionally suggests not only that those dimensions be taken into account, but that they be taken into account in a way that includes the ways that different positions in societies affect not only what people experience and how they experience it but how those experiences and expressions of them are filtered, read, and understood.

For example, the *Diary of a Young Girl*, written by Anne Frank and published by her father, is one of the best-known narratives of how war is experienced and felt. It has been read in schools across the world, as well as popularly. Frank was a Jewish teenager who hid in Amsterdam during World War II for two years before being sent to Nazi prison camps where she ultimately died. The diary was edited both by Anne Frank's father and by the publishing house. It has recently been revealed that some of the things that were edited out of Anne's diary were about sexuality – sexual jokes, descriptions of her romance with a boy, and attraction to a girl: "[O]nce when I was spending the night at Jacque's, I could no longer restrain my curiosity about her body ... I asked her whether, as proof of our friendship, we could touch each other's breasts ... I also had a terrible desire to kiss her, which I did. Every time I see a female nude ... I go into ecstasy ... if only I had a girlfriend."[35] The censorship of this passage and others resembling it was overdetermined: Sexuality is not one of the ways it is sanctioned to talk about war, narratives about women portrayed them as asexual, and homosexuality was taboo inside and outside of war. The part of Frank's war narrative that fell outside of expectations and acceptability was omitted, silenced, and delegitimized. Even for one of the most well-known narrators of war experience, gendered and heterosexist notions of what people should be played a role in what was told and how it was told.

DISCOURSES OF SECURITY

Anne Frank's diaries are an example of how narratives of security and insecurity are framed by who tells them and what is socially understood as acceptable or important to tell. Feminist scholars have frequently pointed out that states often seek their security at the expense of their most insecure citizens. Wars are often fought on the backs of the most marginalized members of those states, where poor people and minorities are most likely to fight in wars, and women and children are most likely to suffer many of wars' ugly side effects. States often spend countless billions of dollars on "national defense," while many of their citizens are ill, malnourished, or living in unsanitary environments, creating insecurities for their own citizens. States' narratives about security often (though not always) focus on military security and state sovereignty, ignoring many of the other facets of security. As Lene Hansen notes, "defining what constitutes threats to 'national security' relies upon a set of discursive practices that inscribe state sovereignty and national identity as the privileged reference point for security."[36] Who gets to author security discourses has a heavy influence on what those security discourses look like.

Critical theorists have discussed the construction of security by security discourses, calling it *securitization*. Securitization theory suggests that security is in significant part a speech-act – the things that are called "security" by state elites are the things that become security.[37] But even what securitization is recognized is heavily dependent on authorship and privilege.[38] Securitization is "located within the realm of political argument and discursive legitimation," where the utterance of things as security is itself a powerful move that sets a landscape of policy priorities.[39] The US White House's page on national security and defense describes the

Trump administration's security priorities: "rebuilding U.S. deterrence to preserve peace through strength must be our Nation's top priority. The unprecedented era of peace that followed World War II revealed that the free world is safest when America is the strongest. The slow depletion of our military has resulted in an escalation of threats the world over, which President Trump is committed to reversing."[40] In this statement, security is related to the military strength and physical integrity of the state, which needs to be built up through military stockpiling and the amassing of **nuclear deterrence**. Many people, especially at the margins of society, are not made secure by nuclear deterrence – it does not address hunger, illness, disability, domestic violence, environmental hazards, or other insecurities that militarized states do not treat as "security."

Privileged, statist perspectives on security not only ignore and minimize the multiple kinds of security and insecurity in global politics but also mainstream a narrow (in this case, wealthy, white, male, hetero, cis) perspective as a universal perspective. Traditional security discourses tend to promote the security of the state over the security of people and to obscure the security experiences and needs of most people. Creating the space for an inclusive discourse of security necessitates asking important questions about security in *all* lives, including asking how the lives of scholars, politicians, and even students are secured or made insecure. This means talking about how people live security.

Feminist scholar Annick Wibben suggests that it is possible to use a narrative approach to security to look at the ways that people talk about security rather than the ways that leaders and states dictate it. Wibben describes narratives as "essential because they are a primary way by which we make sense of the world around us, produce meanings, articulate intentions, and legitimize actions," and therefore key to understanding what people see as sources of security and insecurity.[41] She explains that "the difference among stories and storytellers, which characterize personal narratives" can be "explicitly acknowledged" rather than glossed over or ignored. In this context, "narratives are always contextual; securities are likewise."[42]

Rather than accepting top-down **security narratives** as accurate (and therefore self-fulfilling), an intersectional approach to security pays attention to the narratives of people who are traditionally excluded from state security narratives. This approach, "based on personal narratives," can "challenge conventional narratives of security not just because security is different ... but because narratives have the ability to capture a variety of concerns and events" from the experiences of an individual narrativizing to the context in which that individual had their experiences.[43] This turns security discourses upside down, both in terms of who tells security and in terms of what security is told.

SUMMARY

- **Intersectional security** means that what counts as "security" and whose security receives attention is different than the ways the word "security" is usually thought about.
- Traditional meanings of security are gendered, raced, and classed, and looking at those dynamics shows not only that the things that should count as security are deeper and broader than traditional interpretations, but also that defining security should start at a contextual evaluations of people's lives and experiences.
- Looking closely at contexts shows that security and insecurity are distributed unevenly among people, both locally and globally. Often, women, minorities, poor people, disabled people, or queer people experience insecurities different in kind and severity than persons who are in positions of privilege.
- There is not and cannot be a single experience that defines security for women, or security for non-binary persons, or security for economically disadvantaged persons. Though people may fall into these categories, their experiences are not the same just because they share a category. Also, the intersection of those categories may be different than or more than a sum of their parts.
- Looking at the distribution of security, then, it is important to see on what axes security and insecurity are distributed among people. The distribution of security is more than the distribution of material advantage and disadvantage – it is about how security is sensed, experienced, and felt.
- Replacing traditional, top-down, narrow but universalized discourses of security about militaries and states with personal narratives about living different securities can reframe conflict and security in a more plural way for the study of global politics.

CONCLUDING QUESTIONS

1 How do security concerns affect your life?
2 How does intersectionality apply to security?
3 How is security distributed around you and around the globe?
4 Suggested class activity: With a proper understanding of your peer's willingness to participate and discuss personal issues, discuss the following questions with a partner:
   a. How is their life experience different from yours in terms of economics and physical security? How is it similar?

b. Discuss how we can see through the eyes of others and walk in their shoes.

c. Reflect and discuss how being bound by your own lived experiences affects your ability to empathize with other lives in a global community.

NOTES

1 Kristen Chick, "Ending the Shame of Kosovo's Rape Victims," *Foreign Policy* 22 (2016).

2 Annette Ekin, "Rohingya Refugees Share Stories of Sexual Violence," *Aljazeera*, September 29, 2017, https://www.aljazeera.com/indepth/features/2017/09/rohingya-refugees-share-stories-sexual-violence-170929095909926.html.

3 Kimberlé Crenshaw, "Demarginalizing the Intersection of Race and Sex: A Black Feminist Critique of Antidiscrimination Doctrine, Feminist Theory and Antiracist Politics," in *Feminist Legal Theory: Readings in Law and Gender*, ed. Katharine T. Bartlett, 57–80 (London: Routledge, 1989).

4 Kimberlé Crenshaw, "The Urgency of Intersectionality," YouTube, 2016, https://www.youtube.com/watch?v=akOe5-UsQ2o&feature=youtu.be.

5 Crenshaw, "The Urgency of Intersectionality."

6 Stephen M. Walt, "The Renaissance of Security Studies," *International Studies Quarterly* 35, no. 2 (1991): 211–39.

7 Yuen Foong Khong, "Human Security: A Shotgun Approach to Alleviating Human Misery," *Global Governance* 7 (2001): 231.

8 Barry Buzan, Ole Wæver, and Jaap de Wilde, *Security: A New Framework for Analysis* (Boulder, CO: Lynne Rienner, 1998).

9 Ken Booth, *Theory of World Security* (Cambridge: Cambridge University Press, 2007).

10 Lloyd Axworthy, "Human Security and Global Governance: Putting People First," *Global Governance* 7 (2001): 19; Mary Kaldor, *Human Security* (Cambridge: Polity, 2007).

11 Laura Sjoberg, *Gendering Global Conflict: Toward a Feminist Theory of War* (New York: Columbia University Press, 2013); J. Ann Tickner, *Gender in International Relations: Feminist Perspectives on Achieving Global Security* (New York: Columbia University Press, 1992); Annick T.R. Wibben, *Feminist Security Studies: A Narrative Approach* (London: Routledge, 2010).

12 USDA, "Definitions of Food Security," Economic Research Service, 2017, https://www.ers.usda.gov/topics/food-nutrition-assistance/food-security-in-the-us/definitions-of-food-security.

13 Office of Disease Prevention and Health Promotion, "Food Insecurity," 2017, https://www.healthypeople.gov/2020/topics-objectives/topic/social-determinants-health/interventions-resources/food-insecurity#4.

14 MercyCorps, "Quick Facts: What You Need to Know about Global Hunger," 2019.

15 Michelle Andrews, "Some College Students Go to Class Hungry," *Washington Post*, August 13, 2018, https://www.washingtonpost.com/national/health-science/some-college-students-go-to-class-hungry/2018/08/07/4e39f5ec-94d0-11e8-80e1-00e80e1fdf43_story.html?noredirect=on&utm_term=.b9e8f936b768.

16 Jennarose DiGiacomo, "Never Give Up the Fight: Food Insecure," 2018, http://servingfoodsolutions.com/the-problem/economics/personal-story-barbie-izqiuerdo.

17 Andrews, "Some College Students."

18 Drew Silverthorn, "Hungry for Knowledge: Assessing the Prevalence of Student Food Insecurity on Five Canadian Campuses," Meal Exchange, 2016, https://www.mealexchange.com/what-we-do/hungryforknowledgereport.

19 Silverthorn, "Hungry for Knowledge."

20 Laura Beeston, "Nearly 40 Per Cent of Canadian Post-Secondary Students Experience 'Food Insecurity': Study," *Toronto Star*, November 2, 2016, https://www.thestar.com/news/gta/2016/11/02/nearly-40-per-cent-of-canadian-post-secondary-students-experience-food-insecurity-study.html.

21 Silverthorn, "Hungry for Knowledge," 14–15.

22 HIV.gov, "The Global HIV/AIDS Epidemic," July 7, 2020, https://www.hiv.gov/hiv-basics/overview/data-and-trends/global-statistics.

23 UNWomen, "Facts and Figures: HIV and AIDS," 2018, http://www.unwomen.org/en/what-we-do/hiv-and-aids/facts-and-figures.

24 Centers for Disease Control, "COVID-19 in Racial and Ethnic Minority Groups," 2020, https://www.cdc.gov/coronavirus/2019-ncov/need-extra-precautions/racial-ethnic-minorities.html.

25 Lisa Hornak and Erin Stone, "The Next Wave of Climate Refugees," *The Atlantic*, 2019, https://www.theatlantic.com/video/index/591832/climate-refugees.

26 Elizabeth Kolbert, "Louisiana's Disappearing Coast," *The New Yorker*, March 25, 2019, https://www.newyorker.com/magazine/2019/04/01/louisianas-disappearing-coast.

27 Jessica Leann Urban, "Interrogating Privilege/Challenging the 'Greening of Hate,'" *International Feminist Journal of Politics* 9, no. 2 (2007): 251–64.

28 See, for example, Jamie J. Hagen, "Queering Women, Peace and Security," *International Affairs* 92, no. 2 (2016): 313–32.

29 Jean Friedman-Rudovsky, "The Women Who Bear the Scars of Sierra Leone's Civil War," *The Telegraph*, November 16, 2013, https://www.telegraph.co.uk/news/worldnews/africaandindianocean/sierraleone/10450619/The-women-who-bear-the-scars-of-Sierra-Leones-civil-war.html.

30 Neta C. Crawford, "Emotions and International Security: Cave! Hic Libido," *Critical Studies on Security* 1, no. 1 (2013): 121.

31 Ronni Alexander, "Popoki, What Color Is Peace? Exploring Critical Approaches to Thinking, Imagining and Expressing Peace with the Cat, Popoki," *Factis Pax* 2, no. 2 (2008): 211–28; Ronni Alexander, "Remembering Hiroshima: Bio-Politics, Popoki and Sensual Expressions of War," *International Feminist Journal of Politics* 14, no. 2 (2012): 202–22.

32 Sarah Kruger, "Rwanda's Sounds of Genocide," *Houston Chronicle*, September 23, 2007, https://www.chron.com/opinion/outlook/article/Rwanda-s-sounds-of-genocide-1839647.php.

33 *Irish Times*, "Besim Lives to Recount His Story of Kosovo War Survival," March 23, 2000, https://www.irishtimes.com/news/besim-lives-to-recount-his-story-of-kosovo-war-survival-1.258704.

34 Cynthia Enloe, "Womenandchildren: Making Feminist Sense of the Persian Gulf Crisis," *The Village Voice*, September 25, 1990.

35 Anne Frank, *Diary of a Young Girl: The Definitive Edition*, eds. Otto H. Frank and Mirjam Pressler, trans. Susan Massotty (New York: Doubleday, 2010), 162.

36 Lene Hansen, "The Little Mermaid's Silent Security Dilemma and the Absence of Gender in the Copenhagen School," *Millennium* 29, no. 2 (2000): 285–306.

37 Buzan, Wæver, and de Wilde, *Security*.

38 Alison Howell and Melanie Richter-Montpetit, "Is Securitization Theory Racist? Civilizationism, Methodological Whiteness, and Antiblack Thought in the Copenhagen School," *Security Dialogue* 51, no. 1 (2020): 3–22.

39 Michael C. Williams, "Words, Images, Enemies: Securitization and International Politics," *International Studies Quarterly* 47, no. 5 (2003): 512.

40 Whitehouse.gov, "National Security & Defense," 2019, https://www.whitehouse.gov/issues/national-security-defense.

41 Wibben, *Feminist Security Studies*, 2.

42 Wibben, *Feminist Security Studies*, loc. 2298.

43 Wibben, *Feminist Security Studies*, loc. 2688.

RESOURCES AND SUGGESTIONS FOR FURTHER READING

Alexander, Ronni. "Popoki, What Color Is Peace? Exploring Critical Approaches to Thinking, Imagining, and Expressing Peace with the Cat, Popoki." *Factis Pax* 2, no. 2 (2008); 211–28. *This piece talks about the different ways security can be read and experienced.*

Crenshaw, Kimberlé. "Demarginalizing the Intersection of Race and Sex: A Black Feminist Critique of Antidiscrimination Doctrine, Feminist Theory, and Antiracist Politics." In *Feminist Legal Theory: Readings in Law and Gender*, edited by Katharine T. Bartlett, 57–80. London: Routledge, 1989. *This piece is one of the foundational writings of intersectional feminism and includes many of the principles used in this chapter to frame an intersectional approach to security.*

Hagen, Jamie J. "Queering Women, Peace, and Security." *International Affairs* 92, no. 2 (2016): 313–32. *This essay talks about the intersection of gender and sexuality in the women, peace, and security (WPS) agenda.*

Wibben, Annick T.R. *Feminist Security Studies: A Narrative Approach*. London: Routledge, 2010. *This book outlines a decolonial feminist approach to theorizing security narratives.*

CHAPTER FIFTEEN

International Law and Human Rights

Dr. Malliga
Och

Dr. Susanne
Zwingel

LEARNING OBJECTIVES

1 Explain the importance of statism for international law and recall the sources and types of international law
2 Explain the history and conceptualization of human rights
3 Identify the core international human rights instruments
4 Analyze and evaluate the claim of universalism in international law and human rights

KEY TERMS

crimes against humanity   acts that are purposely committed as part of a widespread or systematic attack directed against a civilian population

customary international law   rules that result from the long-term practice of states based on what they consider to be their legal obligations

general principles   international legal principles recognized by nations

genocide   the intentional action to destroy a people – usually defined as an ethnic, national, racial, or religious group – in whole or in part

human rights   a set of rights that all human beings are entitled to without discrimination in order to live in dignity and free from fear and want

Indigenous peoples   ethnic groups who are the earliest known inhabitants of an area, in contrast to groups who occupied or colonized these areas later. Indigenous rights claims condemn exploitation through colonialism and aim at collective self-determination.

international conventions and treaties   written agreements between two (bilateral) or more (multilateral) states

International Court of Justice   the main judicial body of the United Nations that settles disputes between states

International Criminal Court   an intergovernmental organization and international tribunal with the jurisdiction to prosecute individuals for genocide, crimes against humanity, war crimes, and the crime of aggression

international law   legal rules that regulate the relationship among states

international organizations   organizations established by a formal intergovernmental treaty, charter, or statute between three or more states with activities in several states

public versus private spheres   areas of public interests, most commonly business and politics, versus areas of home and family

self-determination   the right of nations and states to determine their own internal and external affairs and organization

slavery   any system in which principles of property law are applied to people, allowing individuals to own, buy, and sell other individuals

socioeconomic rights   rights that allow a dignified life free from material want, including access to housing, decent working conditions, social security, and education and absence of child labor

statism   the idea that states are central to the functioning and working of the international system

torture   the act of deliberately inflicting severe physical or psychological suffering on a person for the purposes of obtaining information, punishment, intimidation, or coercion carried out or tolerated by state officials

universalism   the assumption that some ideas have general applicability or moral standing. It is a position that is often criticized or rejected as disguised particularism (e.g., Western-centrism, a worldview centered on and biased toward Western civilization).

war crimes   actions carried out during the conduct of war that violate accepted international rules of war, including intentionally killing civilians or prisoners, committing rape, and recruiting child soldiers

women's rights   entitlements of women and girls to live as autonomous and self-determined as men and boys; requires overcoming *androcentrism*, meaning attitudes and practices that universalize male perspectives and thereby marginalize or subordinate female perspectives

WHAT IS INTERNATIONAL LAW?

The most enduring feature of international affairs is anarchy, the absence of a world government. Yet the absence of a world government does not mean that international affairs is steeped in chaos and unpredictability. Quite the contrary, global affairs are characterized by a dense network of rules, norms, and expectations that govern the behavior of states. In this chapter, we will discuss how international law and international human rights law provides guideposts for the behavior of states not only in how they treat each other but also in how they are expected to treat people. By setting up legal standards and expectations, international law and international human rights law mediate the effects of anarchy, making international affairs a little bit more predictable and regulated.

International law is mostly written with states in mind. Despite the existence of other global actors such as international non-governmental organizations, transnational activist networks, and transnational corporations, states are the fundamental building blocks of international relations now and in the foreseeable future. Thus, international law sets the standards for what states can and cannot do.

States as Building Blocks of International Law

The building blocks of **international law** are states and **international organizations** (which are made up of states, and which will be discussed extensively in the next chapter); only very recently and under special conditions have other entities, such as individuals, become subject to international law. **Statism**, the idea that states are central to the functioning and working of the international system, is the basis of international law. International law thus governs the relationship between states and determines what states can or cannot do in international politics.[1]

States display several characteristics: They dispose of a territory, a population, a government, and they are politically independent and recognized by other states. States are sovereign entities with exclusive control over their territory. This means that interference of external actors in their inner affairs is not allowed. International law therefore focuses on relations *between* states and recognizes statehood as the *only form* of political representation. For example, international trade law describes how trade ought to occur among *states* – not individual companies. Likewise, *states* – not individuals, groups, or companies – are members of international trade organizations such as the World Trade Organization or the International Monetary Fund.

As today's world is mostly made up of states, it might not appear necessary to mention this basic function of the state in international law. However, international law has developed over time, and states were created along the way. The idea of state sovereignty first took root among European states as a form of mutual recognition of their territories and sovereignties. When European powers set out to colonize territories and peoples all over the globe, they denied such recognition to non-European peoples and rather declared them less than human (or "uncivilized") and the spaces they inhabited as not occupied (the principle of *terra nullius*).[2]

Based on this construction of inferiority, Europeans then assumed the land was there for them to claim. Centuries later, it required massive decolonization movements to create independent states in Latin America, Africa, and Asia. The territories of many of these states followed the borders drawn by colonial powers, not the will of the people inhabiting them. Further, statism has replaced other modes of political organization that are *not* based on exclusive territorial control. Such types of collaborative use of land are practiced by many **Indigenous peoples** around the world. They are based on the understanding of human dependency on their land, which creates a sacred relationship to the land and requires preservation rather than exploitation of resources, and on the willingness to share resources in ways that are beneficial to all parties involved (see Box 15.1).

BOX 15.1: INDIGENOUS NOTIONS OF SELF-DETERMINATION

The tension between state sovereignty and Indigenous self-determination can be seen in the story of Cayuga chief Deskaheh's European visit … to the League of Nations in 1923. In his capacity as the Speaker of the Six Nations of the Haudenosaunee, he felt compelled to make the long trans-Atlantic journey as conflicts between the Haudenosaunee and Canadian peoples had reached an impasse. He felt it unjust that his people were being imprisoned for protesting the Canadian state's imposition of its self-declared sovereignty over their lands, claiming it to be tantamount to an invasion and stating that "we are determined to live the free people that we were born" … The lands were, and still are, subject to treaties expressing an alternative vision of shared authority over shared lands and mutual respect between peoples as equal nations cooperatively governing the same territory – an idea that is largely antithetical to the Westphalian vision of exclusive territorial authority by one people … Chief Deskaheh's appeals fell on deaf ears … as the states concerned refused to interfere in the domestic affairs of one of their peers, namely Canada.[3]

In sum, the category of "state" is more complicated than we may at first think; it does include the notion of sovereignty and **self-determination**, but it is also a product of colonial conquest and violent extermination of other forms of political organization. Hence, it is useful to think of the state not so much as a universal form of political organization, but a historically grown concept that has embodied the idea of "self-rule" to varying degrees.

Sources of International Law

Unlike domestic law enforcement, there is no world government that establishes and enforces laws globally. Instead, international law stems from four sources as recognized by Article 38 of the **International Court of Justice** statute: international conventions and treaties, customary international law, general principles, and precedent.

International conventions and treaties are written agreements between states. Bilateral treaties are agreements between two states. For example, the United States and Russia have committed themselves to a number of bilateral arms control agreements, including the New Start Treaty to reduce and limit strategic offensive arms in 2011. Multilateral treaties are treaties that bind more than two states and are deposited with the United Nations, which was established in 1945 to preserve international security and world peace. To date, over 560 multilateral treaties have been registered with the United Nations Office of Legal Affairs covering topics as diverse as narcotic drugs, law of the sea, the environment, and educational and cultural matters. In theory, treaties apply to all people equally; in practice, this is not always the case – as you will see in Box 15.2.

BOX 15.2: THE OTTAWA TREATY

The Convention on the Prohibition of the Use, Stockpiling, Production and Transfer of Anti-Personnel Mines and on their Destruction (also known as Ottawa Treaty or Mine Ban Treaty) was negotiated over a course of several meetings in 1997 and came into effect six months after 40 states had ratified the treaty (Article 17). State parties commit themselves to abstain from using, producing/developing/acquiring, or assisting in the use of anti-personnel mines. In addition, states are required to destroy any remaining anti-personnel mine arsenals (Article 1). The Ottawa Treaty also includes a reporting mechanism detailing the number and location of anti-personnel mines and measures adopted to comply with the treaty's obligations (Article 7) and allows for fact-finding missions to verify treaty compliance (Article 8). Finally, the Ottawa Treaty is of unlimited duration (Article 20).

At first look, the issue of landmines seems gender neutral – after all, landmines kill people indiscriminately. Yet in reality, landmines affect men and women differently: Gender determines the likelihood of individuals becoming victims of landmines and determines access to care afterwards.[4] Women's and men's risks to landmines differ based on their economic responsibilities: Women are more likely to fall victims to landmines when they gather water, firewood, or food, while men are more likely to step on landmines when traveling on public roads. Similarly, in countries where female literacy is low, women and girls are less likely to be well-informed about the risks that landmines present as they cannot read educational materials.

Overall, women and girls make up the minority of landmine victims worldwide. Yet when women are injured by landmines, they are more likely to become isolated from their community and cast aside by their families, especially if they become disabled because they are now considered a burden to their families, unable to take care of household and familial chores. At the same time, women are the majority of indirect victims as they are the ones who need to take care of family members injured by landmines, often without financial support that puts them at greater risk for poverty. The Ottawa Treaty thus shows that seemingly gender-neutral issues can have gendered implications that must be addressed if international law aspires to truly be universal in its application.

International treaties are typically negotiated among national delegations with input from experts and civil society actors at international conferences and meetings. Each treaty specifies when it becomes legally binding, what state obligations are, how compliance with treaty provisions will be monitored and measured, and whether there is an end date to the treaty. Once the treaty text is finalized, representatives of the state governments sign the treaty, signifying their intent to follow the treaty's provisions. However, signing a treaty does not make it legally binding. To become legally binding, states must ratify the treaty. Once a specific number of states (the exact number varies by treaty) have done so, the treaty comes into force and is legally binding on all state parties.

The process of ratification is governed by national law. In some states, the signature of the government is sufficient for ratification, while in other states ratification requires parliamentary approval. For example, in the United States both the signature of the president and approval by the US Senate with a two-thirds majority is required to ratify any international treaty. In the case of the Convention on the Elimination of All Forms of Discrimination Against Women (CEDAW), President

Carter signed the treaty in 1980, but the US Senate has never called CEDAW to the floor for a vote. This means that the United States has not ratified CEDAW and that the treaty is not legally binding on the United States, as is the case for only seven other states in the world (the Holy See, Iran, Niue, Palau, Somalia, Sudan, and Tonga).

Customary international law are rules that significant numbers of states follow in practice because they feel a legal obligation to do so. Many of these rules are so fundamental to state behavior that they have never been codified (written down as law) and are referred to as *jus cogens* (fundamental laws), but many of them are also honored in treaties.[5] Prominent examples are the prohibition of **genocide**, **slavery** and the slave trade, **war crimes**, **crimes against humanity**, or appropriation of outer space and celestial bodies.

Because *jus cogens* is so central to international law, violators are often ostracized from the international community and targeted with economic sanctions or military retribution. For example, the prohibition of the use of chemical and biological weapons goes back to 1685 and today has risen to the status of *jus cogens*.[6] When Syria used chemical weapons in August 2013, the reaction by the international community was harsh and swift: The United States considered retaliatory action, several other states called for Syria to hand over its chemical weapons to international oversight for destruction, and the UN General Secretary called Syria's actions a war crime. Even though Syria was not part of most legal international instruments that prohibit the use of chemical weapons, Syria suffered immediate public ostracization for its actions. However, and as the Syrian example demonstrates, most violations of *jus cogens* only draw verbal condemnation rather than military action against the offending state. As a result, violations often continue. In Syria, chemical attacks continue to this day even after the strong worldwide condemnation in 2013.

General principles are legal principles "recognized by civilized nations" (Article 38(1)a ICJ) that are applied to international law. Often, general principles fill in the gap when international treaties or international customary laws do not provide an answer. It is best to think of general principles as largely unwritten rules that everyone follows. One of the oldest legal principles is *pacta sunt servanda* – treaties once made, should be followed. Others include that judges need to be impartial and that a person cannot be held criminally responsible for actions that were not prohibited by law at the time they were committed (principle of *nulla poena sine lege*).

Judicial decisions and scholarly writing "of the most highly qualified publicists of the various nations" (Article 38(1)d ICJ) represent the last source of international law if the issue cannot be adjudicated by the preceding three sources. This means that, on the one hand, past decisions by judges on particular cases can be used as precedents on how to judge similar current cases. On the other hand, court decisions and judges' opinions sometimes reinterpret or broaden the understanding of an international concept because of changed circumstances. For example, that rape as a tool of war is punishable by international law was first recognized when the International Criminal Tribunal for the former Yugoslavia and the International Criminal Tribunal for Rwanda issued court rulings recognizing rape as a crime against humanity, a war crime, and a form of genocide. Keep in mind that most international courts are a blend of the civil law and common law traditions you read about in Chapter 10 – and the civil law tradition is not reliant on precedent.

In 2016, Jean-Pierre Bemba Gombo became the first individual who was ever sentenced by the **International Criminal Court** (ICC) to prison for 18 years for conducting a campaign of rape and murder against thousands of men, women, and children in the Central African Republic from 2002–3. Referring to article 28(a) of the ICC Rome Statute for the crimes against humanity of murder and rape and the war crimes of murder, rape, and pillaging, the ICC recognized rape as a war crime for the first time in history. Unfortunately, in 2018, the Appeals Chamber acquitted Bemba due to trial errors. While the case of Bemba might not have ended as many had hoped, the ICC's decision to hold someone criminally accountable for rape remains historically significant. The ICC is discussed at length in Chapter 16.

Questioning the Universalism and Objectivity of International Law

While international law is often presented as objective and universal (a concept known as **universalism**) and as an antidote to pure power politics among states, this is not completely accurate. For one, laws are never created in a vacuum but reflect political, socioeconomic, and cultural interests within a particular historic context. Think of the slave trade as an example. Before the nineteenth century, the slave trade was not considered illegal. It was only with the 1807 Act for the Abolition of the Slave Trade that the slave trade came to be viewed as prohibited under international law.

As critical theorists rightly point out, international law is both Western-centric (i.e., steeped in Western traditions that are rooted in white culture) and androcentric (i.e., centered on (white) men).[7] Thus, international law needs to be interpreted by not only taking into account who created the law (European white men) but also who it is applied to (non-Western states). Acknowledging the Western- and androcentric nature of international law does not dismiss the value or state-centrism of international law, but instead draws attention to the concerns and states who are marginalized in the international legal order and discourse – namely women and states from the Global South.

Calling international law out for being Western-centric means acknowledging it as a largely European project that evolved over the last 400 years as a byproduct of European nation building and colonial expansion. Rather than seeing the norms, customs, and rules enshrined in international law as universal, it is more accurate to see them as *European* norms, customs, and rules that were first applied *among* European states and later became global standards. This extension was based on the assumption of superiority of Western-centric international law over other forms of legal systems, such as customary law practiced by Indigenous peoples. European colonial expansion as well as the differentiation of humanity into superior and inferior races developed parallel to international law.

The international (i.e., European) community differentiated between civilized and uncivilized nations, considered their own colonial "civilizing mission" of non-European peoples legitimate, and took a long time to recognize non-European states as equals.[8] Consider, for example, Japan's attempt after World War I to include in the Treaty of Versailles a clause about the equality of all nations regardless of race. This proposal was rejected by the majority of the European states negotiating the peace treaty.

Similarly, calling attention to the androcentric nature of international law means acknowledging that international law was written by men, thus silencing and marginalizing the voices of women.[9] First, looking at individuals who are heads of state and government, the absence of women is glaring. As of early 2019, 11 women were serving as heads of state and 10 as heads of government *worldwide*.[10] Likewise, women are notably absent in international decision-making structures, such as international organizations, international courts, or the diplomatic core, which not only govern interstate relations but also the creation and implementation of international law.

This absence is based on the division of societies into a **public sphere** in which men regulate the affairs of society – in other words, where they do politics – and the **private sphere** of the family, in which women play a nurturing and subordinate role. From this division of labor comes a direct connection of women to their husbands and families, and a remote connection to the broader public and the state. While we have seen some challenges of this disconnect between women and public affairs, women remain underrepresented in all public office. This means that international law is created and international legal disputes are settled with little or no input from women, thus ignoring the lived experiences, rights, needs, and interests of women.

Second, international law more often than not privileges male concerns, which are considered "universal," while women's concerns are a special category that is neglected or ignored. Take the prohibition of **torture** as an example. The Convention against Torture and Other Cruel, Inhuman or Degrading Treatment or Punishment (1987) defines torture as

> any act by which severe pain or suffering, whether physical or mental, is intentionally inflicted on a person for such purposes as obtaining from *him* or a third person information or a confession, punishing *him* for an act *he* or a third person has committed or is suspected of having committed, or intimidating or coercing *him* or a third person, or for any reason based on discrimination of any kind, when such pain or suffering is inflicted by or at the instigation of or with the consent or acquiescence *of a public official or other person acting in an official capacity.* (emphasis added)

Note how the legal text refers to *he/him*, indicating that women were not considered to be regular subjects of torture. Likewise, it is only torture when it can be linked to public authorities through either direct involvement or encouragement/ consent of the act. As important as the prohibition against torture is, it does not reflect the experience of women who are most likely to be victims of terror campaigns by militias or subject to violence in their own homes committed by their spouse or other relatives.[11] This is one of many examples of how international law privileges the needs and experiences of men over those of women.

As you may have heard before, and to paraphrase critical theorist Robert Cox, international law is always for someone and for some purpose.[12] To post-colonial legal theorists, international law is for Western powers to enshrine Western dominance, while to feminist legal theorists, international law is for men to preserve male dominance over women. Together, critical legal theory questions the objective and universal nature of international law.

THE CONCEPT OF HUMAN RIGHTS

Just like international law, the concept of human rights originates in a European cultural context. The difference between the two lies in the subjects of concern: International law addresses states and interstate relations; the human rights framework focuses on individual humans and the conditions they require to live dignified lives. These two areas have long been separate from each other, and it took until the war crime tribunals after World War II in Nuremberg and Tokyo to recognize individual responsibility for crimes committed in the name of states (in particular, war crimes and crimes against humanity). Since then, the standing of individuals in international law has become stronger. One expression for this is the 1948 Universal Declaration of Human Rights, the first document of global reach with a focus on individual rights. It is nonetheless important to recognize the conceptual distinction between the two – state sovereignty and relations on the one hand, human dignity on the other.

Background and Conceptualization of Human Rights

Human rights have been described as a vision of "equal citizens endowed with inalienable rights that entitle them to equal concern and respect from the state."[13] The concept of human rights becomes historically relevant during the seventeenth- and eighteenth-century Enlightenment in parts of Europe and the United States. In the American Declaration of Independence of 1776, the basic idea of human rights is laid out as follows: "All men are created equal, that they are endowed by their Creator with certain unalienable rights, that among these are life, liberty and the pursuit of happiness." Over time, the concept has developed: Human rights do not mean the same thing today as they did centuries ago, and people in different parts of the world do not think of human rights in uniform ways. But fundamentally, the aim of human rights is "to realize the worth of human beings in the face of prejudice, discrimination, exploitation, oppression, enslavement, persecution, torture, and extermination."[14] In other words, human rights are more than a concept: They are also a tool to achieve social justice.

Four components are important: First, human beings are seen as individuals. This is radically different from the medieval vision of society as a *body politic* in which everybody had a function within the organic, hierarchal order. Second, each human being has value. Because of this value, humans possess and do not have to earn rights. This entitlement cannot be taken away from them – their rights are "inalienable." Third, all humans are *equally* worthy. Our shared humanity functions as an equalizer, and nobody is of inherently higher or lower value. Fourth, entitlement to rights can only be guaranteed by a powerful actor – that is, the state. However, the state plays an ambivalent role in the human rights framework, as it is also a potential violator of rights, for example when state agents torture people or incarcerate them without reason. Ideally, human rights describe a relationship between the state and individuals in which the state respects, protects, and fulfills the rights of all without discrimination.

Which Rights and Which Humans? Historical Developments

Two of the central questions are which rights should humans have, and should all humans enjoy the same rights? By following some of the prominent human rights struggles in history, we see that the claims made were directed *against* context-specific injustices and *for* particular humans. Over time, both the substance of rights claims and the imagined group of rights bearers has expanded, but limitations and exclusions remain to this day.[15]

The first articulation of human rights (or *droits de l'homme* in French) took place in the context of the American and French Revolutions of the late eighteenth century (1765–83 and 1789, respectively). These revolutions were based on the idea of the British seventeenth-century philosopher John Locke that humans had the right to life, liberty, and property, and that the task of the government was to *serve* these individual rights. However, in the view of the revolutionaries, the French and British governments of the time did the opposite – they arbitrarily abused, killed, and unfairly taxed their subjects.

Therefore, they fought *against* abusive governments and *for* freedom of expression and political participation in public affairs. In this way, governments could be created in the interests of citizens. However, this project of political self-determination was not extended to all. The French political activist Olympe de Gouges demanded that women be granted the same rights as men, but this demand was considered too radical and led to her execution in 1793. Other groups that were not considered full rights holders were men who did not own property, Indigenous inhabitants of territories colonized by European powers, and enslaved people. Jews gained some rights, but their emancipation was contingent on assimilation.

The Haitian Revolution under Toussaint Louverture that started as a slave rebellion against plantation owners and led to Haiti's independence in 1804 is a profoundly relevant, but often unrecognized, part of the human rights struggles of the time. This rebellion was inspired by the French Revolution and the resulting abolishment of slavery in France's colonies. However, Napoleon reinstated slavery in 1802, and Haitian revolutionaries had to fight *against* France to gain independence. In other words, while Black Haitians were first included in the French call for *"liberté, égalité, fraternité"* (liberty, equality, fraternity), this inclusion was soon revoked. At the time, European-descendant, white, middle-class men could see only themselves as autonomous subjects and rights holders. They thought of women as their dependents, the poor and the Jews as inferior, and non-Europeans as subhuman. This means that the (male) subject of the European Enlightenment era was *based on* the devaluation of the female, non-European, and otherwise undesirable other.

Nineteenth- and twentieth-century human rights struggles brought an expanded understanding of humanity as well as of the rights to be enjoyed. Due to increased abolitionist activism in Europe and the Americas, first the slave trade and later slavery itself were legally banned. These steps did not lead to the *de facto* eradication of slavery, but according to the law, humans could not be treated as property anymore. The 1926 Convention to Suppress the Slave Trade and Slavery (ratified to date by 99 states) is an international manifestation of this step.

Women's rights activists across the world also started to articulate their claims to be recognized as full human beings. They mobilized to improve their legal status, both in regard to their subordination in marriage and in public life, to have better access to education and employment, and to gain the right to vote. Many of these activists were European or of European descent, of middle-class status, and internationally connected, but their struggle nevertheless took several generations to bear fruit.

New Zealand's women were the first to gain the right to vote in 1893 (without the right to stand for national elections), and Finland first granted universal women's suffrage in 1906. In the United States, this goal was only achieved in 1920 after over 70 years of struggle, which started in 1848 with the first Women's Rights Convention held in Seneca Falls, New York. There is no doubt that achievements toward full personhood of women have been made, but the concept of *dependent citizenship* is still a reality in many legal systems around the world today. Dependent citizenship means that a woman is not by herself a rights holder but is through her connection to a man who represents her – typically her husband. For example, in Iran and Madagascar, if a non-citizen woman marries a male citizen, she automatically acquires his and loses her own citizenship, and in Jordan and Lebanon, a married mother does not have the same rights as her husband to pass on her citizenship to their children.[16]

Another group that stood up for their rights was the working class. Capitalist industrialization in Western states had created wealth, but also a new impoverished class of workers who owned nothing and had only their labor to sell. Men, women, and children worked long hours in factories under dangerous conditions for minimal pay. Karl Marx exhorted workers in his *Communist Manifesto* of 1848 to fight this misery: "Die Proletarier haben nichts zu verlieren als ihre Ketten. Sie haben eine Welt zu gewinnen. Proletarier aller Länder, vereinigt Euch! [The proletarians have nothing to lose but their chains. They have a world to win. Workers of the world unite!]"[17]

Marx was not the only one to decry the inhumane fate of the working class. Workers' organizations demanded that workers have a voice, which meant universal suffrage, not suffrage contingent on property ownership or formal education.

They articulated new rights that focused on socioeconomic well-being, including access to adequate housing, decent working conditions, limitation of work time, and social security in case of injury, illness, and old age. It was a crucial part of these claims for a better *material* life to free children from hard labor and grant them access to education. This set of rights did not so much ask for "freedom from" an oppressive government but rather for "freedom to" live a dignified life. The state is a crucial guarantor of these rights, for example through labor regulations and investment in public education and healthcare.

Another rights claim that began to be articulated in the early twentieth century was that of *collective* self-determination. As we have seen above, a rights-ensuring state is the crucial base for the enjoyment of individual rights, but at the beginning of the twentieth century, many peoples were not allowed to govern themselves – these included colonized nations in Africa and Asia as well as minorities within existing states in Europe. After World War I, some demands for self-determination were heard and new sovereign states were created, including Poland and Yugoslavia, but others were ignored, including the demand for a Kurdish state. Also, for colonies and so-called mandates and protectorates, overseen mostly by Great Britain and France, it took until the 1960s to reach self-determination, against strong resistance of the colonial powers, which deemed them not capable of self-government.

The development of human rights standards is often described in historical generations – the first being the claim for civil and political rights starting in the eighteenth century, followed by the second generation of economic and social rights articulated in the nineteenth century, and finally the right to collective self-determination, combined with the right to development, as the third generation. This narrative points to the dynamic character of the human rights concept, and to this day the scope of human rights is evolving to include new demands and unrecognized interests. The 2006 adoption of the Convention on the Rights of Persons with Disabilities expresses this dynamism. However, it is noteworthy that there is no convention to protect gender non-conforming individuals, including LGBTQ+ persons, from discrimination. Also, in light of massive anthropogenic environmental degradation, the human rights framework has not – yet – been modified to contain a right to a life-sustaining planet, which is the foundation for the right to life.

The Post–World War II Standard: Drafting and Content of the UDHR

The rise of fascism in Nazi Germany and elsewhere led to the atrocities of World War II as well as to state-committed crimes against humanity and the genocide of the Jews. The massive scale of these crimes triggered the "moral demand" for an international mechanism to protect human rights. Never again should it be possible that a state so blatantly dehumanizes and kills people, including its own citizens. In the context of the newly founded United Nations (1945), with its mission to preserve world peace, the plan to create such an international bill of rights was well placed. Two context factors are important to understand the result of this endeavor.

First, while the process was multilateral, state sovereignty was its most fundamental building block. Sovereign governments were the ones *asked* to follow human rights principles, but they could not be *forced* to do so. In the drafting process, undertaken in the UN Commission on Human Rights under the leadership of Eleanor Roosevelt, it soon became clear that the most powerful states, the United States and the Soviet Union, were not interested in comprehensive, enforceable obligations. In light of this opposition, the commission decided against drafting a binding treaty and resolved to produce a declaration, the Universal Declaration of Human Rights (UDHR), which was adopted in 1948 by the United Nations. The UDHR sets out 30 rights and freedoms that to this date form the basis of international human rights law. In international law, declarations are mere proclamations of states' intents and do not contain legally binding provisions and enforcement mechanisms. While this defeated the original purpose of the endeavor, it may have been a blessing in disguise that the UDHR ended up being a document of ambitious aspirations without enforcement. This non-threatening form has helped create widespread global acceptance of the human rights framework.

The second important factor to understand the outcome of the UDHR is that it was drafted by experts with a wide range of cultural backgrounds. There is no doubt that this group remained rather exclusive, as only 58 states were UN members at the time and could send representatives to the commission. Today, the UN counts over 190 member-states, and many of them were colonies in the 1940s. However, within these parameters a wide range of world civilizations, not only Western viewpoints, were present in the debates, including Egyptian, Chinese, Indian, Russian, Lebanese, Chilean, and South African, among others. During the process, much diligence was applied to synthesizing principles from these diverse cultural traditions.

In the words of Glendon and Kaplan, this led to a "flexible universalism" that included not only individualistic but also collectivist principles, as well as notions of freedom, solidarity, and responsibility.[18] It was of utmost importance for many of the non-Western delegates to connect individual rights and freedoms to duties and respect toward the community. Nevertheless, the possibility of drafting a normative catalog that would universally apply to all humans despite their manifold cultural differences was hotly contested at the time and prominently opposed in a statement issued by the American Anthropological Association (AAA) in 1947. This statement warned that the UDHR would not be universally liberating as intended, but incompatible with and therefore disrespectful of many cultural traditions around the world. The AAA modified this position in its 1999 Declaration on Anthropology and Human Rights.

The UDHR consists of 30 individual articles (see Box 15.3) that should be read as an interdependent whole. Articles 1 through 5 spell out the general meaning of living a life in freedom, security, and without discrimination. Articles 6 to 11 cover legal dimensions, ranging from each person having equal standing before the law to a spectrum of due process rights. Articles 12 to 21 spell out civil rights, including rights to privacy, property, and having a family; rights to freedom of belief, conscience, and expression; and political participation rights. Articles 14 and 15 on the right to seek asylum and a nationality are a reaction to the displacement and statelessness caused by World War II. Articles 22 to 27 represent the right to basic socioeconomic well-being. The last articles specify the need for an international, not only national, order to enhance human rights and determine limitations of rights for individuals and duties toward their communities. One could say that the UDHR collects diverse rights claims that had been made over time and integrates them into a comprehensive whole. However, it is not a strong document when it comes to collective self-determination, and it does not address its own inherent tension between human rights protection of individuals and the prerogative of state sovereignty.

BOX 15.3: THE ARTICLES OF THE UNIVERSAL DECLARATION OF HUMAN RIGHTS

Article 1: "All human beings are born free and equal in dignity and rights."

Article 2: Prohibition of discrimination

Article 3: Right to life, liberty, and security

Article 4–5: Prohibition of slavery and torture

Article 6–7: Recognition as a person and equal treatment before the law

Article 8–11: Due process rights (effective remedy, prohibition of arbitrary arrest or exile, fair and public hearing by independent tribunal in case of criminal charges, right to be presumed innocent until proven guilty)

Article 12: Right to privacy

Article 13: Freedom of movement

Article 14–15: Right to seek asylum and to a nationality

Article 16: Right to marry and have a family

Article 17: Right to own property

Article 18–19: Freedom of thought and religion, opinion and expression

Article 20: Freedom of assembly

Article 21: Right to participation in government and elections

Article 22: Right to social security and realization of economic, social, and cultural rights

Article 23–24: Right to decent work without discrimination, to form trade unions, and to rest and leisure

Article 25: Right to a decent standard of living

Article 26: Right to education

Article 27: Right to participate in cultural life and to intellectual property

Article 28–30: Right to international order conducive to human rights; duties to the community and limits of rights; prohibition of destruction of any right listed

The UDHR was not greeted with universal enthusiasm. While the large majority of UN member-states (48) voted in favor, eight abstained and two did not vote at all; yet no state directly opposed its adoption. Also, there have been reactions to the UDHR that question its universal character, such as the Cairo Declaration on Human Rights in Islam issued by the Organization of Islamic Cooperation (OIC) in 1990. This declaration – which is a statement by the OIC and should not be confused with a general Muslim perspective on human rights – declares Islamic sharia law as the source of all human rights. This means that some rights enshrined in the UDHR are adapted to the norms enshrined in the sharia; for example, freedom of expression is granted as long as the views expressed are not in contradiction to the principles of the sharia. In general, the UDHR enjoys wide support around the world, to the degree that many scholars now consider it customary international law. It also holds the record of being the most translated document in the world – as of 2020, into 523 languages!

Steps of Codification and Clarification of Rights since the UDHR

The UDHR is a crucial normative point of departure, but as we have seen it is not legally binding for states. What is more, the declaration does not spell out the responsibilities that states have to promote, protect, and fulfill human rights – rather, it simply lists the rights humans should be able to enjoy. Hannah Arendt famously criticized this undertaking. Based on her experience of statelessness as a Jew fleeing Nazi Germany, a declaration of rights made no sense unless the rights in it could be guaranteed. In her view, only a state could ensure for its citizens "the right to have rights" (and would most likely deny such privilege to anybody else).[19] Following this logic, the UDHR was supplemented with legally binding human rights treaties that spell out state responsibilities and that have, over time, added further dimensions to the human rights catalog.

The acceptance through ratification of these treaties is a free decision of each state. Once taken, a state indeed assumes a legal responsibility. Also, all human rights treaties contain a monitoring procedure in which a committee of experts periodically assesses each state party's progress and state of compliance with the treaty. While evidence exists that this dialogue between states and expert committees trigger some positive changes, a large gap between rhetorical adherence to and actual realization of human rights nevertheless persists in many states.

The nine UN human rights treaties that currently exist (see Table 15.1) do different things. The covenants on civil and political rights and on economic, social, and cultural rights (ICCPR and ICESCR of 1966) specify state responsibilities *related to the entire scope of the UDHR*, even if they do so in the separation that was characteristic for the time of capitalist–socialist bloc confrontation: Capitalist states emphasized the importance of civil and political rights, and socialist states as well as many newly independent states focused on **socioeconomic rights**. The major difference is that a state that grants civil and political rights refrains from violating individual rights (such as freedom of expression), but it does not support individuals to live a materially dignified life; a state that focuses on the latter provides access to resources such as housing and healthcare but considers individual expression rights secondary. Many states combine these two imperatives. Together, the UDHR and the two covenants are often referred to as the *international bill of rights*.

Two treaties focus on one particular dimension of the UDHR, namely the Conventions against Torture (CAT of 1984) and against Enforced Disappearance (CPED of 2006). Forced disappearance is not mentioned in the UDHR, yet since the 1970s it has become a particularly heinous tactic of oppressive regimes who clandestinely capture thousands of their opponents and make them disappear. Torture also became an urgent area of human rights protection because of its massive use in dictatorships. However, its use is unfortunately also widespread among democratic regimes – between 2009 and 2013, Amnesty International received reports of torture in 141 states from all world regions.

The other five treaties look at the human rights catalog from the perspective of a particular constituency whose concerns are not sufficiently considered under the UDHR. These are the Conventions against Racial Discrimination (CERD of

Table 15.1. **The UN Human Rights Treaties**

Treaty	Entered into force	State parties
International Convention on the Elimination of All Forms of Racial Discrimination (ICERD)	1969	182
International Covenant on Civil and Political Rights (ICCPR)	1976	173
International Covenant on Economic, Social, and Cultural Rights (ICESCR)	1976	170
Convention on the Elimination of All Forms of Discrimination against Women (CEDAW)	1981	189
Convention against Torture and Other Cruel, Inhuman or Degrading Treatment or Punishment (CAT)	1987	169
Convention on the Rights of the Child (CRC)	1990	196
International Convention on Protection of the Rights of All Migrant Workers and Members of Their Families (ICMRW)	1990	55
Convention on the Rights of Persons with Disabilities (CRPD)	2006	180
International Convention for the Protection of All Persons from Enforced Disappearance (CPED)	2006	62

Source: United Nations Treaty Collection, https://treaties.un.org; state parties as of October 2019.

1965), Convention on the Elimination of All Forms of the Discrimination Against Women (CEDAW of 1979), Convention on the Rights of the Child (CRC of 1989), International Convention on Protection of the Rights of All Migrant Workers and Members of Their Families (ICRMW of 1990), and the Convention on the Rights of Persons with Disabilities (CRPD of 2006).

All of these conventions implicitly make the point that the "general" human rights framework oversees the most pressing needs of specific groups. In reaction, these conventions have reconsidered what human rights mean from the particular perspective of racial minorities, women, and so on, and as a result they have integrated new issues into the human rights framework. For example, CERD addresses discrimination against Black and other non-white people by requiring state parties to repeal any discriminatory laws, including non-discriminatory policies or laws that nevertheless have discriminatory effects;[20] the CRC focuses on the right of the child to be protected and to develop into a full human being, a pair of concerns that sometimes have to be weighed against each other; and the CRPD demands inclusion and support for self-determined living for people with disabilities rather than separation and external control. These interventions have also shown that there is no "general" human rights framework if the needs of particular groups of humans are not included. Hence, they have increased recognition of intersectional forms of discrimination and significantly improved the human rights framework.

The development of the women's rights catalog is a good example of this improvement. Women's issues were long seen as development issues rather than rights issues within the United Nations. This changed at the 1993 UN Conference on Human Rights in Vienna. At that conference, violence against women was framed for the first time as a human rights violation – this means that individual incidents of violence against women are understood as part of a larger misogynistic structure, that this structure is unacceptable, and that states have the duty to work against it.[21] For women, it means that they are not just victims, but that they have a right to protection from gender-based violence.

We already mentioned that there is no world government that can enforce laws. Instead, human rights treaties usually establish a monitoring body, which brings together human rights experts, that is tasked with monitoring compliance with treaty standards and enforcing compliance when states are found in violation of the treaty. For example, under CEDAW it is possible to bring complaints to the monitoring committee of CEDAW if a state is believed to violate the rules of CEDAW and call on the committee to enforce the responsibilities of the state under the convention.

In 2008, a complaint against Brazil was brought to the committee regarding the state's responsibility for the death of an Afro-Brazilian women from complications during childbirth (*Pimentel v. Brazil*). The committee held that the state had not taken its responsibility to prevent maternal mortality seriously because its reproductive health services infrastructure was insufficient. Further, poor Afro-Brazilian women were at additional risk because their neighborhoods were particularly underserved. At the time, Brazil took the CEDAW committee's assessment seriously, compensated the complainant (the mother of the deceased), and made efforts to improve its health infrastructure. Of course, enforcement of any human rights standards depends on the willingness of the offending state to address the issue; in many cases, demands are ignored as monitoring bodies have few resources and little leverage to force a state into compliance outside of public shaming.

In the past decades, several other collectives have mobilized to add their claims but are not (yet) represented in their own human rights treaties. Two prominent movements include Indigenous peoples and LGBTQ+ individuals. For the former, the most important rights are collective self-determination, preservation of traditions, and connection to ancestral lands. This vision of human dignity stands in sharp contrast to a world based on statehood, as many states were built based on the exclusion and even extermination of Indigenous populations. For LGBTQ+ people, the most important right is to be respected as complete human beings and not devalued as deviations from the heteronormative (cis-heterosexual) standard. As it stands, the claims of both LGBTQ+ individuals and Indigenous peoples have met with resistance in many parts of the world, but the UN human rights framework has also offered a stage to articulate concerns that were previously silenced. The formulation of the Yogyakarta principles (2006) as well as the Declaration of the Rights of Indigenous Peoples (2007) are a testament to that.

CURRENT CHALLENGES AND CONCLUDING ASSESSMENT

As this overview has shown, human rights are a concept in development, and controversies over their coverage and subjects of entitlement have been ongoing. At the present moment, human rights are increasingly connected to environmental concerns. The right of future generations to a healthy environment that enables their survival is, after all, the most fundamental of all rights: the right to life. It is hard to think about this right in the traditional human rights concept of state responsibility toward the individual. In essence, this claim is a criticism not of a particular state but of the collective human lifestyle that has been depleting natural resources to a degree that the foundations of future human life are in jeopardy. It is a claim that fundamentally questions the centrality of the human species (or *anthropocentrism*) on the planet in the face of the rapid extermination of species through human influence, and it demands radical transformation of human behavior. It is doubtful if a rights framework, or rather one of collective responsibility, is a more suitable tool to reach this goal.

However, even if we stay within the parameters of anthropocentrism, there are sufficient controversies between the different dimensions of human rights. Many voices from non-Western contexts consider the human rights approach too individualistic and representative of Western rather than universal values. For example, the 1990s debate on "Asian values" painted a picture of Asian societies as oriented toward the common good rather than individual status. Sometimes such criticism is not convincing, especially when articulated by authoritarian leaders who use it to justify their own governments' human rights abuses. But many critics of human rights put a finger on human suffering that the rights framework has a hard time including, especially when this suffering is a result of global hierarchical structures and not of a clearly identifiable "evil" perpetrator. Examples include child mortality from lack of clean water and sanitation (a far too common experience among the world's poor) or civilian casualties resulting from military interventions and drone wars. Note that in the latter case, these interventions are justified by protecting other humans' lives.

On a more positive note, the human rights framework has also provided synergies between different grievances. For example, the idea that women should not be subordinated to men paves the way for questioning oppressive heteronormative standards, and the right of children to develop goes hand in hand with the right to a future healthy environment. Human rights have also served for countless activists around the world to make justice and equality claims, most of which have to do with recognition, respect, and access to resources for a dignified life. Clearly, human rights are not the only ethical lens that can support struggles for justice. But all things considered, the greatest achievement of human rights thinking and activism has been to help increase cultures of mutual respect – between state and individual, but also among the diverse members of the human family.

SUMMARY

- International law governs the relationship between states and determines what states can or cannot do in international politics.
- International human rights law specifies how states must treat their citizens and protect them from human rights abuses so that all human beings can lead a dignified life.
- States are both violators and protectors of human rights.
- International law is far from objective and universal, since laws are never created in a vacuum but reflect political, socioeconomic, and cultural interests within a particular historical context. International law is both Western-centric (focused on the needs and interests of the West) and androcentric (reflects the experiences and will of men) while being applied to the Global South and women who had little say in the creation of the legal order or international treaties that are applied to them.
- Human rights – or the question of who is considered human – have changed and expanded over time. Today, there are several human rights treaties that address the human rights of specific groups such as women, the disabled, children, racial minorities, or migrant workers. Other groups, such as Indigenous peoples and the LGBTQ+ community, are still fighting to be recognized as humans under the human rights framework.
- Globally, violations of civil and political human rights, such as torture or extrajudicial killings, receive most of the attention as these violations are done by states against mostly male citizens. In contrast, socioeconomic and cultural human rights abuses are often ignored as these largely affect women and minorities and are perpetrated by private citizens and thus do not fit neatly into the state-centric and androcentric nature of the international system.
- The universality of the Universal Declaration of Human Rights – and human rights in general – has been contested by those questioning whether there can be a moral framework that fits all humans or if instead legitimate moral standards must arise from specific cultural contexts.

CONCLUDING QUESTIONS

1 Because international law governs the relationship between states, the andro-centric nature of international law is inconsequential. Discuss.
2 How do we know that an international norm has risen to the status of *jus cogens*?
3 What do you think is the reason that the international community has yet to create a binding human rights treaty for LGBTQ+ or Indigenous peoples?
4 The Universal Declaration of Human Rights together with the ICCPR and ICE-SCR are sufficient to guarantee human rights to all humans. Discuss.
5 The Black Lives Matter, Me Too, and Bring Back Our Girls movements are all examples of how human rights are still under threat today. Discuss.
6 Climate justice is a universal human right. Discuss.

NOTES

1 Beth Simmons, "International Law," in *Handbook of International Relations*, eds. Walter Carlsnaes, Thomas Risse, and Beth A. Simmons, 352–78 (Thousand Oaks, CA: Sage Publications, 2013).
2 Simmons, "International Law."
3 Jeff Corntassel and Marc Woons, "Indigenous Perspectives," in *International Relations Theory*, eds. Stephen McGlinchey, Rosie Walters, and Christian Scheipflug, 131–7 (Bristol, UK: E-International Relations Publishing, 2017).
4 Edward Laws, "The Impact of Mines and Explosive Remnants of War on Gender Groups," 2017, https://assets.publishing.service.gov.uk/media/59844e0c40f0b61e4b00005c/149 -the-impact-of-mines-and-explosive-remnants-of-war-on-gender-groups__1_.pdf.
5 Marjorie M. Whiteman, "*Jus Cogens* in International Law, with a Projected List," *Georgia Journal of International and Comparative Law* 7 (1977): 609.
6 Charles Hyun, "The Prohibition of Chemical Weapons: Moving toward *Jus Cogens* Status," *Southern California Law Review* 88 (2014): 1463.
7 Maja Zehfuss, "Critical Theory, Poststructuralism, and Postcolonialism," in *Handbook of International Relations*, eds. Walter Carlsnaes, Thomas Risse, and Beth Simmons, 145–69 (Thousand Oaks, CA: Sage Publications, 2013).
8 Antony Anghie, "The Evolution of International Law: Colonial and Postcolonial Realities," *Third World Quarterly* 27, no. 5 (2006): 739–53.
9 Hilary Charlesworth, "Feminist Methods in International Law," *American Journal of International Law* 93, no. 2 (1999): 379–94; Hilary Charlesworth, Christine Chinkin, and Shelley Wright, "Feminist Approaches to International Law," *American Journal of International Law* 85, no. 4 (1991): 613–45; Fernando R. Teson, "Feminism and International Law: A Reply," *Virginia Journal of International Law* 33 (1992): 647.

10 UN Women, "Facts and Figures: Leadership and Political Participation," United Nations, 2019, http://www.unwomen.org/en/what-we-do/leadership-and-political-participation/facts-and-figures.

11 Mark Ellis, "Breaking the Silence: Rape as an International Crime," *Case Western Research Journal of International Law* 38 (2006): 225.

12 Robert W. Cox, "Social Forces, States and World Orders: Beyond International Relations Theory," *Millennium* 10, no. 2 (1981): 126–55.

13 Jack Donnelly, *Universal Human Rights in Theory and Practice* (Ithaca, NY: Cornell University Press, 2013), 71.

14 Pauls Gordon Lauren, "History of Human Rights," in *Encyclopedia of Human Rights*, ed. David P. Forsythe, 394–407 (New York: Oxford University Press, 2009), 394.

15 For more on the history of human rights, see Ratna Kapur, "Human Rights in the 21st Century: Take a Walk on the Dark Side," in *Wronging Rights?*, 28–65 (India: Routledge, 2012); Lauren, "History of Human Rights."

16 Equality Now, "Report: Ending Sexism in Nationality Laws," 2016, https://www.equalitynow.org/report_ending_sexism_in_nationality_laws.

17 Karl Marx and Friederich Engels, *The Communist Manifesto* (1848).

18 Mary Ann Glendon and Seth D. Kaplan, "Renewing Human Rights," *First Things* 290 (2019): 1–10.

19 Hannah Arendt, "The Decline of the Nation-State and the End of the Rights of Man," in *The Origins of Totalitarianism*, 267–302 (Orlando, FL: Harcourt Brace & Company, 1973).

20 Audrey Daniel, "The Intent Doctrine and CERD: How the United States Fails to Meet Its International Obligations in Racial Discrimination Jurisprudence," *DePaul Journal of Social Justice* 4 (2010): 263.

21 Dorothy McBride Stetson, "Human Rights for Women: International Compliance with a Feminist Standard," *Women & Politics* 15, no. 3 (1995): 71–95.

RESOURCES AND SUGGESTIONS FOR FURTHER READING

Indigenous Peoples and the United Nations Human Rights System. 2013. https://www.ohchr.org/Documents/Publications/fs9Rev.2.pdf.

International Campaign to Ban Landmines. http://www.icbl.org/en-gb/home.aspx.

LGBTQ+ Rights: Born Free and Equal. https://www.ohchr.org/Documents/Publications/BornFreeAndEqualLowRes.pdf.

Living Free and Equal. https://www.ohchr.org/Documents/Publications/LivingFreeAndEqual.pdf.

The Prosecutor v. Jean-Pierre Bemba Gombo. ICC case information. https://www.icc-cpi.int/car/bemba.

United Nations Human Rights Office of the High Commissioner. https://www.ohchr.org/EN/Pages/Home.aspx.

United Nations Treaty Collection. https://treaties.un.org.

UN Women. http://www.unwomen.org/en.

CHAPTER SIXTEEN

International Organizations

Dr. Jillienne Haglund

LEARNING OBJECTIVES

1 Identify some of the most prominent intergovernmental organizations (IGOs) and describe their structure, design, and purpose
2 Describe the challenge of global governance for international organizations
3 Evaluate the influence of IGO design on the globally governed
4 Describe and assess the role of international non-governmental organizations in global governance

KEY TERMS

austerity measures   policies that aim to reduce government budget deficits, including spending cuts and tax increases; often used by governments that find it difficult to pay their debts

balance of payments   the difference in total value between payments into and out of a country over a period

distributional problems   problems resulting from the existence of one or more possible cooperative agreements in which some actors benefit more than others

export-processing zones   areas within developing countries that offer incentives and a barrier-free environment to promote economic growth and attract foreign investment for export-oriented production

global governance   cooperative problem-solving arrangements usually structured as a set of rules or institutions, often taking the form of formal international organizations

intergovernmental organizations (IGOs)   formal organizations with members from multiple states that place a variety of obligations on states in pursuit of a common goal

loan conditionality   conditions placed on loans by the International Monetary Fund, often requiring loan recipients to make adjustments to national economic policies

mandate   obligations specified by IGOs, often in an official agreement or treaty, and required of states

multinational corporation   an enterprise that operates in a number of countries with production or service facilities outside its country of origin

non-governmental organizations (NGOs)   private, voluntary organizations whose members are individuals, groups, or associations from more than one country who come together in pursuit of a common goal or purpose

subsidies   a sum of money granted by the government to assist an industry or business so that the price of a commodity can remain low or competitive

veto power   the ability to prevent the passage of a measure through a unilateral act, such as a single negative vote

Washington Consensus   a collection of policy recommendations generally advocated by economists and policymakers in the Global North, including trade liberalization, privatization, and openness to foreign investment, among others

WHAT ARE INTERNATIONAL ORGANIZATIONS?

International organizations (IOs) provide the basic architecture of global governance in world politics. **Global governance** is defined as the development of cooperative problem-solving arrangements to achieve a common goal or outcome. Cooperative problem-solving arrangements are usually structured as a set of rules or institutions and often take the form of formal international organizations. States join international organizations to facilitate cooperation around significant global problems and challenges, such as managing threats to international peace and security, the continued threat of global terrorism, international economic stability, the protection of human rights, and climate change, among various other issues.

International organizations generally fall into two broad categories, intergovernmental organizations (IGOs) and non-governmental organizations (NGOs). IGOs, like the United Nations (UN) and International Monetary Fund (IMF), represent some of the most important and powerful IOs globally. **Intergovernmental organizations** are formal organizations with members from multiple states that place a variety of obligations on states in pursuit of a common goal. The UN, for example, represents a formal organization with a variety of goals, including the maintenance of international peace and security, and obligates states to dedicate resources toward this goal.

States, not individuals, make up the membership of IGOs, and members work to resolve global issues collectively by gathering and disseminating information, providing a forum for the exchange of views and ideas, defining appropriate standards of behavior, creating rules and legally binding treaties, and supervising compliance with rules and imposing punishment, among other activities. For an international organization to be considered an IGO, it should consist of at least three member-states, hold plenary sessions at least once every 10 years, and possess a permanent secretariat and headquarters. Scholars have identified nearly 500 IGOs globally.[1]

The second type of international organization, **non-governmental organizations**, are typically private, voluntary organizations whose members are individuals, groups, or associations from more than one country who come together often in pursuit of a common goal or purpose, such as greater protection of human rights, better protection of the environment, or greater provision of humanitarian aid. Examples of NGOs range from Amnesty International to Greenpeace to the International Committee of the Red Cross and Red Crescent Societies.

The key difference between IGOs and NGOs involves membership and power. Whereas states are members of IGOs, NGO membership includes a larger set of actors in pursuit of policy change. Moreover, NGOs are not powerful in the traditional sense, so NGOs rely on informal sources of power, such as their legitimacy and ability to leverage more traditionally powerful actors, like state officials and IGO representatives.

IOs are often associated with images of well-connected wealthy bureaucrats working at large organizations like the UN in New York or Geneva. Images of refugees fleeing conflict-ridden countries; rice farmers in Wangting, China; or sex trafficking victims in Bangkok, Thailand, rarely come to mind when thinking about the work of IOs. Yet global governance facilitated by international organizations profoundly shapes the lives of such groups. For example, the lives of individuals like refugees are shaped by the presence of UN agencies like the World Health Organization, as well as NGOs like Refugees International. Groups like refugees represent the globally governed, which Weiss and Wilkinson define as "populations whose past, present, and future behavior is directly influenced by the actions and activities of actors and institutions that we commonly consider part of contemporary global governance."[2] A focus on the globally governed requires examining how global governance is encountered and experienced by individuals.

The remainder of this chapter examines questions related to the role of IOs in global governance, including a focus on the influence of IGO design and governance on the globally governed. As Weiss and Wilkinson point out, governing globally often takes place in the Global North, but large segments of the globally governed are located the Global South, and the effects of IGO design and governance are often experienced by some of the most marginalized, vulnerable groups in society, such as women, children, Indigenous peoples, racial minorities, and others.[3] As a result, "many of the world's most precarious communities have a more intimate relationship with global governance than do citizens of states where global governors reside."[4]

BASIC ARCHITECTURE OF GLOBAL GOVERNANCE: IGOS IN WORLD POLITICS

Although there are nearly 500 IGOs globally, we will be looking at four of the most important IGOs in the provision of global governance: the United Nations, the World Trade Organization (WTO), the International Monetary Fund (IMF), and the International Criminal Court (ICC). Each of these organizations varies in its history, membership, **mandate** (obligations placed on states), as well as the mechanisms of enforcement designed to ensure compliance.

United Nations

The United Nations was established by the UN Charter in 1945 following World War II and is currently made up of 193 member-states, making it a truly global organization. The UN represents a collective security organization, designed to promote peace and security among member-states, though the UN has taken on a much wider range of responsibilities. The UN is composed of six principal organs (pictured in Figure 16.1), which include the following:

- Security Council (UNSC)
- General Assembly (UNGA)
- Economic and Social Council (ECOSOC)

Figure 16.1. **The Principal Organs of the United Nations**

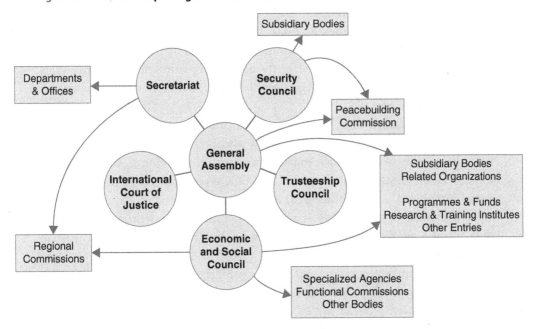

- Secretariat
- Trusteeship Council
- International Court of Justice (ICJ)

The Security Council is charged with responding to threats to international peace and security globally and can authorize the use of force in pursuit of that goal. The UNSC is composed of 15 members, including five permanent members (China, France, Russia, the United Kingdom, and the United States) and 10 non-permanent members. Each of the five permanent members (also known as the P5) possess **veto power**, which allows the permanent members to defeat any substantive decision of the UNSC with which they disagree. The 10 non-permanent members are elected to two-year terms by their regional caucuses, with five states coming from the African and Asian group, one from Eastern Europe, two from Latin America and the Caribbean, and two from the "Western Europe and Other" group.

The second constitutive body of the UN, the General Assembly, has a broader mandate and can discuss any matter under the jurisdiction of the UN, including peace and security matters as well as social and humanitarian issues. Although the General Assembly grants every member-state one vote, the UNGA is only authorized to pass resolutions and make recommendations to states and other international actors (like the UNSC). Although UNGA resolutions do not represent legally binding directives, they do hold substantial political influence as they reflect the view of the international community more broadly.

The third principal organ of the UN, the Secretariat, represents the bureaucratic staff of the UN, including over 43,000 people from 186 different countries headed by the Secretary-General.

The fourth organ of the UN, the Economic and Social Council (ECOSOC), is a subsidiary body of the General Assembly and is charged with discussing and researching issues beyond peace and security, including economic, social, cultural, educational, and health-related matters. ECOSOC is composed of 54 member-states elected from the UNGA for three-year terms.

The fifth body of the UN, the Trusteeship Council, was operational until 1994, when its primary functions were completed. The Trusteeship Council was designed to oversee former colonies that were placed under the council's care to help them move toward self-government or independence. Despite having fulfilled its mandate, the Trusteeship Council still exists as a result of the difficulty of amending the UN Charter.

The final body of the UN, the International Court of Justice (also sometimes called the World Court), represents the main judicial body of the UN. The ICJ is composed of 15 judges elected by the UNGA and UNSC for nine-year terms. The ICJ is primarily charged with settling disputes between member-states and offering advisory opinions to various actors. The ICJ does not possess compulsory jurisdiction, meaning that for the ICJ to gain jurisdiction, states must explicitly refer a case to the ICJ, be party to a treaty that explicitly authorizes the ICJ to resolve disputes over the interpretation of the treaty, or issue a general declaration that the ICJ has jurisdiction over all future legal disputes. From 1992–2014, the ICJ considered 68 contentious cases, which averages to around three per year.

World Trade Organization

The World Trade Organization (WTO) was created in 1995, succeeding the General Agreement on Tariffs and Trade (established in 1947). The WTO governs international trade relations among states. With a membership of 164 states, the WTO stipulates how countries can regulate their imports and exports, with an emphasis on the reduction of barriers to trade. When countries join the WTO, they agree to "bound" tariffs, or a ceiling for the import tariff they charge on each imported good that they cannot raise unilaterally. States also grant all other member-states "most-favored nation" status, meaning that concessions (e.g., reductions in tariffs) to one state are granted to all WTO members. Finally, states commit to the principle of "national treatment," meaning that states cannot discriminate between imported goods and domestically produced goods.

The WTO also plays an important role in resolving trade disputes among countries. When states are not following WTO rules, other member-states can file a complaint with the WTO's Dispute Settlement Body (DSB). The DSB is composed of all member-states, which appoint a panel of experts to investigate the alleged violation. The panel issues a report that becomes a ruling within 60 days. Each side can seek to overturn the ruling through a formal appeals process. However, once binding, the dispute settlement process allows for economic sanctions against countries that refuse to comply. Although states are supposed to impose sanctions on the same area of trade, in practice retaliation is often carefully considered to impose a large political impact and change the behavior of the rule violator.

International Monetary Fund

The International Monetary Fund (IMF) (along with the World Bank) was created in 1945 as part of the Bretton Woods monetary regime. Powerful countries believed that the failure to establish economic order in the interwar period (between World War I and World War II) had produced international monetary *dis*order and exacerbated political tensions among states. As a result, the United States and Great Britain led the charge and created the IMF to monitor and oversee currency relations among states. Over time, the IMF has become a powerful IO, charged with assisting countries facing economic crises. The IMF provides emergency short-term loans to states when capital is so quickly fleeing a country that it threatens the country's financial and social stability. These crises often happen when the country is importing more than it is exporting, which can create a **balance of payments** deficit. IMF membership consists of 189 countries and is governed by a board of governors made up of finance ministers or central bankers of all 189 member-states, including both borrowing and lending countries. All member-states have a vote on the activities of the IMF, but votes are proportional to the member's financial contribution to IMF resources, or its "quota."

In practice, a country facing debt problems (largely as a result of balance of payments deficits) can request a short-term loan from the IMF. The IMF holds a substantial pool of resources, including around $650 billion and access to another $1 trillion in pledges from member-states that it can call upon in a short period of time. However, for a state to receive a loan, the IMF negotiates a program of economic policies with which a state must comply. With respect to **loan conditionality**, the IMF states, "when a country borrows from the IMF, its government agrees to adjust its economic policies to overcome the problems that led it to seek financial aid. These policy adjustments are conditions for IMF loans and serve to ensure that the country will be able to repay the IMF."[5]

Conditions placed on loans typically include **austerity measures**, which are designed to reduce consumption, typically by cutting spending, raising taxes, and restricting wages. The conditions placed on loans can create political and economic issues for a debtor country. However, in return for implementing the IMF's conditions, the IMF grants an inexpensive loan to the country, and perhaps more importantly the IMF certifies the debtor government as being in compliance with IMF policies, making the country more attractive to creditors and subsequently increasing the flow of capital into the country.

International Criminal Court

The International Criminal Court (ICC) entered into force in 2002 after 60 states ratified its founding treaty, the Rome Statute. The ICC consists of 123 member-states from all regions of the world. The ICC is charged with ending impunity for perpetrators of war crimes, genocide, and crimes against humanity. A key mandate of the ICC is to prevent or deter the future commission of such crimes, and to do so the ICC investigates, tries, and prosecutes individuals accused of grave human rights violations. The ICC represents a court of last resort, meaning that the ICC is designed to complement national legal systems; the ICC can only prosecute individuals for grave crimes when it judges that the national legal system is unable or unwilling to do so. Also, the ICC only has jurisdiction if:

- the accused is a national of a state party,
- the crime took place on the territory of a state party, or
- the UN Security Council refers a case to the ICC prosecutor.

As of September 2020, 28 cases have been brought before the ICC for investigation or trial and there have been four convictions.[6] The ICC has no machinery for apprehending suspects, so for its policing function it relies entirely on member-states, who are obligated to help apprehend suspects under the Rome Statute. Some suspects are sheltered and protected by governments. There are currently 14 defendants at large, primarily nationals from several African countries (see Box 16.1).

BOX 16.1: THE INTERNATIONAL CRIMINAL COURT AND AFRICA

Since its inception in 2002, the ICC has faced criticism related to its preoccupation with Africa and its failure to investigate conflicts in other parts of the world. In the first decade of ICC activity, the focus of the ICC prosecutor was on cases in the Central African Republic, the Democratic Republic of the Congo, Ivory Coast, Sudan, and Uganda. In response, several African states, including South Africa, Gambia, and Burundi, all pursued withdrawal from the Rome Statute of the ICC in 2017. Notably, South Africa and Gambia remain members.

As a result of these criticisms, the ICC has taken several steps. For one, Fatou Bensouda, a Gambian citizen, was elected as prosecutor of the ICC in 2011. The ICC also initiated investigations in other parts of the world, including the Philippines and Afghanistan, both of which have been unsuccessful. The ICC initiated a preliminary inquiry in the Philippines as a result of accusations that the Duterte administration had committed crimes against humanity in the course of the war on drugs. In 2019, the Philippines officially withdrew from the ICC. In 2017, Prosecutor Bensouda also opened a request to investigate alleged crimes against humanity and war crimes in Afghanistan, including human rights abuses committed by the Taliban as well as foreign forces including the United States, but ultimately the ICC stepped back and chose not to proceed in 2019.

IGOS AND THE PROBLEM OF GLOBAL GOVERNANCE

Although IGOs represent institutions designed to resolve important global problems, they have weak enforcement mechanisms and are often designed in a manner in which the interests of the globally governed are not adequately represented. IGOs cannot require and ensure that state behavior aligns with IGO legal obligations because states are sovereign, meaning they have legal and political supremacy within their borders. The failure to comply with the rules of an IGO represents a violation of international law, but IGOs generally have weak international enforcement mechanisms to ensure state compliance.

A second problem of global governance involves a disconnect between global governors – those that create and make decisions in IGOs – and the globally governed – those experiencing the effects of IGO design and decision making. As the creators of many IGOs, powerful, developed, Western democratic states often maintain significant influence in IGO governance. As a result, decision making in IGOs is often biased toward the most powerful states in the international system, and such biases often result in the inequitable distribution of benefits of IGO governance. Weaker, less-developed countries are often marginalized in IGO governance. The following sections examine the ways in which the structure and design of IGOs can adversely influence the globally governed.

Designing IGOs: The Influence of Power

States, often in the Global North, design IGOs in an effort to further their individual and collective goals.[7] IGO design varies on several dimensions, including the rules of membership, the scope of issues covered, the centralization of tasks, the rules for controlling the institution, and the flexibility of the agreement. The structure and design of IGOs is chosen purposely by states to solve issues of global governance, such as distributional problems, enforcement challenges, the number of actors affected by a global governance issue, and uncertainty about the behavior of states, the state of the world, or state preferences.[8]

For example, states facing severe **distributional problems** may design an IGO with a wider issue scope to allow states receiving large gains at the expense of others to compensate one another on a different issue.[9] Although design features are rationally chosen by states, they are often chosen with the interests of global governors (i.e., powerful states in the Global North) in mind, and such interests may directly conflict with the interests of the globally governed (i.e., less powerful states in the Global South). Below, I discuss several dimensions of IGO design, including the rationale or justification behind the selection of particular design features and the influence of IGO design on the globally governed.

Membership

Membership rules stipulate who can belong to an IGO and can be exclusive or inclusive, regional or universal. Membership in the United Nations is inclusive and nearly universal, while membership in the UNSC is exclusive, as permanent membership is restricted to a small subset of states. Arguments for the maintenance of the small permanent UNSC membership stipulate that a small number of actors should facilitate decisive and quick collective action in matters involving international peace and security.

However, the membership rules can also produce policy outcomes that negatively affect not only the legitimacy of the institution, but also the lives of the globally governed. Consider the permanent five members (P5) of the UNSC (China, France, Russia, the United Kingdom, and the United States). The permanent membership of the UNSC reflects the power distribution in the international system at the time the

UN was created (the end of World War II), and notably absent from the P5 are large less-developed countries, like India or Brazil. The P5 hardly reflects the diversity of views among the UN membership. Members of the Non-Aligned Movement (NAM; see Box 16.2 for more on the NAM), a group of states pledging not to align with the United States or Soviet Union during the Cold War, note that global diversity should be reflected in the composition of the Council. For example, Cuba has argued that the diversity within a regional caucus should be taken into account when deciding how many seats a particular region should hold.[10] The composition of the UNSC means that the views and interests of many important states and individuals are not reflected in decision making on important matters of peace and security.

The Security Council can invite non-member states specially affected by an issue to participate in deliberations, giving non-member states an avenue to add their voice to formal deliberations of the council (Article 32). Notably, however, voice typically does not translate into formal decision-making power. In practice,

---

BOX 16.2: REPRESENTING THE INTERESTS OF THE GLOBALLY GOVERNED: THE NON-ALIGNED MOVEMENT

The Non-Aligned Movement is a forum of 120 developing countries that claim to not be aligned with or against any major power bloc. The NAM was founded during the collapse of the colonial system as countries in Africa, Asia, and Latin America were struggling to gain independence. The primary objectives of the NAM focused on supporting self-determination, national independence, and sovereignty, among other goals. The NAM eventually led to the development of other developing country coalitions, such as the Group of 77 (now 130 members) at the United Nations.

In the 1970s and 1980s, the NAM played a key role in the struggle to establish a New International Economic Order (NIEO), which focused on the economic emancipation of countries of the Global South. The NIEO was largely focused on ensuring that the international economic order fell more closely in line with the needs of poor countries. The NIEO's proposals included better regulation of multinational corporations, revising trade agreements that favored the products of the developed world, and granting greater voice to developing countries in international economic organizations.

The NAM and other similar organizations were able to use the power of numbers to gain a voice in IGOs like the UN. However, the membership rules still tend to favor the global governors (large developed democracies) over the globally governed.

for the UNSC to take action, the permanent members must not have a vested interest in inaction (see Box 16.3), and all members must have the political will to recommend taking action.

BOX 16.3: THE UNSC AND DARFUR

The bloody conflict in Darfur (western Sudan) provides an example of the way in which the membership of the UNSC adversely influences the globally governed. Widely acknowledged as a genocide by members of the international community, government-supported militias have carried out systematic killings of civilians in Darfur. Since 2003, around 200,000 to 400,000 people have been killed, and up to 3 million others have been displaced from their homes. In the mid-2000s, UNSC discussions of sending forces to Darfur were met with stark opposition by members of the P5, notably China. China was interested in diversifying its oil sources beyond the Middle East to Africa, and in 2006, 7 per cent of Chinese imported oil came from Sudan.[11] Further, China is wary of any action that might open the door to unwanted meddling in its own affairs and invite criticism of Chinese human rights practices. Because of China's privileged membership on the UNSC, China has sought to block sending UN peacekeepers to Darfur without the government's consent and has blocked expanded sanctions.[12]

UN failure to act in situations like Darfur result in continued widespread suffering. The Arab-dominated Sudanese government's pursuit of a genocidal policy resulted in the deaths and displacement of large segments of the population. The government sought to empower local militias to engage in racially targeted killing and rape, and the effects of this policy are still being felt in Darfur today.[13] Although the Sudanese government issued a ceasefire in 2015, paramilitary groups continue to attack villages, causing many to flee their homes. There are around 2.7 million Darfuris suffering in internally displaced person camps. Reports of harassment, arrests, systemic rape, and forced disappearances have been reported in such camps, and when women leave camps to find work, they are often vulnerable to labor exploitation and rape.[14]

Scope of Issues Covered

IGO issue scope varies on a continuum from broad coverage like UN involvement in issues related to security as well as economic, social, and humanitarian issues, to narrow coverage like the issue scope of many environmental agreements.[15] For some IGOs, scope is not open to choice (e.g., law of the sea negotiations necessitate discussion of coastal environments). However, negotiations over the design of other IGOs involves deliberate choices about the scope of issues. For example, the WTO was designed with a fairly narrow issue scope, governing trade among nations and promoting greater trade liberalization. However, international trade impacts many other issues, such as health, labor, and environmental standards, raising concerns over the extent to which the WTO incorporates such standards into its issue scope.

Consider the case of public health and access to medicine. Although advances have been made in global access to important medications and prices for medications have declined globally, many of the poorest countries in the world still have weak health infrastructure and diseases like malaria, HIV/AIDS, and tuberculosis kill millions of people every year. Intellectual property represents a key challenge for granting access to affordable medication as large pharmaceutical companies often possess patents on such medications.

The WTO oversees an agreement on intellectual property, the Agreement on Trade-Related Aspects of Intellectual Property Rights (TRIPS). TRIPS, which entered into force in 1995, introduced minimum standards for protecting and enforcing intellectual property rights, but critics of TRIPS have focused largely on the impact of this agreement on public health. TRIPS regulates the introduction of patents, including patent protection for pharmaceutical products. In practice, the agreement allowed for the protection of wealthy **multinational corporations**, including pharmaceutical companies, from the development of cheaper generic drugs. Generic drugs are copies of brand-name drugs, typically sold at a discounted rate. Many countries in the Global South, like India and Brazil, had developed strong generic drug industries, producing and selling generic drugs under patent in developed countries. The TRIPS agreement required all countries to protect patents after 1995, with the primary beneficiaries being developed countries and large pharmaceutical companies.[16] Developing countries, NGOs, and other IGOs have been highly critical of TRIPS. The UN Development Programme noted that TRIPS "has the potential to restrict access to medicines, technology, and knowledge, with disturbing implications for indigenous knowledge and food security."[17]

The global AIDS epidemic in the 1990s placed the TRIPS agreement front and center at the 2001 Doha round of negotiations among WTO member-states. The result was a declaration providing developing countries with an extension for implementing parts of the TRIPS agreement through 2016. However, powerful countries like the United States have worked to strengthen intellectual property standards beyond TRIPS through the use of bilateral and regional trade agreements.[18] One scholar notes, "As the WTO has worked towards making TRIPS acceptable to poorer countries, so the US, at the instigation of Big Pharma, has worked toward circumventing concessions."[19] Controversy and conflict still exist around whether the WTO represents a narrow economic institution solely designed to facilitate trade or whether the WTO must also expand its reach to address some of the negative impacts of global trade and intellectual property on the globally governed.

Centralization

Centralization represents another important design feature of IGOs. Centralization refers to whether important institutional tasks are performed by a single focal entity or by many different actors. Centralization occurs around the gathering and dissemination of information, bargaining, and enforcement.[20] States design IGOs with greater centralization to protect against uncertainty about state behavior or state compliance with an institution. Greater centralization enhances cooperation by providing a centralized system of monitoring state behavior. The International Criminal Court represents a centralized institution in the realm of gathering information as well as decision making regarding global involvement. The prosecutor of the ICC has significant independent authority in initiating investigations. Moreover, the ICC has the ultimate authority to determine whether the local investigation or prosecution was considered "genuine" or not. With respect to enforcement, the ICC's ability to enforce arrest warrants is largely decentralized, as the ICC has no centralized body to apprehend suspects.

For IGOs that have centralized processes in place, considerable authority is vested with the bureaucratic actors responsible for making decisions for the organization. As a result, diverse representation among centralized bodies is necessary for ensuring that the voices of the globally governed are represented. Specifically, the participation of women lends greater legitimacy to IGOs, ensures that issues affecting women are addressed, and changes people's understanding of politics, particularly international politics, as a man's domain (see Box 16.4).

BOX 16.4: WOMEN'S REPRESENTATION IN THE ICC

Women's representation in international courts is important for ensuring that the voices of the globally governed are heard. Research in political science shows that female judges in international courts are more favorably disposed toward discrimination cases filed by women.[21] Of the 20 judges of the International Criminal Court, six are women (around 30 per cent). Representation of women in international criminal law is a necessity, because women represent the principal victims of displacements associated with combat and military campaigns and suffer disproportionately from crimes like rape, other sexual crimes, and forced labor. Substantive representation indicates that women judges may demonstrate a sensitivity and understanding of the specific nature and degradation suffered by female victims of such crimes.[22] Because information gathering in the ICC is highly centralized, female judicial representation in international criminal law is particularly important in ensuring that the prosecutors' offices give gender crimes the priority they deserve.[23]

In 2012, Fatuou Bensouda became not only the first female prosecutor of the International Criminal Court, but also the first African prosecutor. Bensouda's appointment was meant to bring a voice of the globally governed into the leadership on the ICC. Moreover, on International Women's Day in 2017, the first female president of the ICC, Judge Silvia Fernández de Gurmendi, stated "The ICC, with an all-female Presidency, a female Prosecutor and several female Judges, is an example of how women can lead in achieving justice and pursuing security."[24]

In IGOs where decision making is highly centralized, like the ICC, representation of women in high-level posts is of particular importance for ensuring that issues that disproportionately affect women, like violence against women during conflict, are heard and represented.

In the United Nations, an organization committed to supporting and advancing gender equality and women's rights around the world, women have gained considerable representation in high-level posts. In fact, 20 women have held top jobs in the UN, including leadership positions in the World Health Organization, the UN Population Fund, the UN Children's Fund, and the World Food Programme. However, there are 14 agencies in the UN that have never had a woman leader, including the UN Office on Drugs and Crime, the International Labour Organization, the Food and Agriculture Organization, and the World Bank, among others.[25] When it comes to leadership positions, many women in the UN have been channeled into specific portfolios that are considered gender appropriate, such as issues involving the environment, children and women, gender equality, education, health, and human rights. Women are often left out of leadership positions in offices governing security-related issues, as well as agriculture, industry, trade, and technology. Evidence shows that women continue to face barriers in many appointment processes of particular UN agencies, creating glass walls that are hard for women to break.[26]

Control

Control within an IGO is determined by rules governing how collective decisions will be made.[27] Control can manifest in rules for electing representatives to key positions of power or in rules governing how an IGO is financed. In designing IGOs, states may choose to grant some members more control than others as a result of the size of the membership and uncertainty about the state of the world. States that are considered to be more important to the IGO may be granted more control over decision making. For example, the more some members contribute to an IGO (via resources or otherwise), the more important the state is perceived to be to an IGO, and the more asymmetric control will be within the institution.

The International Monetary Fund represents an IGO in which several members maintain substantial control over decision making. Because the IMF is involved in short-term lending to countries suffering balance of payments deficits, the IMF needs access to a large pool of resources. Although membership in the IMF is composed of developed and developing countries, votes in the IMF are proportional to each member's financial contribution to the IMF pool of resources, or its quota. Financial contributions are determined based on the size of a country's economy and economic influence in the international system. In practice, the United States provides around 18 per cent of the IMF's total resources and the member-states of the European Union provide another 32 per cent. IMF decisions generally require 85 per cent majorities, which means that as a group, the United States and European Union (members of the Global North) can block IMF actions. Research indicates that although economic considerations, like need and creditworthiness, influence the likelihood of receiving IMF lending, powerful states in the IMF (e.g., the United States) have substantial control over IMF lending decisions.[28]

In addition to lending decisions, control in the IMF manifests heavily in the conditions placed on loans. Such policies typically emphasize reduced government spending, including a reduction of subsidies on basic consumer goods, higher taxes, and policies designed to reduce inflation. Such policies, called neoliberal policies, include liberalization, privatization, openness to foreign investment, and restrictive monetary and fiscal policies. Beginning in the 1980s, developed country economists began advocating neoliberal policies, and the general acceptance of this array of market-oriented policies by Western democracies (particularly the United States) became known as the **Washington Consensus**. Developed democracies like the United States advocated for neoliberal policies as important for encouraging future economic stability. However, wealthy democracies in the Global North have interests in requiring countries in the Global South to implement such policies, such as gaining greater access to imports of cheaper goods produced in the Global South.

Such neoliberal policies can have detrimental effects on the lives of individuals in the Global South. Studies suggest that such policies often fail to generate economic gains in debtor states,[29] and neoliberal policies required by IMF loans often have the most detrimental effect on the least well off in society, "reducing the size of the 'economic pie' to be distributed and resulting in more unequal distribution of the economic pie itself."[30] For example, women disproportionately hold public sector jobs that are often cut as part of the IMF's required programs, and women are disproportionately hurt by cuts to social programs.[31] Though, importantly, women's overrepresentation in informal employment means that women may avoid some of the negative effects of such policies.

Moreover, many IMF loan recipients are required to emphasize production for export. Although women have gained greater employment opportunities in **export-processing zones** (EPZs), increasing women's participation in the labor market, the primary goal of EPZs is to help countries adjust to meet debt service payments. As a result, governments often offer incentives to multinational corporations to attract foreign direct investment. Governments, then, are prone to respond favorably to multinational corporations' demands for few regulations as well as cheap labor. EPZs offer a source of employment for women, but also offer women little in terms of pay and benefits. In the Dominican Republic, for example, EPZs are characterized by "strict discipline, sexual harassment, low pay, occupational health hazards, excessive and forced overtime, arbitrary suspension and dismissal for protesting and organizing."[32] When IGO design endows powerful states (the global governors) with control, the interests of powerful states become paramount, often marginalizing the interests and needs of individuals and groups in less powerful states (the globally governed).

Flexibility

Flexibility of institutional arrangements also constitutes a design feature along which IGOs vary. There are two types of institutional flexibility: adaptive and transformative. Adaptive flexibility allows members to respond to unanticipated international and domestic circumstances, while still maintaining their standing in an IGO. Escape clauses, which allow states to temporarily suspend their IGO commitments, are an example of adaptive flexibility. Transformative flexibility represents a deeper type of flexibility, including sunset provisions or clauses allowing for or requiring periodic renegotiations of an agreement. Flexible arrangements may be used when there is uncertainty about the state of the world or about how the benefits of IGO membership will be distributed in practice.[33]

The World Trade Organization represents an institution that has adopted several flexible design features. The national treatment principle in the WTO stipulates that countries cannot apply rules, such as safety standards, labeling requirements, or taxes to imported goods, unless they are also applied to domestically produced goods. However, agricultural goods are treated differently from manufactured goods. Agricultural goods are largely exempt from the rules of the WTO, covered by a separate, weaker set of rules adopted as an annex to the WTO's charter. Most developed countries have placed protectionist policies on agricultural goods. The United States, Japan, and the EU provide farmers with **subsidies** and support programs. In fact, the government of Japan maintains a tariff of 700 per cent to protect rice farmers, and the EU transfers tens of billions of dollars to farmers every year.[34] Since 2008, the top 10 farm subsidy recipients in the United States received an average of $18.2 million ($1.8 million annually).[35] The strength of agricultural lobbies in developed countries plays a key role in ensuring protectionist policies persist. Because these policies disproportionately harm developing country exports, they can have substantial effects on poverty reduction, including food security and the livelihoods of poor, marginalized individuals, specifically in sub-Saharan Africa (see Box 16.5).[36]

BOX 16.5: AGRICULTURAL SUBSIDIES AND COTTON PRODUCERS IN SUB-SAHARAN AFRICA

The majority of Africans earn a living through agricultural production. Cotton is grown in many states in Africa; however, cotton growers in countries like Mozambique find that they can barely make a living from their crops. Mohammed Lamine, who works for Oxfam International (an NGO) in Dakar, Senegal, claims that billions of dollars in subsidies paid each year to farmers in the United States and Europe are undercutting African farmers. Oxfam estimates that between 2001 and 2003, US subsidies cost African cotton farmers roughly $400 million.[37]

In northern Mozambique, cotton farmer Americo Candido Asan claims that US subsidies drive cotton prices lower, making it difficult to earn a living. He claims, "Here in Mozambique we don't have any help from the government. So if they have subsidies, it means American farmers have everything prepared for them. But here we are using our own money, our own labor, and the price always becomes lower and lower because of them – the Americans – it's not fair."[38] Despite WTO renegotiation procedures, powerful countries in the organization are able to ensure that the interests of the Global North (the global governors) remain paramount in the WTO.

The WTO includes transformative flexibility features by allowing for periodic rounds of negotiation over tariff-reducing measures, as well as rules governing trade policies. This built-in flexibility allowed for renewed discussion over issues of agriculture in the Uruguay round of negotiations from 1986–94 and the Doha negotiations, which began in 2001. Despite this built-in flexibility, the Doha round of negotiations failed to achieve an agreement. Agriculture played a key role in the collapse of the Doha negotiations, as delegates from developing countries walked out of negotiations, arguing that the developed world was unwilling to compromise on big issues like agriculture. The agricultural sector accounts for 50 per cent of the labor force in developing countries, but due to opposition from the United States and the EU, there has been little progress in trade liberalization in this area.[39] Despite the existence of flexible mechanisms in the WTO, gridlock over trade issues like agriculture that directly impact poor, marginalized individuals in less-developed countries render such built-in flexibility ineffective in generating an equitable distribution of benefits for WTO members.

COUNTERING THE POWER IMBALANCE: THE ROLE OF INGOS

Although the design of IGOs can generate policy outcomes that disproportionately affect the experiences of many individuals in the Global South (the globally governed), international non-governmental organizations (INGOs) can play a key role in ensuring the voices of the globally governed are heard. INGOs operate within large advocacy networks and behave as principled actors, helping to spread norms and advocating for state and non-state actors, like multinational corporations, to align behavior with emerging and established norms.[40] INGOs often work alongside domestic actors to stimulate policy changes, including improved human security.[41]

Additionally, while the design of IGOs often privileges powerful states in the Global North, INGOs can work to ensure that the inequitable effects of IGO governance are addressed. INGOs are not powerful in the traditional sense, so they rely on other strategies to initiate change. INGOs provide and spread important information to various actors about issues they wish to influence. They also work to leverage more powerful actors, like IGOs, states, and private sector actors, by calling them out for inappropriate behavior.[42]

For example, the World Trade Organization's implementation of TRIPS led many INGOs to pay special attention to the impact of TRIPS on access to medication, particularly in light of the HIV/AIDS epidemic in the 1990s. In 1997,

South Africa passed a law that allowed the health minister to override patent laws in a health emergency.[43] Large pharmaceutical companies demanded repeal of the South African law, and a group of South African multinational drug companies brought a lawsuit against the South African government. Motivated by a concern for public health and affordable access to medication, INGOs like South Africa's Treatment Action Campaign, Doctors Without Borders, and Oxfam participated in demonstrations in Washington, DC.[44] The companies eventually dropped their South Africa case in 2001 as a result of public backlash, and subsequently many pharmaceutical companies began to reduce the price of HIV/AIDS medication.

As another example, INGOs have also been successful in ensuring that the interests of the globally governed are taken into consideration in the design of IOs. Because centralization within an IGO has the potential to profoundly influence the activities of an IGO, INGOs can play a pivotal role in ensuring equitable representation of marginalized groups in centralized bodies. For instance, the Women's Caucus for Gender Justice (WCGJ), comprising more than 300 women's organizations, worked to ensure that the International Criminal Court was able to effectively investigate and prosecute crimes of sexual and gender violence.[45] The WCGJ participated actively in the 1998 Rome Conference, where the ICC was created, by lobbying delegates to adopt specific definitions of sexual violence and incorporate such crimes into definitions of war crimes and crimes against humanity. Women's INGOs also played a key role in their influence on structural aspects of the ICC, including lobbying for the representation of women on the court. Largely due to their efforts, the Rome Statute includes a statement that there should be "fair representation of female and male judges" (Article 36, 8(a)) on the court. The WCGJ remains active during nomination and election periods, calling on state parties to nominate and elect women to these positions.[46]

Despite the importance of INGOs in countering power imbalances and the lack of representation of the globally governed in IGOs, not all INGOs are altruistically motivated. Research shows that INGOs are interested in longevity and appeasing international donors, and they often make decisions based not on shared values but on what fits with their personalistic agenda.[47] Such motivations can include INGO biases toward powerful states, like the United States.[48] However, research also shows that the underlying motivations of INGOs vary, and INGOs often use costly signals to indicate their true motivations, such as policy statements or involvement in IGOs.[49] As a result, in assessing whether INGOs will be effective at giving the globally governed a voice within IGOs, it is important to consider the signals INGOs send of their true intentions and motivations.

SUMMARY

This chapter provided a short introduction to international organizations. The following points summarize the major issues discussed:

- International organizations provide the basic architecture of global governance and work to solve global problems by ensuring cooperation among states.
- States, often in the Global North, design IGOs in an effort to further their individual and collective goals. Design of IGOs varies along several dimensions, including membership, scope of issues covered, centralization, control, and flexibility.
- The design of IGOs can produce policy outcomes biased toward the Global North and can have harmful effects on the globally governed who are largely concentrated in the Global South.
- INGOs can play a key role in countering biases in IGO design, including by ensuring that potential biases are considered at the design stage and by raising awareness and stimulating mobilization efforts.

CONCLUDING QUESTIONS

1 What role do states in the Global North and Global South play in global governance?
2 How does the design of IGOs influence the globally governed?
3 In what ways can IGOs be designed differently to ensure that the interests of the globally governed are taken into account?
4 What is the role of INGOs in global governance? How can INGOs work to ensure that the voices of the globally governed are taken into account in IGO decision making?

NOTES

1 Jon Pevehouse, Timothy Nordstrom, and Kevin Warnke, "The Correlates of War 2 International Governmental Organizations Data Version 2.0," *Conflict Management and Peace Science* 21, no. 2 (2004): 101–19.
2 Thomas G. Weiss and Rorden Wilkinson, "The Globally Governed: Everyday Global Governance," *Global Governance* 24, no. 2 (2018): 194.
3 Weiss and Wilkinson, "The Globally Governed."

4 Weiss and Wilkinson, "The Globally Governed," 195.

5 IMF, "IMF Conditionality," 2019, https://www.imf.org/en/About/Factsheets/Sheets/2016/08/02/21/28/IMF-Conditionality.

6 See https://www.icc-cpi.int/cases for more recent information.

7 Barbara Koremenos, Charles Lipson, and Duncan Snidal, "The Rational Design of International Institutions," *International Organization* 55, no. 4 (2001): 761–99.

8 Koremenos, Lipson, and Snidal, "The Rational Design of International Institutions."

9 Koremenos, Lipson, and Snidal, "The Rational Design of International Institutions."

10 Ian Hurd, *International Organizations: Politics, Law, Practice* (Cambridge: Cambridge University Press, 2011).

11 "China and Darfur," *New York Times*, August 4, 2006, https://www.nytimes.com/2006/08/04/opinion/04fri3.html.

12 "China Seeks to Block U.N. Report on Darfur, Diplomats Say," *New York Times*, October 20, 2010, https://www.nytimes.com/2010/10/20/world/asia/20sudan.html.

13 John Hagan, Wenona Rymond-Richmond, and Patricia Parker, "The Criminology of Genocide: The Death and Rape of Darfur," *Criminology* 43, no. 3 (2005): 525–62.

14 Ahmed H. Adam, "Displaced in Darfur," *World Policy Journal*, March 30, 2018, http://worldpolicy.org/2018/03/30/displaced-in-darfur/.

15 Koremenos, Lipson, and Snidal, "The Rational Design of International Institutions."

16 Tamar Gutner, *International Organizations in World Politics* (Washington, DC: CQ Press, 2016).

17 UNDP/Earthscan, "Making Global Trade Work for People," 2003, http://ctrc.sice.oas.org/trc/Articles/UNDP_FULL.pdf.

18 Gutner, *International Organizations in World Politics*.

19 Adrian Flint, *HIV/AIDS in Sub-Saharan Africa: Politics, Aid and Globalization* (New York: Springer, 2011).

20 Koremenos, Lipson, and Snidal, "The Rational Design of International Institutions."

21 Erik Voeten, "Gender and Judging: Evidence from the European Court of Human Rights," *Journal of European Public Policy* (2019), https://dx.doi.org/10.2139/ssrn.3322607.

22 Patricia Wald, "Women on International Courts: Some Lessons Learned," *International Criminal Law Review* 11, no. 3 (2011): 401–8.

23 Margaret deGuzman, "Giving Priority to Sex Crime Prosecutions: The Philosophical Foundations of a Feminist Agenda," *International Criminal Law Review* 11, no. 3 (2011): 515–28.

24 ICC, "On International Women's Day, the ICC Calls for a World with No Fear or Violence," Press Release, 2017, https://www.icc-cpi.int/Pages/item.aspx?name=PR1283.

25 Kirsten Haack, "Breaking Barriers: Women's Representation and Leadership at the United Nations," *Global Governance* 20 (2014): 37.

26 Haack, "Breaking Barriers."

27 Koremenos, Lipson, and Snidal, "The Rational Design of International Institutions."

28 Strom C. Thacker, "The High Politics of IMF Lending," *World Politics* 52, no. 1 (1999): 38–75.

29 James R. Vreeland, *The IMF and Economic Development* (Cambridge: Cambridge University Press, 2003).

30 M. Rodwan Abouharb and David Cingranelli, *Human Rights and Structural Adjustment* (Cambridge: Cambridge University Press, 2007).

31 Joan Acker, "Gender, Capitalism and Globalization," *Critical Sociology* 30, no. 1 (2004): 17–41.

32 Bharati Sadasivam, "The Impact of Structural Adjustment on Women: A Governance and Human Rights Agenda," *Human Rights Quarterly* 19 (1997): 630.

33 Koremenos, Lipson, and Snidal, "The Rational Design of International Institutions."

34 Kimberly Ann Elliott, "The WTO, Agriculture, and Development: A Lost Cause?," *Bridges Africa*, 2018, https://ictsd.iisd.org/bridges-news/bridges-africa/news/the -wto-agriculture-and-development-a-lost-cause.

35 Adam Andrzejewski, "Mapping the U.S. Farm Subsidy $1M Club," *Forbes*, August 14, 2018, https://www.forbes.com/sites/adamandrzejewski/2018/08/14/mapping-the -u-s-farm-subsidy-1-million-club/#6b70fa533efc.

36 Samuel K. Gayi, "Does the WTO Agreement on Agriculture Endanger Food Security in Sub-Saharan Africa?," Research Paper No. 2006/60, United Nations University, 2006.

37 Jason Beaubien, "U.S., European Subsidies Undercut African Farmers," *National Public Radio*, October 13, 2006, https://www.npr.org/templates/story/story.php?storyId =6256274.

38 Beaubien, "U.S., European Subsidies."

39 Gutner, *International Organizations in World Politics*.

40 Martha Finnemore and Kathryn Sikkink, "International Norm Dynamics and Political Change," *International Organization* 52, no. 4 (1998): 887–917.

41 Alison Brysk, "From above and below: Social Movements, the International System, and Human Rights in Argentina," *Comparative Political Studies* 26, no. 3 (1993): 259–85.

42 Margaret E. Keck and Kathryn Sikkink, *Activists Beyond Borders: Advocacy Networks in International Politics* (Ithaca, NY: Cornell University Press, 2014).

43 Gutner, *International Organizations in World Politics*.

44 Gutner, *International Organizations in World Politics*.

45 Louise Chappell, "Women, Gender and International Institutions: Exploring New Opportunities at the International Criminal Court," *Policy and Society* 22, no. 1 (2003): 3–25.

46 Chappell, *Women, Gender and International Institutions*.

47 Clifford Bob, *The Marketing of Rebellion: Insurgents, Media, and International Activism* (Cambridge: Cambridge University Press, 2005).

48 Sarah Sunn Bush, "When and Why Is Civil Society Support 'Made-in-America'? Delegation to Non-State Actors in American Democracy Promotion," *Review of International Organizations* 11, no. 3 (2016): 361–85.

49 Amanda Murdie, *Help or Harm: The Human Security Effects of International NGOs* (Palo Alto, CA: Stanford University Press, 2014).

RESOURCES AND SUGGESTIONS FOR FURTHER READING

Barnett, Laura. "The International Criminal Court: History and Role." Library of Parliament, 2008, 2013. https://lop.parl.ca/staticfiles/PublicWebsite/Home /ResearchPublications/BackgroundPapers/PDF/2002-11-e.pdf.

Goldstone, Richard J., and Adam M. Smith. *International Judicial Institutions: The Architecture of International Justice at Home and Abroad*. New York: Routledge, 2015.

Narlikar, Amrita. *The World Trade Organization: A Very Short Introduction*. Oxford: Oxford University Press, 2005.

Steil, Benn. *The Battle of Bretton Woods: John Maynard Keynes, Harry Dexter White, and the Making of a New World Order*. Princeton, NJ: Princeton University Press, 2013.

United Nations. *Basic Facts about the United Nations*, 42nd edition. https://doi.org/10.18356/2faf3279-en.

United Nations. Charter of the United Nations. https://www.un.org/en/charter-united-nations.

Conclusion

Dr. Amy L. Atchison

LEARNING OBJECTIVES

1 Recognize the politics of division
2 Understand that identity politics are not bad politics
3 Appreciate that student evaluations of teaching are biased

KEY TERMS

politics of division   the intentional creation of wedges (divisions) between groups of people to help the majority maintain power in the face of growing numbers of minorities

student evaluations of teaching (SET)   end-of-term surveys given to students ostensibly to evaluate professors' teaching abilities

white supremacy   the belief that white people are racially superior to all other groups and therefore should dominate society

SUMMING UP

There are so many important points that I want you to take away from this book that I could not do justice to a true summary. In lieu of that, I decided to pick just one example from each chapter – stick with me here, because I am building up to a point (I promise).

Part I:

- Chapter 1: I made the point that while the classics in political theory claim to be seeking universal truths, the home truth is that the lessons of the classics aren't at all universal – they're largely predicated on the experiences of men.
- Chapter 2: Dr. Lindsay detailed the myriad ways that the canon of political theory is not only biased in gendered ways, it also contains considerable racial bias.
- Chapter 3: Dr. Xydias discussed how we can see patriarchy as an ideology that is embedded in most societal structures.
- Chapter 4: Dr. Townsend-Bell revealed that the playing field is not equal for all social movements or interest groups – level of resources and membership matters to their success.
- Chapter 5: Dr. Kenny showed you that minorities and/or women experience both direct and indirect discrimination in candidate recruitment.
- Chapter 6: Dr. Piscopo demonstrated that proportional representation electoral systems provide better odds that minorities and/or women will become members of the legislature.

Remember: I'm going to make a point at the end of this – but this part is important for making the point.

Part. II:

- Chapter 7: Drs. Erzeel and Mügge made a very strong point that it isn't just that political theory has distinct white-male biases; it is all of political science.
- Chapter 8: Drs. dos Santos and Jalalzai gave the example of parity cabinets but noted that very few cabinets achieve gender parity (and fewer ensure that minorities receive adequate representation).
- Chapter 9: Dr. Barnes and Beall provided evidence that descriptive representation matters, yet women, minorities, and particularly minority women continue to be underrepresented almost everywhere.
- Chapter 10: Dr. Fields presented compelling evidence of disparities in majority group versus minority group incarceration rates.
- Chapter 11: Dr. Pacheco-Vega demonstrated that public policies do not have uniform effects – they affect different groups in different ways, yet many policy analysts do not take intersectional concerns into consideration in their analyses.

Still with me? Almost there.

Part III:

- Chapter 12: Dr. Ackerly and Carella demonstrated that although "mainstream" (mostly male) international relations scholars doubt the objectivity of women or minority scholars who write about gender and race, those same scholars fail to acknowledge that their own "mainstream" research is built on a non-objective platform.
- Chapter 13: Drs. Brassett, Elias, Rethel, and Richardson noted that when scholars of "everyday international political economy" began to study women's labor, it became clear that IPE had vastly underestimated how much of women's economic activity is conducted informally.
- Chapter 14: Drs. Whooley and Sjoberg demonstrated that no one experiences security exactly the same, but that people's identities – gender, racial/ethnic, class, religion – often make them more or less vulnerable depending on the security situation.
- Chapter 15: Drs. Och and Zwingel revealed that how a person experiences both international law and human rights is highly contingent on who (and where) that person is.
- Chapter 16: Dr. Haglund showed that women's representation in intergovernmental organizations, like women judges at the International Criminal Court, matters to the outcomes generated by these organizations.

Have you figured out my point yet? It's that *all politics are identity politics.* That's the main takeaway I want you to get from this book. Every example I just gave you demonstrates that your identities – race, gender, sexual orientation, class, religion, even ideology – matter to how you experience politics and political institutions.

THE POLITICS OF DIVISION

The term *identity politics* is a highly contested one – as columnist Carlos Lozada recently said, it's "a term so contested that even writing it down can exhaust."[1] He's not wrong. Coming up with a solid definition of identity politics is challenging, but the academic definition I favor comes from sociologist Nancy Whittier, who says identity politics happen (1) when people organize around the collective identity of a given group and (2) when people organize specifically to make an identity visible.[2] For example, people who are non-cis/non-heterosexual have organized around their LGBTQ+ identities to press for equal rights in society, and members of the LGBTQ+ community and allies have organized to increase trans visibility.

One of the more honest non-academic definitions I have seen comes from journalist Matthew Yglesias, who says that identity politics is "shorthand for talking about feminism or anti-racism." He goes on to say "[t]he implication of this ... is that somehow an identity is something only women or African-Americans or perhaps LGBT people have. White men just have ideas about politics that spring from a realm of pure reason, with concerns that are by definition, universal."[3] Basically, people who decry identity politics are saying that when non-majority groups agitate for change, they're practicing *identity politics* (biased, bad), but when the dominant group digs in to defend the status quo, they're just practicing *politics* (unbiased/good).

Pundits on both the left and the right decry identity politics as divisive. They claim that identity politics is the **politics of division**, driving wedges between different groups in society. The identity-politics-cause-wedges claim is disingenuous (at best), however. The wedges have existed for generations. They were deliberately driven by elites from majority (white) groups because wedges help the majority to maintain power in the face of growing numbers of minorities. A good example comes from US race relations, where poor white and poor Black Americans should have more in common politically with each other than they do with wealthy members of their respective racial groups. However, if the poor were allowed to band together they might have had a shot at political success, but it was not in the interest of the powers-that-be to allow that to happen. How, though, to prevent unity? Drive wedges. As US President Lyndon B. Johnson, speaking about the tactics of division, explained, "If you can convince the lowest white man he's better than the best colored man, he won't notice you're picking his pocket. Hell, give him somebody to look down on, and he'll empty his pockets for you."

The politics of **white supremacy**, as critical race theorist Derrick Bell identified decades ago,[4] have benefited the (white) ruling class in many parts of the world:

- During the apartheid era, white South Africans were encouraged to adopt a strong Afrikaner political identity that was aimed at keeping white supremacy firmly entrenched.[5]
- As you saw in Chapter 3, right-wing populist parties across Europe are exploiting nativist fears about immigrants to gain power.
- Brexiters leveraged nativist fears about immigration to engineer the United Kingdom's exit from the European Union.
- In Australia, the majority of white Australians believe that Aborigines and Torres Strait Islanders receive too much government assistance – despite the fact that these Indigenous groups have been systematically disadvantaged *by the government* for centuries.[6]

- In Canada, which has arguably made more progress on racial issues than either the United States or Australia, there are both native/immigrant wedges and white/Indigenous wedges.[7]

In each case, the wedges serve to help maintain the status quo. If we are looking at politics as *who gets what, when, and how*, then the wedges help the dominant group get what they want, when they want it, and without having to work as hard to get it (because they control the distribution).

IDENTITY POLITICS ARE NOT BAD POLITICS

In essence, the identity groups being so loudly condemned by politicians were *created by* the politics of division. People are coming together around identities that have been used to exclude them from the benefits of full citizenship. As political scientist Courtney Jung puts it, "movements form around issues of gender, race, or class, not because people feel a need to express a primary commitment to such shared identities, but rather because these categories have regulated the distribution of the goods [in their] society."[8] As such, these identity movements are not *creating* divisions, they are *exposing* divisions.

Exposing these divisions seems contentious, but only until you consider that we can't unify if we never acknowledge that we have been divided – that some people have been deliberately cast as *less than* in order for other people to maintain societal control. In exposing the *less-than* treatment of their group(s), activists are bringing to light flaws in our democratic societies. They are "making visible the invisible boundaries that have excluded them" so that they, too, can partake in the benefits of society.[9] Yes, it's a messy process to try to change existing power structures, but if you believe in democratic principles, then it is a necessary process. To quote civil rights activist Dr. Martin Luther King, Jr.: "Freedom is never voluntarily given by the oppressor; it must be demanded by the oppressed."

FINAL THOUGHTS

There is one last thing I want to say before I let you go. We are likely at the end of your institution's term. At many institutions, this means it is time for you to fill out **student evaluations of teaching (SET)**. I want to talk to you about SET.

Ostensibly, the main purposes of SET are (1) to guide faculty improvement in teaching, (2) to influence tenure or promotion decisions, and (3) to provide evidence of quality control procedures for accreditation/institutional evaluation.[10] These purposes share an underlying assumption that people are good judges of their own learning, therefore these evaluations are a fair assessment of faculty effectiveness and quality of teaching. Unfortunately, the majority of evidence indicates that we are relatively poor judges of our own learning (look up the Dunning-Krueger effect). The fact that people are terrible judges of their own learning calls into question the validity of SET.[11]

If SET do not measure student learning, what *do* they measure? At least some evidence indicates that "SET measure students' gender biases better than they measure the instructor's teaching effectiveness."[12] While there are a handful of studies that show no bias,[13] the preponderance of research provides consistent evidence of gender and race bias in SET.[14] Indeed, available evidence indicates that SET are demonstrably downward biased for women, scholars of color, and (in English-speaking places) non-native English speakers.[15]

Studies have found that gender affects students' expectations of faculty behavior; students expect men to be authoritative and women to be nurturing – yet women are penalized in evaluations because nurturing behavior is "less than professorial."[16] Relatedly, students' gendered expectations of leadership factor into women's lower scores when students evaluate large lecture classes.[17] Additionally, Mitchell and Martin find that "a man received higher evaluations in identical courses, even for questions unrelated to the individual instructor's ability, demeanor, or attitude"; they further clarify that "even in identical online courses with almost no opportunity for variation, [students] evaluated a man more favorably than a woman."[18] Note: The same person taught the same online class – one class was told that the instructor was male, the other that the instructor was female. Same class, same instructor, but they got worse evaluations from the class that thought the instructor was a woman. In the same study, Mitchell and Martin also find that (1) students evaluate women more heavily on both personality and appearance than are men and (2) student language indicates women are viewed as less competent.

Far fewer studies of bias in SET focus on race, likely due to the comparatively small pool of scholars of color in the academy.[19] The available evidence indicates, however, that racial bias in SET is a problem, at least in US higher education. Most studies on this have been done in the United States, but I doubt (given the discussion of racial wedges above) that the picture is much different in other countries. In the studies, students consistently rate Black, Asian American, and Hispanic faculty lower than they rate white faculty.[20] Also of note is that there is evidence that students write racist comments on their SET; Delgado notes that faculty regularly report being "trashed" on SET; furthermore, "course evaluations provided some students with the opportunity to express their dissatisfaction with [minority faculty] presence as well as [minority faculty] performance."[21]

Intersectional research on bias in SET is even less common, but here too the available evidence (gathered at predominantly white institutions) is not positive. For example, in a study that examines both race and gender, of the six faculty groups studied both graduate and undergraduate students ranked Black women and Black men fifth and sixth, respectively, on overall value of course and overall teaching ability.[22] Similarly, Reid finds that "Racial Minority faculty were rated less favorably with respect to both *Overall Quality* and *Clarity* than White faculty."[23]

Why am I telling you this? First, because in a textbook devoted to bringing the voices of marginalized political scientists to the fore, it would be negligent *not* to present you with this information. Second, and most importantly, I am telling you this because research indicates that when we tell you about the biases in SET, it makes you think harder before you evaluate your faculty.[24] It matters. Administrators use SET in their evaluations of faculty – SET are part of the package that determines who gets promoted and who doesn't. The fact that SET are consistently biased against women, scholars of color, and especially women scholars of color means that those groups are less likely to be promoted. Losing those voices from political science means that we lose perspectives that matter to our understanding of the political world.

And if you take nothing else from this book, I hope you remember that *political science is for everybody.*

NOTES

1 Carlos Lozada, "Show Me Your Identification," *Washington Post*, October, 18, 2018, https://www.washingtonpost.com/news/book-party/wp/2018/10/18/feature/identity-politics-may-divide-us-but-ultimately-we-cant-unite-without-it.

2 Nancy Whittier, "Identity Politics, Consciousness-Raising, and Visibility Politics," in *The Oxford Handbook of Us Women's Social Movement Activism*, eds. Holly J. McCammon, Verta A. Taylor, Jo Reger, and Rachel L. Einwohner, 376–97 (Oxford: Oxford University Press 2017), 376.

3 Matthew Yglesias, "All Politics Is Identity Politics," *Vox*, June 5, 2015, https://www.vox.com/2015/1/29/7945119/all-politics-is-identity-politics.

4 Derrick A. Bell, Jr., "*Brown v. Board of Education* and the Interest-Convergence Dilemma," *Harvard Law Review* (1980): 518–33.

5 Courtney Jung, "Why Liberals Should Value 'Identity Politics,'" *Daedalus* 135, no. 4 (2006): 32–9.

6 Jill Vickers and Annette Isaac, *The Politics of Race: Canada, the United States, and Australia*, 2nd ed. (Toronto: University of Toronto Press, 2012).

7 Vickers and Isaac, *The Politics of Race*.

8 Jung, "Why Liberals Should Value 'Identity Politics,'" 32.

9 Jung, "Why Liberals Should Value 'Identity Politics,'" 38.

10 Pieter Spooren, Bert Brockx, and Dimitri Mortelmans, "On the Validity of Student Evaluation of Teaching: The State of the Art," *Review of Educational Research* 83, no. 4 (2013): 598–642; Terry A. Wolfer and Miriam McNown Johnson, "Re-Evaluating Student Evaluation of Teaching: The Teaching Evaluation Form," *Journal of Social Work Education* 39, no. 1 (2003): 111–21.

11 Nicholas A. Bowman, "The Meaning and Interpretation of College Student Self-Reported Gains," in *Methodological Advances and Issues in Studying College Impact: New Directions for Institutional Research*, eds. Nicholas A. Bowman and Serge Herzog, chap. 4, 59–68 (Hoboken, NJ: Wiley Periodicals, 2014); Robert M. Gonyea and Angie Miller, "Clearing the Air about the Use of Self-Reported Gains in Institutional Research," *New Directions for Institutional Research* no. 150 (2011): 99–111; Justin Kruger and David Dunning, "Unskilled and Unaware of It: How Difficulties in Recognizing One's Own Incompetence Lead to Inflated Self-Assessments," *Journal of Personality and Social Psychology* 77, no. 6 (1999): 1121.

12 Anne Boring, Kellie Ottoboni, and Philip Stark, "Student Evaluations of Teaching (Mostly) Do Not Measure Teaching Effectiveness," *ScienceOpen Research* (2016), 11.

13 Pascal Wallisch and Julie Cachia, "Determinants of Perceived Teaching Quality: The Role of Divergent Interpretations of Expectations," *PsyArXiv* (2019); Stephen L. Wright and Michael A. Jenkins-Guarnieri, "Student Evaluations of Teaching: Combining the Meta-Analyses and Demonstrating Further Evidence for Effective Use," *Assessment & Evaluation in Higher Education* 37, no. 6 (2012): 683–99.

14 Mirya Holman, Ellen Key, and Rebecca Kreitzer, "Evidence of Bias in Standard Evaluations of Teaching," 2019, http://www.rebeccakreitzer.com/bias/.

15 Anne Boring, "Gender Biases in Student Evaluation of Teachers," 2015, http://www.anneboring.com/uploads/5/6/8/5/5685858/aboring_gender_biases_in_set_april_2014.pdf; Daniel S. Hamermesh and Amy Parker, "Beauty in the Classroom: Instructors' Pulchritude and Putative Pedagogical Productivity," *Economics of Education Review* 24, no. 4 (2005): 369–76; Lillian MacNell, Adam Driscoll, and Andrea N. Hunt, "What's in a Name: Exposing Gender Bias in Student Ratings of Teaching," *Innovative Higher Education* 40, no. 4 (2015): 291–303.

16 Kristi Andersen and Elizabeth D. Miller, "Gender and Student Evaluations of Teaching," *PS: Political Science & Politics* 30, no. 2 (1997): 217.

17 Lisa L. Martin, "Gender, Teaching Evaluations, and Professional Success in Political Science," *PS: Political Science & Politics* 49, no. 2 (2016): 313–19.

18 Kristina M.W. Mitchell and Jonathan Martin, "Gender Bias in Student Evaluations," *PS: Political Science & Politics* 51, no. 3 (2018): 648–52.

19 Holman, Key, and Kreitzer, "Evidence of Bias in Standard Evaluations of Teaching."

20 Kristin J. Anderson and Gabriel Smith, "Students' Preconceptions of Professors: Benefits and Barriers According to Ethnicity and Gender," *Hispanic Journal of Behavioral Sciences* 27, no. 2 (2005): 184–201; Hamermesh and Parker, "Beauty in the Classroom"; Bettye P. Smith and Billy Hawkins, "Examining Student Evaluations of Black College Faculty: Does Race Matter?," *Journal of Negro Education* 80, no. 2 (2011).

21 Richard Delgado, "Minority Law Professors' Lives: The Bell-Delgado Survey," *Harvard Civil Rights-Civil Liberties Review* 24 (1989): 350, 361.

22 Bettye P. Smith, "Student Ratings of Teaching Effectiveness for Faculty Groups Based on Race and Gender," *Education* 129, no. 4 (2009): 622.

23 Landon D. Reid, "The Role of Perceived Race and Gender in the Evaluation of College Teaching on RateMyProfessors.com," *Journal of Diversity in Higher Education* 3, no. 3 (2010): 143–44.

24 David A.M. Peterson, Lori A. Biederman, David Andersen, Tessa M. Ditonto, and Kevin Roe, "Mitigating Gender Bias in Student Evaluations of Teaching," *PloS One* 14, no. 5 (2019): e0216241.

Appendix: Safeguarding Democracy through Civic Engagement

As mentioned at several locations in the book, democratic backsliding is a real and pressing concern. The good news, though, is that you can do things at any level of politics to try to push back against creeping authoritarianism – the authors and I have come up with a list of suggestions to help. It's not comprehensive, but it's a good start! I've separated our list into personal, local/subnational/national, and international ideas for getting involved in political action, but they don't separate neatly and you should keep in mind that many of these ideas work at any level.

PERSONAL

- Vote in any election in which you are eligible to vote.
- Listen to the everyday experiences of those around you and invite them to put these in (non-partisan) political terms.
- Start a blog/webpage that explores how intersectionality shapes life on your college campus.
- Read and cite research from scholars from marginalized groups and disciplines in your own research.
- Write an op-ed or letter to the editor for a local newspaper about a social justice issue you care about.
- Donate to local activist organizations who are engaged in political change work.
- Put a sign up in your yard or window demonstrating support for a local cause or politician.

- Join your neighborhood association and attend meetings.
- Become an active volunteer for a local advocacy non-profit working at changing an unjust policy that you care about.
- Plan or participate in a student strike, labor strike, or rent strike.
- Plan or participate in a consumer boycott when asked by workers to be in solidarity.
- Plan or participate in a divestment campaign on campus or in your community.
- Start or join a local mutual aid network.
- Participate in a political training program like New Leaders Council, Vote Run Lead, Emerge, She Should Run, and so on.
- Run for something yourself – student government, local executive committee, local council, state/provincial representative – or work on a campaign of someone who shares your values.
- Host or attend a debate watch party in your community.
- Establish or join a student group about an issue you care about.

LOCAL/SUBNATIONAL/NATIONAL

- Did we mention that you should vote in any election in which you are eligible to vote? (Students in EU countries, this includes European Parliament elections!)
- Write a letter, make a call/tweet/social media post, or sign a petition to your local council/municipal government, county commission, provincial/state government, or your national legislator(s) (i.e., members of parliament, congresspersons, or senators).
- Attend and speak at local council meetings, committee hearings, school board meetings, PTA meetings; if you cannot be there to speak up on an issue, write your council member.
- Provide public comment on local, state/provincial, and national decisions.
- Participate in a grassroots/citizen lobby day and speak to state/provincial or council representatives in person on issues you care about.
- Ask to get coffee with your council person to talk about issues you care about in your neighborhood.
- Plan or attend a protest, sit in, teach in, rally, walk out, vigil, march, or parade about a social justice issue you care about; if you can't attend the protest in person, research how you can help from home – like donating to a bail fund to help bail out protestors.

- Help get other people registered to vote and help send reminders about elections.
- Start a petition regarding a social or political issue of importance to you.

INTERNATIONAL

- Participate in a student exchange program (either as a host or participant).
- Establish or join a chapter of United Students Against Sweatshops.
- Visit the Toolkit & Guides section on the Amnesty International website and create your own human rights advocacy campaign.
- Establish a student chapter of Amnesty International on your college campus (or join an existing chapter) to fight for human rights.
- Become an activist for Amnesty International – visit its website for current calls for action.
- Join the Urgent Action Network of Amnesty International and protect human rights around the globe.
- Join Amnesty International's letter-writing campaign every December.
- Establish a student chapter of the United Nations Association on your college campus (or join an existing chapter) to advocate for the work of the United Nations.
- Establish or join a Model UN group on campus.
- Look at the labels on products you buy and then find out where it was made, by whom, and under what conditions (e.g., www.followthethings.com).

Contributors

Dr. Amy L. Atchison is an associate professor of political science and international relations at Valparaiso University. Her research interests include gender and politics, social welfare policy, and the status of marginalized groups in political science. She is the co-author of *Survive and Resist: The Definitive Guide to Dystopian Politics* with Shauna Shames (Columbia University Press, 2019). Her research has been published in a variety of journals, including *Poverty and Public Policy*; *Politics & Gender*; *PS: Political Science and Politics*; the *Journal of Women, Politics, and Policy*; the *Review of Policy Research*; and the *European Journal of Politics and Gender*.

Dr. Brooke Ackerly is a professor of political science at Vanderbilt University and co-editor-in-chief of the *International Feminist Journal of Politics* (2018–21). In her research, teaching, and collaborations, she works to clarify without simplifying the most pressing problems of global justice, including human rights and climate change. Using feminist methodologies, she integrates into her theoretical work empirical research on activism and the experiences of those affected by injustice (grounded normative theory). She is the author of several books, including *Political Theory and Feminist Social Criticism* (Cambridge University Press, 2000), *Universal Human Rights in a World of Difference* (Cambridge University Press, 2008), *Doing Feminist Research* with Jacqui True (Palgrave Macmillan, 2010, 2019), and most recently, *Just Responsibility: A Human Rights Theory of Global Justice* (Oxford University Press, 2018). Dr. Ackerly teaches courses on justice, ethics and public policy, feminist theory, feminist research methods, human rights, contemporary political thought, and gender and the history of political thought.

Dr. Tiffany D. Barnes is an associate professor and a director of undergraduate studies at the University of Kentucky. She completed her PhD in political science at Rice University in 2012. Her research is in the field of comparative politics with an emphasis on comparative legislatures, comparative political institutions, gender and politics, and Latin America. She employs both quantitative and qualitative research approaches to examine how institutions shape elite and mass political behavior. In 2017, her book, *Gendering Legislative Behavior: Institutional Constraints and Collaboration* (Cambridge University Press), was awarded the Alan Rosenthal Prize, for the best book or article written by a junior scholar that has potential to strengthen the practice of representative democracy, by the American Political Science Association Legislative Studies Section. She has published in many journals, including the *American Journal of Political Science*; the *Journal of Politics*; *Comparative Political Studies*; *Political Research Quarterly*; *Governance, Politics & Gender*; and *Politics, Groups, and Identities*.

Victoria Beall is a fifth-year PhD student and teaching assistant at the University of Kentucky studying political science with a focus in comparative politics and international relations. Currently, her research focuses on three central questions: How does the composition of the UN Security Council influence the goals of UN peacekeeping mandates? How do UN General Assembly members strategically donate resources to peacekeeping missions? How do the goals of UN peacekeeping mandates affect on-the-ground outcomes, such as conflict-related sexual violence and overall peacekeeping mission success? She is interested in leveraging language as a tool to understand how women and gender issues are prioritized and conceptualized by the UN in peacekeeping missions and conflict more generally. Her recent publications can be found in *Legislative Studies Quarterly*; *Women, Politics & Policy*; and *PS: Political Science*.

Dr. James Brassett is a reader in international political economy at the the University of Warwick, UK. His work engages the everyday politics of globalization with a focus on questions of ethics, governance, crisis, and resistance. Dr. Brassett's research has been published in journals such as the *European Journal of International Relations*, *International Political Sociology*, *International Studies Quarterly*, *International Theory*, *Review of International Political Economy*, and *Security Dialogue*. His most recent book is *The Ironic State: British Comedy and the Everyday Politics of Globalisation* (Bristol University Press, 2021).

Anna Carella is a PhD candidate in the Department of Political Science at Vanderbilt University. Her research interests and writing encompass feminist theory, human rights, global justice, and development studies. Her dissertation deals with the rights-based approach to development and strategies for evaluating development projects based on political processes on the ground. Her work is informed by her time serving as a social scientist on a Human Terrain Team in Khost, Afghanistan (2011–12), providing social and political data to soldiers engaged in counterinsurgency. Her research can be found in the *International Feminist Journal of Politics*, and she is the recipient of a Human Rights Rising Advocate award from Tennessee United for Human Rights. She is on leave from her PhD to serve as co-executive director of Healthy and Free Tennessee, a state-based reproductive freedom advocacy organization.

Dr. Pedro A.G. dos Santos is an associate professor of political science at the College of Saint Benedict and Saint John's University and has also taught at Luther College. He teaches courses on comparative politics and international relations, including courses on sustainability in Latin America, gender and development, and race and politics in Brazil. He has two main areas of research in Brazilian politics: women's representation in the legislative and executive and the rise of evangelical politicians in the country. He has published numerous book chapters as well as articles in *Latin American Politics and Society* and *Politics & Gender*. Dr. dos Santos coauthored with Dr. Farida Jalalzai the forthcoming book *Women's Empowerment and Disempowerment in Brazil: The Rise and Fall of President Dilma Rousseff* (Temple University Press, 2021).

Dr. Juanita Elias is a professor in international political economy at the University of Warwick. She joined PAIS in 2014 from Griffith University, Australia, where she held an Australian Research Council Future Fellowship. Prior to that she worked at the University of Adelaide, the University of Manchester, and Cardiff University. Dr. Elias's research explores the ways in which gender relations and identities operate and are reproduced within a range of political economic settings. This includes work looking at the role of multinational corporations in the production of gendered and racialized forms of inequality; research exploring the construction of vulnerable forms of work and employment, such as migrant domestic work; analyses of efforts to include or "mainstream" gender issues within institutional contexts such as the International Labour Organization and the World Economic Forum; and analyses of how households and (gendered) household relations take shape within and are constitutive of the global political economy.

Dr. Silvia Erzeel is an assistant professor at the Department of Political Science of the Vrije Universiteit Brussel (Belgium). She teaches courses and conducts research on political representation, political parties, elections, gender and intersectionality, and inequality. Her PhD thesis (2012, VUB) dealt with the political representation of women in national and regional parliaments in Europe. Professor Erzeel's current research focuses on three main areas: the integration of gender equality in political parties, intersectionality and ethnic minority women's pathways to power in Europe, and the consequences of economic inequality for representative democracy. Since 2018, she has been the co-convenor of the ECPR Standing Group on Gender and Politics.

Dr. Kimberly P. Fields earned her PhD in political science from the University of Pennsylvania and obtained her BA in political science from Temple University. Dr. Fields's research interests include the political construction and maintenance of race, inequality, environmental policy, state and local politics, political behavior, and government responsiveness. She has current or forthcoming publications in *Environmental Justice*, *The Midwest Journal of Social Science*, and *Environmental Science and Technology* on state environmental justice efforts and anti-discrimination ordinances. Dr. Fields is working on a book-length manuscript, *Just States: Evaluating State Approaches to Environmental Justice*. The book will present the first in-depth analysis of state efforts to address the racial dimensions of environmental inequality through public policy. It also evaluates the development, implementation, and political consequences of these efforts and analyzes the role of political discourse, issue framing, and policymaking processes in shaping government responses, institutional outcomes, and political participation.

Dr. Jillienne Haglund is an assistant professor of political science at the University of Kentucky. She received her PhD at Florida State University in 2014 and was a postdoctoral research associate at Washington University in St. Louis from fall 2014 to spring 2015. Her research and teaching interests fall broadly in the fields of international relations and comparative politics. More specifically, she is interested in human rights, international organizations, international law, and comparative political institutions. Dr. Haglund's work seeks to illuminate the extent to which international law constrains state human rights behavior. Her research has been funded by the National Science Foundation and she recently published her first book, *Regional Courts, Domestic Politics, and the Struggle for Human Rights* (Cambridge University Press, 2020). Her work also appears in several journals, including the *Journal of Peace Research*, *International Studies Perspectives*, and *Conflict Management and Peace Science*.

Dr. Farida Jalalzai is the associate dean for global initiatives and engagement at Virginia Tech. She was previously the Hannah Atkins endowed chair, professor, and head of the Department of Political Science at Oklahoma State University. Her research analyzes the representation and behavior of women and minorities in politics and the role of gender in the political arena. Dr. Jalalzai's work focuses on women national leaders. Her first book, *Shattered, Cracked and Firmly Intact: Women and the Executive Glass Ceiling Worldwide* (Oxford University Press, 2013), offers a comprehensive analysis of women, gender, and national leadership positions. Her second book, *Women Presidents of Latin America: Beyond Family Ties?* (Routledge, 2016), is a comparative analysis of women presidents in Latin America. Dr. Jalalzai is coeditor of the volume *Measuring Women's Political Empowerment Worldwide* (along with Amy C. Alexander and Catherine Bolzendahl; Palgrave, 2018). Her latest book, *Women's Empowerment and Disempowerment in Brazil: The Rise and Fall of President Dilma Rousseff*, coauthored with Dr. Pedro dos Santos, is forthcoming.

Dr. Meryl Kenny is a senior lecturer in gender and politics at the University of Edinburgh. She joined the subject area of politics and international relations in August 2015, having held previous positions at the University of Leicester and the University of New South Wales (Sydney, Australia). At Edinburgh, Dr. Kenny convenes the Gender Politics Research Group, which hosts the genderpol blog (@genderpol on Twitter). She sits on the steering group of the university's genderED initiative. She is also a member of the steering group of the cross-party Women5050 campaign for legal gender quotas in Scotland, co-director of the Feminism and Institutionalism International Network (FIIN), and associate editor of the *British Journal of Politics & International Relations*.

Dr. Keisha Lindsay is an associate professor in the Department of Gender and Women's Studies and the Department of Political Science at the University of Wisconsin-Madison. Her research and teaching interests include feminist theory, intersectionality, black masculinities, and gender-based politics in the African diaspora. She is the author of several article-length manuscripts as well as *In a Classroom of Their Own: The Intersection of Race and Feminist Politics in All-Black Male Schools* (University of Illinois Press, 2018). She is also the recipient of the Caucus for a New Political Science/American Political Science Association's 2019 Michael Harrington Book Award and the National Conference of Black Political Scientists' 2019 Alex Willingham Best Political Theory Paper Award.

Dr. Liza Mügge is an associate professor in the Political Science Department and research theme leader of the Diverse Europe group of the Amsterdam Research Centre for European Studies, both at the University of Amsterdam (UvA). Dr. Mügge is a founding editor of the *European Journal of Politics and Gender* and the previous director of the Amsterdam Research Center for Gender and Sexuality (2016–19). Her research expertise and interests include political representation, intersectionality, gender, ethnicity, transnationalism, and social safety. She is the principal investigator of a five-year research project on political representation and diversity in Western Europe funded by the Dutch Research Council (NWO). During the academic year of 2020–1 she is an Alexander von Humboldt fellow at the Berlin Social Science Center (WZB).

Dr. Malliga Och is an assistant professor of global studies at Idaho State University where she teaches classes on human rights, gender, global governance, and European politics. She is an expert on gender and politics with a particular focus on conservative parties in the OECD region. She is the co-editor of *The Right Women: Republican Activists, Candidates, and Lawmaker*s and multiple journal articles. Dr. Malliga is the 2018 recipient of Deborah "Misty" Gerner Award for Professional Development given by the Women's Caucus for International Studies of the International Studies Association, and the 2018 recipient of the Yellow Rose given by Zonta International Pocatello Club for her contribution in the community to advance women's equality. She received her PhD from the University of Denver and also holds a Magister Artium in political science, communications, and law from the Ludwig-Maximilians University in Munich, Germany, and an MA in political science from the University of Colorado.

Dr. Raul Pacheco-Vega is an associate professor in the Methods Lab at the Facultad Latinoamericana de Ciencias Sociales (FLACSO-México). Previously, he was an assistant professor in the Public Administration Division of the Centro de Investigación y Docencia Económicas (CIDE). He is a specialist in comparative public policy and focuses on North American environmental politics, primarily sanitation and water governance, solid waste management, neoinstitutional theory, transnational environmental social movements, and experimental methods in public policy. Dr. Pacheco-Vega's current research program focuses on the spatial, political, and human dimensions of public service delivery from a comparative perspective. He is the editor for the Americas of the *International Journal of Qualitative Methods*, associate editor of the *Journal of Environmental Studies and Sciences* (JESS), and assistant editor for *Policy Design and Practice*, and he sits on the editorial board of *Water International, Global Environmental Politics*, the *Journal of Environmental Policy and Planning, Regions and Cohesion, International Studies Review, Environment and Planning C: Politics and Space*, and *Politics, Groups & Identities*.

Dr. Jennifer M. Piscopo is an associate professor of politics at Occidental College. She has published over 20 peer-reviewed articles in leading academic journals, including *The American Journal of Political Science, Comparative Political Studies, Latin American Politics and Society,* and *Politics & Gender.* With Susan Franceschet and Mona Lena Krook, she co-edited *The Impact of Gender Quotas* (Oxford University Press, 2012). She is co-editor of the journal *Politics, Groups, and Identities.* Her popular writing has appeared in the *New York Times,* the *Los Angeles Times,* the *Washington Post, Ms. Magazine,* the *Boston Review,* and international outlets. Dr. Piscopo consults regularly for international organizations such as UN Women and has extensive research, travel, and speaking experience in Latin America, Europe, and Asia.

Dr. Lena Rethel is an associate professor of international political economy (IPE) at the University of Warwick. Her research interests include the relationship between finance and development, financialization and the politics of debt, alternative globalizations, and the disciplinary parameters and spatial location of contemporary IPE. Substantively, her work to date has concentrated on both the theories and common sense that underpin financial policymaking, the question of how this leads to institutional change (in particular the expansion of capital markets and the development of Islamic finance), and the socioeconomic implications of these changes. Her research has been grounded primarily in insights from the Southeast Asia region. Dr. Rethel's current project examines the growth of transnational Islamic economic flows and their governance. This research is funded by a Leverhulme Trust Research Fellowship.

Dr. Ben Richardson is a reader in international political economy. His research interests include international trade and sustainable development, the global governance of labor and land rights, and the political economy of food. His first two books, *Sugar: Refined Power in a Global Regime* (Palgrave, 2009) and *Sugar* (Polity, 2015), looked at the global inequalities linked to the production, trade, and consumption of sugar. His third book, *Free Trade Agreements and Global Labour Governance: The European Union's Trade-Labour Linkage in a Value Chain World* (Routledge, 2020), studied the effects of EU trade agreements on workers' rights.

Dr. Laura Sjoberg (BA, University of Chicago; PhD, University of Southern California School of International Relations; J.D. Boston College Law School) is a professor of political science at the University of Florida and British Academy global professor of politics and international relations at Royal Holloway University of

London. Her research interests are in the area of gender-based and feminist approaches to the study of international relations generally, and international security specifically. Dr. Sjoberg is author or editor of more than a dozen books, including, most recently, *International Relations' Last Synthesis?* (Oxford University Press, 2019, with J. Samuel Barkin), *Gender and Civilian Victimization in War* (Routledge, 2019, with Jessica Peet), and the *Routledge Handbook on Gender and Security* (Routledge, 2018, with Caron E. Gentry and Laura J. Shepherd). Her work has also recently been published in *Security Dialogue, Review of International Studies*, the *Journal of International Political Theory, Conflict Management and Peace Science*, and the *Journal of Conflict Resolution*.

Dr. Erica Townsend-Bell is an associate professor of political science and director of the Center for African Studies at Oklahoma State University. She obtained her MA, Certificate in Gender and Women's Studies, and PhD (2007) from Washington University, St. Louis. Her BA in political science and Spanish is from Xavier University of Louisiana (1997). Her areas of expertise include intersectional politics, comparative race and gender politics, and social movements. Her work has been published in *Political Research Quarterly, Signs, JILAR, The Revista de Ciencia Política, Latin American and Caribbean Ethnic Studies, The Oxford Handbook of Gender and Politics, The Palgrave Handbook of Intersectionality in Public Policy*, and other outlets.

Dr. Jon Whooley is a full-time lecturer at San Francisco State University, where he teaches human rights, strategy and war, American foreign policy, gender, critical security studies, and global politics. His research interests include the historical construction of American foreign policy as related to the Middle East, identity, gender, human rights, and security. Dr. Whooley earned his PhD from the University of Florida in 2015 with a successful dissertation on the securitization and construction of US foreign policy toward Iran from the administrations of Lyndon Baines Johnson through Ronald Reagan. He has also co-authored book chapters with Laura Sjoberg in *The Arab Spring and Arab Thaw* (2013) and with Mahmood Monshipouri in *Human Rights in the Middle East* (2011).

Dr. Christina Xydias is an associate professor of political science at Bucknell University. She was previously on the faculty at Clarkson University, where she received the institution's Outstanding New Teacher Award in 2016. Dr. Xydias is a comparativist with a regional focus on Europe; her substantive interests include gender and politics, elections, and legislatures. She has published journal articles and book chapters on women and gender in the German Bundestag, the European Parliament, and US Congress. Dr. Xydias's work on gender and politics has been published in numerous journals, including *Political Research Quarterly*; *Politics & Gender*; *Political Studies*; *Polity*; and *Politics, Groups, & Identities*. She has also written about political protest in Greece and Iceland, an article for which she won the 2017 Polity Prize.

Dr. Susanne Zwingel is an associate professor in the Department of Politics and International Relations at Florida International University. Her research interests are women's human rights and their translation, women's movements and public gender policies around the world, global governance and gender, and feminist and post-colonial IR theories. She is the author of *Translating International Women's Rights: The CEDAW Convention in Context* (Palgrave Macmillan, 2016) and co-editor of *Feminist Strategies in International Governance* with Elisabeth Prügl and Gülay Caglar (Routledge, 2013). Her work has appeared in a number of edited volumes as well as a wide range of journals, including *International Feminist Journal of Politics*, *International Studies Quarterly*, *Politics & Gender*, *International Studies Review*, and *Third World Thematics*. She currently works on transnational gender norm translation in South Florida and the Caribbean.

Index